The Peasants of Languedoc

THE
Peasants
OF
Languedoc

Emmanuel Le Roy Ladurie

Translated with an Introduction by
John Day

George Huppert, consulting editor

UNIVERSITY OF ILLINOIS PRESS
Urbana   Chicago   London

Originally published as *Les Paysans de Languedoc* by the Centre de Recherches Historiques, École Pratique des Hautes Études, VIᵉ Section (Paris: S.E.V.P.E.N., 1966). Translated from the paperback edition published by Flammarion et Cie (Paris: 1969).

Library of Congress Cataloging in Publication Data

Le Roy Ladurie, Emmanuel.
  The peasants of Languedoc.

  Bibliography: p.
  1. Peasantry—Languedoc—History. 2. Agriculture—Economic aspects—Languedoc—History. I. Title.
HD649.L33L413   301.44'43'09448   74–4286
ISBN 0-252-00411-6

SHIPPED AS PAPERBACK

Contents

PART THREE
The Rent Offensive

PART FOUR
The Depression

Conclusion

£ = *livre tournois*
s. = *sou tournois*
d. = *denier tournois*

One *livre* = 20 *sous*; one *sou* = 12 *deniers*

Foreword

Professor Emmanuel Le Roy Ladurie's *The Peasants of Languedoc* is an outstanding work of historical scholarship in the best tradition of that uniquely French institution, the monumental *thèse d'Etat*. It is, at the same time, a remarkable demonstration of the continuing vitality of France's *Annales* school of historiography (so named from the title of the journal founded in 1929 by Marc Bloch and Lucien Febvre). Certainly no major study by an *Annales* historian since Fernand Braudel's classic *The Mediterranean and the Mediterranean World in the Age of Philip II*[1] comes closer to realizing the purposes of a history without frontiers, "the sum of all possible histories." What is implied in such expressions is a readiness on the historian's part to employ the tools and concepts of the other social sciences in his reconstruction of the past. Pride of place is reserved for the study of economic, social, and—increasingly—intellectual (or sociopsychological) structures and structural change—the "unconscious" history of human collectivities as distinguished from the surface history of individual events (*l'histoire événementielle*). *Annales* scholars, in other words, tend to concern themselves with what is recurrent, or at least comparable, in the history of past societies (and hence translatable into the common scientific language of statistics) rather than with what is unique—the delight of traditional historiography, with its noted bias in favor of great events and great personalities.

Le Roy Ladurie set himself the particular task of writing just such a "total" history of peasant society in the ancient French province of Languedoc between the Middle Ages and the Enlightenment. His work combines elements of historical geography, demography, and sociology; of economic

---

[1] Paris, 1949; revised edition, Paris, 1966; English translation, New York, Harper & Row, Publishers, 1972.

history; and of psychohistory in a single construction, baptized "a great agrarian cycle." These different structures are studied in their reciprocal relationships as component parts of a whole. Great events of the period—the Calvinist Reformation, the religious wars, the Camisard revolt—are reconsidered in the changing perspectives of this polymorphic *histoire inconsciente* (which is not to minimize their role or significance).

The author's two key statistical sources are land tax registers, or *compoix*, for shifting patterns of landownership and tithe accounts for the evolution of the gross agricultural product. But the successive phases of the long-term movement he has studied are also delimited and analyzed in terms of more familiar kinds of quantitative data: hearth lists, prices, wages (including wages in kind), land rent, interest rates, and profits. The various series and samplings, like most Old Regime statistics, tend to be disparate and discontinuous, unsuited to the ingenious model building of the "new economic history." To make them speak at all requires not only a perfect understanding of their nature and limitations but also a generous measure of improvisation (see, in particular, Part I, chapters 3 and 4, and Part IV, chapter 2).

The combined results of Le Roy Ladurie's calculations, which are carried out without resort to difficult statistical concepts (and, for that matter, without computers), serve to illustrate the book's central theme—the Malthusian dilemma of a traditional agrarian society incapable, over the long run, of preserving a balance between population and food production.

In the late Middle Ages, Languedoc—in common with the rest of Europe —had suffered a major demographic setback that resulted in the retreat of agriculture and sometimes rural land settlement. But the situation contained within itself "the seeds of a new advance": high wages, improved nutrition, consolidated (that is, viable) peasant landholdings, low rents, and a "frontier" of potentially productive farmland. The sixteenth century was characterized, in the first instance, by a veritable population explosion (the "Malthusian Renaissance") which touched off a whole series of interrelated processes: a progressive division of landholdings, a decline of real wages, a rise in prices (also induced by the notorious effects of bullion imports from the New World), and accumulating profits from direct cultivation in its various forms.

The first sixty years of the *grand siècle*, with profits shrinking and agricultural wages at rock bottom, were the heyday of the parasitic rentier landlord —the "feudal reaction" of an older historiography. If the ensuing "general crisis" (to borrow a term favored by English historians), with its predictable negative repercussions on population, brought some relief to the rural proletariat, it proved almost fatal to farm profits and to all forms of rente. The guilty variables, at this juncture, were soaring taxes, under Louis XIV, and a gross product that still obstinately refused to budge. It was not, in fact, until the age of the Enlightenment that improved yields, the spread of wine growing, and progress in manufacturing finally succeeded in exorcizing the Malthusian specter of recurrent subsistence crises in rural Languedoc.

Le Roy Ladurie breathes life into his statistical blueprint of economic developments with innumerable concrete examples; the career of Guillaume Masenx, a cynical back-country capitalist, symbolizes "primitive accumulation" in the inflationary sixteenth century, and the story of the Lalle family debt to the canons of Béziers illustrates the unhappy predicament of borrowers during the Colbert depression (likened to that of American farmers during the Hoover depression).

But the book's horizons are not bounded by the facts of economic life—by what, with luck and ingenuity, can be counted and quantified. The work also represents a pioneer venture in the history of popular culture inspired, in turn, by the concepts of a Freud, a Weber, a Lévi-Strauss, a Foucault. Thus, for example, if the extended peasant family of the late Middle Ages constituted a practical solution to the labor shortage, it also provided a needed psychological anchorage in an age of violence and insecurity. Or again, the primitive rebels of the late Renaissance (to say nothing of the acolytes of rural witchcraft) were motivated as much by irrational fantasies and Freudian anxieties as by a reasonable resentment against depressed wages and the "uneven growth of wealth." In the post-Revocation period, as a matter of fact, what passed for economic self-interest was often completely submerged in a sea of religious fanaticism. Finally, not all the roadblocks to sustained economic growth were economic in nature. What was also wanting, prior to the eighteenth century, was a spirit of initiative and a minimum level of education. In short, the complex processes described in the book were not determined by economic and demographic factors alone.

The *Peasants of Languedoc* contributes in numerous ways to our understanding of the problems and contradictions of peasant societies both past and present. At the same time, it offers the example of a new and demanding kind of historical synthesis inspired by the *Annales* ideal of a unified science of man.

The original French edition of *The Peasants of Languedoc* was published in 1966 in two volumes. In the shorter paperback edition of 1969, on which this translation is based, Part One of the original version (devoted to climate and human geography), much of the statistical appendix (tables and graphs), and a number of shorter sections were sacrificed, and Part Four (now Part Three, "The Rent Offensive") was summarized. The bibliography and the list of manuscript sources, which were also eliminated from the second French edition, have been restored, and an index has been added.

Professor Emmanuel Le Roy Ladurie occupies the chair of Modern History and European Civilizations with the Collège de France. His other publications include *Times of Feast, Times of Famine: A History of Climate Since the Year 1000* (New York, 1971), *Histoire du Languedoc* (Paris, 1967), *Les Fluctuations du produit de la Dîme* (in collaboration with Joseph Goy, Paris, 1972), *Le territoire de l'Historien* (Paris, 1973), and many articles, especially in *Annales: economies, sociétés, civilisations.*

Paris   JOHN DAY

The Peasants of Languedoc

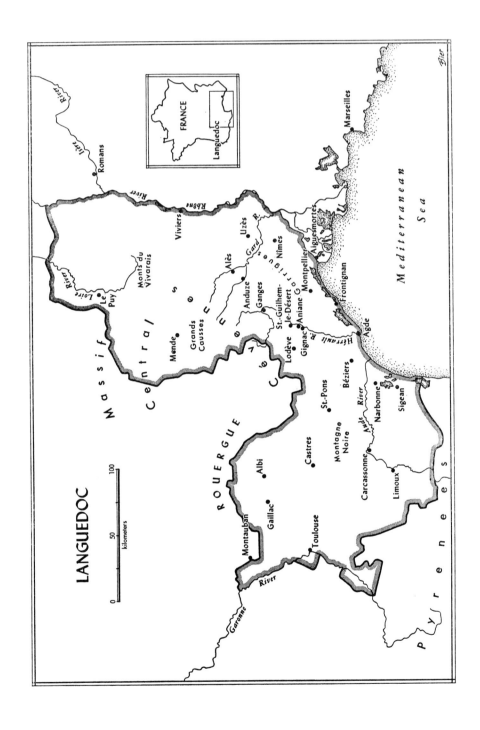

LANGUEDOC

FRANCE

Languedoc

Isère River

Romans

Loire River

Rhône River

Viviers

Le Puy

Monts du Vivarais

Alès

Uzès R.

Gard R.

Nîmes

Anduze

Ganges

Montpellier

Aiguesmortes

Frontignan

Marseilles

Mediterranean Sea

Massif

Central

Mende

Grands Causses

St-Guilhem-le-Désert

Aniane

Gignac

Lodève

Hérault River

Agde

Cévennes

Garrigues

ROUERGUE

St-Pons

Béziers

Sigean

Narbonne

Aude River

Montagne Noire

Castres

Limoux

Carcassonne

Albi

Gaillac

Montauban

Toulouse

Garonne River

Pyrenees

0   50   100
kilometers

Bier

Introduction

It was in 1955 that Raymond Dugrand first spoke to me of the *compoix* of Languedoc and suggested I undertake a study of them. The *compoix*, he told me, are old master cadastres composed solely in regions subject to the taille on real property. The earliest date from the fourteenth century. They describe in detail the extent, nature, and value of landholdings. They make a long-range history of property possible and can therefore be made to shed critical light on the long-ago conquest of the land on the part of capital—on one of the essential aspects, in other words, of the birth of capitalism.

It seemed like a forbidding assignment. The departmental and village archives contained literally hundreds of discouragingly voluminous *compoix*. But I was young at the time; I was teaching at Montpellier, close to the sources; I had my *sixièmes* and my vacations; I was interested in agrarian history and loved the Mediterranean countryside; and I was fascinated by the problem of the origins of capitalism. I decided to follow my friend's advice.

The first results did not disappoint me, and from the start I discovered in the *compoix* exactly what I was looking for, namely, the classic activity of capitalist land engrossers already described by Febvre, Bloch, Merle, Raveau, Vénard, and a host of others. Lattes, in the countryside of Montpellier —a city of notables—was a perfect illustration for the sixteenth and seventeenth centuries of the time-honored and still valid model of the progressive accumulation of rural property by city-dwellers. Has this very model not become a mainstay of agrarian history? I published an article on the subject in 1956.

Little by little, however, these happy convictions began to strike me as insufficient if by no means inexact. My methods of sifting the statistical material in the *compoix* improved with practice and became more exhaustive. I

3

broadened my investigation to take in the almost purely peasant countryside as well as the mountain districts far from the small cities of the land engrossers. Here, certain phenomena that did not fit the traditional picture or confirm my original hypothesis attracted my attention. The process of concentration lost its linear simplicity, and I began to discern the outline of phases, lasting well over a century, of almost unrelieved subdivision of landholdings. Peasant property, during the course of several generations, seemed to be disintegrating, while the *number* of landowners—of diminutive properties for the most part—increased at a dizzying rate. This relentless process of decomposition tended to make a mockery of the persistent efforts of the land engrossers, whether nobles, bourgeois, or *coqs de village*.[1]

At other times—that is, in the subsequent phase—the consolidation of landed property resumed while the number of individuals subject to the taille diminished. The process seems to have continued for a century, more or less, but it was neither definitive nor irreversible. Once again, landholding subdivision became the order of the day, and once again the taxable landowners increased in number as the average holding contracted in size. I observed these great secular movements with growing fascination, and I thought I could perceive the immense respiration of a social structure.

By that time I was immersed in agrarian history pure and simple. I had come a long way from the "origins of capitalism" that had preoccupied me in the beginning. Mine was the classic misadventure; I had wanted to master a source in order to confirm my youthful convictions, but it was finally the source that mastered me by imposing its own rhythms, its own chronology, and its own particular truth. My initial presuppositions had been stimulating, but they were now outmoded.

Little by little, a periodization imposed itself; it was confirmed, despite the usual exceptions, in the case of a hundred-odd rural circumscriptions, with the cadastres and land tax rolls of the empires, monarchies, and republics of the nineteenth and twentieth centuries serving as relays for the *compoix* and the books of the taille. This periodization offered immediate access to the long-range movements of agrarian history.

The starting point was the state of relative concentration of landholdings in the middle or at the end of the fifteenth century—relative, that is, to the preceding period (before 1350) and the succeeding period (after 1500). It

---

[1] *Coq de village*: "cock of the walk," that is, a well-to-do peasant, a village kulak (tr. note).

was not a question, in all probability, of a passing phase of capitalistic consolidation, but rather the consequence of rural depopulation born of the crises, plagues, and wars which had reversed the process of land subdivision still raging in the first half of the fourteenth century.

For that matter, following this passing phase of concentration at the end of the Middle Ages, the subdivision of landholdings recommenced with renewed vigor after 1500; it was strongly manifest throughout the sixteenth century, and it continued at a somewhat slower pace for a good portion of the seventeenth century until it reached a sort of critical threshold, a point of saturation and congestion of smallholdings, generally by about 1680.

At this juncture it came to a halt and slowly gave way once again to the reverse process of land concentration. Marginal holdings were sorted out. The better-qualified, the better-off, and the luckier individuals were cast in the role of engrossing landowners. The process favored surviving heirs and urban land buyers. The smallholders were decimated while the big and medium-sized landlords rounded out their properties from the spoils.

In the period about 1750–70 there was a new inflection, or rather a new inversion, and a resumption of the process of fragmentation spurred by the growth of population and stimulated by the spread of viticulture (which raised income per land unit and reduced the minimum size of a viable, taxable holding). This final offensive of land subdivision was unmatched by any similar movement in the past. It lasted fully a century, up to the phylloxera debacle of 1870–73 and up to the beginning of the rural exodus. Then, with slow deliberation, the contemporary movement of land concentration got under way. It has spared, right up to the present day, some solid blocks of peasant smallholds, but it is far from over.

Such a history of landed property, as outlined briefly above, would have been of little interest except from a juridical or purely technical point of view if it had not served as a sort of secular indicator and if it had not provided us with a concrete insight into the long-range evolution of agrarian society itself.

The outcome might have been different regarding the chronology and the real significance of the vicissitudes of landownership if I had studied the countryside of northern France, which was dominated by large farming units, but in the French Midi, characterized by small-scale agriculture and by the multitude of scattered tenements, the ebb and flow of smallholds constituted evidence of the greatest importance. It underscored the difficulties of an entire society; it served as a partial control, or cross-check, for other kinds of long-term movements; and on several occasions it helped delimit the frontiers of southern agriculture.

Three times, it appears, peasant society in Languedoc, at the end of a long period of expansion, reached one of these frontiers which deflected but never entirely blocked its slow, secular growth from the eleventh to the nineteenth century. The first time, apparently, was in the fourteenth century on the eve of the great collapse symbolized, as a rule, by the Black Death and the Hundred Years War. The second time was under Louis XIII or Louis XIV at the critical juncture of the seventeenth century—in some cases by about 1630, but more generally about 1675–80, depending on the region, as we shall see later in detail. A third time was about 1873–76, when the long period of expanding viticulture which had lasted from Louis XV to the Second Empire was terminated by the phylloxera epidemic and also by the economic depression of the seventies.

The present study is concerned essentially with the problems of the second frontier that marked the conclusion, in the last quarter of the seventeenth century, of the phase of agrarian development under way since the Renaissance. It was not possible, in fact, to exploit the long-term data furnished by the *compoix* and the cadastres in their entirety. Once the overall chronology had been determined and the main points of inflection had been situated on the time scale, it was necessary to stake out a period for a study in depth. Three major phases of expansion and contraction suggested themselves for this purpose: the medieval phase (from the eleventh century to the fifteenth century); the modern phase (from the end of the fifteenth century to the beginning of the eighteenth); and the contemporary phase (from 1750 to 1950).

The third phase, everything considered, is well known and fairly well understood thanks to the studies of various geographers, agronomists, and historians of Languedoc. It could still be enriched in detail, but it promised little in the way of new discoveries. It was during this last phase, in fact, that a good many cultivators of Languedoc ceased being *peasants*, who by tradition practice forms of polyculture and subsistence farming, and became modern winegrowers, purchasing their food and producing exclusively for the market.

As for the first, or medieval, phase, just the contrary was true. It was difficult to study because in its case the *compoix* were rare and, above all, late, dating from the fifteenth century at the earliest.

I have therefore chosen to ignore—except for brief glimpses where strictly unavoidable—the problems raised by the medieval expansion and by the great agrarian crisis that brought it to a close. I have concentrated instead on the strategic middle phase, or "second wind," when at the end of the fifteenth century the rural society of Languedoc raised itself from the ruins and set off on the highroad of modern development.

The *compoix* can serve to delimit this long, cyclical movement lasting from Louis XII to Louis XIV. They fix the basic chronology and reveal certain major inflections. But one must not expect them to shed light on every last detail. The problems raised by the expansion of a preindustrial society, and by the inevitable limits to such an expansion, require a multiple approach and the appeal to documents and statistics of the most diverse sort, for it is a question of discovering the actual movements behind the abstract data of the cadastral records.

In 1958, therefore, I forsook the history of rural property in order to study variables and constants other than land structures. First were the constants: Trained as a historian, was I going to have to describe the geographic structures of Languedoc because of a sister discipline's failure to do so? Fortunately, no. Raymond Dugrand, a geographer by trade, had spared me that task thanks to the remarkable thesis he defended in 1963. I could therefore practice the true historian's craft with a free spirit. I was able, in the first place, to isolate certain anthropological constants. We shall see how these were rooted, paradoxically, in the very mobility of the men of the past, in their regular migrations and those of their flocks and herds, and in the migrations of their cultivated plants.[2]

Next come the variables, whose moving chronology and ever-changing interrelations constitute, basically, the fabric of my book. I have not omitted the variable of climate, which is so important in agrarian history. It helps us to account for harvest fluctuations and the vagaries of supply, at least in the short run. But above all, I was interested—in connection with the long-term tendencies—in the major variables susceptible to lasting inflections and to secular fluctuations; that is to say, population, the different sectors of production and the regional gross product, nominal as well as metallic prices, aggregate income (both nominal and real), revenues, and exactions of various sorts (land rent, tithes, taxes, interest, farm profits or income, money wages, wages in kind, and mixed wages). Behind these abstract, if by no

---

[2] The sections dedicated to these problems are to be found in the original French edition of the present work (Paris, S.E.V.P.E.N., 1966).

means immutable, categories I began to perceive, at the end of a long journey, the living individuals—the peasants of Languedoc in their social context.

I had begun, in the early stages, by adding up hectares and cadastral units. By the end of my research I could observe the activities, the struggles, and the thoughts of the people themselves. In fact, economic and quantitative history by itself, no matter how rigorous or exhaustive, did not entirely satisfy me. It furnished only a rough, if indispensible, framework to build upon. I realized, as a matter of common sense, that the Malthusian stumbling blocks in the way of expansion were not all of a material nature. I sensed the presence of a formidable obstacle in mental attitudes and divined invisible frontiers of the human spirit, the most difficult of all to traverse. Little by little I learned to identify these spiritual stumbling blocks in the chronicle of hopeless popular revolts and in the bloody history of peasant religions.

With the best tools at my disposal, and within the framework of a single human society, I embarked upon the adventure of a "total" history.

PART ONE

Malthusian Renaissance

1

The Low-Water Mark of a Society

The Century of Rarified Population

The tragic demographic situation of the fifteenth century—the scarcity of people—was the overriding fact that lent land settlement, economic life, and social relationships their peculiar coloration on the eve of the great advance of the modern period.

People were rare, first of all, in relation to earlier centuries. Was not Languedoc the scene of an extraordinary demographic expansion between the year 1000 and the Black Death of 1348? The proof, in the absence of population figures, lies in the great reclamation and colonization movement of this period toward the coasts and toward the mountains simultaneously.

In the coastal sector the advance took place across the plain—across the stagnant swamps which were reclaimed and settled en masse. It was the abbeys, employing vast amounts of capital and labor, that drained the marshes. The three monasteries of Psalmody, Saint-Gilles, and Fourque-vaux, the latter a Cistercian abbey founded in 1147 on the banks of the ma-larial backwater of Scamandre, transformed the brackish waters between Nîmes, the Rhône, and the sea into virgin soil and the marshland into plowland. Elsewhere, at the foot of the ancient hill of Ensérune, a star-shaped network of radiating drainage canals remains as tribute to the skill of the unknown master who originally conceived and carried out the project.

In contrast to the colonization of the plains, which was carried forward by the abbeys and the feudal landowners, the demographic advance toward the mountains tended to be democratic and individualistic. Here, numerous colonists came to settle on their own initiative, and the abbeys' role was confined to granting them certain privileges thanks to the organization of *sauvetés*—"those lands delimited by crosses where every immigrant received

11

a plot on which to build, a few fields to assart and the protection of the Church." This was the case in the Montagne Noire and in central Langue-doc between 1045 and 1102. Elsewhere—in the Cévennes, for example—colonization proceeded in a simpler manner still; a spontaneous settlement sprang up next to an ancient *castrum*, or fortified locality. On the rocky soil, the pioneers laid out a whimsical field system—a mosaic of diminutive plots, each of which was barely the measure of a seeding unit. A few olive trees clung to the slopes. Petty farmer-knights, too poor to live as rentiers, pre-sided over a swarm of settlers. The role of the Church was limited to cre-ating a new parish when the time was ripe.

Finally, under the relentless pressure of population, an urban network of mushrooming towns sprang up. This urban growth in turn stimulated the rise of irrigated market gardening on the alluvial bottomlands nearby; the Trencavels, lords of Béziers, were collectors of cabbage tithes before they became pillars of heresy.

A mighty rise in population filled the parish network to overflowing, settled the towns, whose radius of attraction extended from the Rhône to the Pyrenees, contributed to the resettlement of Spain by French colonists, and set the stage for the miracle of the twelfth-century *pays d'oc*, with its booming spice trade, troubadour poetry, and Catharist ferment.

What was of capital importance was the drawn-out character of this population advance. It continued well beyond the Albigensian Crusade, which historians once mistakenly regarded as having broken the movement of expansion. At Montpellier in 1232, four years after the Treaty of Paris, six additional bakeries were being built to feed the inhabitants. And the de-mographic advance continued; land clearing, or *débroussaillement*, culmi-nated between 1222 and 1340 with the creation of between four hundred and five hundred *bastides*. These new rural circumscriptions, asylums of liberty, succeeded in attracting colonists. To the east the Cévennes persevered in their development, and, stimulated by deforestation, the first peasant collier-ies—the "foxholes" of the rustic coal miners—appeared in 1240. One begins to hear of the coal of Alès, the first mined in France and as old as the oldest in Europe. Around 1300 the wave of settlement was still spreading, as at-tested by hearth lists which suggest a population increase of 23 percent be-tween 1293 and 1322 in the rural lordships around Nîmes. In this region by 1293 the desolate *garrigues* had attained a level of population density ap-proaching that of the eighteenth century. The lowland plains country, for its part, was still riding the crest of the colonization movement at the beginning of the fourteenth century. The census takers of 1322 themselves did not fail to note certain aspects of population pressure such as immigration and the excessive atomization of inheritances.

Harvest failures afflicted this superabundant population with redoubled frequency and fury. Out of a period of forty-six years (1302–48) Languedoc was desolated by famine and dearth for a total of twenty. The overpopulated fourteenth century was ushered in by four bad years in a row (1302–1305). Embargoes were imposed on cereal exports, the granaries were searched, and grain stores were disposed of in forced sales. The Jews were singled out as scapegoats. Torrential rains in 1310 introduced another ill-starred cycle of lean years (1310 and 1313). Next came the harvest failures of 1322 and 1329, and the populace, following the example of the fanatical Pastoureaux, vented its anger on the Jews, the lepers, and the sorcerers. In 1332 the poor subsisted on raw herbs all winter long. The period 1335–47, finally, with its succession of bad harvests, must have been especially terrible. The poor, during these dozen years, suffered recurrent hunger. What a "magnificent" field of action for the Black Death of 1348, that holocaust of the undernourished.

We know of the effects of the pandemic in Languedoc from contemporary texts. They inform us that over half the members of corporate bodies were wiped out. They also attest to the high mortality in the religious communities, where the contagion was abetted by the cloistered life; at Montpellier, out of 140 preaching friars only 7 appear to have survived the plague.

Statistical sources confirm, with shades of difference and added precision, the sinister eloquence of the texts. At Albi, where the plague is neatly bracketed by the *compoix* of 1343 and 1357 and where the documents are much more complete than at Toulouse, the ravages of the epidemic were appalling; out of a total of ten thousand Albigeois, at least five thousand disappeared—a mortality rate of 50 percent. In the countryside, various statistical records, some published, others not, supply concordant figures. At Marsillargues, a large village on the plain, the "events" of 1348 constituted a veritable hecatomb that carried off more than 50 percent of the population. At Ganges, a township in the Cévennes, the story was the same. In 1339, there were 305 electors present and accounted for at "the universal assembly of the men of the town of Ganges" for the election of syndics; in 1366 the

Cévennes were prostrate, and more than half of the electors of Ganges had disappeared, leaving only 132 heads of families to answer the roll; by 1433 their number had fallen to 89.

Languedoc, in short—in common with the entire coast of the Gulf of Lion, the first zone attacked by the assault waves of microbes—was severely affected by the plague; more so, no doubt, than certain remote mountain districts like the Rouergue or the Béarn, which reported fewer victims in 1348/49. But fifteen years later, in 1363, the "mountain plague" would begin to equalize the casualty count.

For the disaster was anything but transitory in nature. The population of Languedoc, having picked up momentum, if that is the word for it, continued to decline long after 1348, right up to the 1430's, in fact. Afterwards, it stabilized at an extremely low level up to about 1480 or perhaps 1500. This was the case at Toulouse, at Montpellier, and also at Nîmes, where half the dwellings were still uninhabited as late as 1498.

A simple reflection, perhaps, of the decline of the urban economy? Of the contraction of large-scale trade? No, it was more than that. Parallel studies carried out for villages both large and small reveal a veritable regional unanimity. In every instance in which we dispose of a series of *compoix* or of books of the taille, the same basic tendencies for the period 1348–1480 are evident: a demographic collapse followed by stagnation. Sometime near the middle of the fifteenth century, the population of Languedoc touched bottom. The demographic low-water mark of 1450 was, as a matter of fact, not only the lowest since 1300; it represents at the same time the lowest population level, the absolute minimum, recorded for the entire period 1450–1790. The indications of this depopulation are extremely plentiful. For numerous villages or large rural centers it is possible to reconstitute the series of books of the taille, *compoix* or cadastres for which the tax base—in this region of the taille on real property—remained invariable for centuries. The series, in other words, are homogeneous and reflect the long-range secular movement (1450–1790). It would be a simple matter, thanks to the cadastres and the property tax rolls, to extend them right up to 1950.

Now, never did these villages, on the whole, possess so few taxpayers—so few heads of families, in reality—as in the fifteenth century. In 1450 there were two to three times fewer persons subject to the taille than in 1680 or 1780. The expression "demographic low-water mark" seems perfectly appropriate for the period. Between the Middle Ages and the modern and contemporary periods—between the great medieval colonization movement and single-crop viticulture—the population of Languedoc, like that of neighboring Provence, for that matter, sank to its lowest level.

The demographic shallows of 1450 (or thereabouts) momentarily bequeathed a particular physiognomy to the region of Languedoc. Land settlement, the rural landscape, the crop systems, landed property, modes of exploitation, and the peasant life style all bore the deep imprint of this unique demographic situation—of this "zero degree" of population.

Consequences: The Rural Landscape

Depopulation and the decline of towns and markets was, to begin with, a fatal blow to specialized cash crops such as market gardens and vineyards, which were so thriving prior to 1350. By 1401 the moats of Montpellier, "once planted with gardens, orchards and vines," were "filled with briers and thorns, snakes and lizards." As for the vineyards, it seems they reached the height of their prosperity about 1250–1350. Local and foreign demand—that of Genoa, and in some cases Paris—had stimulated their spread. For example, the fields of Lattes, which was a center of cereal culture in the sixteenth and seventeenth centuries, had been covered with vineyards in the thirteenth. As late as 1353 in a certain village of the region of Béziers there were forty vines for every hundred parcels of land. The depression of the late Middle Ages completed the destruction of this vineyard, leaving only six vines for every hundred parcels at the end of the fifteenth century. In 1520 recovery was under way, and the count was already back to twenty vines per hundred parcels. The retreat of viticulture in the declining Middle Ages was, for that matter, a phenomenon common to the entire Midi. It is met with in the Côtes du Rhône as well as in the Guyenne.

On the whole, the marginal vineyard on poor land was the most seriously affected. It was the least profitable and hence the first to be sacrificed. For example, in the countryside of Lodève, on the good alluvial land, the manorial dues in wine remained at exactly the same level in 1393 as in 1236, while the dues in grain declined by half—a sure sign of the persistence of viticulture. But a few leagues away, in the desolate *ruffes*—sterile red clay soils— the vineyards which were well attested in the manorial accounts of 1236 had completely disappeared by 1393. These *ruffes* no longer produced a single drop of wine. During the great retreat of viticulture (1350–1500) it was the profit motive (primitive though its calculation may have been) that decided the issue. The smaller number of peasants, producing for contracting mar-

kets on less congested lands, chose to concentrate their efforts in the vineyards of the plain, where the yields were higher and the profits surer. The
garrigues, for their part, were abandoned to their unhappy fate. The reaction of the winegrowers of Lodève was no different from that of the Floren-
tine peasants who, on the morrow of the Black Death, were no longer
willing to work any but the best land and left the inferior soils untilled.

Cereal culture was also retreating in the fifteenth century, and the plowlands, the *ager*, contracted significantly. The double frontier conquered by
the pioneers of the eleventh century—the swampy flatlands and the rocky
mountainsides—reverted to woods and waste. In the coastal zone, the lands
afflicted by "bad air" or creeping salinity—those bordering the sea or the
swamps, eroded by saltwater and infested by the malarial mosquito—were
the first to be surrendered. Entire parishes created during the great colonization movement of the eleventh century were abandoned forever after 1350.
Maureilhan, on the coast, counted three churches in the twelfth century. In
more recent times, all that remained were a few miserable tenant farmers
wasted by disease. At Fréjorgues, the French Air Force recently built an air-
field, never suspecting that a fifteenth-century desertion had paved the way
to expropriation. Sometimes, however, a large isolated farmstead (*mas*)
or ruined chapel still bears the name of the lost village.[1] The desertions
of Languedoc, although fairly numerous, were much less serious than the
German desertions of the same period, which in some areas affected up to
40 percent of the nucleated settlements.

Are they comparable, on the other hand, to the English desertions of the
late Middle Ages, when the lords, capitalizing on the anarchy of the War of
the Roses, seized the opportunity offered by depopulation to evict their remaining tenants and convert the plowlands into sheepwalks? No, in
Languedoc the *Wüstungen* do not have this premeditated character. In this
respect, the example of Coussergues is significant.

Coussergues, an ancient Roman villa, its soil riddled with antique coins
and broken pottery, was a small fortified village, a *castrum* surrounded by
walls and towers, in the thirteenth century. In 1317 it counted twenty-four
heads of families, a church dedicated to Saint Martin, some plots of land
sown with barley and wheat, a few vines, some meadows, and some *garrigue*, where the inhabitants procured faggots of heather for their bakeovens
and collected the trunks of evergreen and white oak trees. This democratic

[1] *Lost village* in English in the French editions (tr. note).

settlement existed side by side with a number of isolated farmsteads surrounded by large domains.

In 1348–55 Coussergues was visited by two disasters: the Black Death and the Black Prince. The first decimated the *castrum*; the second sacked it, forcing the survivors to flee. At the end of the fifteenth century the site was deserted. In 1496 a veteran of the Italian wars, a certain nobleman by the name of Pierre de Sarret, appeared on the scene. He shared with his mother a rich inheritance which enabled him to purchase the ruins, lands, and lordship of Coussergues. And not content with the acquisition of a dead village, this rapacious personage married, at the age of fifty, a young woman with a large dowry, one Jaquette de Bozène, the granddaughter of a money changer. Thanks to the dowry, Sarret was able to exploit his vast new domain; thus, the foundations of a great landed fortune were laid for the next four centuries.

The *Wüstungen* of Languedoc do not appear to have been the result of premeditation on the lords' part as was the case in England. They were more a simple natural consequence of the catastrophes of the late Middle Ages, and the lords contented themselves with taking advantage of the situation. The final outcome, in any case, was much the same, if on a much more modest scale than in England: the reconstitution, in the course of time, of a certain number of great estates in the coastal region out of what had once been village lands.

But these handsome landed estates were still a thing of the future. In the fifteenth century the coastal plain of the Gulf of Lion presented a depressing spectacle. The abandoned drainage canals filled with stagnant water became the breeding grounds of malarial mosquitoes, and creeping salinity invaded the forsaken furrows. The salicorn, or soda plant, returned in force. In the 1480's it even paid the tithe. On the desolate coasts, the ports almost ceased to function. This was the fate, for example, of Lattes, the port of Montpellier where a single Romanesque capital and remnants of the ramparts are all that is left to evoke its ancient glory, and above all of Aiguesmortes, a precocious fossil of a town which has preserved intact the geometric street plan of its thirteenth-century founders.

On the mountain frontier of the old rural colonization movement, the collapse was less sweeping. Here, at least, one was safe from the ravages of malaria, which eventually wiped out the last islands of human habitation—already eroded by the plague and the English war—in the coastal regions. In the mountains the villages and parishes were reduced in size, but at least they managed to survive, afflicted not so much by a mortal illness as by a process of chronic anemia. The villages survived, but the hamlets succumbed. At Cessenon in 1374 there is mention of six associated hamlets in addition to the main village. In the *compoix* of the sixteenth century (1560), three of the six have disappeared. A mortality rate of 50 percent is high, even admitting that it was the smallest hamlets, hence the least resistant, that expired.

The fact is confirmed by the bourgeois of Cessenon in their complaints to a visiting commissioner for the Montagne Noire and the Espinouse in 1401: numerous *masages*, they reported, were in fact deserted; population was at its lowest point, with half of the land lying fallow; and the inhabitants had to stand guard over the harvests to protect them against the depredations of deer, stags, boars, and other wild animals. The forest, which was one-eighth of a league from the village, was encroaching on their pasture. Poverty was so widespread that the people were no longer able to pay the taille. The inhabitants petitioned the king to allow them, therefore, to cut wood in the surrounding forest for sale at Béziers.

Nothing is more striking in the complaints of these mountain-dwellers than their obsession with a luxuriant nature, whether animal or vegetable. It was nature's revenge for the great land colonization movement. The depopulated mountain valleys stopped producing grain and began, as one would expect, to produce wood. A forester like Lannoy, who was superintendent of waters and forests understood these problems and the magnitude of the danger. He endorsed the idea of a counteroffensive. "Go into the forest," he told the natives of the Montagne Noire in 1401, "cut the trees, assart, burn charcoal, break the soil to the plow, make ash, plaster, lime, graze your sheep and cattle, hunt stags, partridges, rabbits, boars and other wild animals; fish in the Orb and the Vernazobres to your heart's content." Lannoy's successors confirmed his prescriptions in 1444 and 1467. It was not until 1559, when the forest was retreating once more before the plow, that the superintendent of waters and forests would resume his vocation as protector of the wooded areas and contest the century-and-a-half-old forest rights of the local population.

The advancing forest carried all before it. It was not just wasteland or *garrigue*—a postcultivation association of plant life, a zone of sheepwalks and grazing land (the *saltus* of the ancient agronomists)—that replaced the abandoned plowlands. What was involved over and above this development was a return to the original vegetation—to the climactic holm oak forest of the phytogeneticists. The *ager* gave way to the *saltus*. The *saltus*, in turn, retreated before the *silva*. The *ager-saltus-silva* balance shifted in favor of the last two elements. In the Bas-Rhône at the site of Glanum, a stratum of burned woodland just above the archeological level of the thirteenth century could very well indicate, in this zone, too, the counteroffensive of the holm oak forest at the end of the Middle Ages.

In these spreading woodlands the invasion of wild game reached alarming proportions between 1360 and 1500. By the end of the fourteenth century, the lords of the Cévennes could no longer cope with it unaided, and in 1361–77, for the first time, the peasants of the barony of Hierle were granted the right to hunt and trap bears, wild boars, and stags. There was enough work to keep everybody busy; the brown bear of the Cévennes returned in force to the slopes of the Aigoual, herds of deer roamed the *garrigues* and the evergreen oak forests, the Causses were infested with wolves, and partridges were as common as chickens. And up to the beginning of the sixteenth century the peasants enjoyed unrestricted hunting rights, so unlimited did the reserves of wild game appear to be. The history of hunting that Marc Bloch advocated has its conjuncture, too.

The Concentration of Landed Property

In this depopulated countryside of advancing forest and teeming wildlife, what had happened to land distribution? The *compoix*, cadastres, and tax records provide abundant information on this subject. In Languedoc, as a matter of fact, taxes were paid on real property, and the *compoix* attained a degree of precision not unworthy of a master cadastre of the nineteenth century. Studies of the earliest of these documents lead to the conclusion that the immense network of landownership was extremely loose at the end of the fifteenth century. Instead of the close-knit fabric of small properties and diminutive tenancies paying insignificant quitrents of the period around 1300, the dawn of modern times was characterized by a loose pattern of landholdings composed for the most part of medium-sized properties. It would be a mistake to see in this substitution an example of capitalistic concentration. It was simply a question of the inevitable consolidation of landholdings which went hand in hand with the demographic contraction of the period 1350–1450. A phase of atomization—of subdivision, as the census takers of 1322 called it—was succeeded by a phase of consolidation through inheritance.

Let us have a look at the oldest series of *compoix* for Languedoc, those of Albi. In 1343, the 1,623 taxpayers of this town shared a total of £68,000 in cadastral property—real property, essentially, and above all land and vines. In 1357 only 686 taxpayers were left. Their capital in real property was reckoned at 55,000 cadastral pounds, only some 20 percent below the prepandemic figure. Total property remained almost constant, but thanks to inheritance, individual properties had increased in value from £400 to £800, on the average, and in size from 0.5 to 1.3 hectares.

A closer examination of real wealth confirms our preliminary diagnosis. If we arrange the taxpayers of Albi in a table according to the value of their property and compare the distributions of wealth in 1343 and 1357, we perceive that the number of petty taxpayers, especially the very poorest whose property (a cottage and a croft) was evaluated at less than ten *livres*, diminished considerably in the interval. In 1343 this category represented 30.7 percent of all the taxpaying citizens of Albi. It represented only 17.8 percent of a total now reduced by half in 1357. The plague had decimated the ranks of these miserable property owners, who were so poor they were practically paupers. In 1343 they were crowded into two overpopulated quarters of the town. Between 1343 and 1357 these two islands of poverty lost 62 percent of their taxpaying population. The high mortality had contributed to the concentration of holdings in the hands of less numerous heirs: in 1343, 11 percent of all property owners were worth more than one hundred *livres*; in 1357 the figure had risen to 20 percent. The victims' goods had been joined to those of the survivors. Among these "nouveaux riches" was a certain Bernard Davisat, who tripled his holdings by 1357 thanks to the legacies of Guilhem Davisat and the widow Teisseire, both deceased sometime after 1343. This concrete example only serves to confirm the rule; the total number of individual properties declined by half, the average size of each increased in proportion, and as a consequence there were many fewer small-holds and more medium-sized properties and even great estates. Innumerable family dramas lie hidden behind these dry statistics. It is easy to imagine, as at Florence in the same period, and also in Normandy, the secret delight of certain heirs consoled in their hour of mourning by a deluge of unexpected legacies.

Does the subsequent history of Languedoc confirm that land structure was in an advanced state of concentration and consolidation in the fifteenth century? To find out, let us take the *compoix* of a random village in the province, a *compoix* based on a land survey carried out between 1400 and

1500, and compare it by surface areas or land values—depending on the documentation—with a *compoix* for the same locality dating from the sixteenth or seventeenth century.

Take the case of one large village of the Hérault. At Saint-Thibéry, 357 landowners were crowded together on 4,922 *setérées* in 1690.[2] In 1460 at the dawn of the Renaissance, on the other hand, 189 landowners found themselves relatively disencumbered on roughly the same land area (4,569 *setérées*). And among these, a veritable middle class, comprising 62 taxpayers, or one-third of the total, possessed proper estates of 20 to 100 *setérées*. This well-to-do group laid claim, all told, to half the village lands (2,354 *setérées*). Two centuries later, in 1690, a table of the distribution of landed properties arranged from top to bottom in order of increasing size indicates that this middle class had practically melted away since 1460 (see Table 1). In 1690 the "middle" category of landowners (20–100 *setérées*) represented no more than 10 percent of the total and owned barely a quarter of the village lands. On the other hand, a multitude of small plots appear at the top of the table. They constitute the poorest category—properties of 20 *setérées* or less. This group doubled in number and in overall acreage between 1460 and 1690, representing a veritable pulverization of rural property and leading to the emergence of a class of microlandowners. The decomposition of landholdings as projected in the *compoix* was the normal effect, in short, of an increase in rural population, and this sort of decomposition is not necessarily the sign of a healthy peasant economy. Many of the petty landlords of 1690 owned little more than a *champ al Causse*,[3] where yields were barely three times seed in the good years! And more than one would disappear forever in the crisis-ridden late years of Louis XIV's reign; the *champs al Causse* of 1690 were the "vacant holdings" of the next century.

The proliferation of holdings appears even more unhealthy when one considers how it came about. At whose expense, in fact, did the multiplication of village smallholds of the modern period occur? Was it at the expense of the great estates of the fifteenth century? In this particular parish, that was certainly not the case. The category of great estates (of over 100 *setérées*), far from breaking up to the advantage of the small peasants and landless laborers, carved itself out a bigger share of the cake between the age of Louis XI and that of Louis XIV. Holdings of over 100 *setérées* in 1460 comprised nine great landed estates which covered 1,490 *setérées* and

---

[2] *Setérée*: generally between one-fifth and one-fourth of a hectare (tr. note).

[3] *Causse*: limestone uplands of the Massif Central (tr. note).

accounted for 30 percent of the village lands. By 1690 there were twelve great domains covering 2,237 *setérées* and accounting for almost half of the land. The great landowners progressed, the small ones proliferated, and the middle ones, caught in the squeeze, retreated prodigiously. It was the medium-sized holding, which was literally ground to pieces in the sixteenth and seventeenth centuries, that bore the brunt of the process of atomization. In the fifteenth century, on the other hand—in this particular village—the medium-sized landholding for a brief time reigned supreme.

From a social point of view, these middle properties were not manorial or noble any more than they were bourgeois or urban. No more than a handful of strangers from the neighboring town or noblemen whose names were adorned with the title *moussen* ("lord of ————") turned up in the *compoix* of 1460. The immense majority of the estates, especially of the medium-sized estates (twenty to one hundred *setérées*), which constituted the typical form of landownership in this parish in 1460, belonged to ordinary villagers who were neither nobles nor bourgeois nor artisans, but well-to-do peasants, farm managers, or simple cultivators endowed with mule or ox teams. They formed a sort of substantial yeomanry well provided with land and solidly ensconced on their domains.[4]

Paradoxically, this balanced land structure was the fruit of depopulation. How different from the polarized structure of the seventeenth century; in 1690 we have on the one hand the great landlords—Noble de Nattes, the abbot of Saint-Thibéry, and others—holding half the village lands, and on the other the petty landlords crowded onto their miserable little plots. The old yeomanry of the fifteenth century retreated before the attacks of the big land engrossers and disintegrated under the pressure of increasing numbers and the effects of partible inheritance. One is reminded (without insisting unduly on the comparison) of certain phenomena of land dispersion characteristic of underdeveloped countries with rapidly growing populations in the twentieth century.

A similar process occured at Lespignan. In the fifteenth century the middle-sized and big estates (in excess of twenty-five *setérées*) predominated. A century and a half later, this land structure had collapsed. The largest estates survived, but the middle-sized ones had vanished, giving rise to a multitude of "microproperties" of doubtful economic viability.

Except in the case of Albi, up to this point I have used estimates of land area expressed in *setérées* (or hectares). For the two villages just considered,

[4] *Yeomanry* in English in the French editions (tr. note).

it was impossible to proceed otherwise. Let us now see if the conclusions based on assessed land values confirm the deductions based on estimated land areas.

The assessments of surveyors, land experts, and *compesieurs* of the Old Regime are, as is well known, of great interest to the historian. They represent a serious attempt to appraise the quality of the land and are thus an inestimable boon to scholarship, for in certain cases a blind faith in surface areas leads to the absurdity of equating, for example, an acre of *garrigue* and an acre of good bottomland. Weighted land valuations, on the contrary, furnish a concrete and at the same time quantitative picture of the lands in question. A hectare or a *setérée* of "good" land was assessed by the *compesieurs* at anywhere from three and one-half to ten times the value of a hectare of "poor" land or *garrigue*. This procedure, which was common to all the *compoix*, makes it possible to transcend the geometric abstraction of hectares and arrive at the realities of weighted land measures based on comparative assessed values.

For various reasons, however, the indispensable comparison between the assessments of two *compoix* executed fifty or one hundred years apart is a delicate operation. On the one hand, changes in the value of the currency and price movements must be taken into account; in order to compare land values in the *compoix* of the same village between, say, 1480, 1560, and 1650, one must eliminate these sources of error by converting the figures for each successive survey into their equivalent in weight of gold or silver or, better still, their equivalent in grain. The undertaking, in these circumstances, is hazardous, to say the least.

Furthermore, these delicate calculations are likely to be in vain. The *compesieurs* were concerned with fiscal effectiveness, not economic verities. Often they chose to ignore the real market value of the lands "assessed" and contented themselves instead with establishing a scale of relative values for the different soils from the most sterile to the most fertile, the latter to be taxed two, three, or four times the former. The scale of values adopted for taxing purposes undoubtedly represented the real hierarchy of land values, but the figures themselves were generally chosen arbitrarily. The scale, in fact, was graduated in fictitious pounds—*livres de compoix* or *livres livrantes* —completely detached from the fluctuating market values of the lands in question. Comparisons of absolute values in two *compoix* using different yardsticks—one from the fifteenth century and the other from the sixteenth or seventeenth—are of little or no interest.

The fact is that in this difficult domain only two kinds of comparisons appear legitimate. First, there is the case of a family of *compoix, brevettes*, and rolls of the taille. Take the example of a *compoix* executed around 1500, a register used by the consuls, or by the *greffier* (tax registrar) under their orders, to draw up the annual taille or tax roll. If, for example, the total of individual property assessments entered in the *compoix*—the total *allivrement*—was one thousand *livres de compoix* (cadastral pounds) or, as the tax collectors preferred to say, one thousand *livres livrantes*, and if, on the other hand, the taille demanded of the village by the king was three thousand *livres* (current), one has only to multiply the property valuation for each taxpayer by a coefficient of three to find the sum of his tax for that year. The annual *rôle des tailles*, keeping in mind that the coefficient varied according to the taille and the year, represented, therefore, simply a résumé of the *compoix*. And if the latter is lost, it is still possible to reconstruct the valuation for each taxpayer with the help of the rolls of the taille.

Not only that, but the *greffier*, in drawing up the tax rolls in 1510, 1520, 1530, and so on, took into account changes in landownership which "unburdened" the valuation of one taxpayer and "burdened" that of another. These changes, noted down year after year in the margins of the *compoix* in reference to the individual taxpayer's *manifeste*,[5] were later incorporated in the successive rolls of the taille. A given *compoix* composed, let us say, in 1500 might be used by the consuls for half a century (1500–50), giving birth in the interval to a whole family of tax rolls (1501, 1502, 1503, and so on to 1549). These tax rolls, if properly studied, tell the story of landownership at the village level.

Thus, in a given parish the mass of land parcels, fields, vines, houses, and other properties might be compared to a deck of playing cards. The *compoix* informs us, in the first case, what cards were dealt to the different players—in other words, the distribution of holdings among taxpayers or landowners. But as the years pass, the deck is continually reshuffled and redealt as a result of land transfers, legacies, consolidations, and subdivisions of properties. One taxpayer, who as a young man in 1500 owned three cadastral pounds of property, by 1540 has added to his possessions and is now worth perhaps fifty-five pounds. Another has died, and his twenty cadastral pounds of property have been divided among his four children, five pounds going to each. The book of the taille, *allowing for the relation between tax*

---

[5] *Manifeste*: a detailed enumeration of the taxpayer's real property (lands or houses), including confines, land surfaces, and assessed value.

coefficient and allivrement (assessed value) in that particular year, provides a complete picture of the distribution of "cards" at the date of its composition as well as the current *allivrement* of each individual taxpayer.

It is perfectly legitimate to compare the original *compoix* and a book of the taille derived from it fifty years later. The cards that keep circulating among the players are, in fact, always the same from start to finish. The indications of relative fertility—of poor land or good land—retained their validity from generation to generation. Ours is not a perfectly airtight comparison (no comparisons of land values or, for that matter, of land areas are), and there will always be an irreducible dose of incertitude in quantitative social history to delight the hypercritical. In the present case, difficulty arises from the fact that the face values of certain cards in the deck have been altered slightly—some wheat fields have been planted with vines and vice versa. It is possible, nevertheless—and herein lies the *approximation* proposed here—to determine beyond any doubt who has won and who has lost, and how. (To complicate matters, certain cards have also been torn into two or three fragments through acts of inheritance which subdivide fields and vineyards.)

A good example is furnished by the village of Fontès, which boasts as fine a series of fiscal documents as anyone could hope for. A little before 1505, a *compoix* was compiled which, as we know, came out to £2,010 of *allivrement* in all. This *compoix* served as a base for the books of the taille of 1505, 1533, and 1539. The first of these "books," that of 1505, still bears the mark of the indigent demographic situation of the fifteenth century. The 105 local taxpayers came very close to the figure of 100 for 1427. After 1505 the usual advance in the taxable population raised the figure to 136 in 1533 and 172 in 1539, which represented an increase of more than 65 percent in one generation (1505–39).

To compare the books of the taille of 1505 to those of 1539, therefore, is to compare two ages separated by the demographic revolution. It permits us to view two documents of the same family, of the same *compoix*, in perspective and—keeping to the figure—to follow the same card game from the first deal in 1505, when the players were relatively few, to the last deal in 1539, when they were much more numerous.

A table of landed wealth at Fontès, arranged in order of assessed value, confirms the process reflected in the tables based on land areas studied earlier; namely, the progressive subdivision of holdings. The watershed, in this case, is the assessment of 20 cadastral pounds. In 1505 one taille payer out of every three or four (30 out of 105) had more than 20 cadastral pounds in the *compoix*, which represents a minimum individual holding equal in value to 1 percent of the village's lands (which amounted, all told, it will be recalled, to £2,010 in assessed value). A generation later, the basis of calculation still being the original *compoix* revised to reflect transfers of ownership, only one taxpayer in nine attained or exceeded this figure of 20 cadastral pounds, beyond which lay the domain of middle-sized or large landholdings. There were, therefore, fewer winning players with a fistful of cards and more losing players with only one or two cards or fragments of cards in their hands. In fact, 152 petty taxpayers with assessments below the critical threshold of £30 found themselves at the top of the table in 1539, compared to only 75 in 1505. Thanks to the rise in population, low assessments sprouted like mushrooms, reflecting the rise of a numerous taxpaying cottager class. Conversely, the very end of the fifteenth century appears to be dominated still by middle-sized properties, the same that were destined to disintegrate with the population explosion of the sixteenth century. In this particular case, the study of land values serves to confirm the conclusion of the previous tables based on surface areas.

However, a family of books of the taille derived from a unique *compoix* does not take us very far in point of time. After sixty, eighty, or one hundred years, the original *compoix* or "matrix," crammed full of corrections and hopelessly disfigured by the record of countless transfers, had outlived its usefulness. It was necessary to compile another based on a new land survey and destined to give birth, in its turn, during the course of two or three generations to a new family of tax rolls serving to chronicle the constant changes in landownership. As previously noted, two such *compoix* and their respective families of tax rolls are hard to compare in absolute figures because of monetary and price fluctuations and above all because of the fictitious character of cadastral property assessments, which were concerned more with a scale of relative land values than with determining the actual market price of landholdings.

Must we then give up the attempt to compare the different series of *compoix* or tax rolls of a single village for lack of either a common system of land measurement or a common base of assessment? In this difficult impasse, one is forced to work with percentages—to content oneself, as is often necessary in the statistics of preindustrial societies, with indications of trends rather than with absolute figures.

Saint-Guilhem-le-Désert is located in the canyons of the Hérault on a steep mountainside of limestone cliffs that are broken here and there by ranks of ascending terraces planted with olive trees. The lands of such a village scarcely lend themselves to appraisement in hectares. What counts is the value of the land. In one place, a patch of barren *garrigue* or an out-cropping of virgin rock appears in the jagged *lapiaz* or amid the stony scree. Elsewhere, on the banks of the Hérault, there are verdant meadows worth a fortune compared to the *garrigue* of cistus and rosemary.

Now, it happens that this village, where the taille was imposed on real property, as was everywhere the case in Languedoc, boasts a splendid series of tax rolls based on successive land assessments, or *compoix*, which give the scale of wealth of all taxpayers for the years 1398, 1442, 1486, 1570, 1615, 1654, 1675, and 1750. But how is it possible to compare these different documents, which are homogeneous in regard to content but heterogeneous in regard to form? No two of them have the same *compoix* or the same cadastre as a common ancestor. Quite by chance, each of them is based on a different assessment and is therefore impossible to compare in absolute figures with the one that preceeds or the one that follows. Thus, the total *allivrement*, or rather, in certain cases, simply the total tax imposed on the village, was £47 in 1398, £321 in 1442, £37 10s. in 1486, £84 16s. in 1570, £64 2s. in 1615, £1,043 in 1654, £397 in 1675, £352 in 1750, £8,364 in 1791, and so on. These are arbitrary totals in terms of absolute value, varying according to the method of land assessment used in compiling the *compoix* or according to the rate of taxation. All that mattered, to tell the truth, was the repartition among the different taxpayers.

Let us abandon, in this particular case, any hope of being able to compare absolute land values from one document to the next. In recompense, it is still possible to conceive of comparisons in terms of percentages. True, we do not know how big the "cake" to be divided up among the "guests" actually was (that is, the actual value of the lands portioned out among the village landowners). Still, it is possible to determine precisely the number of "guests" (variable) and the relative value of the portion assigned to each one. Those at the head of the table cut themselves a large slice of the cake. The others, who were more numerous, had to content themselves with crumbs. Is it not of some interest to discover how the partition was effected in each generation? Our ignorance of the actual value of the allotted land-holdings is of less importance than it would be in the case of an urban economy, which is dynamic by its very nature. The elasticity of village lands, on the contrary, is strictly limited, as can be seen by comparing their dimensions in different periods. The possibilities of growth of the total agricultural income of a given village in a preindustrial economy are fairly restricted, even when that economy is an expanding one. Because of this relative stability of the land areas and land values to be portioned out among the different landowners, problems of changes in the repartition, of changes in the percentages of land held by the various categories of owners, large and small, are of the greatest interest.

Saint-Guilhem, between 1398 and 1442, offers a classic example of the reconstitution of landed wealth during a decline of the taxpaying population (from 132 to 115). The critical threshold—the break line—in comparing the two years in the table of the distribution of wealth is situated at a point corresponding to an assessment equal to 0.8 percent of the total for the village: £0.38 in 1398 and £2.60 in 1442. The number of petty taxpayers holding a lesser percentage declined from 98 in 1398 to 68 in 1442. This movement was counterbalanced by the trend toward middle-sized holdings (each comprising *more* than 0.8 percent of the village lands). There were 34 that fell into this category in 1398 compared to 47 in 1442. This is an important fact of social history. The reconstitution of landed property in the fifteenth century was not, in 1442, the result of capitalist concentration in the interest of one or two big village "caciques," whether nobles or bourgeois, but rather a movement that favored some four dozen middle landowners, the survivors or replacements of the more numerous peasantry of 1398; it resulted from the classic accumulation of legacies by a reduced number of possible heirs. In the sixteenth century, the middle-sized holdings reconstituted in the days of Charles VII tended to fly to pieces again under centrifugal pressures; the taxpaying population doubled between 1442 and 1570 (from 105 to 210), and as usual, the middle-sized properties caved in and splintered into a series of diminutive holdings.

On the other hand, as often (but not always) happened, the large properties toward the bottom of the table were also making progress between 1442 and 1570. By a process of polarization, and by virtue of a dialectic of opposites, middle-sized property was being eroded from both sides by small holdings and by large estates. In this particular case, the apogee, about 1450, of a yeoman class of rural landowners favored by the demographic lows of the fifteenth century is twice confirmed—by comparison with what went before and by comparison with what followed. The other villages, where it is possible to compare percentages, offer analogous evidence.

Thus, however one approaches the problem of landownership, whether from the point of view of size, of absolute assessed values, or of assessed values expressed in percentages, the conclusions converge (and a study of the sixteenth century will furnish further proof on this point). A wide-mesh network of landownership was forged in Languedoc on the eve of modern times with the help of a rarified population. It represents the projection of the demographic situation onto the pattern of landownership as reflected in the cadastres. With the modern period, some of the largest of these holdings were joined together and came to resemble veritable capitalistic units of exploitation. But this modern development toward concentrated landownership was not of the same importance as it was in certain regions of the north—England, for example, or Poitou. In fact, under the impact of the population explosion after 1500, most of these large units splintered anew into a fine network of smallholds.

The Reconstitution of Lineages

Up to this point we have been concerned with the abstractions of land structures. It is time now to consider the realities of human relationships and in particular the basic unit of rural life, the peasant family. How was it affected by the *Wüstungen* and the great demographic depression on the threshold of modern times? The complementary processes of disintegration and integration appear to have been at work here.

In the first place, a large number of families and even entire lineages disintegrated altogether. As yet fragmentary studies of family names in the cadastres shed some light on the phenomenon. Take the earliest example, that of Albi. A study of this nature concerning two important quarters of the town where the information in the two *compoix* is complete is extremely revealing. Out of 638 names inventoried in the Le Vigan quarter in 1343, 74 were still encountered in the same quarter in 1358 and another 66 in other quarters of the city. On the other hand, a total of 498 names, or 78 percent, had disappeared altogether. "Family names were sufficiently stabilized in the towns of the fourteenth century to reduce the incertitudes resulting from possible name changes to negligible proportions" (Prat, p. 18). At Albi, in short, with the first major catastrophe of the times, eight out of ten families purely and simply disappeared from the tax rolls (as a result of physical extinction, of emigration, or of complete property loss). This incredibly high figure is confirmed by other studies. Take the case of a hamlet near the Montagne Noire—the *masage* of Prades. In 1375 a census taker counted six poor families, or hearths, all but one of which were deemed to be paupers. All were destined to disappear, at least in the male line. In 1634 in this same hamlet, in fact, not a single person bore one of the old names. They must have been replaced by new immigrant families, forty-three members of which turn up in the tax rolls of 1634, twenty-five bearing the same name. Thus, the break between the late medieval and postmedieval family lineages is complete. The second have completely replaced the first, to whom, at most, they may be related through the female line. Let no one presume to speak of the stability of the peasant family in this region in pre-modern times.

Is it possible to measure, approximately, and to compare the ratios of broken and uprooted lineages in fifteenth-century Languedoc? Below are some figures on the subject: at Saint-Guilhem-le-Désert, out of the 132 tax-payers of 1398, 78 bear a family name which is not to be found in the book of the taille of 1442. The same goes for the 117 taxpayers of 1442, 62 of whose names are absent from the book of the taille of 1486. Family attrition, in other words, was intense; in every decade from 1398 to 1486 an average of 12.7 percent of all taxpayers disappeared without taxpaying male heirs (to be exact, 13.4 percent per decade between 1398 and 1442 and 12 percent per decade between 1442 and 1486). To be sure, we are still a long way from the terrible hemorrhage of the plague period at Albi (when eight out of ten families were uprooted or destroyed in fifteen years), but the loss of substance was in any case considerable.

The counterproof is not hard to come by. After 1500 the rate of attrition of family names in the cadastres declined to a more reasonable level than that of the fifteenth century. In the same parish of Saint-Guilhem, for which there is a book of the taille about every forty years up to the eighteenth century, one finds that the peasant families were much more solidly rooted in modern times than in the late Middle Ages. After 1500, between one tax list and the next only about a quarter of the taxpayers disappear from sight without leaving a trace of their names, as compared to well over 50 percent in the fifteenth century. If one compares the rates of attrition by decade, it appears that the turning point came about 1500. From that time on in the sixteenth, seventeenth, and eighteenth centuries, the figure oscillates around 4.5 percent, never exceeding 6 percent, per decade. On the other hand, between 1400 and 1500, as we have seen, the rate held steady at 12–13 percent. The fifteenth century was without any question the age of broken family lines.

For Fontès an excellent series of *compoix* and books of the taille afford analogous statistics. In this village, too, the rate of attrition of family names in the cadastres by ten-year periods reached its maximum between 1427 and 1505 (8.5 percent per decade). It declined thereafter, dropping to 3.0 percent in the seventeenth century, an age of relative security (when families could multiply peacefully in place and a fair portion of the prospective immigrants would be driven off by *chasse-gueux*)[6] which finally succeeded the late medieval "Time of Troubles." The villages knocked down their stone walls, but they erected social walls in their place.

In the fifteenth century, matters had not yet reached this pass. The ancient lineages unraveled and disappeared. The immigration of new families, no matter how intense, did not suffice, for the moment, to compensate for the losses. The reaction of the surviving families can be summed up in a few words: close ranks and reconstitute the solidarity of the lineage. Families were reconstituted in the same way that properties were—stitched together like the fields and meadows. In fifteenth-century Languedoc there was a move to substitute the extended patriarchal family for the nuclear family, to reconstitute the "great household" of archaic rural societies.

This passage from ménage to *lignage* took place in Languedoc, and especially in the Cévennes, in the depression environment of the period 1350–1480. Naturally, some extended family groups, fraternities, or, *frérèches* existed prior to this time, even in the prosperous twelfth and thirteenth centuries, but as Hilaire has pointed out, "these communities spread rapidly beginning in the second half of the fourteenth century, a phenomenon closely connected with the economic crises of the fourteenth and fifteenth centuries." In fact, economic difficulties and social regression in the late Middle Ages laid bare, underneath the formalisms of written law—of Roman law, which was theoretically sovereign in the Midi—the old bedrock of customary law. And family structures inherited from the distant past experienced a surprising revival on the eve of modern times.

For the Montpellier countryside there are notaries' registers going back to the end of the thirteenth century. Beginning abruptly about 1350, these records attest to the presence of a series of patriarchal or lineal or fraternal institutions in peasant society that were practically unknown to preceding generations. From this time on, these practices spread and developed without interruption. The following examples are found in the deeds: the fictitious transfer of one-third, one-half, or even the entire patrimony to the

---

[6] *Chasse-gueux*: "beggar chaser," a person charged with expelling vagrants and migrants (tr. note).

children's names during the lifetime of the father (a legal fiction thanks to which the latter expressly retained the usufruct of all his property and continued as long as he lived to exercise paternal authority over the household, including his married children and their families); and family communities composed of three couples tightly bound to one another, like one case dating from 1452 in which a father gave his two daughters in marriage to two brothers, sturdy but penniless fellows from the mountains, and the young couples promised to live under his roof (*à feu et à pot*) in total obedience *under the parents' yoke*.

Another characteristic of these extended families of the fifteenth century, in addition to the phenomenon of subordination, was the almost total promiscuity of the old couple and the young ménages. They lived under the same roof, eating and drinking "the same bread and the same wine." There was a sole money box, and the patriarch retained the keys. Without the express consent of the parent, the married son did not have the right to more than five *sous* for himself (a pathetic figure, this forty-year-old scion of an extended family with two or three coppers in his pocket). The father's oppression was compensated for, however, by the obligation he assumed to nourish the young couples, to administer wisely the common grain bin and wine cellar, and to anticipate the family's food needs. The function of command implies the reciprocity of services rendered.

The strict cohesion of the family group created severe strains among its members—strains which reached a breaking point if the father, a widower, remarried and introduced a stranger into the family circle. For that matter, certain widower patriarchs did not hesitate to resort to this "blackmail of the stepmother" vis-à-vis their married offspring who shared the same roof. "If you do not treat me fairly, I'll remarry," Hugues, a peasant in the Cévennes, warned his newly married children who were living in his house. In our own day, the Dominici case, extreme though it is, serves to remind us that it is not always easy to live under the law of a mountain patriarch, a mixture of Jupiter and Ubu.[7] The *grande maison* of Languedoc is a far cry from the bucolic ideal of a Florian. André Chamson's novels of

---

[7] Gaston Dominici, a septuagenarian peasant of Lurs in the southern Alps, was convicted in November, 1954, for the brutal murder of a family of English tourists. The most remarkable aspect of the celebrated *affaire* was the strongwilled patriarch's ascendancy over his numerous clan, which included everyone with any direct knowledge of the crime (tr. note).

the Cévennes picture those mountains as filled with family rivalries and repressed passions and sometimes as the scene of crime and incest.

Moreover, special clauses were inserted in the contracts in order to forestall the revolts that were always brewing against the old man of the house. A contract providing for the community of goods specified that the grandfather's bed was sacred, as was his ration of food. Cursed be the young couple who would sell the one or reduce the other! And cursed be the grandchild who would sell her grandmother's bedstead and bedspread!

A study of the dowry clauses in these contracts is essential to an understanding of the phenomenon of community subjugation in premodern times. The veritable master of the wife's dowry in cases of community of goods was the husband's father. It was he who received and disposed of it. Among the extended family groups that allied themselves to one another through marriage, the dowries passed from father to father, and in the Cévennes in the fifteenth century one finds the classic clauses providing for the reversion of dowries which ethnologists consider one of the characteristics of the extended families of the Maghreb. In the Cévennes at the time of Louis XI, the son-in-law contributed a "dowry supplement" which he might recover if he left the family after the death of his wife. Naturally, before exchanging dowries, the great peasant families of the Montpellier region in the fifteenth century exchanged their young men and women from "power group" to "power group" at the end of astute, drawn-out negotiations.

All these clauses marked the astonishing reinforcement of institutions of lineage in the period 1350–1500. It was a paternalistic institution that was suffocating but protective of the children who resigned themselves to it (and hard on young girls who left it to follow their husbands). A lineage thus constituted was just as solid as a nuclear family. In both cases, divorce was unknown. In the extended family, elderly couples and young couples were riveted together for life—"married" for better and for worse.

The same factors that favored the extended family group also led, in the period 1350–1500, to the creation of innumerable "fraternities," which perpetuated the common exploitation of an undivided domain by the surviving sons after the death of the father. It is true that tacit or contractual "fraternity" is an ancient custom in the Midi, but the institution enjoyed a revival and reached its veritable apogee in fifteenth-century Languedoc. The term *affrairamentum* itself can be dated with certainty to 1420, not to mention its characteristic provisions: the community of goods among brothers, who made symbolic reciprocal donations of half their possessions to one another; and the common life of the brothers' families, who ate and drank at the same table and shared profits and losses. From a psychological standpoint, the figure of the dead father continued to cast its shadow over the associated families of the sons who cohabited and shared in the undivided patrimony. If necessary, it was the lord of the village himself who saw to it that the dead father's will was carried out; it was he who prevented a recalcitrant son from effecting a unilateral division of the inheritance. The common life was all-embracing; hearth, homestead, bread, wine, cooking pot, table, purse, debts, everything was shared. The money of the *frèrèche* was kept in a common coffer. Each brother had a key and the right to no more than five *sous* in pocket money. One of the brothers, usually the eldest, was at the helm and bore the distinction of *gubernator* of the common household. The dowries of the sisters-in-law, naturally, were added to the pool, to be returned to them only in the improbable event of a dissolution of the association. Texts of dissolution of such fraternities are in fact, rare. When one entered into a fraternity it was for life. It was an engagement of enormous import for each of the brothers, for their wives, and for their offspring.

In the fifteenth century, the fraternity in the Cévennes, the classic home of the institution, constituted a basic dimension of social life. It ended by contaminating all sorts of personal relationships. Friends were joined in fraternities; so were fathers and daughters! It was difficult to distinguish unions of interest from unions of affection. Take, for example, the case of Jean Rey. In 1446 his wife, "a bad woman," had left him, but happily Rey had a close friend, one Colrat, of whom he was very fond—a marital breakup and a strong masculine attachment (not without ambiguities in this instance and in certain others). Rey and Colrat, in short, formed a fraternity, bestowed all their goods reciprocally on one another, worked their common holding together, and promised that if Marguerite, Rey's unfaithful spouse, wanted to return "to live with them" and conducted herself "like a good wife," the two friends would be understanding; they would welcome her to their home; they would pardon her.

Beginning in 1440 the Cévennes seem to have been seized by a veritable delirium of "fraternity" which succeeded in contaminating the marriage tie itself. Fraternities between spouses began to multiply. The young couples assumed all the obligations of "fraternity": goods, life, and labor in common, and a common purse with the classic five *sous* of pocket money allotted to each partner. The only special clauses in the case of conjugal fraternities concerned the mutual obligation of faithfulness and the husband's duty to dress his spouse in a befitting manner. Certain young married couples joined by a fraternity contract even promised to be at one another's beck and call, "day and night, like brothers"!

The reconstitution of the extended patriarchal or fraternal family group in the Cévennes region of Languedoc at the close of the Middle Ages is an important fact of ethnological history. The movement's time limits are well defined. It began about 1350, when contracts of this nature suddenly began to proliferate, and it reached its climax about 1450–1510; after 1550–60 acts of family community or fraternity are again rare in the notaries' rolls of Ganges and almost nonexistent in those of Montpellier. The institution did not disappear entirely, but from that time on it played a fairly minor role; it tended to become a relic of the past.

Georges Duby has shown how the crises of the tenth century and of the year 1000, with the collapse of the political-social hierarchies, had led to a short-lived revival of institutions of lineage. In the same way, the crises of the fourteenth and fifteenth centuries favored the next and last revival of the extended family group in France. It was a momentary but widespread phenomenon. Was it not in precisely this period, in 1484 to be exact, that one finds mention, in the region of Caen, of a family of ten couples and seventy souls sharing hearth and pot?

It would be too much of a platitude to account for these phenomena solely in economic, fiscal, or social terms. It was, above all, the anxieties of the fifteenth century and, by contrast, the urgent emotional need for security that these engendered which explain the general return to similar family archetypes. Neither the dislocated monarchy nor the weakened feudality was capable of providing the individual with the moral and material protection he needed. The "libidinous structures of the state" (to paraphrase Freud) collapsed, or proved ineffectual during the course of the wars with England. Needless to say, the individual might still feel a distant affection for his king, an affection mixed with reverence and modeled in an abstract way on the love he felt for his own father, but he knew that from now on he would not receive in return for that affection and obedience the benefits his ancestors normally enjoyed: social order, the right to work in peace, security, and the mutual advantages that come from a respect for legality. And so the individual reappraised—in his ties of affection as in his legal arrangements—his natural protector, the father-patriarch, or his substitute, the older brother.

For all that, psychology, no matter how deeply rooted, was not the only factor. Without any question, the temporary vogue of large family units was tied to the particular circumstances of vacant holdings (*Wüstungen*) and the depopulation that prevailed prior to the great demographic advance of modern times. According to historians of the institution, it was in the mountain regions that the *frèrèches* sprouted like mushrooms in the fifteenth century—in regions of loose and scattered settlement where the land is often unrewarding and difficult to work and during a period when labor was scarce and expensive (bearing in mind fifteenth-century depopulation and the rise of real wages). The large mountain farms, about 1420–50, were faced with a difficult dilemma. Such units could not be operated by a single couple without capital, considerable cash income, and hired labor—impossible conditions. The alternative was to quit the land or else revert to the most archaic and most effective form of mountain land settlement—the large peasant family which supplied its own work force without recourse to hired labor. It is clear that recourse to the *frèrèche* helped maintain islands of human settlement on the rocky mountainsides of the Midi in the fifteenth century. It was the same *frèrèche* that promoted the first attempts to recover the abandoned arable, about 1467–1508, and the new pioneer inroads of the plow in forest and waste. It was not until after 1550, when a dense population (and a numerous labor force) was again solidly implanted in the mountain districts, that the *frèrèches*, the great oppressive, fraternal families of the Cévennes and the Vivarais, their historic mission accomplished, finally gave way to simple nuclear families and small farming units or to great capitalistic farmsteads (*mas*) of the sort recommended by Olivier de Serres.

The Misadventures of Land Rent

These, then, are the problems of land utilization on the threshold of modern times from the point of view of landownership and from the point of view of the peasant family—the basic unit of agricultural production. As always, it is the statistical series that permits one to characterize and compare the same domain or the same type of leasehold from one century to the next.

Let us consider the case of the estates of the cathedral chapter of Saint-Nazaire of Béziers, with its magnificent series of accounts and lease contracts covering a period of four hundred years (1380–1780). In the sixteenth, seventeenth, and eighteenth centuries these estates were always let, either to tenant farmers for rents in grain or money or else to sharecroppers for 50 percent of the grain crop. In contrast, towards the end of the fourteenth century the canons of Béziers were much less demanding. Their tenants of 1384 and 1389 were required to pay only a modest two-fifths of the harvest in rent, even for a veritable wheat factory like the farm of Saint-Pierre, located in the fertile plains country. Not far away was the big farmstead of Viala, whose tenant of 1393 and his successor of 1397 had to deliver a mere quarter of their crop to the chapter. But the sixteenth-century tenants of Viala—in 1544 and 1587—retained only half their crop. They surely would have envied the lot of their predecessors in the days of Charles VI. It was the landowners who were to be pitied, during the reign of the mad king, for their humble quarter of the harvest instead of the portion their successors collected under Francis I or Henry III.

With the coming of the fifteenth century, the landowner continued to lose ground to the working tenant. The good land of Saint-Pierre, which returned two-fifths of the crop to the landlord in 1393, gave up only one-third in 1413. For every thirty sacks of harvest grain, the canons of Saint-Nazaire received fifteen in the sixteenth century, twelve in 1393, and only ten in 1413. Pity the poor canons of 1413! Their tenant, on the other hand, was much better off than his distant replacement of 1585, who was a real fifty-fifty sharecropper on that very same farm of Saint-Pierre.

Four leagues away, on the best soils of the region of Narbonne, in 1430 the richest *condamines* paid a mere quarter of the harvest in rent. In the Lauraguais to the west, another bountiful granary, between 1350 and 1450 "it rarely happened that the cultivator had to pay more than a third of the harvest to the landowner, and often he kept three-quarters or even four-fifths for himself, . . . the system was very advantageous to the farmer" (Wolff, 1954, p. 76).

It is most unlikely that lower yields accounted for lower land rents. The techniques of cereal culture and agricultural productivity scarcely varied in Languedoc from the fourteenth century to the seventeenth century. Languedocian lease contracts and inventories as early as 1384 mention *mi-garach* and *mi-rastouilh*—the classic two-course rotation still practiced without change on the same lands in 1542 and 1780. In regard to the number of plowings, another factor in soil productivity, farmers in the days of Charles VI or Charles VII were at least as industrious as their successors at the time of the Holy League or the Fronde. At Saint-Pierre, Ermengard counted seven plowings per year in 1384, and Agulhon, nine in 1389. The plowmen of the sixteenth and seventeenth centuries would do no better.

Neither the fertility of the soil nor productivity varied significantly, but if agricultural production remained comparatively stable, its distribution was altered markedly. In the modern period it favored the landowner. At the end of the Middle Ages, on the contrary, it favored the peasant. And the causes? One, at least, is well known. In that depopulated world, much land remained idle; it could be had for the asking. And the landlords were no longer in a position to dictate the terms, for if late medieval society was glutted with land, it was short of labor. The peasants could set, even dictate, their conditions and modify the division of the harvest to their own advantage at the landlords' expense.

The landowners of the fifteenth century, consequently, found themselves in a difficult position. It is true that their estates had a tendency to expand as a result of the general consolidation of landed property, but if they wanted to take advantage of this process, to live better off their more extensive properties, they had to learn to exploit them directly and to add the more substantial revenues of the agricultural entrepreneur to the meager rents of the absentee landlord. They had to abandon the role of rentier for that of gentleman farmer. This is exactly what they did. Take the case of the great estates of the canons of Narbonne, for example. After 1550 and in the seventeenth century these lands would often be sharecropped or let for quitrents. In the fifteenth century, on the contrary, direct management triumphed. The canons recruited their harvest hands themselves and directed the haymaking, reaping, binding, and threshing. All of these routine and ignoble tasks were willingly left to their tenants after 1550 and in the seventeenth century just as fast as rising land rents sufficed to meet their needs.

Under Louis XI there was no intermediary between the canons and their farm workers. A simple steward, or *bayle*, transmitted the work orders in 1478–82. His mandate was very limited. He himself worked the land, and his wife did the cooking. The basic direction remained in the hands of the canons, who kept the accounts, paid the *bayle*'s wages and those of the other workers, and distributed their annual rations of wheat, olive oil, salt, wine, and *piquette* ("sour wine"). The *bayle* himself was simply a somewhat better-qualified farm worker, an illiterate corporal from the ranks of the hired hands who was paid the wages of a good plow-hand.

These were the consequences of the low level of population at the end of the period 1350–1480. Landholdings increased in size, but then so did the peasant's share of the harvest. The winner, in these circumstances—or at any rate the one who lost the least—was not, as a rule, the landlord who lived off his rents, but the working landowner, whether peasant, noble, priest, or bourgeois, who personally assumed the role of farm manager.

In view of all this, did the conditions of late medieval society favor the development of rural capitalism and, for example, of a class of large-scale tenant farmers—of agricultural entrepreneurs "without land but with money in their purse" with which to exploit the lands of others? It appears not. Let us return for a moment to the great estate of Saint-Pierre near Béziers. In the sixteenth and seventeenth centuries it is already possible to distinguish certain characteristics (still incomplete) of capitalistic agriculture. A big farmer, the parish kulak, operated Saint-Pierre with dozens of mules and oxen and hundreds of sheep. He produced every year some thousands of *setiers* of grain. One or two centuries earlier, in contrast, according to the disconnected series of land leases at our disposal, the situation was very different indeed. The lands of Saint-Pierre were unified, but not their operation, which was divided—in fact, all but pulverized. In 1389 seven hectares of estate land were let for four years to three peasants in severalty. Then, in 1413, the entire *mas* was let in seven lots for one-third of the produce to seven poor peasants, cultivators from a neighboring parish. One leased thirty *setérées* of plowland for six years, another ten *setérées*, and another six or eight. They had neither money nor tools. The chapter had to sell some of them a plowframe, a heavy iron *reille* ("plowshare") and their only yoke of plow oxen, all on credit (sixteen *livres* in six years). On the contrary, under Francis I, Sully, or Louis XIII a single tenant farmer, a veritable captain of agriculture, assumed command; he was the sole master of the ship apart from the landowner himself.

And yet by the fifteenth century the conditions of landownership necessary, in theory, for the development of capitalistic agriculture were present: broad estates dating back to ancient Gallo-Roman villas or medieval manors. What capitalistic agriculture lacked at the end of the Middle Ages was not land and buildings, but money and labor. One is acutely conscious of the absence of a class of well-to-do, enterprising peasant landowners.

To be sure, there already existed in Languedoc at the end of the Middle Ages a certain number of capitalistic tenant farmers. On September 8, 1395, one Jean Montagnac leased the vast grange of Amilhac for four years at a yearly rental of forty *livres*. By this act alone he qualifies as a rural entrepreneur on a big scale. But individuals like Montagnac did not really begin to appear in large numbers until much later. Without exception, when one compares the tithes, granges, or villages of the fifteenth century with the same tithes, granges, or villages in the sixteenth or seventeenth century one perceives that capitalistic tenant farming was still in its infancy on the threshold of the modern age.

The reasons? Lack of money was the primary one. The monetary famine of the fifteenth century is an established fact. In Languedoc it would not begin to dissipate until the reign of Francis I. Between 1453 and 1504, in more than one village, even the royal taille was payable in olive oil or grain, a fact that was never repeated, to the best of my knowledge, after 1505. The same monetary factors that prevented the emergence of a wealthy land-buying and land-engrossing bourgeoisie in the towns inhibited the formation of a capitalistic farmer class in the countryside.

Monetary difficulties were compounded by other factors relating to the distribution of aggregate farm income. Was not whatever the cultivator gained from the forced self-restraint of the landlord cancelled out by the demands of his hired hands? This raises the next question (after land rent), that of farm wages at the beginning of the period under study.

The Golden Interval of Wages

The period around 1480 was the golden age of wages. The expression is appropriate, with certain reservations, for town workers whose money wages consituted their main income. Is it equally true in the case of the typical farm worker, whose base wages in kind were supplemented every year by a few copper coins?

The lot of the rural proletariat, in fact, depended on the movement, barely studied until now, of mixed wages in money and in kind. Let us consult the archives of the granges administered by a cathedral chapter. One carefully worded contract fixes the conditions of employment of the farm steward, or *bayle*, and his subordinates, the plow-hands or *boyers*. This particular contract was concluded at regular intervals in the period 1475–1510 and is still attested to on different occasions up to 1600–50. If the economic clauses were increasingly severe, the other terms did not change at all from one century to the next, thanks to which fact comparisons are possible. The *bayle* received from his masters (the canons of Narbonne) a fraction of his regular pay in cash. He was also paid a cash pittance or *companage* to contribute to the support of his family and the plow-hands (it was dispensed chiefly for meat). In kind, he received grain, wine, olive oil, and salt, also for himself, his family, and the plow-hands. This represents a typical case of mixed wages for a group of farm workers. If we compare, point by point, the three components of the *bayle*'s wages for the first hundred-year interval at the beginning and the end of our series (1480 and 1580), we shall see to what extent the farm worker of the fifteenth century belonged to a privileged category.

1. Money Wages

In 1478 the *bayle*'s money wages on the two contiguous granges of La Bastide and Védilhan were the same; Béraud Crozat received twenty-four *livres* and twelve *sous* per year "for himself and his wife." His colleague on the neighboring *mas* was paid the same wage. What had happened to money wages one hundred years later? Surprisingly, when one remembers the enormous price inflation that occurred in the interval, the figure had increased only slightly by the end of the sixteenth century. In 1571–75 it was still twenty-four *livres* (eight *écus*) at La Bastide and Védilhan; it was thirty *livres* in 1583, twenty-five in 1590, and thirty-six in 1593, 1596, and 1600. In 1480 the *bayle*'s twenty-four *livres* represented a fairly handsome wage, equal in purchasing power to thirty *setiers* of wheat, or almost the annual wheat ration of three farm workers.[8] On that pay "madame" *bayle* could, in the days of Louis XI or Charles VIII, permit herself the luxury of a few *fantaisies de toilette*. On the other hand, the thirty or thirty-six *livres* that Jean Cassagnol, *bayle* of La Bastide, was paid in about 1583 or 1593 as "wages for himself and his wife" were the equivalent of no more than eight or ten *setiers* of grain (in the measure of Montpellier), barely the annual ration of a single farmhand. The difference spells the radical deterioration (by two-thirds) of the purchasing power of the *bayle*'s annual wage.

2. "Companage"

It is true that the work force of both granges was allocated a supplementary sum of money, the "*companage*," for various purchases, but especially for meat. In 1480 the *companage* at La Bastide for Béraud Crozat, his wife,

---

[8] In *setiers* of Montpellier: one *setier* = forty-nine liters.

and three plow-hands, one a boy, came to £12 6s. per year, or £2 9s. 2d. per head. With respect to this pittance payment, the canons of Narbonne later behaved like certain modern employers. Without tampering with the basic wage, they sweetened the pot with "bonuses" (for productivity, for transportation, and so on). In the sixteenth century, as we have seen, the canons kept the *bayle*'s wages, properly speaking, at a very low level, but they raised the premium of *companage* at both granges from £2 9s. per head per year in about 1480 to £6 in the period 1585–90—an almost threefold nominal increase at a time when the price of meat had increased fourfold. The reduction of *companage* in real terms is unmistakable, but it was not nearly as outrageous as the reduction in the basic money wage examined previously.

3. Rations in Kind

If wages in kind had suffered a decline in the sixteenth century comparable to that of the two components of money wages just studied, the rural proletariat would have had to call it quits.

Nothing of the kind occurred. In terms of quantity, the rations that the canons allowed their farm workers did not diminish between 1480 and 1580; the quality, however, deteriorated—the workers ate white bread under Louis XI and black bread under Henry III. In 1590 the work force of La Bastide received a ration of seven *setiers* of wheat and three *setiers* of rye per person per year.[9] At Védilhan the ration was rather less: five *setiers* of wheat and three *setiers* of rye. The coarse bread that the farmwife made of these eight to ten *setiers* in the grange's bakeoven was no less abundant but a lot darker than that of 1480. Around that time, in fact, the farmhands on the two granges were still eating like bourgeois. Not that their bread was made of the very best flour, but at least it was of pure wheat. Every worker on both granges was allotted eight *setiers* of wheat in 1482, and not a trace of rye or other coarse grains. During the course of the sixteenth century the employers did not cut back on quantity, but they began to skimp on quality.

In certain cases, even, the farm worker was paid less in pocket money but ate more bread at the end of the sixteenth century than in the fifteenth century. At La Bastide, as we have seen, he received eight *setiers* of wheat around 1480 compared to ten *setiers* of grain (seven of wheat and three of rye) around 1580. His bread was darker, but there was more of it at the time of the Holy League. All in all, the fifteenth-century ration was no better than the late sixteenth-century ration in terms of calories, but it was more costly

[9] In *setiers* of Narbonne: one *setier* = seventy liters.

than and not as coarse as it would be a hundred years later towards the close of the religious wars.

Not only did the farm worker of Languedoc in the last third of the fifteenth century insist on having money in his pocket and white bread on his table, but he was also a big drinker of good wine. In 1482 on the same farms, the annual ration of an adult laborer was set at 1 *muid* of red wine supplemented by 0.4 *muid* of *piquette*.[10] A century later, around 1580–90, the ration of red wine had been cut by 20 percent to 0.8 *muid*. The difference was made up by a *piquette* ration of 0.65 *muid* instead of 0.4 *muid*. At the close of the fifteenth century, white bread and good wine; at the end of the sixteenth century, black bread and *piquette*: Was the late fifteenth century a happy age all around? The ration of olive oil was also larger then than it was later.

The question of the salt ration was another one of capital importance, especially since the region of Narbonne lies so close to the saltworks of Sigean. The canons of 1580–90 were close-fisted fellows like their contemporary, Olivier de Serres (who declared naïvely, "with respect to the wageworker, pay him as little as possible"). They neglected to supply their workers with salt. The farmwife, because everything has its price, was expected to pay for salt out of her pittance money, or else each worker out of his personal wages. On this point the canons of 1480 were more generous than their niggardly successors living off fat prebends. Under Louis XI they allotted five quarters of salt to the five adults on each *mas*—one quarter per person per year.

In summary, compared to the miserable devil unlucky enough to be living in the age of Henry III, the farm worker of the late fifteenth century was not badly off at all.

So much for the *bayle* or plow-hand who received a regular food ration from his ecclesiastical employer. The lot of the worker who was paid entirely in kind with a share of the produce (as was the case of harvest hands) was also quite a happy one in the last third of the fifteenth century. Every year, as we have seen, troops of workers came down to the plains to hire out as harvest hands to cut (*segar*) the grain crop. Their leader, or captain, first reached an agreement with the employer, or landlord, concerning the percentage of the total harvest to be set aside for his labor and that of his men. Following a steady decline during the course of the sixteenth century, the figure finally hit rock bottom about 1600–30—on the average the seventeenth sheaf, or barely 6 percent of the total harvest. And sometimes it was even

[10] *Muid*: usually approximately 650 liters (tr. note).

less; in 1620, Jean Escanecabios, an illiterate cobbler, assumed, on behalf of himself and his companions, the "enterprise" of harvesting the wheat fields of La Bastide for the nineteenth sheaf, or 5.3 percent of the crop. These Narbonnese reapers were decidedly "pauperized" compared to their fifteenth-century predecessors. In 1478, in fact, Bernard Fontès and some companions formed a group to harvest the same wheat fields and received, as reward for their labors, exactly the tenth part—*decimam partem*—of the crop, a sort of second tithe, if you like, and twice as much as was allotted their successors of 1620. Seasonal harvest hands, in the centuries that followed, never managed to carry home grain sacks as well filled as that.

In this manner, the fortunate reapers of 1480 reduced the profits of the rural entrepreneur by a like proportion. It is true that the latter's gross income in 1480 was swollen by the depressed level of land rent, but his net income, after meeting expenses, was eroded—amputated, in fact—by the sharp increase in wages.

This rise in wage rates was itself determined by the state of the labor market. The rural work force, reduced by the decline in population, dictated its terms to the agricultural employer. Our conclusions concerning the farm worker's income, whether it consisted of bed and board or of a share of the produce, confirm what is known about the movement of urban wages in Languedoc at the end of the Middle Ages. At Toulouse following the Black Death, the surviving workers took advantage of the labor shortage to demand higher wages. The plague forced the rich to loosen their purse strings; apprentices' salaries rose steadily between 1350 and 1450, and employers, desperate for workers, recruited seasonal labor from as far away as Brittany and set women to work at the hardest tasks.

Meat and Wheat

An increase in real wages and a general improvement in the living standards of the peasantry was brought about by the relaxation of demographic pressures and by the resulting alleviation of the problem of subsistence. The plague of 1348 unquestionably signaled the beginning of the period of rarified population in Languedoc, a period which includes the whole of the fifteenth century. Rarified population meant that wheat was plentiful and cheap. After 1351 the periods of scarcity were less frequent, occurring only once every ten or every twenty years. The demographic depression resolved the problem of subsistence by brutally eliminating the surplus population.

In the long run, this improvement led to changes in diet—in the people's daily bread—and in the agricultural balance of bread cereals. From this point of view, the fifteenth and early sixteenth centuries represent a critical juncture. Prior to that time the peasants ate barley bread; later they would eat bread made of *méteil*, a mixture of wheat and rye. But in the fifteenth and early sixteenth centuries the peasant's loaf was made of pure wheat flour.

First, take barley. For most of the Middle Ages, the rotation of cereal crops in Languedoc followed the ancient Mediterranean pattern. The staple bread grains were hard wheat and barley. In the plains country, in the twelfth century, these two formed the basis of all land leases. In normal years the poor subsisted on barley, and at Nîmes at the end of the twelfth century it constituted the pilot item whose price indicated the state of the market. It is true that rye was already being cultivated in the Middle Ages on soils of the central plateau that were better suited to it, but in the plains of Bas-Languedoc it remained practically unknown as late as the fourteenth century. The inventories of grain stocks in 1323 mention, for the lowlands, nothing but sacks of wheat and barley. The grain exchanges were called *orgeries*.[11]

But perhaps this medieval barley was mainly for porridge, wheat being the only bread cereal? No, this is too simple a view. The barley of Languedoc by 1200 was unquestionably, as far as the populace was concerned, a bread cereal, too, and not just the stuff polenta is made of. A baking ordinance composed in 1196 at Montpellier is explicit on this point. At that time the rich ate bread made of the best wheat flour; the rest of the people ate coarse bread of a mixture of barley and wheat or simply barley bread, heavy and hard to digest even after repeated sifting.

The medieval cultivation of winter barley (still called early barley or *escourgeon*) for bread in two-course rotation with wheat (*escourgeon*, fallow, wheat, fallow, *escourgeon*, and so on) represents a regional practice that has largely escaped the attention of historians. The reason is that in France this particular rotation was found in its pure state (in its heyday) only along the Mediterranean littoral—the Mediterranean of barley eaters. The moment one scales the mountainous amphitheatre that delimits on the north and west the realm of winter barley, the moment one begins to ascend the Alps, the Rouergue, the Haute-Cerdagne or to penetrate the humid regions of the Aquitaine basin, the familiar *ordi* of the medieval documents of Provence and Languedoc is replaced by rye and oats. In contrast to the

[11] *Orgerie*: from *orge*, "barley" (tr. note).

authentic Mediterranean peoples who ate bread made of barley, the natives of the Alps and the Rouergue and other mountain-dwellers had been eating rye bread for centuries.

And indeed, the crop rotation—winter wheat, fallow, winter barley, fallow—is practically unknown in continental France, which practices instead a two-course rotation of wheat and rye with fallowing in alternate years or, farther north, a three-field rotation of winter wheat followed by a spring sowing of barley or oats, followed by a year of fallow. In France and elsewhere, the two-course rotation, with alternate sowings of wheat and winter barley, is a specifically Mediterranean practice. Where, indeed, is it that one finds barley eaters in ancient and prehistoric agrarian societies if not in the Mediterranean countries—among the inhabitants of Ensérune or Jesus' disciples or the starving multitudes of the Apocalypse—none of whom had ever tasted rye bread but were ever faithful to barley like the earliest agriculturalists of the Fertile Crescent? In the Middle Ages, the ancient cropping system based on wheat and barley survived intact from Castille to Greece, and the agrarian landscape was everywhere similar to the landscapes of Languedoc and Provence. The ecology of the Mediterrean lands, where lack of rainfall is favorable to barley, long served to preserve the ancient structures against the invasion of rye and oats, latecomers to the scene from more humid regions.

Now, beginning (very approximately) in 1400, the vast mantle of barley cultivation, which still covered the southernmost region, was rent in different places by gaping fissures. Languedoc offers, in fact, a remarkable example of this process, especially in the region of Béziers-Narbonne. There, as late as 1384–97, the tithes were still paid one-third in *touzelle* wheat, one-third in barley, and one-third in a mixture of the two called *raonage*; in 1391 and 1397 the harvest workers received a food ration consisting half of barley and half of wheat. In all this there is no mention of rye whatsoever.

In 1384–97, therefore, barley cultivation was still in full vigor, but the end of its reign was approaching. In the Lauraguais, the harvest censuses show that barley was still a major crop in 1375, that its importance had declined considerably by 1400, and that it had practically disappeared by 1418. At Béziers-Narbonne, winter barley was still in a very strong position as late as 1400, but by 1480, when the interrupted series resumes, it had almost disappeared. The contracts no longer specify that the harvest workers receive 50 percent of their food ration in barley, as was the case eighty years before, but that they be given the whole amount in wheat. In just three generations the wheat revolution was victorious, and the traditional peasant diet had been radically transformed.

In the early years of the sixteenth century, wheat was the king of bread cereals and all but undisputed lord of a realm it was forced to share with barley in the fourteenth century and with rye in the seventeenth century. The ecclesiastical granges of Béziers in 1527–31 were let for rents in kind consisting of 90 to 100 percent wheat. In the period 1650–90, on the contrary, the same lands paid no more than 40 percent of their rent in wheat, and the rest was in rye diluted with a little oats.

Let us consider for the moment the first step in the process: the passage from a mixed regime consisting of wheat and barley to a single-crop regime of wheat alone. This change took place between 1400 and 1480 (probably about 1400–20) and represents, everything considered, a significant improvement in the standard of living. The proof is that the "old days" of heavy, coarse barley bread evoked nothing but unhappy memories, not the slightest nostalgia, in the sixteenth century. Winter barley, or *escourgeon*, wrote Olivier de Serres, is a vulgar food good for the poor in cases of extreme need, but otherwise fit for horses—a fodder and a cathartic. Estienne was of the same opinion. *Escourgeon* was a famine grain suitable perhaps for the poor devils of Périgord. Rye was infinitely preferable. It gave young girls a firm and rosy complexion. Pliny had once drawn a contrast between the earliest Romans, who were barley eaters, and the citizens of the *Urbs* in his own day, fastidious wheat eaters. "Barley," he said, "was good enough for our forebears, but today it's only good for the horses."

In simpler terms, one may speak of a wheat cycle (fifteenth and early sixteenth centuries) interposed between a medieval barley cycle and a modern rye cycle. Such a phenomenon is of multiple significance. First of all, it is demographic; if one could get along without barley at the end of the fifteenth century, it was because in a normal year there was enough wheat to go around—because, thanks to a sort of reverse Malthusianism, population had retreated faster than the means of subsistence. Its significance from the point of view of land use derives from the fact that the barley-growing areas coincided with the zone of typical Mediterranean agriculture (barley, in fact, is still in our own day a major crop in Spain, Greece, and the Maghreb). By its rejection of barley in the period 1400–80, first mostly in favor of wheat, later for a wheat-rye-oats rotation, Bas-Languedoc tended, in this particular respect, to depart from the classic Mediterranean model (barley in rotation with wheat) and to draw nearer to the continental model of wheat-rye-oats.

Another complex phenomenon, determined both by the retreat of arable and by the rise in the standard of living, was the strong position of stock raising on the threshold of modern times. Take the case of Fontès, a village studied earlier. In 1505 the population was still sparse: 106 native taxpayers, only a handful more than in 1427, when there were 95, and many less than in 1695, when the number had grown to 248. Now, this underpopulated village possessed more livestock in 1505 than it ever would again—2,948 head of sheep and goats as compared to only 1,917 head (a good third less stock for a population three times more numerous) in 1693.

At Coussergues, the deserted village annexed by Pierre de Sarret, the herds of 1503 (comprising 2,500 sheep belonging to the lord or entrusted to the care of a tenant plus 219 goats, 29 oxen, 54 cows, 16 horses, and 98 pigs) were larger by far than any of the herds that have grazed these lands since that time. Sarret, the fifty-year-old former soldier, assisted by his young wife, his ten children, and his two "bastard-matadors," the irascible Jeanny and Michou, was running a real sheep and cattle ranch.

The diagrams of Thérèse Sclafert serve as confirmation. Provence, too, boasted larger herds of cattle, sheep, and goats in 1471 than it ever would again, right up to 1956. Grasse, today the city of flowers, in the fifteenth century was the sheep capital of the entire province.

At the very close of the Middle Ages, the masters of the Midi, a land short of peasants but teeming with livestock, were the insolent graziers. "The four of us carry more weight than all of you, numerous though you be," a group of them declared in 1433 to a handful of family heads who were struggling as best they could to defend the depopulated village lands of Aniane against the depredations of grazing sheep.

The contraction of plowland and the spread of pasture and waste was a windfall for the graziers. Did the rise in the standard of living and the increase in meat consumption similarly enrich the butchers? It is indeed remarkable how well the butchers' guilds seem to have weathered the depression of the fifteenth century. At Montpellier, in the quarter of Saint-Firmin, 458 taxpayers are listed in the *compoix* of 1404 compared to only 294 in 1435. The ranks of the clothworkers were decimated, but there were more butchers, more butchers for fewer people—seventeen *mazeliers* (mutton butchers, for the most part) in 1435 compared to fourteen in 1404. And in the quarter of Saint-Mathieu, where there was not a single *mazelier* in 1404, three turned up in 1435.

The traffic in meat, then, from grazier to butcher, was more intense than ever before, despite the misfortunes of the age. This is not to be wondered at. Pasture was abundant, and, in addition, depressed wheat prices in this period of depopulation, as well as the higher purchasing power of wages, paved the way for a greater consumption of meat.

Thus, fifteenth-century Languedoc offers the example of a dialectic of good and ill fortune. Following the great shipwreck of 1348 and succeeding decades, there emerged, little by little, several remarkable cases of social promotion. The wageworker enjoyed a higher standard of living than ever before. The cultivator dictated his terms to the landlord. The peasant proprietor himself rounded out his plot of land. All these groups were eating better; that is, white bread made of wheat flour, which is more nourishing than the traditional barley bread of their forefathers because it is richer in gluten. A generous nature offered them broader pastures, more wild game, and all the resources of the conquering forests. The virgin lands and abandoned fields provided a challenge to the hardy peasant assarter with only his large family to aid him. A cruelly decimated population discovered new sources of strength in the midst of misfortune, in this contact with the rejuvenated earth. And, like the cleric who hoped to salvage the patrimony of the Church, the lord who sought to safeguard his family's position had no alternative but to follow the peasant's example and become an active farmer, unless he was to take up the life of a bandit chief.

Land alone—that is, landed capital—was, for a time, highly unprofitable. It could be made to yield a profit only if exploited directly, preferably by large peasant families (thereby avoiding the payment of excessively high wages). It was not enough, in other words, to own land. One also had to see that it was worked, by the members of the extended family group itself if not otherwise.

The "primary sector"—the direct production of the fruits of the earth—prospered to the detriment of landed fortunes based on shrinking rents (little matter whether manorial or capitalistic in nature). This reconsecration of active farming laid the groundwork for a new expansion of the rural economy.

About 1480–1500, in any case, we are in the presence of a sturdy, vigorous, well-nourished populace in the process of rapid renewal following the recent uprooting of the majority of family lines. It was a society stimulated by the abundance of colonizable land, which also accounted for the weakness of land rent. It was solidly implanted on its reconstituted domains in powerful family groups. Purified and rejuvenated by a century of trials and tribulations, it was ready, for the second time, to launch an assault on the *hermes* and the waste and to carve out new and larger holdings with torch, ax, and plow. A population reduced to a minimum and concentrated on the best lands contained within itself creative energies that were destined to explode like a nova in the opening decades of the sixteenth century.

By about 1480–90 the first symptoms of demographic increase appeared in the Comtat and in the *garrigues* of the Montpellier region. Beginning in 1500, a new wave of pioneer settlers moved out onto the land.

2

Population, Subsistence, Income: The "Scissors" of the Sixteenth Century

I. The Population Explosion

"Like Mice in a Grange"

The most striking fact about the sixteenth century between 1500 and 1570 was the great boom in population. We possess no civil registers which would permit us to study the phenomenon in detail, but the fiscal records furnish perfectly trustworthy indications of the trend. Every two or three years when the parish *greffier*, or tax registrar, refashioned the books of the taille, taking into account changes in landownership (which had been noted down in the meantime in the margins of the *compoix*), the list of taxpayers grew perceptibly longer. And when every half century or so the land surveyors, at the request of the consuls, compiled a new *compoix* of individual properties, the difference in numbers, reflecting the accumulated increase of one or two generations, was very considerable indeed.

It should be noted that the provincial government put no pressure on the village registrars to add more taxpayers to the rolls. No tax administration attempted to unify their efforts or suggest the proper procedures to be followed. And yet all these parish scribes—all these tiny cogs in the ancient tax machine working for their own consuls in their own tight little circumscriptions—confirm in unknowing chorus the prodigious increase in the number of taxpayers in the two generations separating the accession of Louis XII from the outbreak of the Wars of Religion.

The demographic increase revealed by these records was general in character. The one exception, which only serves to confirm the rule, is the tiny village of Saint-Geniès-de-Varensal deep in the heart of a chestnut forest. The movement does not seem to have gotten off to a particularly early start.

At Lodève and Lunel, for example, it was not under way before 1513–18. In Liguria and even in Provence it seems to have begun sooner (but it began later in Spain, and it is conceivable that the demographic groundswell was moving from east to west along the Gulf of Lion from its Italian epicenter).

In any event, the population increase in Languedoc, if a little late getting started, was truly considerable. Let us try to determine its approximate importance. The rate of growth in the number of taxpayers by decade varies from 6.7 to 21.2 percent, the average for the entire region between 1500 and 1560 being 11.5 percent. At that rate, the number of taxpayers would double in two or three generations. Now, this figure is obviously related, to a large extent, to the increase in the number of heads of families. Is it safe to assume that their number doubled also? In the absence of direct data it is difficult to give an exact figure. For those who are inclined to doubt the extraordinary demographic resurgence of the first half of the sixteenth century, it is worth recalling, nevertheless, that during a somewhat longer time span (1480–1560) Provence, according to impeccable sources, tripled the number of its households.

Whether one considers households, hearths, or enrolled taille payers, the conclusion is everywhere the same—southern France experienced a veritable population explosion in the first sixty-five years of the sixteenth century.

The increase was not only massive; it was also continuous. The case of Gignac, where, thanks to a rich documentation, one can follow the actual ballooning of population almost year by year, is characteristic. There were, to be sure, mortalities, epidemics, and famines that sometimes brought the movement to a standstill, but these constituted little more than brief interruptions. They had nothing in common with the cruel slaughters of the Fronde of 1662, 1694, 1709, and other years which would later dismantle the unhealthy demographic structure of seventeenth-century France.

All the communities saw their numbers increase, and every quarter of every village or town filled up with people more or less at the same rate. At Montpellier the population of each of the six quarters and the suburbs burst its shackles at the precise same moment, in 1500–10.

Twenty-seven communities in all attest to the demographic increase of the sixteenth century. It would be surprising, of course, if the contrary were the case, for the phenomenon, as everyone knows, was not limited to Languedoc. "Between the general census years of 1470 and 1540, the number of households in Provence practically tripled on the average, overtaking the figure for the period preceding the Black Death of two centuries earlier"

(Bautier, p. 267). The Mediterranean countries and certain parts of western Europe were also caught up in this broad population movement, of which Languedoc was only a local case.

The chronology of the rise, however, presents certain peculiarities. In Spain it seems to have reached its height between 1560 and 1600, a time when the peninsula was being inundated by the flood of precious metals from America. In neighboring Languedoc, on the contrary, the movement clearly ran out of steam after 1560–70. If we attempt, sources permitting, to isolate and analyze the period 1560–1600 in detail, we find that the rates of demographic growth, in the majority of cases, had become mediocre, zero, or even negative. The powerful upswing of the first half of the sixteenth century had definitely spent its force after 1560–70. The culprit was probably not the economy. Economic conditions were in fact quite favorable to population growth, as can be seen in the case of Italy or of Spain under Philip II. Rather, the causes are to be sought in the ravages of the civil wars which were peculiar to France. The parishes in which population declined or stagnated were the very ones most sorely tried by the religious conflict; Bessan, which was taken and pillaged by partisans of the League in 1587, is an example. Beyond these brief if bloody episodes it is certain that the classic hardships wrought by war were responsible for the sluggish demography of the years 1560–1600: the massacres, the theft of work animals and other farm stock, the requisitions, and the impossibility of plowing or sowing. And finally, the exodus of Protestants to Switzerland and of Catholics to Spain also served to sap the vitality of population growth.

The caesura of 1570 was, in a sense, definitive. After 1600, despite the return of peace, the wild exuberance, the joyful demographic frenzy, of the days of Louis XII, Francis I, and Henry II, when the Languedocians were breeding "like mice in a grange," never returned. The growth of population resumed, to be sure, after 1600 and continued up to about 1675–80, but in a slow and sensible manner. A similar abatement was perhaps inevitable. Between 1500 and 1560 the high rates of demographic growth in Languedoc and Provence, which were probably also stimulated by immigration, can only be understood in terms of the low level and low density of population at the beginning of the period. Even without the Wars of Religion a deceleration was bound to occur—in fact, did occur in the seventeenth century—when village lands, productive resources, and the labor market all reached a point of saturation.

For all that, the population of Languedoc during the years of maximum increase (1500–70) revealed, in comparison with the preceding period, some original and very healthy symptoms. The plague is one example. From 1481 at the latest, and up to 1516, it remained endemic, an almost annual occurrence in Languedoc, forcing the Parlement of Toulouse to decamp at each new outbreak. And in 1510 Languedoc was still considered the most pestiferous province of the realm.

After 1516, on the contrary, the terrible disease was less virulent, and outbreaks were less frequent. This is particularly evident in the case of Toulouse, where the sanitary and policing attentions of the Parlement make it possible to establish for the first time a veritable statistical series. Between 1481, when the series begins, and 1516, epidemics of the plague were reported almost yearly. Recurrences were discontinuous, on the contrary, after 1516. Once the violent epidemic of 1529/30 had passed, new outbreaks were rare, and they were rarer still after 1564 (and for that very reason all the more terrifying to contemporaries). The scourge of the plague, as we know, finally disappeared from western Europe in the eighteenth century, retiring to its home grounds in eastern Europe and Asia. At Toulouse the epidemic of 1653 was the last. The plague that broke out at Marseilles in 1720 just grazed the eastern corner of Languedoc (Gévaudan and the Cévennes). In short, by the fifteenth century the plague in Languedoc had generally lost the apocalyptic character of the Black Death of 1348. From 1516, moreover, it was no longer endemic. After 1530, and especially from 1564 to its ultimate disappearance, outbreaks were rare and unexpected. The data for other regions confirm those for Toulouse.

Similarly—in connection with the dynamics of population change—one also witnesses the decline of leprosy. The records of admissions to the leper asylum at Nîmes constitute a statistical series and suggest a sort of chronology of the disease. As late as 1535 there were one or two new patients every year, sometimes more. After that date, admissions grew increasingly rare. Long years passed sometimes without a single new case. In 1523 the lepers of Nîmes were still crowded for space in their common quarters. By the end of the century, on the other hand, they had plenty of room to move around in and comfortable furnishings, and they were initiating one lawsuit after another from their forced confinement while their *majoral*, the healthy son of a leper, busied himself investing the now superfluous funds of the common purse. The period around 1519 was also marked by the disappearance of the "white leprosy" of the so-called *capots*, *cagots*, or *ischaureillats*, who were very numerous in the region of Narbonne, the Pyrenees and

northern Spain and whose descendants, the *cagots*, remained legally segre-
gated up to the eightteenth century, with their own hamlets, cemeteries,
holy water vessels, and so on. But these social pariahs, at least as early as
1519, were considered healthy from a medical standpoint.

Thus, the demographic upswing of the sixteenth century, which sprang
from the unique circumstances of the late fifteenth century, was fostered,
in addition, by the attenuation of the old communicable diseases of the late
Middle Ages. Were the microbes in question less virulent than in the past,
was the population more immunized (the latest studies question the validity
of the latter hypothesis), or was it a question of the replacement of the
plague-bearing rat by a different species? Dr. Pollitzer, a specialist in the
study of the plague, favors the first two hypotheses. Whatever the reasons,
there is no question about the attenuation of the ancient kinds of contagion
of Asian or African origin. Even the introduction of New World diseases
destined to take their place—like syphilis, which was propagated right and
left around 1535 by the prostitutes of Montpellier and Avignon—did not
manage to upset the medical and demographic balance, which remained,
compared to the earlier period, emphatically positive. People, in short, were
getting healthier; the plague microbe had lost much of its virulence, and
the mortality rate, caught between two fires, so to speak, was attenuated,
giving free rein during the course of several generations to the rise of
population.

The "Extensive" Solution: The Recovery of Marginal Land

Land settlement (*peuplade*) and land reclamation were practically syn-
onymous terms in the sixteenth century just as they were around the year
1000. Beginning in 1520, the authorities, who had remained indifferent or
even favorable to the practice prior to that time, were aroused by the serious
encroachments on forest and waste ("trees or thistles") by fire, ax, and
mattock. In 1520–21, the first cry of alarm was addressed to the peasants by
the Parlement of Toulouse: "When are you going to stop *depopulating* the
forests and cutting green wood and dead wood there?" In 1539 and again
in 1546 the first complaints were heard from the Estates of Languedoc: "the
country is being entirely cleared of wood." Royal commissioners defended
the integrity of the king's domain and expressed apprehension over the
number of people who went there without license to break "the barren
lands and possessions" to the plow. They waxed indignant over the fever
of mill building that gripped the riverains of Languedoc, like those of the

Franche-Comté, and left the driest of wadis cluttered with dikes and water-wheels.

By about 1555–58 the devastation of the poor woodlands of Mediterranean Languedoc was an accomplished fact. The bakers' ovens were devouring holm oak logs, and the *garrigues*, in the absence of trees, were being denuded of their scrub. Long columns of asses, staggering under faggots of rosemary, supplied the towns with wood fuel.

Even more important than the cutting of firewood was the advance of arable. The *compoix* bring to light some individual examples of land assarters, male and female. Isabelle de Lerm laid claim, in a village of the Hérault in 1534, to some meadow and woodland, doubtless very poor, which she proceeded to "break" or assart, to sow with grain, and to plant with almonds and young olive trees (for even the meadows in this parish, like the meadows of Béziers in about 1530–40, were sown with grain, so great were the food requirements of a growing population).

The *compoix* of Langlade, in the Vaunage of Nîmes, which have been closely studied by taking careful note of place names, permit one to follow the advance of the pioneer fringe of cultivation up into the *garrigue*. In 1500 the village arable measured 306 hectares, all of it (except for a patch of 3 hectares) in the plain, which was entirely under cultivation. The *garrigue*, which accounted for another 520 hectares, was, except for the 3 hectares just mentioned, entirely virgin land. By 1576 the rape of the *garrigue* was well under way. Forty-four hectares had been plowed under, increasing the figure for 1500 fifteen times over. Demographic pressure, the rise in demand, and the increase in prices had made their combined effect felt. One had to resign oneself to the working of poor, rocky soils that had never been worked before or that had been abandoned after 1350 or 1400.

This assarting was of a predatory sort at the expense of field and forest, and it was not very profitable. It required a heavy outlay of human and animal effort and promised only meager returns. Very few of today's farmers would be interested in the poor soils that were then being reclaimed. Was there perhaps another solution to the compelling pressure of population of the sixteenth century?

The "Intensive" Solution: Mixed Cultivation

One can either reclaim virgin or vacant land, thereby increasing the total acreage under crop, or one can plant trees or vines on old or new assarts, thereby increasing the returns from agriculture by more intensive forms of land utilization. The latter is the classic response of Mediterranean agriculture to a rise in population. Indeed, it is often the only form of "high farming" known in the absence of soil-renewing rotations, fodder crops, manuring, and, more often than not, irrigation. The sixteenth century, then, concentrated on arboriculture and viticulture. The agricultural renaissance was characterized, first of all, by a cycle of olive cultivation. Beginning in 1500, in *compoix* after *compoix* one can almost see the ranks of trees advancing down the furrows, transforming certain regions into prime olive oil producers. It was not so much a question of regular orchards, land set aside for olive monoculture, as it was of the so-called *camp en holieu* or *camp en olivas*; in other words, a wheat field planted with rows of olive trees. The arbored wheat field was, in reality, an all-purpose piece of land. On the terraced slopes bordering the Rhône, the Hérault or the torrents subjacent to the Cévennes it produced at the same time wheat, oil, millet, and a few rows of "vegetables" (that is, beans). At Gignac, on the banks of the Hérault—the scene of great activity at this time—the olive tree made continuous progress from the fifteenth century to the end of the sixteenth century. In the earliest *compoix*, which dates from the beginning of the fifteenth century, 6 parcels of land out of 920, or less than 1 percent, were planted in olives. By 1462 the figure was 19 percent, and the revolution was under way. In 1519 olive orchards were marking time (15 percent of the land parcels), but by this time another 16 percent were arbored wheat fields. One-third of the land parcels, in one way or another, were producing olive oil. As the demographic tide mounted and the ranks of the taille payers filled up, the olive made new inroads on every side until, in 1534, 42 percent of the parcels were orchard and 14 percent arbored wheat fields. Finally, by 1596, the revolution was accomplished. The hillsides were carved up into steps and terraces, and olive trees were growing everywhere. Fully 34 percent of the land plots were planted in orchards, and more than 34 percent were mixed, producing both oil and wheat. The silvery tufts of the olive trees even began to emerge from among the more somber mass of vines. *Coltura promiscua* had carried the day. The winegrowers and plowmen abandoned their old trades to devote themselves to the production of vegetable oils of whatever variety (*amelliers*, "almonds," and *nouguiers*, "walnuts," were also being planted in large numbers in the wake of the olive).

Thus, one common denominator in the sixteenth century was the progress of the oil-producing fruit tree, sometimes picketed insidiously on the plowland, but pushing ahead elsewhere in the compact formation of closely planted olive orchards.

The evidence of the *compoix* is remarkably unanimous on this score, but leaves something to be desired from the point of view of detailed chronology. Let us see what the olive tithes can tell us. The long series of tithe accounts, beginning in the period 1480–1500, constitute the most realistic (because they are the most direct) evidence of agricultural fluctuations. Every year at Narbonne and in the surrounding villages the canons of Saint-Just sold the tithe in olive oil to the highest bidder a few days before the fruit was gathered. The tithe farmer made only a modest profit because he was not involved in the cycle of cultivation, his role being limited to claiming his share of the fruit and extracting the oil. The rente in olive oil that he agreed to deliver to the chapter therefore represented a very important fraction of his gross returns. In any event, the variations in the volume of this rente, whether by year, by decade, or by century, were strongly influenced by the volume of the tithe, which is to say, by the volume of production. An abundant harvest meant a big tithe which meant a big rente and vice versa.

Let us consider four of these production curves: Narbonne and Gruissan beginning in 1479, Moussan beginning in 1480, and Cuxac beginning in 1498. At first, one is struck by the extreme irregularity of the graphs, their violent ups and downs and numerous lacunae. The olive tree in those days was subject to a sort of spontaneous fallowing and produced a real crop of fruit only every second year, following which, exhausted for lack of fertilizer, it rested; it recuperated for a year. This accounts for the sawtooth effect. The gaps in the curve, on the other hand, can be explained by crop failure due to severe freezes or parasites, by the decision of the canons to collect the tithe themselves instead of farming it out, or, finally, by an oversight on the part of the scribe.

These, in truth, are minor drawbacks. The reading of the curves is clear; they attest to an increase in olive oil production in the sixteenth century, especially in the major production centers. In certain parishes, tithe receipts doubled between 1500 and 1560. At Narbonne and Cuxac, where the olive was less important, the rising trend, if not so marked, was nevertheless easily discernible during the course of this same sixty-year period. The movement was general; the tithes of the Aude confirm the *compoix* of the Hérault.

The olive groves of Narbonne, which were so important up to 1709, began to take form in the early sixteenth century.

After 1560–70, during the last thirty years of the civil wars, the returns from the olive oil tithes declined. Was this decline actually a case of declining production, or was it the result of cunning resistance to the tithe on the part of the peasants? We shall return to the problem later. For the moment let us concentrate our attention on the first half of the sixteenth century, for which the sources all agree. During the economic renaissance of 1500–1560, olive cultivation was spreading. By 1560 it was in full vigor. No one could have foreseen that four severe winters between 1565 and 1573 would momentarily reduce the olive trees of Languedoc to stark skeletons, blackened and twisted by the freezing cold.

These Renaissance olive planters turn up on almost every page of the ancient registers. In 1533, for example, Bernard Pomayrols, a ropemaker of Béziers—actually a part-time ropemaker with one foot always in the orchard—agreed to plant twelve *estaques* (young olive stocks) at the behest of the canons. The latter furnished the saplings and paid the ropemaker a daily wage for his labor. Bernard assumed all other expenses, brought his own lunch, and undertook to water, dig, hoe, and cultivate the twelve *estaques*. I have often encountered similar individuals in the acts of the notaries. Moreover, on every farmstead, about 1530–50, the tenant was encouraged to plant ten or twelve *estaques* every year at his own expense, making a thousand in a century on a medium-sized property. Thus, it is easy to comprehend the spread of mixed cultivation in the countryside and how the "adornment" of the naked plowlands came about.

The movement also had the effect of extending the limit of olive cultivation farther north. Olivier de Serres, who was an observant geographer, noted that "century by century" the olive "is retreating inland." It flourished in various localities formerly considered unsuitable to its spread because of their "coldness." This northward progress was destined to continue well beyond the sixteenth century. In 1552 Félix Platter, journeying down from Lyons on the left bank of the Rhône, saw his first olive trees laden with their red, green, and black fruit (already mature and very bitter) at Pierrelatte. Three centuries later Flahault encountered olive orchards ten kilometers farther north at the latitude of Viviers. On the right bank of the Rhône, the difference from one century to the next was even more remarkable. In 1595, according to Thomas Platter, the northern limit was at Bourg-

Saint-Andéol. In 1886 it was thirty-three kilometers farther upstream! The olive, in short, was advancing northward at the respectable rate of one kilometer per decade or ten kilometers per century.

The rise of olive cultivation in the sixteenth century was not confined to Languedoc. It affected the other Mediterranean regions as well. Provence, the Comtat Venaissin, Andalusia, and the Tunisian littoral were being planted with olives in the age of Francis I, Charles V, and Barbarossa. Underlying this expansion one can divine the growing local demand of the traditional Mediterranean cuisine: cabbage soup laced with olive oil and interminable fast days with mackerel or small sole cooked in olive oil. Poor Félix Platter, who liked his cooking done with butter in the Swiss manner! Moreover, there was the growing demand of woolen cloth and soap manufactories and of the great Mediterranean cities like Genoa about 1557–60, not to mention that of the distant northern markets. Finally, one suspects that there may have been an African trade in olive oil for Sudanese gold. We know for a fact that in the nineteenth century olive oil was carried by camel caravan as far as Timbuktu in five successive relays. By the time it arrived it was so dear, due to the costs of transport, that it was dispensed a drop at a time for luxury uses or for emergencies—for a lady's toilette or for dressing wounds.

Be that as it may, the olive tree won its place in the sun in the sixteenth century. When climate and location were propitious, it succeeded in occupying a quite respectable position. Thus, in the diocesan cadastre of Nîmes-Alès in 1552, the olive, on the whole, came third behind cereals and vines and only about even with the chestnut. But in the southern part of the diocese, olive orchards accounted for almost a third of the cultivated land in terms of value. The point is that here not only was climate favorable, but seaports specializing in the oil trade were near at hand. Hence, although the rise of olive cultivation was real enough, it was also highly localized; taking the diocese as a whole, the olive, which ranked fourth in terms of production, accounted for only 6 percent of the arable in terms of land values, and not much more than that in the diocese of Uzès.

The agricultural expansion of the sixteenth century was accompanied by important changes in the rural landscape. The olive was introduced in some localities, and woad in others. What was the fate of viticulture under these conditions?

From the evidence of the *compoix*, one sometimes gains the impression of a certain animation in the wine industry. For example at Bessan, a large

village in the plain linked to the nearby port of Agde by the Hérault, 19 percent of the land plots were planted in vineyards (*vinha*) in 1502 compared
to 32 percent in 1523. Or take the tiny port of Sérignan on the coast. In 1521
its inhabitants were busy building terraces and planting vinestocks.[1] Thirty
years later, in 1550–62, viticulture still seemed to be progressing at a goodly
pace in the parish. The marginal soils, *garrigues, vaccans* (vacant holdings),
and *cosse haulte* (chalk uplands) were being planted with young vines
(*maillols en broque*) in this zone of ancient wasteland. The local lord was
the richer for it. He was able to dispose of useless *garrigue* in exchange for
a quitrent, or *nouvel acapte*. His peasants were only too happy to plant it
with vines.

But one swallow doesn't make a summer. These few new vine plantations were doubtless symptomatic of a favorable economic climate, but they
did not suffice to transform the region into one great vineyard. The excellent series of *compoix* of Sérignan make it possible to evaluate the real importance of these scattered vines in terms of overall agricultural activity.
Their importance was, in fact, limited, and their progress was quickly arrested. In the *compoix* of 1521, 17 percent of the land plots were planted in
vines; more than half (11 percent to be exact) were in *maillols*, or young
vine shoots, suggesting that these were new vineyards like those of Bessan
at that date. The rest was wheat fields (72 percent) and olive groves (11 percent). It was a vigorous vineyard but far from ubiquitous. The *compoix* of
1550 gives the following figures: 66 percent in grain fields, 11 percent in
olives, 3 percent in arbored grain fields, and 20 percent in vines. The progress of viticulture since 1520 was a fact, but it was of minimal importance.
Furthermore, it was soon to be arrested by the civil war, which undermined
both olive cultivation and wine growing in this particular parish. The *compoix* of 1603 reports only 11 percent of the land planted in vines and 8 percent in olives, leaving a total of 81 percent in grain fields.

Sérignan is a good example. Isolated references seem to suggest a boom
in viticulture, but the *compoix*, which are complete and all-encompassing,
enable us to take the true measure of the movement, which was in fact quite
modest. It should also be borne in mind that the vineyards of these particular
parishes were stimulated by nearby currents of long-distance maritime
trade. The merchants of Marseilles were active in the sixteenth century in
the string of little port towns along the coast (Sérignan, Frontignan, and

---

[1] "Item, un tras de terra que a romput ... que de present a plantat de malhol ['young
vines']."

Aiguesmortes), loading hogsheads of wine for Genoa and Leghorn. It was "the call of the deep" that incited the peasants of the coast to convert some of their wasteland into vineyards. The same influence was felt in the diocese of Montpellier. By 1500–20 a maritime vineyard had been created there which was centered in a few parishes in the neighborhood of Frontignan. On these lands, under Francis I, the acreage planted in vines approached and sometimes exceeded the acreage sown with grain.

But this was an exception. Elsewhere in the remaining coastal and inland parishes of the diocese (today entirely devoted to viticulture) the vine occupied at the most one-fifth and generally no more than one-tenth of the amount of land surface consecrated to cereal crops. The figure dropped to 1–2 percent in the more remote villages.

In conclusion, according to the testimony of the *compoix*, wine growing in the sixteenth century seems sometimes dynamic but more often lethargic. What do the wine tithes have to tell us?

Not really very much. In the sixteenth century we do not as yet dispose of a good series of this kind of tithe. For that series we have to wait until the period 1600–50. There are a few indications for the small towns, however. At Béziers in 1560 the canons—as yet undisturbed by the Huguenots—farmed "the great tithe" on wine for the territory for fifty *muids* of wine and ten of *piquette*. The figure was exremely low compared to the voluminous tithe farms of 1615–50. One does not encounter tithed vintages as poor as this again until the worst years of the crisis in viticulture at the end of the seventeenth century.

Thus, tithes and *compoix* complete and confirm one another. In central Languedoc (Montpellier-Béziers), despite the population boom and despite the demand of overseas markets (a decisive factor in a few cases), viticulture in the sixteenth century was afflicted by a sort of torpor. This was true in central Languedoc. Was it also true in the east, in the countryside of Nîmes and the Côtes du Rhône?

Let us turn again to the *compoix*. In 1500, Langlade (near Nîmes), today a village of winegrowers, reported 155 hectares of plowlands, 50.2 hectares of vines—all in the plain—and 29 hectares of olives. In 1552, when the figures are only given in cadastral pounds, the proportions are even less favorable to the vine: £18 5s. 10d. of grain fields, £5 6s. 11d. of vines, and £3 8s. 6d. of olives. In the compoix of 1576 only 35 hectares were planted in vines, compared to 50 hectares three quarters of a century earlier. The actual regression of viticulture is all the more remarkable when one remembers that it occurred at a time when both village arable and village population were on the increase. Thus, the inhabitants of Langlade chose to neglect their wine production at the very time their numbers were multiplying and their lands were breaking up into a shower of scattered plots.

These indications are perfectly credible. The sixteenth-century ancestors of the inhabitants of today's village were not natural-born winegrowers. Submerged by the demographic tide, harried by problems of subsistence and rising bread prices, their one thought was to produce more and more and still more grain. To this end, they did not hesitate to sacrifice part of their vineyard in the plain, which was a creation of the less demanding demographic situation of the preceding century. If they cleared and assarted the *garrigue*, it was not—at least in the Vaunage—in order to plant vine-stocks (wine growing being the true vocation of this arid zone) but, contrary to all common sense, for the sake of the miserable grain crops that sometimes struggled to maturity on these rocky soils, at least when the weather was not excessively dry.

The *compoix* of the diocese of Nîmes for 1552 tends to confirm this picture. The vineyards, which constituted only 16 percent of the territory of the whole diocese in terms of value, were concentrated, for the most part, near the towns. The villages had nothing but the scattered leavings.

From Béziers to Uzès there was no expansion of wine growing worthy of the name in the sixteenth century. For this to occur, as will be seen, one must await the reigns of Henry IV and Louis XIII. Under Francis I and Henry II the vineyards of Languedoc managed, on the whole, to preserve the not unimportant gains of the fifteenth century. There was some progress along the coast, thanks to trade, and near the towns, where every craftsman preferred to make his own wine, but elsewhere viticulture sometimes lost ground, especially in competition with the olive. All in all, the gains barely compensated for the losses, and the wine industry was largely stabilized. Why should this be so? To answer this question it is necessary to consider the state of the wine market in the sixteenth century.

First, take the case of the local market. It was extremely important. In 1480 the average farm worker consumed 1.71 liters of pure wine per day. This high level of wine consumption is sufficient to explain the existence of vineyards covering 10 percent of the productive land area.

Popular consumption was relatively inelastic. In the sixteenth century the individual wine ration did not increase. The average worker was already drinking almost two liters a day under Louis XI. He was not going to raise his consumption to four liters under Henry II just to stimulate the spread of viticulture. It is well known, for that matter, that the Languedocians have no particular penchant for drunkenness. The "drunkard and baby-killer," as the troubadours called him, was the northern Frenchman. At Montpellier in 1556, as Platter gravely noted, the town drunks were all Germans. There was not a single native among them except for the sharecropper Antoine, who, as it turned out, during his travels in Germany had contracted the two Germanic vices—Lutheranism and drunkenness. Platter, who could not find words strong enough to condemn the drinking habits of his compatriots at Montpellier compared to the sobriety of the local populace, describes Germans, red as lobsters, dousing their heads with wine—wetting their breeches, dead drunk, while their playful comrades cut off their beards and stuff them inside their vests. For that matter, one finds similar remarks concerning Barcelona in 1595; in the dives of the port quarter one encountered a hundred prostitutes, but not a single drunkard.

In fact, the tendency in the sixteenth century was, if anything, to drink less. The wine ration of farm workers near Narbonne was actually reduced between 1480 and 1580. On the whole, the regional wine market remained important but not expansionistic. It did not serve as the basis for a significant increase in wine production. The torpor of the local market was matched by the sluggishness of foreign markets. At best, wine merchants of Genoa and Marseilles frequented the villages along the coast because water transport was cheaper than land transport, and it cost less to import wine by bark from Languedoc than to fetch it by mule and cart from their respective hinterlands. But foreign demand for the wines of Languedoc did not penetrate more than a few leagues from the coast in the sixteenth century. There was a good reason for this. The wine of Bas-Languedoc was not worth the cost of transport, especially of land transport, which was very expensive. It was not worth exporting simply because it was not worth much at all and also because, except for *muscats* or liqueurs, it did not keep.

There is no question about this; one only has to read the accounts of the Platters. At Montpellier, they remarked, wine, because it is not tapped, rarely lasts beyond the carnival season without going sour. Enlightened natives, like Olivier de Serres, were ashamed of their vintages and above all of their cellars, where the wine went bad before the year was out, especially when they compared them to the sulfurized German wine cellars of the day, with their casks industriously scoured, rinsed, and scented and with wines that lasted twelve, twenty, or even thirty years—from the birth to the marriage of a daughter. Olivier de Serres admired them; he did not imitate them. His own cellars were infested with rats whose stench penetrated the wine vats. As for old father Catelan, he had so few illusions about *his* cellars (in 1556) that he was careless about the keys ("wine doesn't last out the year in this country anyway"). The result was that some German student lodgers went down to the cellar, drank themselves blind, and had to be dragged out from under the casks, where they had passed out, by the feet. The mediocre wine of Languedoc, in short, did not keep, did not travel well, and found few outlets abroad. The cellars were not alone responsible. The grape harvests were also much too early. It was not until the seventeenth and, especially, the eighteenth centuries that the wine growers of Languedoc discovered the secret of late vintages, thereby raising the sugar content of their grapes and eventually the alcoholic content of their wine. With this discovery, the now conservable wines of Languedoc could embark upon the conquest of the foreign market.

In the sixteenth century this was not yet the case. At Dijon, in Switzerland, and in Old Castile the wine harvest, by this time, took place regularly in October; but the winegrowers of Languedoc and the Comtat persisted in cutting their clusters early in September at the very first signs of maturity. It was in vain that the agronomists admonished them to "wait for the complete maturity of the fruit in the hope of better conserving the wine." The peasants ignored them and hurried to gather in the vintage the moment the first grapes tasted right. On both banks of the Rhône, between 1530 and 1562, the grape harvest invariably took place in the first two weeks of September (in August, according to the Julian calendar). The Cordeliers of Avignon, from whom one would expect more care and patience, since they were monks, were in just as great a hurry as everybody else.

In 1528, when because of a terribly cool, wet summer the grape harvest in the Bas-Rhône took place October 9 (September 30, old style), a notary exclaimed that "nobody ever saw the like before." To be sure, but in the eighteenth century, an age of prudent winegrowers concerned about quality and maturity, vintages as late as this were almost yearly occurrences. At Béziers, and Montpellier as well, in the years 1520–50, the grape harvests were almost three weeks earlier than those of the eighteenth century.

The vineyards of Mediterranean Languedoc in the sixteenth century were, in short, inferior vineyards without standards and without a clientele. It is true that some two centuries later they were considered almost on a par with the vineyards of Burgundy and Bordeaux (and their success was consecrated by the practice of fixing the vintage in the fall, like their rivals, and no longer late in the summer). But in the sixteenth century the Languedocian vineyards were, from a quantitative and qualitative point of view and in a pejorative sense, underdeveloped.

The Case of the Cévennes: Chestnuts, Coal, Silk

As Félix Platter rightly observed, the Languedocians of the sixteenth century, even the city-dwellers, were not so much wine drinkers as chestnut eaters. All winter long by the fireside the young girls gorged themselves on roasted chestnuts until it made them ill. Consumer demand stimulated production. On the siliceous soils the chestnut took root and flourished at the expense of the *herms* and the *boscs*. The *compoix* sometimes mark the stages of its prudent progress. For example, in one village devoted mainly to cereals 11 percent of the land plots were *castanedas* in 1526 and 16 percent in 1566. On the other hand, in the seventeenth century in the same parish the advance seems to have been arrested. The figure for 1649 was still only 17 percent.

The surveyors from Nîmes traveled throughout the great Châtaigneraie (chestnut zone) of the Cévennes in 1552, measuring the land surfaces for purposes of cadastral assessment. Very frequently, next to the mature fruit-bearing trees they noted the existence of *plantades* of young chestnuts fresh from their nurseries, the outcome of recent investments that had yet to bear fruit. These new plantations appeared in the very heart of the mountains, but sometimes, too, on its pioneer fringes northwest and southwest of the chestnut forest, where prior to this time the "bread tree" was not cultivated at all. There were good reasons for this new development. The *peuplade* of 1540–50 ended by provoking the *plantade*; the demographic advance, in other words, necessitated the utilization of the only plant that offered reasonable prospects of producing food on that acid soil.

It is necessary to dwell for a moment on this part of the Cévennes, with its great chestnut forest, which was both a focus of settlement and a center of mountain industries. In the middle of the sixteenth century, at the very time they were being swept by the winds of Protestantism and revolution, the Cévennes gave proof of great economic vitality. These active mountain districts corresponded to the central and southern zones of the French chestnut forests of the sixteenth century as delimited by Olivier de Serres: "Dauphiné, Haute-Provence, part of Languedoc, Vivarais, Gévaudan, the Velai; as well as the Auvergne, the Limousin, Périgord, and some areas of

Guyenne"—in other words, the primary geological formations south of the Loire preserved in the Massif Central or recaptured in the younger folded mountains of the southern Alps.

In Languedoc itself, a too hasty analysis would tend to minimize the importance of the chestnut. In the diocese of Uzès (according to a diocesan *compoix* of about 1550) it was unknown. In the diocese of Nîmes-Alès, the chestnut groves were assessed at £568, equal to 7 percent of the total valuation for the diocese or only a fraction more than the meadows (£514), half as much as the vineyards, and one-eighth as much as the plowlands.

But for once statistics are misleading. The geography of the chestnut has nothing in common, for example, with that of meadowland. Green patches of meadow were disseminated "in small parcels" among the vines and plowlands of every village. They were present everywhere but nowhere preponderant. The chestnut, on the other hand, was portioned out in solid blocks. It was completely absent in the plains and in the great river valleys. But in 1552, on the flanks of the Cévennes on both sides of the Alès–Le Vigan axis, a mighty, somber mass of chestnuts clung to the mountainsides, presenting a violent contrast to the treeless country all around. This is perhaps the only case in which it is possible to speak of a single-crop economy in sixteenth-century Languedoc. More than 90 percent of the chestnuts were concentrated in 43 villages out of a total of 179 communities existing in the diocese at this time. In these 43 villages, which were strung out without a break from Alès to Le Vigan, the chestnut was not just one form of cultivation among others. It was lord and master of the village lands and sometimes practically the only occupant. True, it was favored in singular fashion by geology. The zone of the chestnut coincided with the primary geological formations of the Cévennes wedged between the Causses and the *garrigue*. To be more precise, it corresponded to the great vein of granite outcroppings running from Saint-Jean-du-Gard to Soudorgues and Mandagout. Cereals —in this case rye, because the acidity of the soil is unfavorable to wheat— played a minor role in the 43 communities surveyed in 1552. It accounted for £152 in assessed value, less than a third of the *compoix* figure of £521 for chestnuts. This was the only zone in the entire region where cereals were not the number-one crop. With all the more reason, the olive and the vine were rare on that "cold" soil.

Thus, it was the chestnut that was big business in these mountains, and it was tasks like trenching, pruning, and grafting that occupied the landlord's thoughts. For example, in January, 1586, and again in May, a number of laborers working in pairs were engaged to cut (*stirpar*) and to graft (*reboudar*) the *castanets* of the lord of Barjac near the borders of Lozère. Others were busy on the steep slopes building or repairing the support walls (*murailhes*) of the terraced fields. They were paid in pounds of fatback and in white chestnuts, the everyday food of the people of the region. Even at the castle, the lord's diet was based on wheat, wine, fatback, and chestnuts. When the chestnut prospered, so did the *métayer*. In 1586 Christophe de Barjac wrote his sister, the demoiselle Aulnes, that everything was doing well that year; the young girls were in full flower, strong and healthy (*fort galhardes*); there was a fine crop of chestnuts; and if the market held steady, Penarié (the sharecropper) was going to be rich "because there are such a lot and he is a hard worker."

The chestnut of the Cévennes was an all-purpose fruit in the sixteenth century. It was sometimes exported to the cities of Italy and Languedoc, but it served above all as "the basic food of the Cévenols themselves," who consumed it raw or well pared, dried, and cooked or else pounded into flour and made into bread that was black as coal. It also served the mountain people, who were afflicted with giant goiters, to pay the doctor (our example is from 1595). The Cévennes of the sixteenth century were still, and were long to remain, an ill-nourished "land without bread," a member of that wretched international community of chestnut eaters stretching from the highlands of the Estremadura to the mountains of the Rouergue and Savoy. All of these regions shared the same privations—and the same traditions.

The Cévennes were wretched but not resigned, differing in this respect from the Rouergue. The peasants of the thankless Cévennes, with their acid soils, sought salvation and supplementary resources in mines and rural industries. Near Sumène, one of the chief localities of the chestnut region, the poor local peasantry, throughout the sixteenth century, was gripped with gold fever. They expended great effort in digging up the yellow clay earth and washing the debris in a thin stream of water in search of the tiny flakes of gold, light as a leaf, that assayed well enough for the Lyons market. The coal diggers of the Cévennes had a more important role to play. Their activity must have been reduced to a very modest scale in the fifteenth century, when the mines of La Grand' Combe were farmed out for some two hundred pounds of lard, but beginning in about 1528 the process of deforestation gave them a new lease on life. By that time, in fact, the *garrigues* had been devastated by the bakers and even more by the limeburners who supplied the building industry. The resulting rise in the price of wood made rock coal a cheap fuel. In 1553 the *patus* in the neighborhood of Alès were riddled with coal shafts (*balmes, espiraux, charbonnieres*). In the 1560's and 1570's new mines worked by a new breed of peasant-miner appeared at Saint-Félix and Saint-Andéol-de-Robiac. The abbot of Cendras, about 1552–62, lived off his chestnut trees and coal pits, both of which were farmed out to a merchant of Alès. Soon, all these mine tunnels, dug without any plan, like the Paris sewers, began to run into one another, and in 1581 a miner had to promise one of his fellows, a certain Dardailhon, before a notary, to stop the working (*tirement*) of his mine tunnel "there where Dardailhon is working underneath" at the risk of a cave-in, naturally.

Coal was not all. Various chestnut- and sometimes charcoal-producing villages also possessed surface deposits of iron ore. On the banks of the mountain streams were water-driven forges (*molins à batre fer*), a certain number of which are mentioned in the diocesan *compoix* of 1552 in the chestnut forest of the Cévennes, especially in the vicinity of Alès. More than one of these forges dates from the beginning of the economic renaissance. On September 3, 1487, a baker of Alès, a breadmaker doubling as an ore crusher, stepped barefoot into the waters of the Gardon and groped about for a few moments before erecting a symbolic pile of rocks where he intended to build the *resclause* (dam and sluices) of a water-driven mill for pounding iron ore. At that precise moment, the registrar, who was also standing in the stream, recited and signed the minutes of the baker's new claim, which paid water rights to the lord of Portes. The construction of the mill could then proceed.

Thus, the black coal of Alès was supplemented, by about 1550, by the "white coal" of the torrents of the Cévennes. Water mills sprang up everywhere. The chestnut region, with less than a quarter of the villages in the diocese Nîmes-Alès, accounted for one-third of the mills reported in the *compoix*. The geographical distribution of these sources of energy was curiously autonomous for that age; oil presses appeared in parishes devoid of olive trees, and water-driven millstones were installed in villages that cultivated chestnuts but no cereals. There were also *masiers* for fulling cloth, processing paper, and working iron.

The chestnut itself had its role to play in all this industrial activity. In every live *chastanet* the owner saw to it that the trees were cut and transformed into vats, kegs, or barrels. In March of each year, the rustics invaded the copses of wild chestnuts, or *jourguieiros*, to appropriate the raw material for wooden barrel hoops, which they then fashioned, stacked into "wheels," and sold. The small towns resounded with the ring of the coopers' hammers. Between 1490 and 1600 the coopers of Sumène marketed their products throughout Languedoc and as far away as Marseilles, where they were filled with wine, tuna, salted anchovies, and sardines. From the parishes of the Cévennes, Marseilles imported hoops, casks, wicker, and staves already assembled into barrels or else destined for the coopers' workshops of Provence.

It was a new industry. In 1242 and again in 1340 the magistrates of Languedoc petitioned the *sénéchal* of Beaucaire to outlaw the manufacture of barrels made from chestnut wood, "which putrifies the wine." Two centuries later the oak had lost the contest, and popular prejudice had swung around in favor of the chestnut, which "didn't lend any odor to the wine," while wine that was kept "in oak furniture" took on "an awful odor that is offensive to some people." Thus, we find oak wine barrels in the thirteenth and fourteenth centuries and chestnut wine vats in the sixteenth century. Other woodworking industries were sometimes even located above the line that marked the upper limits of the chestnut forest. Thomas Platter, in 1595, discovered numerous carpenters at work in the highest hamlet of the Cévennes making planks and wooden cases that they sold to the towns, thereby providing the mountain communities with a source of cash income.

The Cévennes in the sixteenth century seems to have possessed a sort of dynamic unity of interrelated activities. The chestnut, or "bread tree," provided subsistence for the numerous peasants-workers who were busy mining, weaving, milling, and working in wood and in leather. Members of the last-named trade, of which we shall have more to say later, played a decisive role in the development of the Huguenot heresy in the Cévennes. The density of population was indeed surprising. In the diocese of Nîmes-Alès in 1552, the three chestnut-oriented vicarates of the Cévennes—Alès, Anduze, and Le Vigan—counted 82 villages, large and small, numbering 10,774 households out of a total of 23,710 households in the 179 communities of the diocese as a whole. With 132 households per village on the average, the mountains were just as densely settled and heavily populated as the plain of Nîmes. When one remembers the limited agricultural resources of the mountains, a population balance with the plains meant overpopulation in these commanding villages of the sixteenth century, clinging to their rugged hillsides. The population density of the Cévennes in 1552 was almost frightening—depressing, too, when one considers the low living standard and deplorable state of health of the inhabitants. Sixteenth-century doctors described the wretched condition of the gold miners of the Hérault; the monstrous goiters of the people of Aigoual and Espérou; the poor scrofulous weavers of the woolen cloth centers who were forced to marry among themselves and went in quest of a cure to the fountain of Beaucaire or else sought out the thaumaturgic touch of the kings of France. Even the gentlemen glassblowers, standing before their furnaces in velvet and taffeta doublets, had a seedy look about them.

Such was life in the Cévennes in the sixteenth century, with its poor, its goiters, its scrofula, and also its nobles in silks. Silk dress was, in fact, an isolated example of unwonted opulence and serves to remind us of the presence of the mulberry, *l'arbre d'or*, in the midst of chestnuts. The chestnut zone of the Cévennes was the oldest and once the most active center of silk culture in France. As early as 1234 the existence of a silk industry supplying Marseilles is mentioned in this region. In 1296 Raymond de Caussargues, a resident of Anduze in the heart of the Châtaigneraie, was practicing the trade of silk throwster (*trahandier*), the man who drew and twisted, or "threw," the first filaments of raw silk from the cocoon. The text is of capital importance; it is the first of its kind in France. It helps us to date the beginnings of French sericulture and proves that the silkworm, which was probably imported from Italy, was being raised in the Cévennes at least as early as 1296.

In the fourteenth century the silk throwsters' guild of Anduze was well established and flourishing. There followed a period of eclipse corresponding to the depression of the late Middle Ages, but beginning in 1497 the silk of Anduze, also called "mountain silk," reappeared on the markets of Avignon, where it was much prized by the braid and taffeta makers. From about 1510, secondary centers of sericulture began to spring up elsewhere in the Cévennes. Outside the Cévennes as early as 1494 there were silk-raising centers in Provence and in the Comtat, near Montélimar, thanks to the lord Alan, a companion of Charles VIII who returned from Naples with some white mulberry plants for his parish.

Black or white, a veritable mulberry mania broke out about 1540–50. There were new plantations at Montpellier, at Narbonne, and—in the Cévennes—at Anduze, which continued to supply the market of Avignon. There were others in the Comtat, where, beginning in 1527, a tree nursery supplied the silkgrowers with white mulberry plants. In Provence and in the Bas-Vivarais, between Aix and Salon, more than ten thousand young mulberries were planted. This craze for silks and silk raising coincided, beginning about 1540, with the influx of American silver and the spread of luxury.

As one would expect, the rise of silk culture led, during the course of the sixteenth century, to a decline in the price of silk, which tended to become an item of popular consumption. The age of Louis XII, when no one wore silk hose, was long past, not to mention the days of Emperor Aurelius (A.D. 270–75), when silk, according to a famous text, was worth its weight in gold. The silk of the Cévennes, in the 1540's, was worth only about a hundredth part of its weight in gold; to be more precise, according to a simple if somewhat involved calculation, a kilogram of this silk sold for 7.86 *livres tournois*, the equivalent of 11.48 grams of gold. Here we have a point of contrast between two ages in the history of the western Mediterranean: the Roman age addicted to Chinese silk imported at great expense by the caravans of Lob Nor and Pamir, and the modern age of short hauls on the back of the humble and inexpensive mule, which delivered the raw silk of Anduze to the market of Avignon. Perhaps one also ought to contrast two refusals: Aurelius wisely rejected the pallium of purple silk as being too dear, since it cost its weight in gold, while Henry II, with less reason, forbade the wearing of silk hose, "though the usage is everywhere accepted in his realm." Aurelius was wise; Henry II, just old fashioned.

It would be useful to take the measure of this spread of the mulberry. If it seems considerable in terms of the regression of the fifteenth century, it remained modest compared to the plant's future progress. The mulberry, it is true, gained ground, but not at the expense of the arable. It was not a field crop but a garden crop, and as a consequence, its role was limited and of a complementary nature. For certain villages of the Cévennes it represented a source of cash income but little more. In 1550–60 it still had not altered the foundations of the rural economy.

This is yet another example of the generally limited character of the economic expansion of Languedoc in the sixteenth century. Olive cultivation was spreading, but its dimensions remained modest. It was basically a secondary supplier (of the local demand for cooking oil). The vineyards, too, constituted a sluggish sector of minor importance. Finally, mulberry cultivation suffocated within the narrow walls of Mediterranean horticulture. The bulk of agricultural production was still represented by high-calorie basic food crops; by carbohydrates, in other words—chestnuts on the siliceous soils and cereals everywhere else. Vegetable fats, meat, alcohol, textiles, luxuries, and items for the urban market still counted for relatively little. If the *compoix* of the diocese of Nîmes are to be believed, 63 percent of the land in terms of value (almost two-thirds of a large and economically diversified region) was still consecrated in 1552 to the production of bread or chestnuts—to the coarsest of carbohydrate food crops.

In other words, despite some successful but marginal initiatives (notably olives and mulberries), the expansion of the sixteenth century occurred essentially within the framework of a subsistence agriculture, not one of specialized cash crops (*cultures riches*) dependent on changing market conditions, as was to be the case in the nineteenth century in Languedoc and the Comtat. Even though staked out with olives and vines and scattered with meadows, the rural landscape consisted essentially of plowland and fields of grain.

Did this subsistence agriculture achieve its hoped-for objectives? Did it manage to preserve the standard of living of the growing population that it was called upon to nourish? Or was it governed by the implacable logic of the Malthusian equation? In the race between population and subsistence, between bread and the birth rate, which was the winner? It seems best to pose the problem first in terms of overall production and subsequently in terms of income.

II. TOWARDS AUSTERITY

The Tragedy of Grain

For the production of "*bleds*" (or, at any rate, the production trend) we shall interrogate the curves of the grain tithe. Around 1478–99 the canons of Saint-Just (Narbonne) farmed the grain tithe (payment in kind) of various scattered and representative villages. The bidding took place every June on the eve of the harvest and in function of its predicted size or "appearance." The percentage of the crop set aside for the tithe remained constant—one-thirteenth, for example, for a given village for a period of two centuries. Finally, the tithe farmer's take was modest. Like the farmers of the olive oil tithe, he paid none of the expenses of cultivation but only the costs of carting and threshing out of his share. He retained 11–15 percent of the tithing for profit and expenses and delivered the other 85–89 percent to the canons. The latter figure corresponds to the price of the concession paid in kind. Annual fluctuations in the "price" or rente reflect the movement of the tithe and, by the same token, of the harvests.

One's first impression in studying the graphs, remembering the needs of a

growing population, is reassuring. Cereal production was indeed on the increase after 1480–1500. The data are fragmentary but concordant. At Pé-
pieux the rising trend is clearly marked between 1499 and 1519. At Creissan
the canons collected seventy *setiers* about 1480 compared to more than one
hundred about 1515–20.

Still, in view of the fact that the number of heads of families was in the
process of doubling (between 1500 and 1560), the rise in grain production
seems entirely insufficient. In the most continuous and trustworthy series,
that of Creissan, tithes and harvests increased only by about half between
the lows of 1480 and the highs of 1520. In no case is it possible to report a
doubling of grain harvests between the minimums of the fifteenth century
and the maximums of the sixteenth and seventeenth centuries (1520–30
and 1640–60). What was even more serious was that this gently rising tide
of production did not endure. By 1530 it was beginning to recede everywhere. At Creissan and at Saliès tithe deliveries diminished after that date
until by 1550–60 they had returned to the low levels of the fifteenth century.
At Narbonne the bumper harvests of the years of the Battle of Marignan
are no longer encountered after 1520.

It is possible that resistance to the tithe, which was beginning, almost imperceptibly, to make itself felt, was partly responsible for this decline. The
strike against the tithe, however, was not truly effective, in the case of grain
as well as olive oil, before 1560 and by itself cannot explain the depressed
state of tithe income in the period 1530–60.

In fact, it was not just the tithe; it was the harvest itself that was shrinking. The rising curve of cereal production leveled off about 1525–30. It may
well be that actual harvests did not decline as much as the tithe curves—
which were depressed by the initial resistance of the peasants—seem to indicate. But the remarkable progress of the first third of the century gave
way, at the very least, to a period of stagnating harvest returns. The *tragédie
du blé* had begun. Cereal production was showing real signs of exhaustion,
while population continued to multiply at a rapid rate. Up to 1520–30, growing food supplies almost managed to keep pace with increasing numbers,
but by the second third of the century there was no longer any room for optimism. The famous scissors began to open. Population was still growing by
leaps and bounds while cereal production was just marking time.

Was the competition from cash "plantation" crops in some way responsible? In reality, it was a relatively minor factor, and furthermore, at least in
the seventeenth century, grain, wine, and olive oil showed a tendency to

move together on the production curves. The reasons for the leveling off of cereal production after 1530 were more profound, being related to the basic structure of Mediterranean agriculture and to the peculiar nature of land reclamation in the region. If harvest returns improved hardly at all from one century to the next, it was because this difficult assignment devolved, in fact, upon the new assarts. The problem was the *kind* of land that was being reclaimed and colonized in sixteenth-century Languedoc. The unhealthy but fertile fenlands were not attacked on a broad front before the reign of Henry IV. There were scarcely any forests to be cleared in the region, forests occupying heavy and hard-to-work, but also fertile, soils—none comparable to the woodlands of western France that were cleared in the modern period, in any event. In Mediterranean Languedoc the only possibilities were offered by lands that went under the name of *rouquiers, garrics, herms, pasturals*. Here, the difficult, costly work of reclamation always came up against the immovable stumbling block of diminishing returns. New landbreaking under these circumstances is somewhat absurd, if not to say futile.

On the whole, concordant evidence leaves one with the picture of a society in which "the reproduction of human beings" outran "the production of the means of existence." Population was going at a gallop, while production was advancing at a snail's pace, if it was not merely marking time. This was true of crops like wine, for which the market was depressed, and of sectors which despite a certain dynamism were too marginal and localized, like olives and silk. It was also true of subsistence crops whose expansion was arrested on the granite formations of the chestnut zone and the limestones of the "arable" *garrigue* by the law of declining yields on infertile soils.

All these considerations taken together induce one to accept, as a working hypothesis, the concept of distortion, or in any event of disequilibrium, in regard to economic growth in the sixteenth century. It is a question, in short, of the divergence between demographic expansion and economic development—between the needs of a more numerous population and a level of production incapable of adjusting itself to these needs. A similar divergence is bound to upset the harmony of healthy growth. If the overall product increased a little, the per capita product did not. Ultimately, this situation risked reducing the mass of the population to the status of paupers through the reduction of the level of individual consumption, the population inflation having overtaken the too slow increase in food supplies.

The above tendencies are quite clearly marked, but our "model" is still rudimentary. We have a picture of a growing crowd of people pressing to get at a stockpile of grain which is not being replenished fast enough to meet their needs. Is it a true picture? In reality it is only a preliminary sketch. Between production and consumption a whole series of economic and social factors intervene: global factors concerning general market conditions and individual factors involving questions of distribution. It is only by examining the one and the other that we begin to perceive the concrete realities of the possible processes of enrichment or of impoverishment in the disjointed development of the sixteenth century.

The Stagnation of Real Income

All the crops of a given year constitute a mass of "consumer goods" dissimilar in nature and utilization: grains, wool, wood, livestock, chestnuts, wines, vegetable oils, and others. Happily, they all have a common denominator; each product has its price and each crop its monetary value. And all of these values add up to the aggregate agricultural income of a given region in a given year. This global figure varies from year to year; it rises, falls, or remains stationary, and the general movement is essential. It exerts its influence, in fact, on the formation of, and the variations in, the personal income of every individual peasant.

It is true, and it is important to keep in mind, that this global income was not always *realized* money income in the sixteenth century. The peasant family also produced its own necessities, and the commercialization of the product of its labor was, as a result, severely limited. Even when exchange occurred it often assumed the form of barter—mules for sacks of grain, the labor of harvest workers for a percentage of the crops, and so on.

Yet, paradoxical as it may seem, the general income from agriculture—although still in large part unrealized income in monetary terms and hence an abstraction—was nevertheless the object of serious and systematic, if antiquated, statistical measurement. The amassing of farm products and the rough but regular estimation of their aggregate values constituted, in fact, the very basis of the tithe collector's work and calculations.

Let us leave aside for a moment the tithes in kind. In the case of certain well-situated fertile villages, the canons, anxious to fill their wine vats, oil jars, and grain bins, took actual delivery on their wine, olive oil, and grain tithes. In such cases the statistics are imperfect. The "amassing" took place as usual, but the valuation in monetary terms was absent. In any case, such tithes in kind constitute the exception after 1500. In the great majority of rural parishes the tithing organization (the chapter, the convent, or whatever) conceded all the tithes of a given village—on grain, wine, oil, hay, *salicor* ("saltwort"), new lambs, wool, grazing land, gardens, and so on—to the highest bidder en bloc, sometimes for a year but more often for from three to five years. The successful bidder agreed to pay a certain sum of money every year as the price of his concession. The following is one example among thousands. In 1560 a certain bourgeois offered the canons of Aiguesmortes £308 per year for five years for the right to collect in kind, and for his own profit, all the tithes from the fields, vineyards, and orchards of the village of Malespels, which was subject for tithing purposes to the collegiate church of Aiguesmortes. The concession was "knocked down" at this price, and the good burgher became the tithe farmer of Malespels for the next five years in exchange for the £308 per year he pledged to pay the canons.

The price offered for the concession was arrived at by the future tithe farmer by following some fairly careful calculations, necessitated by the fact that the bidding was competitive. His figuring was based on a series of previsions, more or less statistical in nature, which involved, first of all, the aggregate product of the village lands in a normal year or, to be exact, the approximate overall volume of the various tithes at the local rate—one-thirteenth in some localities, one-eleventh in others. In the second place, the farmer had to anticipate the sale, at current market prices, of the fruits of the tithe and the total sum to be realized from this operation. Because he paid for the lease entirely in cash, our tithe farmer was forced to dispose of those portions of the harvests received in kind also for cash. Let us suppose the tithe farmer of Malespels has estimated his future cash receipts at £342. His next calculation concerns the amount he must deduct from this sum to cover costs and profits. Figures for both items were reduced by competitive bidding to a minimum representing—according to sixteenth-century records—only about 10 percent of the total product of the tithe (the tithe farmer, it will be remembered, unlike the tenant who leased the ecclesiastical estates, had no salaried dependants and bore none of the costs of cultivation but only the modest expenses of gathering and processing). To repeat, the farmer kept about 10 percent of the tithe for himself; the other 90 percent—the surplus, if you will—constituted the net tithe income paid to the canons in cash. It represented, in other words, the price of the tithe lease contracted for in advance—in the case of Malespels, £342 minus £34, or £308.

The movement of tithe rentes in monetary terms can be traced, from three-year lease to three-year lease, for almost three centuries. Generally, since the farmer retained a very modest share, these rentes were determined essentially by the total receipts realized from the sale of the tithes in kind. But of course the tithes themselves only represent one-tenth, one-eleventh, or one-thirteenth (according to the local rate) of overall agricultural income on the lands in question. Gross agricultural income, a theoretical reality but one of capital importance, can be formulated in any given year by the equation

$$A = Rp + R'p' + R''p'' + \ldots + R^n p^n$$

where A represents aggregate income from agriculture; R, R', R'' the size of the various crops (grain, wine, oil, wool, and so on) produced that year; and p, p', p'' the respective prices of these products. A, the symbol of agricultural income, is what is called in François Quesnay's model "annual reproduction"; that is, the gross value of the overall harvest, a portion of which the agriculturalist sells on the market and a portion of which he sets aside for family consumption and next year's seed. In short, tithe rente in money (C) is pegged, over the long term, to tithe income in money (B) and this in turn to cash income from agriculture (A).

We shall never know the value of A in absolute terms for any given year or series of years, but this is of no great importance. What matters, in the present connection, at any rate, is the general movement, the trend, the "diachronic" (and not the "synchronic"). From the movement of C (tithe rente in money) we obtain the approximate figures (about 90 percent) for the movement of B (tithe income in money) and also the closest approximation—the only one possible, for that matter, given the nature of Old Regime statistics—of the general movement of A (theoretical agricultural income expressed in current prices for any given circumscription). Now, it happens that access, however indirect, to information concerning the movement of A opens the door to an important historical reality, namely, general harvest movement as a function of the general movement of agricultural prices.

These calculations concerning the movement of agricultural income, starting with tithe rentes in money, rest on a broad geographical and statistical base, one of the broadest offered by the ancient ecclesiastical and notarial archives of Languedoc. One can judge for oneself. We have records for five major centers of tithe collection—five luminous sources to guide our inquiry—in Mediterranean Languedoc; they are, from west to east, Narbonne, Béziers, Montpellier, Aiguesmortes, and Nîmes. Each of these towns had a cathedral chapter or collegiate church that claimed the right to tithe a large part of the countryside, comprising dozens of villages. A total of 175 localities were covered by the five tithing jurisdictions just named, including a number of large villages, ancestors of the great wine-growing centers of the twentieth century—175 different points on the map between the Rhône and the Aude where every three or every five years the canons and tithe farmers eventually worked out a contractual agreement on the value of tithe income in money, which depended, in the long run, on overall agricultural income. One hundred seventy-five documented villages scattered over a vast region, where the total number of parishes in the modern age (the seventeenth century) did not exceed 570, is a very good sampling even from the point of view of the contemporary science of statistics.

The validity of our ample survey is also shown by the general agreement among the different curves of tithe income in monetary terms that result. What we have is a long-term movement, because the contracts were renewed at intervals of three or five years (hence, there was no way the curve *could* reflect annual fluctuations). The movements of the tithe, expressed in money, follow very similar paths over the course of centuries in the large agricultural regions of Nîmes, Narbonne, Béziers, and Montpellier. Only the curve for Aiguesmortes diverges prior to 1560, after which date it falls into line with the others. We shall see why later.

In the period before 1560 our information concerning the tithes comes from Narbonne, Béziers, and Aiguesmortes. At Narbonne the index number of median tithe income for the years 1500–1505, based on a total of thirty-one series of tithe farms stipulated in money for thirty-one villages, was 14.5 (the base 100 being the average for the years 1610–40). The index for the period 1555–60 was 35. Between 1500 and 1560 the rise in the curve, from index 14.5 to index 35, is uninterrupted. It was a conspicuous but limited movement. Tithe returns stipulated in money—or rather in money of account (*livres tournois*)—were a little better than doubled in the space of two generations. At Béziers the rates of increase were of the same order.

But one must keep in mind that the prices of these tithe farms, which followed an ascending scale decade after decade, were stipulated in *livres tournois*, a money of account. The rise is, therefore, purely nominal, and in order to measure it in *real* terms one has to compare the movement of nominal income with the movement of nominal prices. Every wage earner knows that it is quite useless to raise salaries if prices are rising at the same rate.

There are, in theory, three possibilities:

a. The nominal rise of tithe income (H) is greater than the nominal rise in prices (H'), or $H > H'$. This signifies that at constant prices the real product of the tithes is increasing, and since the tithes are a fixed percentage of the harvests, it also signifies a prolonged rising trend in the size of the crops; that is, a real increase in overall agricultural production.

b. The nominal rise of tithe income is equal to the nominal rise in prices, or $H = H'$. In this case, the two cancel one another out. The tithe expressed in money is automatically pegged to the rise in prices, but the actual volume of the tithes—being a fixed percentage of the harvests—remains unchanged. Prices are rising, but not agricultural production in real terms (in kind), which is stagnating.

c. Finally, if by chance the nominal tithe income is rising more slowly than nominal prices, or $H < H'$, it can only mean that the real product of the tithe has a tendency to diminish. Prices are rising, it is true, but income is falling behind because actual tithe collections are shrinking. A lively rise in prices accompanied by a sluggishness of income signifies a decline in the size of the tithe and hence in the size of the crop. Of the three possible hypotheses, which is correct? To answer this question one has to know the movement of nominal prices.

The *mercuriale* (market price list) of Montpellier furnishes a series of wheat prices from 1477 up to the beginning of the seventeenth century—two, three, or four quotations, and sometimes more, every year without fail. For the hundred years in question, then, we have a continuous series to work with. Five-year medians serve to indicate the secular trend.

Now all the elements of a comparative study of nominal prices and nominal tithe income are at hand. It makes for an interesting confrontation. Between 1500–1505 and 1555–60 *touzelle* (the best wheat) increased in price from sixteen *sous* and six *deniers* to thirty-four *sous* per *setier*; or, in index numbers (1610–40 = 100), from 19.8 to 41.0. In two generations the price of wheat had a little better than doubled. But does this not represent almost the same rate of increase as that of tithe income at Narbonne, which passed from index 14.5 to index 35 during the same interval? The two curves are practically identical. The conclusion that emerges is that in constant prices—or what comes to the same thing, prices expressed in measures of grain (the basic food)—real income from the tithes, reflecting real income from agriculture as a whole, hardly advanced at all between 1500 and 1560. The two curves—prices and income—rose parallel to one another at the same pace.

These observations serve to confirm, extend, and generalize the conclusions that emerged from the study of tithes in kind and cadastral land reclamation. In sixteenth-century Languedoc, if population was growing rapidly, perhaps even doubling, production, in contrast, exhibited a total lack of animation and elasticity. Real agricultural income, assuming constant prices, was stationary or rising almost imperceptibly. This leads to the inescapable if distressing deduction that with population growing rapidly and aggregate income hardly at all, average real per capita income (that is, aggregate real income divided by population) tended inevitably to contract, resulting in a process of "pauperization."

Our preliminary conclusions are subject, however, to certain geographical exceptions. In this connection, the case of Aiguesmortes is very instructive. In the sixteenth century it was a little ghost port lost in the morass of the Camargue, infested with mosquitoes and afflicted with a high rate of unemployment. But at the same time it was the center of a remarkable effort of rural land development. Sacks of spices and bales of cotton were no longer unloaded on its rotting wharves, but its granaries were bursting with grain because the soil was deep, well watered, and drenched in sunshine. Once it was properly drained, the land returned some excellent harvests. In the Camargue of Aiguesmortes in the sixteenth century the tithes literally leaped ahead. Median income from the tithes (in nominal figures) more than doubled at Narbonne between 1500 and 1560. At Aiguesmortes it more than tripled, in fact it nearly quadrupled, during these same sixty years. In 1500–1505 the index was 28; in 1555–60 it stood at 105. This vigorous rise, much more rapid than the rise in prices in this case, originated in the watery circumscriptions tithed by the canons of Aiguesmortes. It was an impressive advance that left rising grain prices far to the rear. It signified an authentic, strongly felt increase in agricultural income expressed in measures of grain. If we eliminate the fictitious rise due to rising prices, real agricultural income (in constant prices) on the lands tithed by Aiguesmortes appears to have increased by at least 50 percent during the period considered.

But the anomaly of Aiguesmortes is readily explained. On these water-logged acres, Mediterranean agriculture finally burst its chains. It was no longer a question of land clearing but of land drainage. Instead of attacking the skeletal soils where the increase in costs was not balanced by an increase in returns, deep, fertile soil was purged of its excess water and annexed to tillage without further ado, doubling the real income of a tithe or of a village, in the space of just a few years.

It so happens that similar endeavors were quite rare in the sixteenth century. The results were impressive, but the human sacrifice was too great. The attack on the swamps and the digging of drainage canals stirred up legions of malarial mosquitoes. It was a murderous zone for human settlement where the very drinking water was polluted. If land reclamation on the *garrigues* ran up against the obstacle of diminishing returns, the draining of the swamps was little by little brought to a halt by the terrible mortality among the workers so engaged. In the sixteenth century, land drainage was strictly localized, and the Camargue, drained and reclaimed at the fringes, remained as always a great festering sore at the center. At the beginning of the seventeenth century, it is true, land drainage would be more widespread. But it was not until the twentieth century, thanks to quinine and improved hygiene, that the coastal plain was to become a flourishing agricultural area. In the sixteenth century, despite its relative animation and an increase in output, the agriculture of the coastal strip remained of strictly marginal importance for the regional economy as a whole. The income of a fenland chapter like that of Aiguesmortes—notwithstanding the boom in its tithe collections—was quite ludicrous compared to the opulent prebends of the healthier zones. Between 1597 and 1607, when we dispose for the first time of overall accounts, the benefices that depended on the *mense* of Aiguesmortes returned, all told, some £5,000 to £8,000 per year.

Now let us leave the watery wastes of the Camargue and turn our attention to the foothills, the rolling country, and the dry, salubrious plain. At Nîmes about 1600 the priories subject to the tithe returned, all told, £25,000 in an average year, four times the revenues of Aiguesmortes. At Montpellier the figure was £45,000! In the sixteenth century, therefore, it was not the narrow skirt of marshy coastland that was typical of Mediterranean Languedoc, but rather the countrysides of Narbonne or Béziers, with their healthy, patchwork plains already entirely under tillage. This fact made further progress out of the question, since the *garrigues* which were still available for reclamation were infertile. In this land of plain and *garrigue*, agricultural production (in real terms) was hopelessly stagnant, and the income from the tithes (again in real terms) faithfully mirrors that situation.

Thus, it was the product of the tithes, and at the same time real agricultural income, that on the whole—with the exception of a few malarial cantons on the coast—refused to budge. Agricultural income had reached a sort of ceiling. The farm population, for its part, had broken through another. Average peasant income per head, therefore, ran a serious risk of contracting. In order to judge the reality of this risk of growing austerity, it is necessary to consider, in addition to production, the problem of the distribution of the goods produced.

3

Land Subdivision,
Land Concentration, Pauperization

The product to be apportioned increased but little, while population was growing by leaps and bounds. As a consequence, the question of distribution was of vital importance. First of all, I would like to consider the initial stage of agricultural distribution, the pro rata apportionment of village production according to the size of the individual holding. Did the sixteenth century in Languedoc, the *"beau XVIᵉ siècle,"* represent a period of land concentration or one of land subdivision and disintegration? The studies carried out elsewhere in France by Raveau, Merle, and others emphasize the concentration of land, beginning with the Renaissance, in the hands of seigneurs and bourgeois. Was this also the case in Languedoc? The inverse hypothesis of a subdivision of landholdings cannot be excluded when one considers the teeming population and the regular practice, in this region, of partible inheritance at every social level. Since diverse hypotheses are possible, let us let the facts—that is, the *compoix*—speak for themselves.

First, a comment on method: the question of landownership has to be envisaged successively from the point of view of surface areas (in hectares or the ancient *setérées*) and from the point of view of assessed land values (in cadastral pounds). In this way it is possible to reach a rough approximation. The two approaches, furthermore, are complementary. The evaluations of surface areas are the more precise and the more suggestive, but the difficulty with them is that lands of unequal value (limestone soils and *garrigues*, for example) are measured by the same yardstick. Such evaluations, moreover, are to be found only in the master *compoix*, which were rarely revised (at fifty- or one-hundred-year intervals) and provide at best a very discontinuous kind of documentation. For example, in order to compare the landed generations of 1500 and 1560 one is forced to resort to two successive land surveys, one executed in 1492 and the other in 1607. The time spread in this case is truly excessive.

On the other hand, the weighted assessments in cadastral units of value, as originally set down in the *compoix* and regularly brought up to date in successive rolls of the taille, make it possible to study the process that interests us close at hand and even step by step for a given period. Thanks to these series, one is able to explore the changes in land structure between 1500 and 1560 decade by decade.

The surveys of surface areas serve as solid points of reference in the initial stages of our research. The assessed values provide us with a weighted index, an instrument of detailed verification and chronological refinement.

Hectares or Setérées

First, let us consider land areas. The village of Lespignan, for example, possesses two *compoix* of landed property, one for 1492 and the other for 1607. In 1492 there were 103 taxpayers; in 1607, there were 174. The classic population explosion of the sixteenth century seems to have assumed relatively modest proportions in this case (but it is also possible that the parish suffered the effects of the civil war with its retinue of misfortunes after 1560). In another place I have sketched a set of long-term comparisons for this particular village based on the widely separated *compoix* of 1492 and 1652. Landownership under Mazarin appeared extremely fragmented compared to the large, well-consolidated holdings of the end of the fifteenth century. Let us see if the sixteenth century played a role in this process of subdivision, and if so, what role, by comparing the *compoix* of 1492 and 1607. To begin with, the village arable remained about the same or increased only slightly in extent. The cultivated land area amounted to 4,984 *setérées* in 1492 compared to 5,605 *setérées* in 1607, representing an increase of 621 *setérées*, or less than 15 percent, in 115 years. Land reclamation and drainage in the sixteenth century, if far from negligible, did not raise the productive capacity of village lands by very much, here or elsewhere. However, if total production just barely increased, the repartition of the land and its fruits was profoundly altered, as if by a major upheaval. To persuade oneself of this it is sufficient to arrange the landholdings in the *compoix* of 1492 and 1607 in a table in order of increasing size from 0 *setérées* to more than 1,000 *setérées*. A comparison of the two years in the table gives one a bird's-eye view of the evolution of landownership. They are indeed very different. One's impression, in short, is that both small and large holdings had progressed at the expense of medium-sized holdings. The problem of determining the limits, or frontiers, between small, medium, and large properties, between groups whose historical behavior was either dynamic or regressive, can be resolved by a comparison of the tabular statistics themselves. The facing columns of the table thus have a determining role to play at the research stage itself. Their function is not merely illustrative but also heuristic.

A confrontation of the two columns shows, in fact, that the critical thresholds—the points at which the tendencies change direction—are situated, in the case of this particular village, at 20 *setérées* and at 110 *setérées*. The landholdings which measured more than 20 but less than 110 *setérées* regressed, while holdings of less than 20 or more than 110 *setérées*, the dwarfs and the giants at either end of the scale, progressed.

Group I (more than 110 *setérées*) comprised, in 1492, the 5 biggest landowners, with a total of 1,854 *setérées*. By 1607 there were 12 in this category, with a total of 2,708 *setérées*. The "more-than-110's" owned 40 percent of the land at the end of the fifteenth century and almost half of it in the reign of Henry IV. Group II (20 to 110 *setérées*), which occupied the intermediate position on the scale of landholdings, numbered 59 at the time of Christopher Columbus and possessed 2,765 *setérées*. At the near term of the comparison, in the age of Sully, there were only 44 left in this group, with 2,066 *setérées* of land. The middle compartment of landed properties was contracting, in other words. Group III (smallholds of less than 20 *setérées*) comprised 39 proprietors, with a total of 365 *setérées* in the first sampling. In the second the number of Lilliputian landlords had increased to 115 crowded together on 831 *setérées*.

The land structure caved in in the middle and was reinforced at the two extremes. The medium-sized or intermediate landholding was being attacked on two fronts. At the top of the table it was being eroded by the rising tide of population, which favored the subdivision of property and led to the breakup, through a process of mitosis, of a total of fifteen properties of more than five hectares into numerous smaller units. It was eroded at the bottom by the land engrossers who invested their sixteenth-century fortunes —as in Brie or Poitou—in the lands of an indebted peasantry.

At this point it might be useful to postulate a "model" of "high-yield" cereal cultivation (which was actually the case). Assuming average yields of 10 hectoliters per hectare (not uncommon in the plains) and a two-course rotation, the village of Lespignan in the period 1490–1500 should have produced 6,000 hectoliters of grain in a normal year, and about 1600–10 its production should have been 6,726 hectoliters. This very modest increase mirrors what has been said concerning the "flattening out" of harvests and of farm income in real terms in the sixteenth century.

Simple division indicates that every landholder, on the average, disposed of 60 hectoliters of grain in 1492 compared to 39 hectoliters in 1607. Since the manual laborer's normal ration in the sixteenth century was 5.6 hectoliters per year, the margin appears quite comfortable in 1492, and even in 1607 the average landholder had enough grain for himself and his family to subsist on with some left over to sell.

But our ideal landholder is an abstraction. In reality, thanks to the table, which like a prism breaks global income down into its component parts, it is possible to know the actual apportionment of the village harvest. In 1492 the six big landowners, with an average estate of seventy-two hectares, harvested 360 hectoliters each. The portion allotted to the majority of fifty-nine landowners who composed group II amounted to a respectable 55 hectoliters per holding, on the average. Finally, the minority, the thirty-nine land-holders in group III, reaped and threshed only 11.2 hectoliters per head—a double ration, in other words, which is not enough to feed a family with children (and for that matter, man does not live by bread alone). As a result, these microlandowners could not live off their land.

It was precisely this "Lilliputian" minority of 1492 which had become a majority by the beginning of the seventeenth century. In 1607 the 12 *coqs de village* disposed, on the average, of 270 hectoliters per landholding. The "middling" proprietors in group II, who now numbered only 44, being reduced to a minority, still managed discretely on the same 55 hectoliters per holding. But the great majority of village landholders (115 out of a total of 171) who now found themselves in group III had been reduced to a bare living. Each miniscule property in this category returned on the average only 9 hectoliters of grain, not even the minimum ration for a childless couple.

The obvious conclusion is that in 1492 the majority of landowners had some surplus grain to sell and were therefore in a position to purchase other necessities—in short, they were living above the "poverty line." In 1607 the great majority of them had to purchase grain for their own subsistence be-cause their properties were too small and their harvests too meager to meet their minimum needs. By the same token, it is easier to understand why the land structure tended to sag in the middle and to be reinforced—to become polarized—at the two extremities. These microproprietors, who had lost their independence and were no longer self-sufficient, had to look for work on the great estates. They supplied an abundant work force for the great landed properties, which, their labor problem thus resolved, never stopped growing and prospering during the course of the century. The two developments were complementary. The petty holding of the day laborer, in the final analysis, was of considerable utility to the great landowner's latifundium. The miniscule plots enabled their owners to survive during the winter months while awaiting the bounties of the busy season, when the lord of the great estate "permitted the day laborer to partake of the pleasures of his purse." This mutual reinforcement of the great and the small at the expense of the middle-sized landholder was a logical if contradictory process.

Cadastral Pounds

After surface areas, let us turn to assessed values. The latter enable us to study at close range, thanks to a more continuous series of data, the effects on land structure of the population explosion of the sixteenth century. Our investigation concerns ten villages.[1] All ten of them, without exception, argue strongly in favor of an intense subdivision of landholdings in the sixteenth century and the proliferation of microproperties. In three of the cases, the movement was so intense that it paralyzed every attempt at consolidation. It led to the disintegration of the medium-sized properties, and it also forced the great estates to give ground. In the other seven villages, land subdivision, although very marked, was nevertheless accompanied by a more or less pronounced movement of land consolidation at the other end of the scale. The chief victim in this group of seven villages was clearly the medium-sized holding. Under frontal assault, as elsewhere, by the process of subdivision, it was simultaneously being attacked from the rear by the consolidations of the land engrossers. It was this two-front struggle that reduced it to extremity.

An Example of Integral Subdivision

At Fontès the exceptional abundance of fiscal documents makes it possible to trace the history of land subdivision between 1500 and 1580 in considerable detail. For 1504 we have a book of the taille based on an old *compoix* which has not survived. At that time the total assessed value of the village

---

[1] See the ten monographs in the original edition of the present work, p. 243.

lands was 2,379 cadastral pounds. A new *compoix* was composed in 1505. This one, too, has been lost, but the first of the taille rolls to issue from it, dated the same year, has been preserved. Its list of tax assessments, in other words, is based on a brand new *compoix*. The new overall assessment is 2,010 cadastral pounds. Of the family of taille rolls descended from this particular *compoix*, three survive: that of 1505, just mentioned, and those of 1533 and 1539. The mutations are numerous but recorded with care. The deck of cards was repeatedly reshuffled and redealt, but the overall assessment remained invariable, which is natural, at £2,017 in 1533 and £2,021 in 1539. Between 1539 and 1543 a new *compoix* was composed. In this case, the total assessed value was 1,025 cadastral pounds. (Let us note in passing that the cadastral pound of 1540 was worth about two cadastral pounds of 1505. A result of deflation? No, in reality, the unit of measure chosen for this village is perfectly arbitrary in terms of absolute values. All that mattered to the land surveyor of 1505 or 1540 was its convenience in measuring and weighing the relative values of commensurate areas of good, of average, and of poor land.)

Fragments—scribblings, really—of the *compoix* of 1540 survive, as well as two of its progeny—two taille rolls in very good condition dating from 1543 and 1581. The sixteenth century in this village, in short, is well staked out with a whole series of taille records, each constituting a sort of cross-section in the social evolution of property during a period of some eighty years (1505–81).

Two series of comparisons suggest themselves: that between the different families of taille rolls (in percentages), and that between rolls belonging to the same family and employing the same unit of assessment (in cadastral pounds). This double operation serves for mutual control and verification. Between 1505 and 1533 comparisons are very easy. The two surviving rolls of the taille are descended from the same *compoix*. The critical threshold, obtained through a confrontation of the columns of the table, is thirty cadastral pounds (1.5 percent of the *compoix*). Toward the bottom of the table below that figure, the number of "less-small" holdings diminished, as a result of land subdivision, from 23 to 18 between 1505 and 1533. Even the largest holdings succumbed to this process. Of the three biggest properties of 1505, only one preserved its former rank. Reading up from this critical threshold, the smallholds, parcels of land assessed at less than thirty cadastral pounds, proliferated from 82 in 1505 to 118 in 1533. The tendency to-

ward land subdivision persisted after 1533. Let us examine the books of the
taille of 1543 and 1581, both of which were based on the *compoix* of 1540.
The land debacle was so serious in 1543–81 that it affected at one and the
same time the large properties, the medium-sized properties, and even the
more viable fraction of the small properties, which were the beneficiaries of
this same process during the course of the preceding generation.

The critical threshold in 1540–81, in fact, was markedly inferior to that
of 1505–33. It was now situated not at 1.5 percent but at 0.4 percent of the
total assessed value of the village lands—at four cadastral pounds, in other
words, on the scale employed in the *compoix* of 1540. The 73 taxpayers
below this threshold in 1543, with holdings assessed at four cadastral pounds
or more, had been reduced to 65 in 1581. Inversely, the 117 "microtaxpayers"
of 1543, with less than four cadastral pounds, had increased to 186 by 1581.

Let us attempt to draw the balance for the century. The largeholding had
been liquidated in less than three generations (1505–81). In 1505 eight *coqs
de village* exceeded the threshold figure of 3 percent of the total assessment.
The eight of them alone accounted for a quarter of the village lands. In
1581 a single landowner surpassed the fatal 3 percent, and his portion represented barely one-twentieth of the total landed wealth of the village. A tidal
wave of small properties had swept everything before it, and the large
landed property did not recover a measure of its former vigor until the
seventeenth century. This volatilization of the middle-sized as well as the
large domains, a fact attested to by the successive taille rolls, is confirmed in
the case of individual families. In 1504 and 1505 the two "headmen" of the
village, Antoine Hébrart and Pierre Peysson, together accounted for 15
percent of the land of the village in terms of assessed value. The landed
properties of Pierre Peysson represented 5.6 percent of the total in the taille
rolls of 1504 (133 cadastral pounds out of 2,379). He also owned 418 head
of *fèdes et cabres* ("sheep and goats"), or 14.1 percent of the 2,948 head for
the village as a whole. Pierre Peysson died sometime between 1505 and
1533. His heir, Guilhem Peysson, preserved the family's position in the rolls
of the taille of 1543 by still claiming 5 percent of the village lands (51 cadastral pounds out of 1,025 pounds in total assessment). But Guilhem subsequently died, and in the book of the taille of 1581 old Pierre's inheritance has
been apportioned among four descendants, Jean, François, "Young Jean,"
and Antoine Peysson. The elder Jean received a share assessed at 10 cadastral pounds (representing 1 percent of the land of the village), Antoine's

share was assessed at 2 cadastral pounds, and the shares of the other two heirs were 3 pounds each. The rest of the inheritance is missing—sold off, no doubt, or transferred into the hands of a son-in-law. This is but one example among many of the disintegration of a landed estate.

The Retreat of the Smallholder

Up to now I have adopted the most optimistic hypothesis in respect to the smallholder. I have assumed an unrelieved subdivision of holdings, a sort of contagious democratization of the village lands. But this hypothesis is only valid in a minority of cases. As a general rule, the process, although intense and everywhere in evidence, was limited to a relatively restricted amount of acreage. It succeeded in undermining the middle-sized domains, but not the solid blocks of great landed properties, armed with capital, which were in fact expanding.

At Serignan the stage-by-stage process was complex, but the final outcome was no less conclusive. Here, the documentation consists of a 1453 book of the taille listing 125 taxpayers and two *compoix*, one dated 1521 listing 207 taxpayers and the other dated 1550 with 268—a good example of the sharp demographic upswing that characterized the Béziers region. But the social evolution that is suggested by changes in land structure is less of one piece. In the beginning, matters proceed in the most democratic fashion. In 1453, in an age of underpopulation, the landholders had plenty of breathing space. Of the four largest, two accounted for 7 percent each of the village lands, and the four combined accounted for over a quarter of the total. They grazed large herds of stock on the marshy soils. One owned 800 *fedas*, 105 *bestias bonas*, 1 *sauma*, and 30 *best-cavalh*[2] besides a *carretta* ("wagon") and an oil press. One of the four was a bourgeois; three were rich peasants. Among the well-to-do taxpayers (but not as well off as the four wealthiest) some were amphibious. One, for example, had five florins' assessed value in land (equal to 2 percent of the total) as well as 700 *fedas*, 14 fat *bestias*, and 1 *sauma* in livestock, and one *carretta*, but in addition he owned three fishing barks, two *files* ("fishnets"), one *boliech* (a small net), and even a gondola. Grazing his cattle in the fens one day, dragging his nets out at sea the next, our seagoing peasant reduced his risks by hedging his bets.

Balanced exploitations like these would be swept away by the great winds

[2] Eight hundred sheep, 105 cattle, 1 mule, and 30 horses (tr. note).

of expansion of the sixteenth century. As elsewhere, land subdivision in the beginning worked to the advantage of the small peasant because the great landed properties—the four big estates of 1453—were dismantled and disappeared. In 1521 the biggest taille payer owned no more than 4 percent of the village lands. A sort of spontaneous agrarian reform resulting from the division of inheritances had taken place. A quantity of small properties, created out of the debris of the big domains, was added to the category of holdings accounting for less than 5 percent of the village territory. A little democracy of peasant cultivators, fishermen, and winegrowers developed around the tiny port.

The next generation—for which the state of landownership is registered in the *compoix* of 1550—was much less fortunate than its predecessors. True, population continued to grow, and the number and social significance of the peasant smallholds multiplied—but no longer their real economic importance. The reason was that the process of subdivision of the period 1520–50 affected a category of ridiculously tiny properties, those constituting not 5 percent or less of the village, as in 1450–1520, but 0.2 percent or less. There were 77 of these tiny landholders in 1521, but the number had grown to 149 by 1550. Their parcels were so microscopic one hesitates to dignify them with the name of landowner. The "reasonable" (economically viable) reapportionment of the preceding generation was a thing of the past.

This "reasonable" category of land parcels, whose caliber ranged from 0.2 to 5 percent of the village total, prospered and multiplied off the spoils of the great estates in the period 1450–1520. But now, after 1520, it fell victim to the same process that had previously assured its development. Land subdivision ended by devouring its own offspring, and the properties it had helped to form in the period 1450–1520 splintered, in their turn, in the following generation, the victims of population pressure and of an uninterrupted process of atomization producing smaller and smaller landholdings. In brief, the category 0.2 to 5 percent, which was flourishing around 1500, was in full retreat between 1521 and 1550, losing thirty-four units in thirty years. The medium-sized domains were breaking up at the rate of one a year.

The incredible subdivision of landholdings is confirmed, in the case of the same village, by nonstatistical sources. In 1550, for example, Durand Roure divided up his single property, consisting of a bit of garden one-quarter of a *quarte de setérée* in area and one *sou* in assessed value in the *compoix*. His beneficiaries were his four children, Guilhem, Jehane, Durand, and Catarine Roure. Each individual portion was a quarter of a quarter of a *quarte*, or three *deniers'* worth in the *compoix*.

However, the retreat of the smallholders onto these tiny parcels of land can be explained by other factors besides the population bomb. Between 1520 and 1550 at the bottom of the table it is possible to trace the growth of a large estate (of a wealthy peasant or *coq de village*), a nebulous property in the process of consolidation. In 1520 this important block of holdings was nonexistent; by 1550 it already comprised 14.1 percent of the village lands (353 cadastral pounds out of a total of 2,500). Here, the medium-sized property was being attacked from two sides. It was being eroded from above through subdivision and being gobbled up from below by the big land engrosser. The process is typical of a great many villages.

In any event, the single common denominator of all these fastidious but indispensable examples is land subdivision, the driving force that dispersed the village lands in an irresistible wave of divided successions. In addition, one also encounters a secondary phenomenon of more modest proportions, the concentration of land into large estates. It occurred fairly frequently but was by no means universal. The victim of both processes was the medium-sized holding, which was breaking up everywhere through inheritance and was also being dismantled, in certain cases here and there, by the activities of the big land buyers.

The second of these two phenomena, capitalistic consolidation, holds no great mystery today. Since Marc Bloch, it has been the subject of dozens of studies. It remains to determine, however, just who the land engrossers were: Were they bourgeois who had fattened on the windfalls of the price inflation? Old feudal lines longing to round out the family estates? The class of officeholders as emphasized by Vénard for the Île-de-France? In sixteenth-century Languedoc all these social groups were hard at work. When the village was fertile and close to a center of judicial administration like Montpellier, the activities of the land engrossers—especially the magistrates and fiscal officers—took on an aggressive character, as I have tried to show in the case of Lattes, a village in the plain.[3] Studies of the *compoix* published elsewhere illustrate the activities of members of the nobility, like Messire de Thézan at Joncels, and of individuals close to the royal financial administration, like Lord Mirman, or Miremand, at Montagnac. The case of these two nobles, however, is more a matter that concerns the seventeenth century, and their operations, carried out far from the towns, were limited in

[3] See my article in *Annales: economies, sociétés, civilisations*, Vol. XII (1957).

scope. The land engrossers Thézan and Mirman, supplied with capital of feudal or fiscal origin, managed to amass barely 3 to 8 percent of the total cadastral assessment of the villages in question.

In reality, if we restrict ourselves, as in the present chapter, to sixteenth-century data, we are bound to emphasize the role of the *coqs de village* of peasant origin. At Saint-Guilhem-le-Désert the consolidation of landholdings was not the work of noble lords, but of three commoners without the shadow of a title, either noble or professional. In this case the engrossers to be found at the bottom of the table were not even bourgeois drawn from the "leading families" of the region. Otherwise they would have the right, if not to the aristocratic particle *de*, at least to a title like *noble, mestre, moussen,* or *monsieur* before their names in the *compoix,* which normally abound in similar honorifics. The new rich in these villages were parvenus with their roots still in the soil—rich peasants and country merchants.

Was this a regional phenomenon peculiar to Languedoc or the Midi? There is little doubt that the land structure of Languedoc, with its alods and its manorial tenancies subject to minimal quitrents, lent itself more readily to peasant progress than the regions of western France, where the nobility held the land and the people more firmly in its grip. But there were other causes of a more general nature. The economic boom of the sixteenth century, as we intend to show, favored the peasant entrepreneur. It stimulated the rise of a rude, purely rural bourgeoisie distinct from the urban bourgeoisie. A process of social differentiation was splitting the peasantry. A small group of *coqs de village* were growing rich from the exploitation and extension of their estates, but the peasant masses were sinking deep into poverty as a result of the subdivision of landholdings.

It is necessary to return to the question of land subdivision. It was the basic phenomenon in this region in the sixteenth century, being of greater social import and much more general than the inverse process of land consolidation. (The latter did not really carry the day in Languedoc until after 1630 or 1680.) Historians preoccupied with the origins of rural capitalism (and rightly so) have paid little attention to problems raised by the accelerated division of inheritances, a characteristic feature of periods and regions dominated by small-scale agriculture (*la petite culture*). It is necessary, therefore, to insist on this point. Otherwise, it is impossible to understand the sixteenth century in the south of France, which was a veritable sea of peasant smallholds.

Diminution of Inheritances; Impoverishment of Heirs

The basic problem is to determine whether land subdivision in this particular time and place signified peasant impoverishment. Should we, in the present case, embrace the view expressed two thousand years earlier by Hesiod, a perceptive observer of the realities of Mediterreanean society? The Greek poet recommended that "there should be an only son to feed his father's house, for so wealth will increase in the home." Did the division of inheritances provoked by the demographic advance of the sixteenth century "decrease the wealth" of the ever more numerous rural households? The best way to answer this question is to reverse the argument. Given the universal character of the phenomenon, under what conditions would land subdivision *not* have led to pauperization?

Our first case concerns the actual reduction in the size of individual holdings in villages where the comparison of successive *compoix* and landholdings in terms of acreage, or hectares, is possible. It invariably turns out that at the end of the sixteenth or beginning of the seventeenth century the individual plots were much more numerous and more exiguous than at the end of the fifteenth century. In these circumstances, only an increase in harvest yields could compensate for the reduction in size of individual landholdings and prevent the impoverishment of the smallholder. Let me repeat that there is not the slightest evidence of any such increase in yields; plowings, cropping systems, and farming techniques remained practically invariable from one century to the next. It is true that there existed, before 1750, one last recourse for the impoverished peasants whose too-numerous properties were visibly shrinking in size—the introduction of plantation crops. It is conceivable that "the adornment of a holding" with olives, and especially with vines or mulberries, would raise the income per hectare to a point at which the purchasing power in grain of a dismembered holding of two hectares in 1600 was equal to the actual grain production of a four-hectare holding of 1500. Something of the sort actually occurred in the nineteenth century. Thanks to single-crop viticulture, the winegrower of 1860 enjoyed a higher standard of living than the diversified cereal farmer of 1760, even though the latter had more land to cultivate. The sixteenth century witnessed no such development. Plantation crops were grown, but their importance was limited, despite some interesting initiatives, and the minimum increase in income per hectare that resulted failed to compensate for the reduced acreage of the average holding. For that matter, we know from the tithes that aggregate agricultural production stagnated, or made very little progress, between 1500 and 1560 or even, practically speaking, from 1500 to 1650. The tithe collections show that the landholders did not, in fact, succeed in raising their yields or in producing more profitable crops that would have served to compensate for the constant diminution of their individual parcels generation after generation. In these circumstances the prevailing tendency is progressive impoverishment, which serves to aggravate the problems peculiar to the *microfundium* and to the phenomenon of rural "dwarfism" so well characterized by René Dumont (1951) as "the disproportionate expenditure of human energy, the excessive exiguity of landholdings, overpopulation."

Let us consider the second possibility, when land subdivision is measured no longer in hectares but either in cadastral pounds (the *livres livrantes* or *compoix* pounds of a single "family" of fiscal records) or in percentages of the total assessed land value of the village in question without any indication of the actual amount of acreage affected by the process. Here again, in order to counter the decline in the individual income of the owner of a subdivided holding compared to the income enjoyed by his predecessors, who were less numerous and better provided for, the overall income from the village lands—or what amounts to the same thing, from every hundredth part or percent of the total land assessed—would have to have increased by a sufficient figure. Let us take a typical and very simple example, a certain village that possesses *compoix* or rolls of the taille for the years 1500 and 1580. Let us assume that the number of landowners, or landed taxpayers, in the village doubled in the sixteenth century—that is, between those two dates—which is what we have been led to expect. At the same time the typical holding, as revealed by the table of village land values for the two years and measured as a percentage of the total, shrank by half between 1500 and 1580. The median holding, let us say, was equal to 2 percent of the total assessment in 1520 but only 1 percent in 1580. If this percentage decline in the size of landholdings was not to result in a decline in the real income of individual landholders from one generation to the next, the aggregate real income of the village would have to have doubled during the same interval of time. This might have been accomplished either by extensive means (land reclamation) or by intensive means (higher yields or plantation crops). In such a case the subdivision would have been simply apparent, or nominal (as in the nineteenth century), without in any way implying pauperization. Nothing, in fact, but the dynamic universe of rapidly rising farm income would have been fragmented. The second factor would have compensated the first; twice the number of participants would have shared twice the amount of farm income. The result is a standoff; the individual landowner's income remains unchanged, and there is no impoverishment.

But all of our evidence points to a less satisfactory outcome. In reality, the rise in yields was insignificant. Arboriculture and viticulture were practiced on a modest scale, and land reclamation was limited and marginal. Real aggregate farm production remained sluggish, and its progressive repartition into ever more numerous and ever smaller portions corresponds to the effective impoverishment of the individual participants.

Here is another example. Suppose the real income, calculated in measures of grain, of a certain village was 3,000 quintals in 1500 and 3,600 quintals in 1560. During the same period, the typical holding, the median property, was reduced through subdivision from 1 percent to 0.5 percent of the village arable. Hence, the output of the typical holding was 30 quintals in 1500 compared to 18 in 1560. The measure of impoverishment was −12 quintals of grain. One is forced to conclude, in the words of René Dumont, that "to increase at all costs an already numerous peasantry can only lead to an increase in the number of participants in the repartition of agricultural income."

What is more, we have been considering here examples of simple subdivision. In reality, in the majority of villages this process was accompanied by a certain consolidation of the largest estates. In such a case, the proliferating peasant smallhold found itself in an even more difficult position. As usual, it had to share in a global village income, which was in a state of stagnation, but at the same time the great estate's portion of this practically stationary global income was more important than heretofore. The impoverishment of the petty landholders, victims of their own high birthrate, was accelerated in this case by the progress of the larger estates.

4

Wages, Rents, Profits: The Impoverishment of the Rural Wageworker

Up to this point we have been studying the problem of distribution in its *horizontal* aspects—in the context of land structures and the land ownership patterns which determine, in the first instance, the repartition of aggregate agricultural income. It is time now to consider the second cycle of repartition, this time in its *vertical* aspect, the problem of distribution at three superimposed levels corresponding to the three categories of social income derived from agriculture—land rent, profits, and wages.

I. THE DETERIORATION OF REAL WAGES

First, let us turn to the problem of wages, including one of the most characteristic forms of compensation in preindustrial economies—wages entirely in kind, which were especially widespread in the case of the great seasonal labors of agriculture. Take harvest work, for example; on May 21, 1570, Thomas del Longe, an inhabitant of Les Corbières, signed a contract with the canons and landlords of La Bastide-Redonde, near Narbonne. He promised in his own name and in the name of twelve companions, described as "laboring personnages," "to cut the wheat properly . . . a half foot from the ground, to bind it . . . , at the proper time to secure the sheaves in bundles, the ears on the inside, to store the wheat and other grain and take the straw to the cowshed" (*"de bien copper les bleds . . . à demi-pied de terre, faire lier . . . , à temps propre mectre les gerbes en molles l'espi en dedans, rentrer les bleds et grains, mectre les paliers dans le boval"*). The group's wages consisted of every twelfth *setier* measure of grain threshed on the threshing floor, "for twelve *setiers*, one" (that is, 8.3 percent of the harvest).

As a matter of fact, as we have seen, the reaper, or *ségaire*, was still getting

every tenth *setier* at the end of the fifteenth century. These were princely
wages equal to the tithe collector's share. In the sixteenth century the latter
did not budge; the *ségaire*, on the other hand, saw his portion steadily reduced. Let us try to establish the exact chronology of the phenomenon,
which has been dealt with in an earlier chapter only in general terms. The
chronology is indisputably correct, because the same estates are involved
throughout. Beginning in 1525 the harvest hands of La Bastide and Védilhan lost 10 percent of their specific real income. Henceforth they only had
the right to the eleventh *setier* (9 percent of the harvest) instead of the tenth
setier (10 percent). Beginning in 1546 another *setier* was sacrificed, and the
harvest worker was left with one in twelve (8.3 percent of the harvest). This
particular type of wage, in other words, had declined 18 percent since the
end of the preceding century. After 1560 the decline assumed catastrophic
proportions, dropping to the minimum rate of 5.5 percent of the crop (every
eighteenth *setier*) in about 1600–30. In this extreme case, impoverishment
measured in real terms, between Charles VIII and Louis XIII, amounted to
45 percent.

For the evolution of mixed wages—a food ration with a cash supplement
—it is necessary to return to the example of the *bayle*, or farm steward, a
wageworker who personifies direct management in traditional agriculture.
The chief traits of this personnage emerge quite vividly from sixteenth-
century documents. Take the example of Antoine Darrieux, a native of the
Narbonne countryside, and his wife, *bayle* and *baylesse* of La Bastide-
Redonde in 1570. Antoine was responsible for four plow-hands (*boyers*),
two of whom doubled as wagon drivers. But he himself was only a subordinate, forced to perform the heaviest tasks, for his masters did not trust
the other workers. His function was to execute rather than direct, and his
wages were little better than those of a simple wagoner. In 1566 the *bayle*
was paid twenty-four pounds in personal wages for himself and his wife,
while the unmarried wagoner (his subordinate) received fifteen. A study
of the *bayle*'s wages, already initiated in the previous chapter, is quite revealing of the lot of the workers in a traditional agricultural society.

In about 1480 the *bayle* was paid £24 12s. plus his individual "pittance" of
£2 9s. 2d., making a total annual cash wage of £27 1s. 2d. This figure remained practically stationary from 1480 to 1551! The wage "curve" was almost horizontal. In a period when the price of grain at Montpellier nearly
doubled, the *bayle*'s money wages were frozen at £27. In 1540 they even fell
temporarily to £24 10s. following a decline in the price of wheat, which

served the canons as a pretext to reduce wages.[1] In 1549, however, the old rate of £27, in effect from 1480 to 1535, was restored. Finally, in 1557 the canons decided "to make a sacrifice" because the inflation of silver was driving prices sky-high and it was impossible to keep a lid on the outmoded wage rates of the fifteenth century. The cash wages of the new *bayle* were raised to £28 10s.[2] This increment was insignificant in view of the fact that the price of wheat in this region more than doubled between 1480 and 1560, and it did not in fact constitute a repudiation of the permanent wage freeze. The purchasing power of the *bayle*'s cash wages had declined drastically, and the worst was yet to come.

There is no question that in the case of mixed wages, in kind and in cash, the monetary component diminished spectacularly in real terms. What about wage payments in kind? They did much better, although they also show a tendency to decline—in quantity in certain cases, in quality in others. The fact itself has already been established. I shall confine myself here to defining the chronology of the movement in the sixteenth century.

Up to about 1530 the food rations that were allotted to the *bayles* of the farms in the region of Narbonne, and to their dependent plow-hands, remained at the high levels of the late fifteenth century. From 1530 on, various symptoms of decline began to appear. In a contract of that same year one notes a reduction in the salt ration from 1 *cartière* measure per person per year to 0.8 *cartière* per person per year. In Languedoc, too, this marks the beginning of a period of rationing which would lead elsewhere to salt riots— for example, in Angoumois (1537) and Guyenne (1548). The olive oil ration was also beginning to decline. From 1478 to 1534 it was fixed in the farm workers' contracts at 14 liters (12.8 kilograms) per person. In a contract dated 1540 it had fallen to 11.6 liters (10.6 kilograms). It would remain

---

[1] Departmental Archives of the Aude, G 31, f⁰ 211, deed dated September 25, 1540. Pierre Manhe, of Moussan, the new *bayle* of La Bastide-Redonde, was to receive twenty-three *livres* per year in wages for himself and his wife (instead of twenty-four *livres*, the usual rate since 1480). He, his wife, three plow-hands, and one *boyerat* (apprentice plow-hand), six persons in all, were to get fifteen *livres* as "pittance" money instead of the twenty *livres* of 1534 (two *livres* and ten *sous* instead of three *livres* and seven *sous* each). The *bayle*'s total annual cash wage was to be twenty-five *livres* and ten *sous*, in other words, instead of the twenty-seven *livres* and seven *sous* his predecessor received in 1534 (cf. Departmental Archives of the Aude, G 31, f⁰ 133, deed dated September 25, 1534).

[2] Departmental Archives of the Aude, G 33, f⁰ 14v⁰, October 11, 1557. The *bayle*'s personal wage was still twenty-four *livres*, but the *companage*, or pittance, of the six personnel increased from twenty *livres* to twenty-seven *livres*, or four *livres* and ten *sous* per person. The steward Bergier therefore earned £24 + £4 10s. = £28 10s.

fixed at this rate at the end of the sixteenth century, and for that matter until much later. In 1850 the agronomist Gasparin still allotted each of the workers on his estates in the Vaucluse and the Camargue 10 kilograms of olive oil per year.

In the case of meat, a key item in determining the living standard of the populace, the cut in rations occurred somewhat later. In 1540 the new *bayle*, Pierre Manhe, was fattening "three hogs without any sows" for the farm's regular personnel. In 1549 there were still six adults to board at the farm, but they no longer had the right to raise more than two pigs for their own table, a condition repeated in subsequent lease contracts up to and including that of 1562. In 1566 a new blow fell when the figure was reduced to a single pig.

A study of the *pitance* or *companage*, a sum of money set aside for the purchase of meat or fatback—sometimes simply listed in the notaries' deeds under the heading *"achept de viande"* ("meat purchases")—fully confirms the above facts. This cash quittance was shared equally by the entire personnel of the farm. It can be represented statistically in terms of its purchasing power in mutton (the price of which is known for the butcher shops of Narbonne):

Purchasing Power in Mutton of the Annual Companage *Paid to Each Farm Worker in the Region of Narbonne*

1480	39.5 kg.
1533–34	40.9 kg.
1549	32.7 kg.
1551	38.2 kg.
1562	35.0 kg.
1563	30.0 kg.

In 1583 the *companage* declined to the equivalent of about twenty kilograms of mutton, barely half the fifteenth-century figure. The farm worker in the age of Henry III was a miserable pariah compared to the simple foot soldier in Montmorency's regiments who gorged himself on seventy-seven kilograms of meat per year. There was a crisis in the popular consumption of meat and also a serious decline in stock raising (a problem we shall return to later) beginning about 1530.

In fact, the years 1530–40 definitely appear to mark the turning point when wages began their downward spiral. Let us look at the wine ration. As late as 1530 the bacchic norms of the fifteenth century were still respected; the wine ration remained the same. It was still 5 *muids* (Narbonne measure) of wine and two of *prenses* (or *piquette*) for five persons, or 1 *muid* of wine and 0.4 of *prenses* per person, the equivalent of 625 liters of wine and 250 liters of *piquette* per person per year (or about 2 liters of wine per day for a manual laborer). The risk of liver cirrhosis was minimal, however, because the alcoholic content remained weak. In 1534 there was a slight change. The canons hired a sixth worker but "forgot" to increase the overall wine ration, which was still fixed at 5 *muids*. The individual ration immediately dropped to 521 liters per year. As a consolation, the landlords substituted quantity for quality by raising the individual ration of *piquette* from 250 to 416 liters per worker per year. These rates remained stabilized up to 1585. What about the bread ration? The deterioration in quality, the "blackening" mentioned earlier, was, strictly speaking, a late-sixteenth-century phenomenon. Up to 1560 the large ration of pure wheat characteristic of the end of the fifteenth century was still the rule despite a few temporary setbacks. In 1475–85 the annual wheat ration per person on these Narbonnese farms amounted to 8 *setiers* (Narbonne measure), or 5.6 hectoliters. In 1551 the ration still consisted of pure wheat, and it was larger than ever—10 *setiers* (7 hectoliters) per person per year. Dark, coarse rye bread did not really come into its own until after the outbreak of the civil wars at the end of the long impoverishment of the sixteenth century. Its final triumph was signaled in the contracts of 1580–90, in which the farm worker's ration consisted of a mixture of seven-tenths wheat and three-tenths rye.

In order to appreciate the impoverishment of the rural wageworker as exactly as possible, we must compare the late fifteenth and the late sixteenth centuries. Whatever the causes—lagging wages in a period of price inflation, demographic pressure that depressed the price of labor and forced up the price of basic foods, restrictions and scarcities provoked by the civil war—the effects were of a considerable magnitude. Several comparisons are possible. The first is by volume or weight of the commodities in question:[3]

	ANNUAL RATION	
	1480	1580–90
Bread	560 liters of pure wheat	700 liters of mixed wheat (7/10) and rye (3/10)
Wine	625 liters of wine, 250 liters of *piquette*	521 liters of wine, 416 liters of *piquette*
Meat	39.5 kg.	18.2 kg.
Olive Oil	14 liters	11.6 liters

[3] It will be recalled that these individual rations are also maximum rations. The presence of children in the home of the *bayle* would have the effect of reducing the food allowance of the adult wageworkers.

The same comparison can be expressed in calories per day:

	1480		1580–90	
	calories	*percent*	*calories*	*percent*
Bread	3,531	84.6	4,417	89.9
Wine-*piquette*	133	3.2	153	3.1
Meat from *companage*	186	4.6	86	1.7
Olive oil	313	7.6	261	5.3
Totals	4,163	100.0	4,917	100.0

In any event, at first sight our farm worker of 1590 is scarcely to be pitied. He was better nourished than the population of today's underdeveloped countries. His diet contained as many calories, more in fact, than that of his predecessor of 1480. Every year, he consumed (at most) more than half a ton of bread and half a ton of wine—almost two kilograms of bread and two liters of wine per day. But his diet was poorer than in the past and lacked balance. Since the end of the fifteenth century, fat and protein deficiencies had become more strongly accentuated. Proteins were supplied by twenty kilograms of meat per year, half what the ration had been in the days of Charles VIII and one-third of the sixty-two to sixty-three kilograms of meat consumed annually by a well-fed people like the Paris populace of 1788—or 1955.

In compensation, the bread ration had been increased (but blackened). This abundance of carbohydrates in no way served to mitigate the deficiency in animal proteins. In reality, "in any given dietary regime, it is the quantity of proteins that determines balance or lack of balance. . . . A protein deficiency is not compensated for by an overabundance of fats (lipides) and carbohydrates. It is irremediable, and the consequences are instantaneous: a weakened biological resistance, a greater vulnerability to epidemic disease, and, as a result, an immediate rise in the mortality rate" (Philippe, 1961*a*, pp. 550–51). The allusion to death is worth emphasis. Is not one of the keys to the demographic turning point that put an end to the vigorous population boom of the period 1500–60 to be sought in the deterioration of diet and especially in the reduced consumption of meat?

In the case of fats and carbohydrates, a direct comparison between the unbalanced rations of the Narbonnese farm workers and the balanced diet of their better-fed contemporaries, the bourgeois of Béziers, is possible. Here, according to their unedited household accounts, is the Rocolles family of Béziers at the dinner table. In 1583–90 the family consisted of a widow, her two daughters, and a female servant (*chambrière*). The four women consumed three *muids* of good wine per year, the equivalent of 495 liters each.[4] In truth, the widow, the serving-maid, and the two girls imbibed liberally— less, however, than their working-class contemporaries, who managed to down 521 liters of wine and 416 liters of *piquette* in the space of a year. Wine, which was a sign of luxury for the wealthy classes of northern Europe, was considered a basic food in the wine-growing south of France— a stimulant, in reality, but not much of a nutrient for the ill-fed manual laborer.

The same remarks hold true in the case of bread. The Rocolles ladies disposed of twenty-seven *setiers* each of wheat per year, equivalent to a daily bread ration of 1 kilogram. This was a respectable portion, but still a lot less than the 1.7 kilograms of daily bread allotted the Narbonnese farm laborer. Did the short bread and wine ration in the case of the Rocolles represent a specifically feminine portion? No, not if a female farmhand in the sixteenth century ate as much as an able-bodied male—more than half a ton of black bread per year, equal to 630 kilograms, or 1.7 kilograms per day.

If the Rocolles ladies drank less sour wine, or *piquette*, and ate less bread, a subsistence food, than simple workers did, it had nothing to do with their being women. It was because they could permit themselves the luxury of a richer diet of meat and olive oil. Their annual olive oil ration, in fact, amounted to seventy-six liters for four persons—nineteen liters per person per year or 47.2 grams per day. This was almost twice the portion of their less well nourished contemporary, the farm worker of the Narbonne region, and more than that of the well-nourished farm worker of 1480—more, for that matter, than the average consumption of a citizen of Marseilles in 1960. It was less, it is true, than the northern Frenchman's consumption of animal and vegetable fats in 1960 (70 grams per day), but olive oil, of course, has a higher calorie count than the butter, margarine, or other fats used in northern cooking.

As for meat, the bourgeois ladies of Béziers consumed considerably more of it than the rural proletarians of their day. The "family budget" of the Rocolles household amounted to more than one hundred *livres* per year for four people. Now, this figure must have represented meat purchases in large part, since it did not include items such as clothing, footwear, servants' wages, wheat, wine, olive oil, or pork, which were either entered under separate headings or received in kind from the family's sharecropper. The

[4] The *muids* and *setiers* in question are measures of Béziers.

figure of about one hundred *livres* in meat purchases for four persons is far in excess of the *pitance* paid to the six Narbonnese farm workers (twenty-seven *livres* in 1580, thirty-five *livres* in 1590).

The agricultural workers did not find themselves in a particularly enviable position compared to these well-fed bourgeois women, who seem to have been especially fond of olive oil. It is easy to picture a plump and matronly madame Rocolles and her two strong-limbed daughters, for the calories in fats are essential to healthy growth in children.

In other words, the workers' ration, with its emphasis on bread, supplied more energy than the normal diet of bourgeois families like the Rocolles, but because of its overwhelming percentage of carbohydrates it was considerably poorer and less balanced.

After considering the above examples, let us attempt to compose an overall balance sheet in terms of values and percentages in the case of mixed wages. The *bayle* in 1480 received a mixed wage broken down as follows:

$$£17.1 = \text{money value of wages in kind}$$
$$+ \; £24.0 = \text{money wages}$$
$$£41.1 = \text{total mixed wages}$$

In 1590 his total wage, composed of the same two homologous elements, came to $£101.8 + £36 = £137.8$.

Reckoned in *livres tournois*, in nominal value, therefore, the *bayle*'s wages had a little better than tripled. In the same interval of time (1480–1590), however, the price of wheat on the markets of Languedoc climbed from £1.6 to £8 per hectoliter. The total real wage of the *bayle* reckoned in measures of wheat, in other words, tumbled from 25.7 hectoliters to 17.2 hectoliters, or, to put it another way, from 3.7 to 2.5 times the annual cereal rations of a manual laborer. The decline was precipitous, and Hamilton's much-debated conclusions concerning the spread of pauperism in the sixteenth century, based on the behavior of money wages, can be extended (for the first time) to include mixed wages, which were the most typical kind in a preindustrial economy.

Furthermore, the very structure of this mixed wage was profoundly altered. In 1480 it was really mixed, and the money part predominated, accounting for £24 compared to £17 in food allotments. By 1590 the roles were reversed. Wages in kind were now equivalent to £101, while money wages amounted to only £36. The *bayle* was little better than a hired hand working for his keep plus a modicum of pocket money.

The effacement of the nongrain rations in the part of his wages that was paid in kind is also worth noting. In this type of wage, the role of bread increased steadily in importance from the reign of Charles VIII to the accession of Henry IV. In 1480 the bread ration was evaluated at £7.8, representing 45.6 percent of the value of all wages in kind but only 19 percent, or about one-fifth, of the total wage (wages in kind plus money wages). However, by the end of the sixteenth century the bread ration, now evaluated at £54, represented 53 percent of wages in kind and 39 percent of the total wage. Bread's share had become the lion's share. It jumped from 20 percent to 40 percent (or from one-fifth to two-fifths) of the total. This passion for bread (and wine) is yet another sign of a certain poverty and especially of a want of meat. The wageworker compensated for this meat deficiency, or imagined he did, by investing half his earnings in the cheap calories supplied by bread cereals.

Under the pressure of mounting poverty, the wageworkers of Languedoc were forced to adopt a mode of existence common to many other centuries and many other poor. They restricted their consumption of salt, meat, and fats, in itself a sure sign of the impossibility of procuring proper nourishment. No doubt they also saved on taverns and clothes—patching up their rags and tatters as best they could—defending at all cost their customary ration of bread and wine, the staple foods of the poor and humble in the Mediterranean countries since the days of the Last Supper. But even so, the quality deteriorated. By about 1580–90 the poor man's bread was black bread, and the poor man's wine was cheap *piquette*.

After wages paid in kind and mixed wages paid in money and kind come money wages of the modern variety. These affected the vast category of day laborers in agriculture and in the artisan trades. In 1480–1500 a master stonemason at Montpellier earned, in normal times, four *sous* per day and sometimes more. His fellow craftsman, the carpenter, earned about the same. Four *sous* at then-current prices was the equivalent of sixteen liters of wheat, enough for fifteen kilograms of bread. The latter represents the daily bread ration of eight manual laborers. This was a comfortable wage, sufficient to feed, house, and clothe the stonemason and his family without much difficulty. The unskilled mason's helper earned three *sous* per day (equal to about eleven kilograms of bread, or six daily rations of a manual laborer). The *terraillon*, or ditchdigger, took home three *sous* and six *deniers* per day, the equivalent of thirteen kilograms of bread or seven rations.

These handsome wages were soon to be eroded by price inflation and especially by the human saturation of the labor market. By 1530–50 the process was well advanced. Despite occasional increments, nominal wages, on the whole, increased little in these two decades as compared to the beginning of the century. The stonemason of 1530–50 earned five *sous* per day, the ditch-digger earned three *sous* and ten *deniers*, and the farm laborer (in the present case, the *poudaire* charged with dressing the grapevines) made three *sous* and three *deniers* per day.

What had happened to the well-being of former times? The five *sous* that constituted the daily wage of the stonemason in 1530–50 would only purchase 9 kilograms of bread compared to 15 kilograms at the end of the fifteenth century—the equivalent of five daily rations of a manual labourer instead of eight. The *poudaire* of 1530–50 was even worse off: he earned three *sous* and three *deniers* per day for his work in the vineyards at a time when wheat was selling for twenty-three *sous* the *setier* (Montpellier measure). His wages were therefore worth seven liters of wheat or 6.6 kilograms of bread, or a little more than three rations.

And the process of progressive impoverishment continued right up to the end of the century. Grain prices between 1480–1500 and 1585–1600 sextupled. The daily money wages of stonemasons, carpenters, and farm workers during the same interval only tripled. Therefore, real wages for a day's work (wages expressed in measures of grain) declined drastically.

But is it sufficient to study the type of wage paid stonemasons and vineyard workers in general terms and without distinction? Were agricultural wages perhaps depressed in some specific way? To answer this question we need to consider the rural wage structure of our preindustrial economy.

The first thing that strikes us is that the scale of wages in agriculture differs from the urban scale. A document from the south of France is very revealing in this connection. It consists of a tariff of wage rates promulgated in 1594 by the Three Estates of the Comtat Venaissin. The text is reproduced below in the form of a table for greater clarity.

It is clear from the table, which provides a rudimentary picture of the old sociology of the working classes, that the wages of urban workers fell into three categories: the skilled worker (ten to fifteen *sous*), the unskilled worker (five to seven *sous*), and the unskilled female worker (three to four *sous*). Agricultural wages, on the other hand, fell into only two categories: day laborers or vineyard workers (seven to eight *sous*) and women of all work (three *sous*). The disparity is evident at once. The top level of the

Daily Wages in 1594

	ARTISAN TRADES	AGRICULTURE
"High" wages	Master stonemason without keep: Winter: 10 *sous* Other seasons: 15 *sous*	
"Medium" wages	Laborer without keep: Winter: 5 *sous* Other seasons: 7 *sous*	Day laborers or vineyard workers without keep: Winter: 7 *sous* Rest of year: 8 *sous*
"Low" wages (women)	Women laborers without keep: Winter: 3 *sous* Other seasons: 4 *sous*.	Women of all work without keep: Winter: 3 *sous*

rural proletariat corresponds, in reality, to the middle level of "industrial" wageworkers. In other words, the qualified farm worker (the reaper, the vinecutter) was paid much less than the qualified craftsman in the building trades. He was on a par, rather, with the mason's helper or the ditchdigger.

Everything we know about the sixteenth-century working class confirms the classification worked out by the jurists of Avignon. We may say that in the sixteenth century—at Montpellier (1530), Béziers (1580), and Avignon (1594)—the craft industries distributed three sorts of wages: low (to women), intermediate (to unskilled laborers), and high (to master masons, joiners, and other skilled workers). In agriculture, on the other hand, there were but two sorts: low wages for women and intermediate wages for men. No top wages were paid for work on the land. The actual rates might vary, but this wage structure, a veritable salary grid, long remained in vigor, and since farm work was poorly rewarded, the impoverishment characteristic of the century assumed a more brutal and tragic aspect in agriculture.

Now, in this two-tiered world of the agricultural day laborer, which was the dominant category from a statistical point of view, the poor male workers or the starving females? In viticulture it was the former, the male worker hired to cut (*poudar*) or to plant (*fogar*) the vinestocks. Women were in a majority only at vintage time, when they were hired to gather in the grape harvest. The development of a more generalized viticulture, beginning in the seventeenth century, corresponded, for this reason, to a rise in the living standards of the rural proletariat because of the importance of better-paid male labor in the wine-growing industry.

But in the sixteenth century viticulture was still a marginal and relatively static sector of the Languedocian economy, far overshadowed by cereal culture and ancient forms of polyculture. In these traditional sectors, the repartition of wage labor according to sex stands out sharply. The great majority of year-round farm workers were men—four *bouviers* (plowhands) for every *chambrière*. In the case of seasonal farmhands, who were paid in a percentage of the crop, the women's role was more important. At the harvest there was one female binder for every two male reapers; at the threshing there were nine women for every ten men. Finally, in the case that interests us at the moment, that of day laborers compensated in cash, women counted far more than men in numbers, if not in their rate of pay.

Take the case of petty notary and rich peasant of Béziers, Jean de Rocolles, about 1580. In his two principal farming activities, cereal and olive cultivation, which together accounted for 80 percent of the income from his lands, he distributed in two years a total of 519 days' wages—29 to men for sowing and 490 to women for weeding the grain fields and gathering olives.

Women, in this case, constitute 94 percent of the labor force. They went by the names of Catherine Birette, La Pastorelle, La Gavachette, and so on, and they represent, at a daily wage of two *sous* and nine *deniers*, a vital day-to-day addition to the year-round labor of the male farmhands hired by Rocolles at an annual salary of twenty *livres*.

This preponderance of women in the day labor force in agriculture, but not in viticulture, continued without change up to the eighteenth century.

Tenant Farms in the Region of Béziers, 1773–74, in Other Than Wine-Growing Sectors (Grains, Alfalfa, Beans, etc.)

	WOMEN	MEN
Number of paid workdays at Saint-Pierre, Amilhac, Les Salles	2,969	1,486
Daily wage	8 *sous*	25–30 *sous*

From the above table it can be seen that, on balance, for every 2 low-paid female workdays there was but 1 high-paid male workday. What the women hired by the day lacked in wages, they made up for in numbers, and the role of this superabundant, underpaid feminine work force appears essential to the traditional rural economy (viticulture excepted) of old Languedoc. It was even more important than the role of the regular year-round employees. Compared to the latter group's 300 workdays, I count 540 workdays furnished by day laborers, principally female, on these same Béziers farms.

Olivier de Serres, writing at the close of the sixteenth century, was fully aware of this numerical preponderance of day laborers over regular farm workers, as his advice to landlords shows: "Have more people by the day than by the year." And again: "Do not assume too many hands on a yearly basis . . . seeing that you can hire people by the day for your money to keep matters moving."

The Difficulties of Women Workers

This was the cold logic of an agronomist. For the mass of day laborers in agriculture, but especially for the underpaid female majority, the pauperization of the sixteenth century was a most merciless process. In order to convince oneself of this, it is enough to study the changes in the relationship between men's and women's wages for the same work. In Languedoc the series of data on this subject begins about 1349–50. The female grape pickers in these years earned, for a day's work, eight-ninths or four-fifths as much as their male counterparts. It is true that this "favorable" situation was due to a scarcity of labor caused by the plague. The sudden labor shortage created incredible havoc in wage structures. At the same time that employers in Languedoc were paying women at almost the same rate as men, farm wages in Italy overtook and passed urban artisans' wages! Later, beginning in 1367 and for the whole of the fifteenth century, the ratio of women's to men's wages in Languedoc remained stabilized at the lower figure of 50 percent. If a male wine harvester at Toulouse, for example, received two *gros* for his day's work, a female wine harvester only got one. The same was true at Nîmes, where a tariff of 1420 fixed a woman's pay at one-half that of a man, or at most, when the need was urgent (during the harvest and the vintage), at five-eighths. Half pay for women, working alongside men at similar tasks, seems to have been a durable institution consecrated by centuries of practice. As late as 1524 the cathedral chapter of Béziers paid women grape pickers ten *deniers* per day plus their food. Men hired as porters or vat workers got twice this amount—twenty *deniers* per day plus their food. In 1536 five men and six women were hired to plant stakes or piles near Béziers. The men earned forty *deniers* and the women twenty *deniers* for a day's work (both groups supplied their own food).

In the second half of the sixteenth century, however, women's wages deteriorated. The two-century-old rule of half pay for female labor was abandoned. In 1579, during the wine harvest at Béziers, the canons paid the women grape pickers one *sou* and three *deniers* compared to four or five *sous* paid the men who carried the *semals* (wooden hampers) or worked with the vats. In 1585 Rocolles, who was especially miserly, allotted one *sou* a day to women vintage workers and four *sous* to men. In these years, too, women were paid two *sous* and six *deniers* for gathering faggots and *trenats* ("stakes") in the woods, while men received eight *sous* for the same work. Hence, by the end of the sixteenth century women were only getting 37 percent of a male farm worker's or unskilled building trades worker's wage instead of 50 percent as in the first third of the sixteenth century or at the end of the Middle Ages. The pauperization of the woman worker was much more severe than that of her husband or father. In the century of American treasure and galloping inflation, the nominal wage of a female vintage worker rose from ten *deniers* in 1536 (with food) to fifteen or eighteen *deniers* at the close of the century. But in the meantime, prices had turned several somersaults.

From the present point of view, the decade of the 1550's represented a turning point, in other words. It was then that female impoverishment, heretofore almost imperceptible, became the rule it was to remain until much later. Let us consider this critical juncture in the light of the only series of women's wages that is complete and continuous for the period 1500–1600—the series for wet nurses, who constituted an important female work guild before the age of the baby bottle.

The abbot Rozier, from his Languedocian residence, describes the ideal wet nurse in his *Dictionaire*, dwelling with obvious relish on her complexion, the size of her bosom, her figure, and so on. These women, in fact, were personnages of a certain importance in the sixteenth century and were recognized by the municipal authorities. The consuls of Montpellier in 1575, for example, confided the infant Jehane and a certain female infant "discovered in a dung heap" to their care. At other times they were paid to care for the little bastards of local worthies like bishops or consuls. What were their wages, these nurses of town or countryside ("whose nurslings suffer much because they devote themselves to work in the fields")? There was a double scale, one wage for wet nurses properly speaking (*lactans et nutri-ens*) and one for dry nurses (*nutriens*) charged with the care of an infant but without breast-feeding (*"enfant norry sans laict"*).

In 1480 the *lactantes*, or wet nurses, earned seventeen *sous* and six *deniers* per month; the *nutrientes* made only twelve *sous* and six *deniers*. Thanks to the accounts of the *clavaires* (municipal treasurers), it is possible to follow the movement of these women's wages year by year right up to the eigh-teenth century. Incredible as it seems, the wage of seventeen *sous* and six *deniers* per month for wet nurses and twelve *sous* and six *deniers* per month for dry nurses remained unchanged up to 1562. I have been able to verify the figures year by year in the sources themselves; month in and month out during the first eighty years of the price revolution the stipend allotted to dozens of women was frozen at exactly the same figure. The wage curve only began to rise in 1563, and then falteringly. It never managed to over-take the enormous advance of wheat prices. Here is evidence of intense impoverishment; wages were blocked at an index of 100 from 1480 to 1562, while the price of wheat passed from an index of 100 in 1480 to 250 in 1560.

The movement of nurses' wages confirms the wage curve of female wood gatherers and grape pickers. The cumulative lag in women's wages was especially serious in the sixteenth century, and women were the principal victims of the process of pauperization. Doubtless, the reason is that their earnings were regarded with condescension as mere extra income which it was legitimate to reduce, the conjuncture permitting.

These facts are relevant to the history of the condition of women in the sixteenth century. The brilliant destinies of a Diane de Poitiers, a Mar-guerite de Navarre, or a Gabrielle d'Estrées should not serve to obscure the distress of the exploited working women, who were all the more tempted by a different sort of livelihood; prostitution, as is known, was widespread in the Mediterranean countries in the sixteenth century. From Avignon to Narbonne to Barcelona, "sporting women" (*"femmes de débauche"*) sta-tioned themselves at the gates of the cities, in streets of the red-light dis-tricts—or *rues chaudes*—and on the bridges. (According to a popular saying of the times reported by Platter, "On the bridge of Avignon you are always certain to encounter two monks, two asses, and two whores.") Prostitutes seated in armchairs played on the lute and—resorting to a trick as old as time—snatched the hats of passers-by, who were then obliged to come re-trieve them in the ladies' chambers. Cleanups were rare. The only trace of one was in 1570, when certain consuls, alarmed by the spread of the new diseases, shut down the *Bon Hostal.* Such measures were ineffective, and in 1594 the "shameful traffic" was flourishing as never before. The pimps set their snares for the more or less gullible serving-girls and chambermaids fresh from the countryside. Economic motivations—the deterioration of women's wages—certainly did not create the phenomenon, but did they not perhaps contribute to its spread?

The important fact is that all wages—male and female, agricultural, rural, and urban—were plummeting in terms of their actual purchasing power in wheat. Whether it is a question of wages in kind, money wages, or mixed wages, the evidence (it is true that we have singled out the two terminal dates for purposes of comparison) is overwhelming. Between 1500 and 1600 wages in kind (for reapers) declined from 10 percent to 6 percent of the harvest, money wages from index 100 to index 54, and the mixed wages of the farm steward, calculated in measures of wheat, from thirty hectoliters to seventeen. The rates of decline are comparable; the trend was general.

The impoverishment of Languedoc is only a local example of a widespread phenomenon. Earl J. Hamilton has shown how Spanish wages deteriorated between 1500 and 1600. The *grande pénitence* of the wageworkers was also raging in Normandy, in Poitou, at La Rochelle, and in the Atlantic sector of the French economy in the sixteenth century.

The causes? Price inflation first of all. Wages were lagging behind prices. But it is also worth noting that wages paid entirely in kind, in a percentage of the harvest, were also amputated by the process of impoverishment.

Hence, one must also invoke, over and above short-lived monetary phenomena, the profound disarrangement of social structures provoked by the strong demographic pressures of the sixteenth century. The rise in population after 1500 convulsed the labor market, where conditions prior to this time favored the workers. Among the rural proletariat it created a "reserve army" of actual or potential job seekers whose presence exerted severe pressure on the wage scales of employed workers. The cruel fate of this "reserve army," which was only called up for the great seasonal labors of agriculture, is evoked by Olivier de Serres; he speaks of "poor laborers" and of "the underfed in their miserable hovels ... who are paid wages only for the days they work in good weather, wages which they have plenty of time to consume when bad weather keeps them idle." Permanent joblessness or seasonal joblessness, which the priests of Languedoc reckoned at four to eight months out of twelve under the economic conditions of the Old Regime, depending on the locality, account in large measure for the phenomenon of rural vagrancy in Mediterranean France in the sixteenth century. In February and March, 1569, two thousand task workers were hired by the bourgeois of Marseilles to cut their vines. Winter passed, and the job was finished; by April they were no longer needed. The consuls of Marseilles decreed that these "jobless" workers were vagrants and expelled them, despite the loud protests of a certain Balthazar Garnier, who had farmed the flour tax. Task worker in March, vagrant in April—this was frequently the fate of the day laborer whether in Provence or in Languedoc.

The pauperization of the wageworkers, with work harder to find and real individual income shrinking, paralleled that of the peasants whose holdings were breaking up and contracting in size. Behind this twin phenomenon, this double impoverishment that often affected the same individuals who were simultaneously hired farm workers and peasant smallholders, was the obsessive hunger for land and for income—for subsistence and for work—of a fast-breeding population. This hunger grew at a time when supplies of land, of subsistence, and of work remained practically static or increased by very little.

II. The Persistent Stagnation of Real Rent

On the threshing floor and in the field, on the farmer's table and in the master's purse, the wageworker's portion diminished. But to whose advantage? Let us recall, first of all the basic terms of the problem; real wages declined, and real aggregate income from the land stagnated or increased very little. Therefore, if the number of wage earners per unit of income did not increase (we shall return to this possibility later), the master's or employer's share (in real terms) was bound to grow between 1500 and 1560–90.

It is necessary, however, to complicate the schema somewhat. In a preindustrial agrarian economy, there were not two players in the game but three: the wageworker, the working tenant farmer, and the landlord or, expressed in terms of income, wages, profits, and land rents.[5] Under these circumstances, the decline in real wages referred to in the preceding paragraph did not result ipso facto in a rise in profits. This theoretical rise could be absorbed or eroded by a parallel rise in land rent, in which case the tenant

---

[5] By land rent I mean, of course, not the token manorial quitrents to which tenancies were subject, but rent from a fixed, short-term lease of land to a tenant farmer, a simple cultivator who thereby acquired no particular title to the property in question.

farmer served as a "go-between" who simply turned over to the landlord the profits which he might legitimately hope to realize from the decline in wage costs.

The question is not an idle one. Behind the abstract categories of rent and profit the destinies of the different social classes were being decided; on the one hand were the beneficiaries of land rent—nobility, clergy, and emerging urban bourgeoisie—and on the other were the peasant cultivators who had assumed the working management of their domains. Of these two groups, which one was destined to profit from the growing exploitation of the rural proletariat in the sixteenth century? In the last analysis, the struggle was between two different social formations—between the nascent rural capitalism of the peasant cultivators and the life style of the rentier class of landed proprietors (for the urban bourgeoisie, to the extent that it accepted the role of rentier, disavowed its capitalistic character at the same time that it adopted the aristocratic life style of the "gentleman of leisure").

It is true that no sixteenth-century documents give the movement of income on typical estates broken down into land rent, profit, and wages. Still, it is possible to determine the evolution of land rent in real terms, not, as in Daniel Zolla's interesting study, based on the aggregate money income of the great ecclesiastical communities. Income of that sort is composed essentially of tithes levied against "priories" or parishes; it is pegged, in other words, to tithe income, which reflects the overall agricultural product and not just land rent.

In order to isolate land rent, one must eschew excessively global calculations like Zolla's. Instead, it is necessary to construct series of lease contracts for specific estates and veritable farming units. One had best forget the "priories," whose principal income—apart from a few vines and gardens—came from the tithe. There is no question that the ecclesiastical records, thanks to their continuity, still constitute the fundamental source, but one has to look beyond the overall monetary income of the tithe-collecting *mense.* One must try to isolate from the mass of accounts and lease contracts all those relating to a particular estate or landholding subject to the religious community or chapter. The correct method, in short, is to begin with a series of statistical monographs. From sources buried in the ecclesiastical and notarial archives, I have succeeded in composing thirteen studies of this sort concerning thirteen different estates. The data—which are not necessarily continuous—cover the sixteenth and seventeenth centuries.

Finally, an ultimate advantage is gained by the student of these estate records. Land rent, in twelve cases out of the thirteen, was paid in grain. It represents real income, therefore, and not income expressed in nominal monetary units.

In the sixteenth century, an age of expansion comparable in some ways to the eighteenth century, one might have expected a rapid and sustained rise in land rent. This was hardly the case at all. Of the thirteen estates studied, only two experienced an increase in rent. In the other cases, farm rents collected by the landlords in kind increased a bit, stagnated for a time, and sometimes even declined slightly between 1500 and 1560. In the sixteenth century there was nothing comparable to the rise of land rent that occurred in the eighteenth century.

Here, to take one example, is the brief but instructive history covering two and one-half centuries (1535–1769), of one large piece of land. It was called *condamine de l'aumosne,* and it was situated in the fertile territories of Coursan (Aude). It belonged to the cathedral chapter of Narbonne. Its extent, which amounted to about five hectares, remained unchanged from 1535 to 1769. In 1535, 1548, 1551, and 1559 the different tenants who leased the *condamine* paid an annual rent of exactly 5 hectoliters of grain—1 hectoliter per hectare. This was a reasonable charge in exchange for a yield—taking into account the two-course rotation practiced in this region in the sixteenth to eighteenth centuries—which amounted in normal years to about 5 hectoliters per hectare. The landowner took a fifth or at most a quarter of the harvest. What a difference compared to the seventeenth century! In 1611 Estienne Arnailh leased the same *condamine* for fifteen *setiers* of wheat per year (2.1 hectoliters per hectare), twice the rate prevailing prior to the civil war. Arnailh suffered the disadvantages of a sharecropper (he handed over practically half the crop to the landlord) without the advantages, notably, an automatic reduction in rent in the event of a poor harvest.

But in the sixteenth century land was cheap, and this *condamine* of the Narbonne countryside, let for a modest hectoliter of grain per hectare, did not constitute an exception. One or one and one-half hectoliters per hectare was the normal rent paid by innumerable tenant farmers in the region between 1550 and 1565. In normal years it represented about a quarter of the crop. This uniform rate was not destined to be raised—at the tenant's expense—until the early years of the seventeenth century.

After considering the case of isolated land parcels that argue for low land rent in the sixteenth century, let us examine some large farmsteads and entire estates. The lands of Creissan formed another holding of the Narbonne chapter comprising, in this case, one hundred *setérées*. A two-course rotation is attested to there, at least from 1540 to 1716. One can follow the vicissitudes of the estate from 1505 to the Revolution as well as the movement of land rent, which is perfectly characteristic. It was invariably low, and even declining, in the sixteenth century, when the property returned to its owners sixty to seventy *setiers* of grain and two *charges* of olive oil per year. In the seventeenth century the rent moved steadily upward. In about 1650 it passed the hundred *setier* mark of wheat plus the two *charges* of oil. In metric measures the tenant farmer of 1540 paid 1.32 hectoliters of wheat per hectare and 0.14 hectoliters of oil, whereas his distant successor of 1665, whose lease was also for a five-year period, had to pay 3 hectoliters of wheat per hectare and 0.14 hectoliters of oil for the same land. Estimating the average yield at 5 or 6 hectoliters per hectare (making allowance for biennial fallowing), the rent levy passed from one-quarter to one-half of the crop. The purgatory of the tenant farmer, in other words, would begin in the seventeenth century.

Land rent, in this case, behaves like an independent variable with respect to secular fluctuations in agricultural production. At Creissan, both the movement of land rent (on the estate in question) and the movement of village production as a whole (from the tithe in kind) are known. Cereal *production* about 1630–70 was still mired at the 1510–30 level. *Rent,* on the other hand, was decidedly higher in the middle of the seventeenth century than in the first third of the sixteenth century. The rent-collecting landowner, in short, was not content to adjust his demands to the level of production. In the seventeenth century he took a bigger slice of the cake for himself at the expense of the other partners. In the first third of the sixteenth century it had been the cultivator who, aided by the immobility of land rent, stood to profit from increased production and the decline of real wages. In the seventeenth century it was the landlord. In the first case, production increments led to profit increments; in the second, they were translated into higher rents.

On the left bank of the Orb there once stood the large tenant farm of Saint-Pierre, which we have already encountered in the fifteenth century. It consisted, in 1542, of an array of spacious farm buildings; a great hall on the ground floor with a large table of poplar wood, *tota de una piessa* ("all of a piece"); a kitchen; a bakeoven; a chapel; a stable with *manjadoires des boeufs* ("mangers for cattle"); a sheep shed, its broad roof resting on six columns; and a *porcayral* ("pigsty") for the pigs, which were let to a swineherd for a share of the natural increase. Notwithstanding all this livestock, or perhaps because of it, the farm was basically a grain factory. As late as 1775 the wine crop accounted for less than 10 percent of its revenues. It was an imposing 154-hectare block of land. The rent charges were light, amounting in 1527 to three hundred *setiers* of wheat and twenty-five of rye, the equivalent of 1.40 hectoliters per hectare and less than the portion set aside for seed. Between 1532 and 1560 rent was a bit higher but still moderate. In the 1550's it amounted, all told, to 1.8 hectoliters per hectare. Contrast this with the rack rents of the seventeenth and eighteenth centuries. In 1603 the canons let Saint-Pierre to a tenant for 3.3 hectoliters per hectare. In the eighteenth century (1706 and 1718) the rate was to rise to 5 and 6 hectoliters per hectare. The tenant, in this case, gave up almost his entire grain harvest to the landlord, retaining for himself only the secondary crops like wine, beans, maize, olives, hay, silk, livestock products, and wood.

In conclusion, it was primarily the wageworker who was sacrificed in the sixteenth century, but the landed proprietor profited little thereby. If he preferred the life of a gentleman of leisure to that of a gentleman farmer, he had to content himself with a meager, stationary land rent. His day would come, but not before 1600.

It is true that the landowner was not being driven to the wall. In contrast to the wageworker, he was not actually reduced to poverty or pauperized by hard times because in the immense majority of cases he collected his rents in kind; that is, in grain. Now, it happened very seldom, during the course of the sixteenth century, that this sort of rent declined. In general it tended to increase slightly between 1500 and 1560, or else it remained stationary. This was important because it meant that fixed real income in grain, converted into money at current market prices, followed the price curve. In this way, rents were automatically pegged to the pilot price, which was that of wheat. Land rent was weak, but it was safe. It was the sixteenth-century equivalent of a low-interest perpetual annuity secured on land, at least if we are to accept the word of jurists and notaries who between 1543 and 1561 agreed in estimating rents at the thirtieth *denier* (3.3 percent) or at most the twentieth *denier* (5 percent) of land values. This was at a time when the moneylender was demanding the tenth *denier* (10 percent) or at least the twelfth *denier* (8.3 percent) as interest on loans. Moneylending, therefore, was more profitable in the short run, but not in the long run, because of the price inflation of the sixteenth century. Land rent in kind, on the other hand, was mediocre and stagnant, but it offered the long-term advantage of being pegged to prices. In the sixteenth century it constituted a safe gilt-edged security rather than a guarantee of quick riches.

Let us now try to imagine a simple "model" of the repartition of the gross product. The secular movement of aggregate production describes a very gentle rise, the movement of real wages shows a sharp decline, and the direction of land rent in real terms is horizontal. The rentier's standard of living was stable while the wageworker's declined. Here we are confronted with a classical situation very similar to the one described by David Ricardo in his *Principles of Political Economy*—that of a society which was in the process of demographic expansion but barely embarked upon the phase of capital formation. Wages were compressed by an "iron law," land rent remained stable, and profits, if we accept Richardo's analysis, were necessarily on the rise.

In actual fact, what was it that in the end "swallowed up" the surplus product that disengaged itself from the modest rise in production combined with the accentuated decline in wages and the stability of land rent? What, indeed, if not "business profits" or, to be more exact, the net income of the tenant farmer?

III. THE TRIUMPH OF PROFIT

Outsiders: Tithes, Quitrents, Taille

The tithe can be exonerated. It was a heavy burden, but its relative importance did not increase. Tithe rates in the sixteenth century remained blocked at the customary levels, and we have seen how the movement of money tithes faithfully followed the price curve without ever overtaking it.

It was not the tithe collector, therefore, who pocketed the surplus value of the sixteenth century, nor was it the lord of the manor. Manorial quitrents in this region of freeholders were in reality insignificant. In the vast circumscription of Béziers, with its thousands of households, fields, and vines, the total value of the manorial quitrents or "customs" (*usages*) of the cathedral chapter in the sixteenth century amounted to one hundred *livres* per year—this at a time when the least of village priories was let for perhaps three hundred *livres* per year.

The hapless lords would have been quite powerless to implement any "feudal reaction" whatsoever. When their customs were settled in pennies and farthings, inflation rendered their situation ridiculous. In the neighborhood of Montpellier, for example, a hectare of land in about 1480 paid on the average six *sous* in manorial dues or *censives*—the equivalent of twenty-five liters of wheat per hectare or 5 percent of the harvest. Yet in 1570–80, at the climax of the rise in prices when wheat was selling for eighty *sous* per *setier*, these same lands went on imperturbably paying their six *sous* per hectare, now equal to four liters of wheat or less than 1 percent of the harvest. In the case of quitrents, therefore, price inflation had practically liquidated the manorial system. The same process could be observed in the vicinity of other cities where fifteenth-century lords who put their trust in the currency had often fixed their *devoirs* (manorial rights) in monetary terms. Thanks to this fortunate naïveté, by the end of the price revolution suburban lands had been practically freed from the yoke of manorialism.

Elsewhere in the countryside, however, manorial rights often continued to be paid in kind, usually in grain. In these cases, the manorial rent held its own in real terms since its market value was linked to current prices. It did not increase, however, and at any rate it was insignificant from the beginning to the end of the period—a few handfuls of grain, generally barley, a relic of the Middle Ages worth less than half the price of wheat. Whether in barley or in *deniers*, manorial dues were a miserable affair in the age of the Renaissance. At Béziers the annual income from the customs farmed out by the canons was frozen at one hundred *livres* from 1500 to 1560. During the same interval of time, nominal tithe income tripled. There was no question of a feudal reaction under Francis I and Henry II; rather, of an antifeudal reaction.

In reality, the crisis of quitrents in the sixteenth century is an established fact. It has attracted every historian's attention, perhaps to an exaggerated degree. Manorial rent, properly speaking, was often weak and inconsequential by 1500, and the price inflation of the sixteenth century served to exorcise an old ghost, nothing more.

What was more important than the inglorious demise of these fossilized manorial quitrents was the stagnation of the real-life rents of the landed proprietor who let his land out to tenant farmers. As for the lord whose rights were limited to a handful of barley, a pair of gloves, or a glass of water, he had long since been consigned, in the democratic Midi, to the land of shadows—unless, of course, he happened to possess clear title to a demesne as well.

The tithe collector and the manorial landlord, in any case, are out of the picture. Was it then the king, with his taxes and taille, who devoured the real surplus value from agriculture in the sixteenth century? The question is certainly legitimate, because taxes, at the local level, were capable of playing just such a role. In Languedoc, agricultural wealth bore the brunt of taxation. The taille fell on real property. Even in important towns like Montpellier, the land census, or land *compoix*, was the basis of most taxation. The *compoix cabaliste*, or census of "industrial" and commercial profits and movables, accounted for an insignificant fraction of the tax revenues.[6]

The crucial question is whether the fiscal charges, which amounted to some 6.2 percent of the gross agricultural product in about 1580–90, were more, less, or the same as they had been, for example, at the close of the fifteenth century. The problem is important because if the percentage increased during the course of the sixteenth century, it was taxes that were going to "soak up," in part, the agricultural surplus value released by the long-term movements of production, land rent, and real wages. If, on the contrary, this percentage stagnated or declined, the surplus value would go straight into the pockets of the farm tenant, by now the only player remaining in the game. Who would the winner be, the king and his followers or the plowman and his brood? The answer, in a word, is that in the sixteenth century it was not taxes but profit that took the pot.

It is true that nominal taxes in Languedoc increased considerably during the course of the sixteenth century, and not a few fine historians have been deceived into describing the mounting taxation in frightening terms. How much truth is there in this somber picture? It is obvious that the nominal increase in the taille signifies nothing in itself. The crux of the question, which is generally ignored by these sensitive scholars, is this: Did taxes rise faster than, just as fast as, or not as fast as prices?

We have the answer for Montpellier, for which it is possible to construct a curve of direct taxes from 1446 to the eighteenth century to compare with the price curve. Taille revenues and wheat prices at Montpellier are two homogeneous and perfectly comparable series. The use of a logarithmic scale permits the direct comparison of percentage change as it appears on the two diagrams. Thus, we learn at a glance that taxes did not keep pace with prices but fell conspicuously behind as the century advanced. At a rough estimate, taxes at Montpellier a little more than doubled between 1480 and 1560, while prices nearly tripled. About 1475–85, wheat cost thirteen *sous* per *setier* and the taille was fluctuating around £5,000 per year. In the decade 1520–30, the taille had only increased about 20 percent to around £6,000 per year. Wheat, in the meantime, had already doubled in price to twenty-four

---

[6] *Compoix cabaliste*: from the Languedocian *cabal*, "chattel" (tr. note).

sous per *setier*. Taxes in real terms had therefore dipped considerably since the reign of Louis XI. Later, the king's commissioners would try to make good the loss, not without provoking ritual wails of anguish from the provincial estates. About 1555 the taille at Montpellier returned £10,300 per year, or twice as much as it had at the end of the fifteenth century, but wheat was selling for thirty *sous* the *setier*, thereby conserving the better part of its lead. Montpellier, which was bigger and richer in 1555 than in 1480, paid less in taxes expressed in real terms. By a curious distortion, taxes did not overtake prices on our two curves until about 1585 and did not really leave them behind until Richelieu's time.

The conclusion is that fiscal pressure did not increase during the century following the death of Louis XI. It actually decreased momentarily under Francis I, after which, under Henry III, it simply returned to its late-fifteenth-century level. All things considered, the tax burden was not yet of the sort to put a serious damper on entrepreneurial profit by absorbing real surplus values and possible profit margins.

The Entrepreneur and His Receipts

In the sixteenth century, then, the agricultural entrepreneur enjoyed a definite advantage. He was able to capitalize, at one and the same time, on the rise in prices and the saturation of the labor market. But let us confine ourselves to real income, real taxes, real rents, real wages, real profit, and real surplus value and leave nominal values aside.

If our man happened to be a working landowner, he had to deduct wage costs, which were declining, as well as fiscal charges, which were also declining or at least stable, from his slightly increasing income. He pocketed, therefore, the entire absolute surplus value (represented by the modest rise in production) in addition to the relative surplus value (the marked decline in wages) engendered by long-term secular movements. The same process favored the simple farm tenant who worked the land of others. He was exempt from taxes,[7] the rent he paid the landlord did not increase, and his workers were poorly paid—more poorly paid than in the past.

Whether landowner or tenant, the active farmer stood to gain. Between the apogee of wages (in the late fifteenth century) and the heyday of land rent (in the early seventeenth century), there occurred a golden age of profits which took form little by little in the course of the sixteenth century.

---

[7] Taxes were imposed on property in land, not on the tenant.

Thus, we have a losing hand (wages), a winning hand (profits), and two tie hands (land rent and taxes—the royal taille and the church tithe). Rent and taxes managed more or less to hold their own against the combined attack of price inflation and real profit. In other words, from the point of view of social history, the sixteenth century ranked the simple working or tenant farmer in first place, followed by the working landlord or "gentleman farmer," then the rentier landlord, and finally, in last place, the big loser of the century—the hired farm worker.

Where did the accrued earnings of the different kinds of farmers end up? One can imagine numerous possibilities: in hoards or in dissipation on jewels, silver, spices, or even books in the case of the rich landowner; in investments in livestock in the case of the tenant farmer; in a building splurge on the part of the landlord who assumed the working management of his estates.

In reality, it appears that investment decisions followed the most obvious course, given the overabundance of labor, in the utilization of new work forces; that is, the hiring of extra workers and also the purchase of supplementary plow animals. The case of the Narbonne farms of La Bastide and Védilhan is no doubt typical. They did not increase in size or importance in the sixteenth century, and yet more and more hands were hired. At the end of the fifteenth century and in the first third of the sixteenth century each of the two farms employed, in addition to the steward, only three workers on a permanent basis. Beginning in 1535 a fourth plow-hand, a *boyerat*, was added. In 1551 provision was made to hire a fifth, but only for the three busiest months of the year—April, May, and June. In a contract of 1557, the same in which the Narbonnese canons, the "gentleman farmers" in the present case, reduced the number of pigs in their workers' ration from three to two, provision was made for the first time for the purchase of a horse "for the transport of food and other things" (*"pour charrier vivres et autres afferes"*). In 1570 an extra worker was hired by the chapter to handle the plow "during sowing and sheaving." In addition, and for the first time, laborers were hired by the day to inspect and help with the harvest, and a *goujat* ("apprentice") was hired to plant (*soumesser*) vinestocks.

The new earnings, in short, created new jobs and led to more hiring. But was this investment in labor profitable and truly productive? In reality, the hiring of a fourth and then a fifth worker on a farm employing three full-time plow-hands meant incorporating a growing number of field hands into the labor force without any change in productivity or in farming techniques. Here, too, the law of diminishing returns comes into play. Only the spread of more productive cropping systems and more profitable forms of cultivation, like wine growing, could make it otherwise.

In summary, in the sixteenth century nascent rural capitalism disposed of an abundant labor force supplied by the dynamic demographic situation. The active farmer seized the opportunity to reduce wages and with his extra earnings hired new hands to help work practically the same acreage. In so doing, his production gains were mediocre, since he persisted in his attachment to primitive techniques and contented himself with absurdly low yields. Extra earnings are not always translated into economic growth.

It must be emphasized, however, that in the sixteenth century landed property was not a divine right which granted automatic access to the rewards of a certain expansion. It was not enough to be born with land. Landed property, if it was to confer riches, had to be combined with management, enterprise and the effective direction of the labor force. This was the key to the surplus product and surplus profits. Inversely, enterprise pure and simple, through the medium of savings, could lead to landownership and sometimes, for a homo novus, to the acquisition of middle- or large-scale properties at a single stroke. The profits of enterprise could be converted not only into labor but also into fields and vines.

In short, the sixteenth century, in this case, was not only a fortunate age for the sons of a good family who took the trouble to be born and who joined the landlord class without further ado. It also tended to favor the "self-made men" who owned no land at the start of their careers.[8]

Up to this point we have been concerned with necessary abstractions. Let us now attempt to discover the social groups—the human beings behind the cold figures of our statistical model—in concrete outline. First are the tenant farmers; there are various indices of their relative good fortune. To begin with, their stability is itself proof of a certain facility in meeting their rent. At the farm of Amilhac (which was to change tenants twenty times in the seventeenth century) a certain Estienne Rebieyre, of Servian, held the lease without interruption from 1538 to 1563 because he was "a responsible person and a good risk."

The tenant farmers of Languedoc of the sixteenth century could make the landlords dance to their tune. Olivier de Serres noted with indignation their rich man's pride, their irreverance, their self-assurance, and their excessively low rents. There is no doubt that a class of rural entrepreneurs had been con-

[8] "*Self-made men*" in English in the French editions (tr. note).

stituted, or reconstituted. The great estates that had been divided up in the fifteenth century into smaller farming units were reunited, beginning about 1500–20, under the management of single large-scale cultivators. The latter might hold sway over 150 hectares, four or five plow-hands, eight pairs of oxen, and dozens of seasonal hands or day laborers, as was the case of the tenant Jean Raissac at La Bastide-Redonde in 1553. Everything was his responsibility. The landlords—in this case the canons of Narbonne—contented themselves with collecting the rent and did not interfere in actual day-to-day operations. In order to assure his managerial functions, Raissac needed practical experience, livestock, and also capital, or at least credit with which to pay his workers or borrow sowing seed. He needed, in short, the attributes of a capitalist "possessing no landed property, but ready money."

In this manner—just as in the Île-de-France, if to a lesser degree—the combination of low land rent and low wages in sixteenth-century Languedoc favored the emergence, or reemergence, of a rural bourgeoisie composed of capitalistic tenant farmers.

"Monsieur le Capital" and "Madame la Terre"

The stage above the tenant farmers was occupied in the sixteenth century by the oligarchy of *fermiers généraux*,[9] businessmen in the service of the abbeys or the great lords who were also served by the rise in "business profits." A picture of these individuals sometimes emerges from their account books and from notarial records.

Guillaume Masenx was born about 1495 at Castelnau-de-Montmirail, in western Languedoc, into a family of landowners, merchants, priests, and simple sharecropping peasants, or *bordiers*. His uncle Antoine, a priest, saw to it that he had a modicum of schooling, but Guillaume would never know French or Latin. He spoke *la langue d'oc* with a peasant accent until, nearing the end of his life, he finally adopted the elegant Romanic speech of the towns, substituting, in the manner of the Auvergne, the *o* for the *a* as in *Madaleno* instead of *Madalena*. To compensate for his lack of formal instruction, Guillaume possessed a good head for business. In 1516 he married the daughter of a tenant farmer who was working one of the estates of the commandery of Saint-Pierre of Gaillac. Guillaume moved in with his father-in-law. In 1518 he took over the lease, overseeing the work of his father-in-law, mother-in-law, and brother-in-law, who together supervised

---

[9] Not to be confused with the *fermiers généraux* who farmed out the royal taxes in eighteenth-century France (tr. note).

the workers, marketed the wine and grain, and collected the rents and dues on his behalf. In 1535 he was promoted to *fermier général*, the general factotum of the commandery itself. The rent he paid for this concession was comparatively low, as shown by the fact that he was able to turn around and sublease the estates which he himself had leased, for one-half of the returns, and still make a profit.

A typical capitalist at the stage of "primitive accumulation," Masenx reinvested his profits and made money on everything he turned his hand to. In the first place, he made loans of grain or money at short term and high interest for a month (*dins un mes*) or for a week (*deo paga d'aysi VIII jorns*) at a time, and he also practiced the cruelest form of usury, lending "from day to day at his pleasure." He lent his *bordiers* (who did not even have sowing seed) the money to marry off a daughter or a sister, and he also furnished, on credit, the silver, the old wine, and the leg of mutton for the wedding feast. He lent money on land, and in time the fields of his debt-ridden clients would help round out Masenx's own properties.

Masenx, the *fermier*-usurer, despite the Church sometimes mentions interest, or *paga*, in his account books. Thus, for example, at one point he lent some grain to Mandret *fils*, of Vors, at 14 percent for twelve days, or 400 percent per year. At other times the interest is masked by bookkeeping tricks. In 1542 Masenx lent a certain Calvet, called "Bean," a peasant from the farmstead of Andrades, ten quintals of hay valued at fifty *sous*. One month later he was reimbursed fifty-four *sous*, a return of 8 percent per month or 96 percent per year. The record of the second operation was poorly camouflaged by an opportune erasure. Was Masenx feeling pangs of conscience, or was he afraid of prosecution? At other times a deliberate error permitted the surreptitious introduction of usury: *deniers* were transformed into *sous*, and *livres tournois* were converted into *écus*; three quintals of hay lent in 1538 turned into five, God knows by what magic, when they were repaid in 1539. The accounts swarm with similar indelicacies and "mistakes" in arithmetic which, by a curious coincidence, always seem to work out to Masenx's advantage.

One of his tricks consisted in making loans of barley, rye, oats, or vetches and demanding repayment measure for measure in wheat. Another was to play on price fluctuations which were often completely fictitious. For example, in 1545 he calculated the value of the wheat he lent at four *livres* and ten *sous* the setier; the following year he demanded repayment (in kind) at the rate of two *livres* the *setier*, forcing the borrower to return over twice the amount of grain he had received. Masenx's cynicism knew no bounds, for at the same moment he was selling his own wheat on the market of Gaillac for five *livres* and six *sous* the *setier*! A dozen similar examples show that he made a regular practice of reckoning the reimbursed grain at half its market price, thereby doubling the size of the loan.

Occasionally our man was assailed by feelings of remorse and perhaps fear. He altered the original loan figure (one *setier*) to include the interest (one *cartière*) that he collected, together with the principal, when the loan came due in two months' time, imagining he had dissembled thereby a usurious interest of 150 percent. But the chemistry of the centuries has un-masked the deception. The black ink of the interlineation contrasts with a different ink, which had in time become a bit reddish in color, used in the original entry. Masenx's conduct is typical. Like thousands of his contem-poraries—businessmen, lawyers, and large-scale tenant farmers—he special-ized in usurious grain loans. He also, if necessary, collected his debts in the form of labor. Paul Bru, from the farmstead Bru, purchased a quintal of hay from Masenx in 1535. He had neither money nor grain to pay for it. No matter; he promised a day's plowing instead. Other needy debtors helped bring in Master Guillaume's harvest, cleared his ditches, did his carting, re-paired his roof, and so on. He was playing, in short, on the spread between the two rates of return. As *fermier* and rent-paying tenant, he benefited from the still very low return on landed capital (about 3 percent in land rent). As a moneylender, on the other hand, he himself collected interest at the normal high rate of 10 percent ("the tenth *denier*") or else at crushing rates of usury. He paid the thirtieth *denier* in interest and collected the tenth denier at the very least. This was one of his secrets for getting rich.

There were others, because he reinvested his earnings above all in trade. He kept a draper's shop at the commandery, where he sold the peasants breeches, capes, blankets, and wedding dresses. He dealt in a little of every-thing: pack-saddles, jewelry for the bride, floorboards, building frames, and oak planks to repair the city gates.

Finally, the circle was closed. The wealth the land produced in the form of profit returned to the land in the form of property. Did our capitalistic en-trepreneur aspire to the consideration that went with landownership and to the economic security conferred by land rent? If he did not own a single in-tegrated estate, Masenx did manage to collect, parcel by parcel, a bizarre array of disconnected holdings scattered to the far corners of four parishes. He bought up alluvial tracts, luxuriant meadows, and bottomland suitable for cash crops like hemp or vegetables.

Once again, it was indebtedness that led to changes in landownership. A certain Ramon Fabre, a neighbor of Masenx, had purchased some cloth from him on credit. In April, 1531, a spring of high prices, he received a loan in grain. Masenx let the debt ride for seven years (1532–39). In 1539 Fabre borrowed more grain. As collateral he pledged various lands from which Masenx henceforth drew an "annual pension." Finally, in 1545 he settled his debt to Master Guillaume by selling him his property of Resals. In 1546, a year of scarcity, the same scenario was repeated. By April 8, the Fabre family was without bread, and Ramon Fabre went to call on Masenx once again. On this occasion it was the latter's brother Jean who handed over the seven half-*cartières* (1.20 hectoliters) of grain the starving man needed to sustain his family of several persons until the harvest. Fabre had his back to the wall. The loan was repayable "from day to day" at the lender's pleasure. In the end he would be forced to sell the last of his land in order to get out of debt—*"paga cant vendet la terra"* ("paid from the sale of the land"), as Masenx dryly noted in his daybook. In 1546, in other words, bread was paid for in land, and the Fabres became Masenx's *bordiers*, reduced to sharecropping the land of their forefathers.

Masenx is a perfectly coherent personage. As a pioneer capitalist he was attracted to the new ideas that were spreading among the business classes and that seemed to suit his style of life. On July 26, 1537, together with three notables of Gaillac—a lumber merchant and two municipal officials—he organized a reception in honor of some *ministres* who had come to preach the Reformation, more or less clandestinely. It was Master Guillaume himself who advanced the money for their room and lodging. If one wants to characterize Masenx, the cold-hearted businessman whose career is known to us quite by chance, he might be regarded as a living symbol of the "primitive accumulation" of capital. As a big tenant farmer in the age of the price revolution, he profited at the same time from the low wages he paid his dependents and the low rents he paid his superiors. He possessed, in addition, loan, land, and commercial capital combined with "industrial" initiative, a head for business, and a Calvinist mentality. Masenx was a go-between who, thanks to the favorable conjuncture of the sixteenth century, was able to introduce the mediation of business enterprise between the great landowners and the mass of the peasantry and in so doing cream a large part of the surplus value for himself.

All in all, Masenx and his rivals invested their capital in enterprise more often than in land. Instead of burying their money in the ground, they put it to work. The landlord mentality so characteristic of the seventeenth century was less highly developed prior to 1600. At his death, for example, Masenx left his liquid capital and his livestock to his direct heirs, but the lands he had acquired by foreclosure and purchase went to a neighboring abbey. Was this a proof of piety, of remorse for his thievery, or of indifference to landownership? The century of fanatic land grabbers, in any case, did not dawn until 1600, when the rise in land rent finally got under way.

Nevertheless, an aristocracy of businessmen, of *fermiers généraux* favored by rising farm profits, had superimposed itself on the roughhewn "middle class" of working tenant farmers.

Bourgeois Peasants and Gentlemen Farmers

In the sixteenth century, the small-scale as well as the large-scale cultivator's income was in a healthy, or fairly healthy, state. How did the rentier landlord react to these circumstances? He reacted, logically enough, by assuming the management of his own estates, appropriating the profits, short-circuiting the tenant by becoming his own tenant, so to speak, and in this manner uniting in his own hands both land rent (which was stabilized) and farm profits (which were growing).

To be sure, the importance of direct exploitation in the sixteenth century from a statistical point of view is difficult to determine. The management of one's own estate is a private matter that does not require the services of a notary. Only the ecclesiastical archives make long-term comparisons possible. These records seem to suggest that direct exploitation was less universal in the sixteenth century than in the period 1380–1480, when it helped mitigate the deficiency of land rent, which had declined to almost nothing with so much land derelict and abandoned. Nonetheless, the direct management of landed properties by the landlord himself was still common practice in the age of the Renaissance and the religious wars and much more so than in about 1630–50, when the great landowners, pampered by lavish rents, relied completely on their tenant farmers to oversee the work of the fields.

At Narbonne, a large rural center, the canons were semipeasants up to the end of the sixteenth century. They managed the lands of the chapter themselves—at least those close to town. La Bastide, for example, would not be let on a continuing basis at short term for fixed rents until the height of the rent movement beginning in 1630. In the sixteenth century the usual practice was direct exploitation, thanks to the services of a *bayle*, or a semidirect sharecropping arrangement (*métayage*). If we look into the residence of certain of these Narbonnese priests about 1524–35, we discover their living quarters—where a copy of some chivalric romance was also apt to be lying about—encumbered with various tools, picks, pickaxes, and hayforks as well as pigs' heads, sacks of grain, barrel rings, and jars of oil.

Like these church notables, and to an even greater degree, the bourgeois of the sixteenth century opted for the direct exploitation of his landed properties. He, too, succumbed to the incitement of dynamic profits combined with sluggish land rent. The personal accounts of Jean de Rocolles, which open in 1550, testify to his intense participation in the working of the land. Jean was careful to sow the best seed. He superstitiously trimmed his vines when the moon was full and cut his willow branches when the moon was new. If time was short, as in April, 1558, he betook himself to the farm together with his wife and children to spade the vinestocks. He marketed his own vintage; he bartered one barrelful of wine for a hundred roofing tiles. Like everybody else, he lent grain at usurious interest rates of 100 or 200 percent. He lent money and demanded reimbursement in wheat reckoned at one-third of its market value. He collected rent on miserable farm shacks from his hired hands. He farmed the tithes on lands lying adjacent to his own. Notary, usurer, landowner, cultivator, tithe farmer, Jean de Rocolles managed to make ends meet by patiently accumulating modest profits here and there. He died in 1568.

His son Gabriel became a canon. His daughter Jeanne married Aubert, the apothecary. Another son, Guillaume, inherited his father's property and profession. Like his father, Guillaume—after office hours—personally managed his properties (consisting of fifty hectares of plowland plus vines and olive orchards). He distributed hundreds of wage-days of work; he recruited women of the vicinity—chambermaids or shepherdesses—to weed his wheat fields and gather olives or collect vine shoots. He supervised laborers hired to dress and to plant (*podar* and *fogar*) his vines. He had "the eye of the master" (*l'œil du maître*). He handled everything in person without hired bailiff or steward (like Sire de Gouberville in Normandy).

The case of the Rocolles was typical of the sixteenth century. It is sufficient to turn to the pages of Olivier de Serres. If your land is well situated, he writes, and your wife is of sunny disposition and in good health, "well suited to household management," exploit the land yourself. In the case of outlying portions, rely on the semidirect control of *métayage*, not on tenant farming. Indeed, never resort to tenant farming except in case of great misfortune—if you are sick or your wife is a grumbler and a spendthrift.

Like the experiences of Rocolles or the timely warnings of Olivier de Serres, statistical studies of forms of land utilization provide an insight into the long-term psychology of the sixteenth century, when the rich and fortunate landowners strove, wherever possible, to combine profit and rent. It would take the sharp rise in land rent of the seventeenth century, combined with shrinking profits, for the sons of the Renaissance entrepreneurs of Languedoc to develop a taste for the noble life of idle rentiers. In the sixteenth century, "the long encouragement of a mounting tide of profit" was conducive in the country, as in the city, to business daring, to "an aptitude for risk-taking," and to a spirit of initiative.

5

General Perspectives

The time has come for us to reassemble the concrete results of our different analyses: those which bear "horizontally" on land structures and those which bear "vertically" on the principal types of income.

The World of the Poor

At the bottom of the social ladder, among the great mass of the populace, twin processes of pauperization were raging. The first process attacked the smallholders whose numbers had multiplied as a result of land subdivision without a sufficient increase in real income per unit to compensate for shrinking individual land parcels; the second affected the salaried workers and resulted from the decline in real wages. It is certain that the same individuals and the same families were very often victims of both processes. The cases of mixed income in which the peasant lived off his wages plus a small plot of land are numerous. It is enough to leaf through the notaries almost at random. In a certain large village of the Cévennes in about 1555, for example, many wageworking *travailleurs* also owned diminutive mountain plots and "half a pair of oxen" (*sic*). It is true that there were also landless wageworkers, but these were the regular hired hands on the estate farms, not the village day laborers.

In the last analysis, this twofold impoverishment represents history's radical solution to the Malthusian dilemma. Because population had taken wing while production was marking time, a double system of rationing went into effect: a rationing of land that confined the peasant to tinier and tinier plots and a rationing of money, because employers cheerfully exploited the economic conjuncture to distribute lower and lower wages to their workers. The living standards of the poor succumbed to this double system of restraints and sank to the vital minimum, and the subsistence crises deepened.

In fact, the poor harvest years (one out of every three or four in this dry region) had relatively benign effects on the sparse population of 1480–1500, whose tenures were ample and whose wages were substantial, but their ravages spread as population grew, landholdings contracted, and wages shrank. A harvest failure about 1550–90 affected living standards that were already depressed and impoverished. For this reason it created acute shortages and sometimes famine.

If our analyses of landownership and wages in the preceding pages are exact, one would expect to encounter, during the course of the century, scarcities and famines of increasing frequency and intensity and at the same time appropriate modifications in the provisioning policies of the authorities. This hypothesis corresponds to reality, at least as far as the century between 1460 and 1560 is concerned. (After 1560 the civil wars, by creating artificial famine conditions, may serve to vitiate the results). In general, it is possible to distinguish three periods: one of relative plenty (1460–1504), one of initial difficulties (1504–26), and one of grave crises (after 1526). The three stages suggest a process of deterioration; the mounting demographic tide was submerging the weak defenses of agricultural production.

First we have the period of plenty from 1460 to 1504, of which the Estates of Languedoc were fully conscious. The delegates had not yet succumbed to the timorous, prohibitionist attitude they would adopt after 1504 and especially after 1526. They did nothing to restrict the exportation of grain from the province. On the contrary, they encouraged it, and they complained of the king's agents who first set restrictions on exports and then granted export licenses "under the table" to their special friends. It was for this reason that the provincial governor, the *sieur* de Chabannes, was censured by the Estates in 1492. In this first period the regional assembly imposed an embargo on grain exports on only three occasions: in 1496, in 1498, and in 1501. In normal years the province enjoyed a surplus. The grain market was strangely becalmed. What a far cry from the human overcharge and recurrent famines of the first half of the fourteenth century, prior to 1348.

There were omens of what was to come, however. To begin with, there was the harvest failure of 1474 in the region of Toulouse. It seems to have spared Mediterranean Languedoc, unlike the one born of cold and rain that devastated the whole of France south of the Loire in 1482/83. At Montpellier the beggars were penned up and given three hundred loaves of bread to share with the plague victims of that same year. Then the curtain falls; for the next fifteen years there was not a single famine alert. In this period of plenty without precedent, the demographic resurgence of Languedoc, which had long been brewing, could materialize under the most favorable of circumstances.

With the mediocre harvests of 1495–96, and especially of 1497, the first discordant notes of *esterillité de vivre* (food shortage) were sounded. The towns were full of panderers and roving packs of hungry roughnecks. The Genoese wanted to buy grain, but the Estates imposed an embargo on the ports. Mule drivers with their pack animals came flocking from the poverty-stricken Rouergue and from the whole mountainous amphitheater of the south-central plateau in the hope of making off with some of the meager stocks of the Mediterranean littoral. These starving wretches were indeed a pitiful sight to behold. There were a few other alarms (the mediocre crop of 1501 caused a brief price flurry), but afterwards everything returned to normal. On the whole, periods of scarcity were rare during these forty-four years.

The second period (1504–26) began with a poor harvest year, which initiated a new phase of austerity. The following winter the Estates placed an embargo on exports. Clients near at hand who were also short of provisions —Genoese, Florentines, and natives of the Dauphiné—were refused grain. The twenty-two bishops sitting in the assembly even confiscated two hundred *charges* of wheat destined for "Our Holy Father the Pope." Throughout the winter of 1504/1505 the cathedral chapters and commanderies distributed alms to a swarm of paupers. The situation remained tense following the harvest of 1505. By fall, food hoarding and shortages were rife. The harvest of 1506 was not much better. In January, 1507, with the new harvest still months off, the Estates panicked and forbade the export of grain. Similar measures followed the harvest of 1507, when exports of grain to Aragon or other destinations were outlawed. The run of bad luck continued; the harvest of 1508 must have been another disappointment if in the spring of 1509 commissioners were appointed to prevent the circulation of grain from seneschalsy to seneschalsy. This phase of uncommon scarcity, lasting from 1504 to 1508, was signaled by a plateau of high prices on the *mercuriale* of Montpellier.

A new hunger cycle set in after a very short lapse of time (something unheard of before 1504), with three lean years in succession (1513, 1514, and

1515). This time it was clear that Languedoc's position as a grain-exporting region was seriously compromised—that the grain market was somehow out of order. The fortunate late fifteenth century—when five or ten or sometimes even fifteen years passed without the slightest hint of scarcity, when export restrictions were measures of exception and were never renewed from year to year—was a distant memory. In fact, if the structure of the market changed, if barriers were raised between the regional economies in a spirit of exclusiveness, it was because there were many more mouths to feed. The "full contingents" of the period around 1500 weighed heavily on the demand side of the supply and demand equation, creating conditions of scarcity.

The situation was irreversible and was getting worse. Export embargoes were imposed in 1517, 1519, 1520, 1522, and 1525. Henceforward, hidden lean periods recurred every second year, like fallowing. Beginning in 1526 the "tragedy of wheat"—a veritable famine cycle—got under way. A period of recurring difficulties gave way to one of permanent crisis. The Estates' laissez-faire attitude was a forgotten memory, and the free grain market of the fifteenth century was dead and buried. For ten years running (1526–36) the provincial assembly prohibited the export of cereals.

A Crisis in Depth

In 1526 the harvest was mediocre; in 1527 disaster struck. A cyclonic period lasting several years (with rainy summers and mild winters that caused the grain to rot in the ground) descended on Europe and the Mediterranean. The harvest of 1527 was a total loss. In August the Estates—ignoring the entreaties of grain buyers from Provence, Florence, and Genoa—prohibited cereal exports. But important personnages like the abbot d'Aniane, who was too close to the court to be refused a favor, managed nevertheless to market their grains abroad at high prices and handsome profits. By April of 1528 famine was raging in Languedoc, and wheat had to be imported from overseas via the port of Marseilles. It sold for two *livres* and ten *sous* in the towns and three *livres* in the villages, always the last to be served. Dearth was attended by plague.

The usurers were having a field day. In the foothills they lent scarce grain to the poor at high interest. This was the way the *sieur* de Carlencas responded to the appeals of a number of hungry weavers in that sinister April of 1528.

June, 1528: the new harvest was not good. Hunger persisted and stocks remained low. August, November, 1528: *"rarité des bleds, cherté plus que ne fut oncques"* ("shortage of grain, prices higher than ever"). The price curve had been climbing steadily since 1525. The borders of the province remained sealed. The spring of 1529 was therefore a difficult time; the Parlement of Toulouse finally beseeched the notables, "for charity's sake unlock your granaries, cart your grains to market, lower your prices." But it was a case of "famine," and the implacable order also went out to "expel the vagabonds and foreigners."

The harvest of 1529 did not succeed in exorcising the shortage of bread. In November the Estates, assembled in the lower hall of a large hospital, rejected the appeals for grain emanating from the cities of Lyons, Avignon, and Arles. The harvest of 1530 was still inadequate, given the growing need and the empty granaries. In September, 1530, restrictions were imposed on nonresident grain buyers. In November exports were again prohibited. The spring of 1531 was one of scarcity and even famine; a reward was posted for denouncing secret stocks. In May requisitioning began, and the price of grain was frozen in the face of the intolerable scarcity and the growing multitude of destitute poor. At Montpellier, for that matter, the seasonal highs of 1529 and 1531 broke all previous records on the price curve. They would not be equaled again until 1545. New prohibitions against exports were promulgated by the Estates in 1531, 1532, 1533—when a bad dry spell paralyzed the sowing—and finally in 1535.

The passage from a free-trade mentality to self-serving protectionism on the part of the notables of Languedoc is evident. Their about-face connotes a simple awareness of economic realities and also a psychological adjustment. Thirty years earlier abundance had been the rule; now it was chronic scarcity. Henceforth, there were too many mouths to feed and not enough bread to go around.

It is necessary to dwell at some length on these ten lean years (1526–35), in the first place because they mark a major turning point in the grain policy of the Estates of Languedoc. In other sectors, that of wine for example, the provincial assembly remained faithful to its fifteenth-century free-trade principles. The export of wine was permitted because there was never a shortage of it, but in the case of grain, freedom to export was only an exception reserved for the bumper harvest years (1536, 1542, 1547, 1549, 1554, and 1556). Interdiction had become almost an automatic reflex. In the period 1537–60, the Estates suppressed (at least in theory) all cereal exports from the province three years out of four. Languedocian wheat after 1526 was in reality a prisoner, if sometimes free on parole.

The crisis of 1526–35, moreover, also marked a social turning point. Vagrancy became a veritable scourge and was, for the first time, systematically suppressed. In 1532, following five years of dearth, the province was full of vagabonds—"murderers guilty of innumerable homicides." According to the Estates, the inhabitants of the region no longer dared go to their fields. In 1533 the countryside of Nîmes was "infested with beggars as a result of the extreme misery that has reigned here in recent times."

Ritual complaints, perhaps? But there was nothing ritual about the following. In 1533 for the first time in their history, the Estates of Languedoc, all out of patience with the profusion of poor wretches, determined to wipe out pauperism by force. They wrote the king that too many poor sought refuge in the lands of Languedoc, that too many of them refused to work, and that they encumbered the churches, troubled the divine service, and disturbed the meditations of the faithful during the elevation of the Host by their clamor—not to mention the sicknesses that followed in their wake.

Francis I granted the petition. From Compiègne, he signed an edict dated April 15, 1534, providing for the arrest of all healthy individuals who "for a certain time" have gone to beg and panhandle (*belistrer*) in the territories of Languedoc. And thenceforth, almost every year up to 1560, the question of the errant poor, "thieves, robbers and evildoers" (*"volleurs, larrons et malvenans"*), "vermin who proliferate day after day in the towns, fields, roads and lanes," led to anxious deliberations in the Estates or in the Parlement of Toulouse.

What was true of Languedoc, where the long subsistence crisis of 1526–35 aggravated by demographic factors led to mass vagrancy and to its repression by the authorities, was also true of the rest of Europe. Everywhere in the west the problem of the poor became acute about 1525–30 because of demographic ground swell, the succession of poor harvests, and the cycle of high grain prices. In 1525 Zwingli set up his relief plan for the indigent population of Zurich. In 1526 Juan Luis Vives published *De subventione pauperum*, a work conceived at Louvain and Oxford. In 1530 Henry VIII promulgated the first antivagrancy statute. By royal order, sturdy beggars were yoked to carts, were whipped until the blood ran, were mutilated by having an ear cut off, or were sometimes hung. In 1537 Charles V took similar measures in the Low Countries. It was precisely in these years that the first timid signs appear of a dream that was later to haunt the *mentalités classiques* of seventeenth-century France: the *"grand enfermement"*—"great sequestration"—of the poor.

Our "microscopic" research concerning farming units and land structures serves to demonstrate the pauperization of the sixteenth century. At the same time, a macroscopic study of the behavior of the public authorities and the popular masses confirms the general advent of pauperism with the crisis of the 1530's. The two phenomena are evidently closely related to one another just as they are related to the underlying movement of society as a whole. The silent demographic expansion was not matched by a rise in the aggregate product; it destroyed Languedoc's capacity to produce a surplus of wheat for export; it forced the ill-fed peasants to eke out an existence on shrinking tenures—on the *peau de chagrin* of subdividing landholdings[1]— it resulted in a sort of wage squeeze, especially after 1525 when prices, which had been rising moderately, suddenly took wing. And it was all this that induced the populace to concentrate its purchasing power on bread cereals, which had the effect in times of scarcity of putting the minimum wheat ration out of reach of the poorest classes. It was the spread of joblessness—the pressure of a growing army of seasonal or year-round unemployed—that accounted for the aggressive vagabonds, divested of land and wages, who infested the countryside. Finally, it was these combined factors (the authorities perceived the effects without comprehending the causes) that resolved the Estates of Languedoc to keep the grain harvest inside the province and drive the destitute out of town and parish.

The crisis of 1526, then, was a "crisis of growth," but of "unhealthy growth." It affected the level of consumption of the populace not only in the case of crude foodstuffs like cereals and bread but also in the case of meat and other animal products, which were the unique symbols of popular well-being.

The year 1530, or thereabout, was the great turning point. It marked the beginning of the decline of stock raising and meat consumption—the beginning of an insidious sort of undernourishment. I have already pointed this out with regard to individual diets in my studies of wages. The same phenomenon, magnified many times, reappears at the level of aggregate production.

---

[1] The *peau de chagrin*, from the Balzac novel, was a leather talisman which enabled its possessor to satisfy every desire but which shrank in size with each new request "as the days of the owner's life" (tr. note).

A mere glance at price behavior suggests the agitated state of the market. The price of wheat increased sixfold and more between 1480 and 1580. Yet in the same interval the price of meat barely quadrupled. The two curves of wheat and meat prices diverged in a "scissors" movement in the French Midi just as they did in Germany. Had the demand for meat perhaps declined in such a way that it discouraged stock raising?

The study of farm incomes more than confirms this diagnosis. For the sixteenth century there exist several good series of *carnencs* (tithes on livestock) for village stock or for the great town herds of Narbonne and Béziers. These revenues, as a rule, were farmed annually by the tithing chapters. The tithe farmers, whose personal expenses were minimal, were charged with gathering the wool "at the shearing" and the lambs and kids "at the feast of Saint Mark, one for ten," plus a pig from every original litter. They paid a sum of money for the concession which approached the actual tithe collections in value. Thanks to the series of *carnenc* leases, it is possible to reconstitute, if not the total volume, at least the trend of nominal income from livestock production. A median curve synthesizing the curves for the different localities provides us with a simplified picture of the movement in question.

The beginning was promising. Between 1475 and 1515 "livestock income" expressed in nominal prices more than doubled and in fact nearly tripled from an index of 30 to an index of 80 (1610–40 = 100). Now, in this first period prices were still stable or rising only slightly. The nominal increase in income corresponds, for this reason, to an actual increase in livestock production. The animal population was multiplying as fast, if not faster, than the human population, and the demographic fires were kindled in about 1490–1500 under the most favorable circumstances from the standpoint of diet. The supernumerary population was guaranteed an adequate amount of protein.

But this situation did not long endure. Beginning in 1515–20, stock raising in Languedoc began to retreat. The retreat quickly turned into a rout, and by 1525–30 livestock production was literally a shambles. The nominal income from the *carnencs* dropped from an index of 80 to an index of 40. At the same time, prices skyrocketed. It was clearly the herds that had fallen apart. It was a fearsome crisis, the worst until the Wars of Religion.

The causes? The epizootic diseases coincident with the general scarcity and the human epidemics of 1529–30, in all probability, were one. It was also a question of a transfer of demand. Grain was so dear around 1530 that it monopolized the people's purchasing power. Meat was omitted from the popular diet, and the livestock industry suffered the backlash.

Finally, it is necessary to invoke a third factor to explain the crisis in stock raising, one that was likewise inseparable from the general movement of the society. Land reclamation reduced sheepwalks. Olive and chestnut plantings, terraces, and stone enclosures restricted common pasture. For all these reasons, stock raising leveled off and then declined. In traditional peasant agriculture, where forage plants were unknown—or confined to gardens—it was impossible for livestock and field crop production to develop simultaneously, since both were competing for the remaining free land which was daily becoming more circumscribed. In the absence of an organization like the Spanish *Mesta* to defend the interests of the graziers, the livestock industry in an expanding preindustrial society was sacrificed without ado.

Once again, the turning point occurred about 1520–30. Grazing rights on the commons and fallow had been liberally accorded stockherders prior to that time, and the Parlement of Toulouse, between 1445 and 1519, had shown itself to be the leading champion of the ancient customs. In 1520 came the first discordant note. Parlement's attitude changed in connection, specifically, with the recent spread of vine and olive cultivation. In that year the inhabitants of Gignac were forbidden to pasture their animals in the vineyards and olive orchards. This was the first time Parlement took such measures. In 1528 the inhabitants of Lunel suffered the same restrictions. The question was henceforth one of public concern, and faced with a choice between livestock and cash crops like wine and olives, one did not hesitate to sacrifice animals to plants—the peasant's common rights to the farmer's private interests. In 1530, for the first time in their history—and then again in 1531 and 1532—the local notables sitting in the Estates demanded the off-limits posting of vineyards, olive orchards, meadows, woods, copses, and fruit trees and the interdiction of common pasture in these posted areas, or *devès*, without the owner's permission. At Pézenas, too, measures against collective grazing in the plantings—decreed in 1306 but fallen into disuse during the *Wüstungen* period of 1350–1500 when stock was king—were resurrected in 1533; overpopulation and land hunger infused new life into the ancient pre-*Wüstungen* legislation dating from an earlier cycle of demographic congestion, vine and tree plantings, and agrarian particularism. And under the pressure of circumstances, the attitude of the public authorities changed radically about 1520–30; by a single impulse, both free trade in grain and common grazing rights were repudiated or restricted. The precious bread cereals and certain cash crops were the objects of every solicitude, while cattle and sheep were regarded with hostility. The reign of the graziers drew to a close.

The livestock industry of Languedoc never recovered from the crisis of 1530. Between the start of the sixteenth century and the civil war, the nominal returns from the *carnencs* passed from an index of 60 to an index of 100 —a nominal increase, but a regression in real terms because in the same interval the price of dressed meat rose 130 percent. This deterioration of real income from the *carnencs* is a sure sign of shrinking herds. While the human population was doubling and food crop production was rising slightly, or at least holding its own, stock raising collapsed, and the popular consumption of meat, as reflected in wages and tithes, caved in.

The period 1526–35, in short, was one of deep crisis arising from the contradictions inherent in the development of the society itself. It was a crisis that affected every aspect of life from its biological foundation to its psychological superstructure.

With regard to biology, the plague of 1530, which proliferated in the wake of hunger and malnutrition, was one of the most violent of the sixteenth century (this at a time when the plague tended to become less virulent in the French Midi). In 1530 Montpellier mobilized practically all its revenues to fight the contagion. The case was almost unique in the financial history of the city, a measure of the seriousness of the epidemic.

With regard to psychology, beginning in 1526 Protestant propaganda evoked a powerful response in a population tormented by material adversity and envious of the wealthy clergy. It was during the Christmas of 1527 and the terrible Lent of 1528, a winter and spring of stark hunger, that the Reformation took root in the Vivarais and in Languedoc with the first heretical preaching of the Cordeliers before excited crowds and the earliest persecutions of religious propagandists in a region heretofore untouched by heresy. In November, 1528, Lutheran sectarians appeared as far away as Toulouse, "invoking the devil," it was said, and "uttering execrable blasphemies." The rural Cévennes, a future bastion of heresy, was already "infected." In 1529 the Rebeine insurgents of Lyons, contemporaries of the Anabaptists of the North, staged food riots, attacked the convents, and mutinied against the tithes. The influence of the Rebeine was perceptible throughout the southeast, a region linked to Lyons by a multiple network of commercial relations. Beginning in 1530, the satiric theme of the monk's head with ass's ears was popularized as a decorative motif by the stonemasons of Languedoc. The peasant masses were contaminated. In 1532 in the Bas-Rhône, entire villages—led by their syndics, regents, and priests—embraced the Reformation. The heresy was thus implanted at the height of a social crisis. It took firm root, giving promise of a brilliant future; five years later its practitioners were beyond counting.

The years 1526–35 were therefore a pivotal crisis, a nodal point of social history as the Fronde was later and elsewhere and in an entirely different context. As a result of these years, the abstract economic indices—the disparities noted in rates of growth and the analyses of landownership and wages—assume a concrete significance, finding embodiment in the great popular disturbances. The crisis first dramatized the lessons of immoderate demographic advance attended by insufficient economic growth. During and after this paroxysm, the popular and rural masses "could no longer live as before"—could no longer work, eat, pray, think, and die as in the past. On the threshold of the second generation of expansion, the crisis of 1530 marked the end of good times and the twilight of a happy age.

Languedoc was not alone. In Spain, Germany, the Low Countries, and England the decade of the 1520's or 1530's commenced the long travail of the old-style proletariat, the repression of the peasants and the poor. In Italy the decade of the 1520's, especially 1528–29, was a time of terrible famine, of the *gran fame*, the "great hunger," at Venice. "What were obliterated in these difficult years were the brightest flowers of the early Renaissance" (Braudel, 1949, p. 373).

A Certain Capitalism Miscarries

It remains for us to consider—over and against the question of poverty—the triumphant history of profits and wealth. To understand the latter, the studies of land and income, the horizontal and vertical analyses, have to be compared and integrated "in their multiple complexity and the reciprocity of their interrelations" (Sartre). In the world of the poor, a comparison of the two angles of vision leads to converging and cumulative results. The two kinds of pauperization, in wages and in land, reinforced one another. The "little man" was impoverished twice over, as a wageworker and as a smallholder. At the other end of the scale, at the level of profits and wealth, the story was different. There, the land or "horizontal" perspective and the social or "vertical" perspective were no longer complementary but apparently contradictory. From the vertical perspective of types and levels of income, land rent held its own while profits rose. Did this signify that rural capitalism was making progress?

In a certain measure, yes. But it remained confined within narrow limits because the surplus value on which it depended was not derived, except in a small way, from a rapidly growing aggregate product, as was to be the case after 1750 and especially after 1850. For once our picture-book clichés happen to be true. That surplus value was extracted drop by drop from the sweat of the impoverished workers, and the good fortune of profits was conditioned by the misfortune of wages. A "growth of wealth" of this type is necessarily limited, for pauperization quickly reaches the level of bare subsistence and can proceed no further. In order to release important sources of surplus value, production would have had to increase on a massive scale, as was the case in neighboring Catalonia in the eighteenth century. But in sixteenth-century Languedoc the process of economic growth was not yet really under way.

The other profit impasse derived from the land structure itself and from its characteristic evolution. True, entrepreneurial profits grew in the sixteenth century, but only within the immutable confines of a given domain. The capitalist class, in order to allow the process ample scope, should have consolidated its lands—enlarged its territorial base. There should have been more and more great estates, big landowners, and large-scale tenant farmers. Land concentration, in other words, should have been the dominant phenomenon.

Practically nothing of the kind occurred. There were, of course, a few attempts at land consolidation, but these constituted exceptions to the rule. Take the case of Eutrope Fabre, of Gaillac, a miserly priest who died in 1532. In a lifetime of saving he barely managed to piece together five or six plots of land, a miserable seven hectares in all. This "magnificent" property, moreover, was destined to be parceled out again to his prolific grandnephews. The basic movement of the sixteenth century is to be sought elsewhere, in the process of land subdivision which dismembered those land units capable of generating capitalistic profits. The great estates of the sixteenth century constituted an isolated archipelago lost (and sometimes swallowed up) in a rising sea of destitute, diminutive smallholds.

Rural capitalism appropriated a greater share for itself on the vertical plane at the expense of the farm worker, but it was largely unsuccessful on the horizontal plane, where success was a question of land aggrandizement.

It failed to appropriate the peasant smallholds. To the extent that this process was taking place at all in the sixteenth century, it was limited to the countryside of Paris or London and was hardly characteristic of the regions around Nîmes or Narbonne. The south of France, between 1490 and 1600, was refractory to land engrossers.

There are three possible sources of surplus value in agriculture: increased production, land concentration, and reduced wages. Rural capitalism in Languedoc in the sixteenth century really only explored the most primitive and the least humane of these three possibilities, the third. In these circumstances it was able to accomplish modest and limited progress at best. The regional economy, nothwithstanding the enormous sacrifices of the rural laborers, remained incapable of secreting a capitalistic social system—capitalism is not built on poverty.

Languedoc and Catalonia

A comparison between Languedoc in the sixteenth century and Catalonia in the eighteenth century is perhaps relevant in this connection. The common features stand out in relief. In both cases population doubled in less than a century—two examples of the incredible demographic resiliency of the Mediterranean peoples, cast into the depths by misery and disease only to reemerge with renewed vitality. Another trait in common was the accelerated subdivision of landholdings that went hand in hand with the rising tide of population.

At this point, however, the comparison breaks down. In Catalonia production kept pace with and sometimes outdistanced the increase in population. An ingenious irrigation policy unchained income per land unit, eliminated fallowing, and transformed the rural landscape into an enchanted world of meadows, *huertas*, and cash crops like flax, maize, rice, alfalfa and clover, and garden plants. Vineyards were planted, stock multiplied, and the heavy plow ousted the scratch plow. The demographic increase served as a multiplier of real wealth. The overall tithe, income, living standards, land rent, profits—all "rode up together, on the tide" and at a much faster rate than prices. Wages were no longer the pariah of economic expansion. They clung to the price curve, picking up momentum and managing even to leave prices behind during the prosperous years of the French Revolution. This was true economic growth in the modern sense, and it contributed to the growth of urban and industrial capitalism. Peasant savings, sustained by Mexican piastres, financed the expansion of the port of

Barcelona, a city of one hundred thousand inhabitants, upsetting the old economic balance and paving the way for an industrial "takeoff."

Nothing of the sort occurred in our mid-sixteenth-century Languedoc. The one dominant factor, alas, was demography. Economic attitudes remained immutable, and Malthusian "scissors" were opening up on every side: between population and production, between agriculture and stock raising, between wages and prices. Wage rationing and land rationing were instituted. The meager savings realized from the squeeze on rural wages were insufficient to initiate large-scale agricultural investment and failed at the same time to stimulate urban development. The biggest "cities" of Mediterranean Languedoc in about 1550, Nîmes and Montpellier, each counted two thousand houses or about ten thousand inhabitants, a quarter of whom were peasants and farm laborers. They were still, in reality, just small country towns.

The Catalonian expansion of the age of the Enlightenment was a modern type of development, the source of individual economic enrichment. The Languedocian expansion of the Renaissance was of the ancient kind, a multiplier of poverty.

PART TWO

New States of Consciousness and Social Struggles

1

The Paths of Scripture

This unequal development, such as it was and for all its shortcomings, was creative of change. It brought in its wake new states of consciousness, social struggles, and conflicts over land; it engendered wars and revolutions. It was attended by a deep and sometimes lasting permutation in peasant mentality. This permutation needs to be defined.

Two Cultural Currents

Two revolutions in mental attitudes, two currents of cultural change, arose in Mediterranean France in the sixteenth century. The first was the linguistic revolution represented by the earliest diffusion of the French language (1450–1590). It took possession of the cities, towns, and large villages, the privileged orders and the urban bourgeoisie, but it only contaminated the highest levels of rural society. It is of considerably more than philological interest because it serves to delimit, by the first half of the sixteenth century two contrasting culture areas. In the east was the main axis of rapid linguistic penetration and precocious bilingualism where, as early as 1450–90, the *langue d'oil* of the notables contrasted with the Romance dialects still spoken by the common people. This zone corresponds to the Rhône Valley and, more generally, to the triangle formed by the Rhône, the Cévennes, and the Mediterranean—by Valence, Montpellier, and Arles. The breach in the old linguistic frontier southward along the Rhône was contained by maritime Provence and especially by western Languedoc and eastern Aquitaine, all of which resisted the invasion of the French language for one or two generations more (up to about 1530–50). These regions were all cultural backwaters and were destined to remain so for a long time to come. As late as 1570, according to statistics on signatures, or 1680–86, according to Maggiolo's charts, the level of culture declined progressively, region by region, as one advanced from the Bas-Rhône to the Haute-Garonne.

A study of the frequency of signatures, from east to west, indicates, in fact, that about 1575 (the date of the earliest statistics) only 25 percent of the artisans at Montpellier were illiterate compared to 33 percent at Narbonne. Moreover, the level of culture was much superior at Montpellier, where the majority of "literate" artisans could write their full names, while half the people in this category at Narbonne signed with just their initials. The same was true of the peasants. About 1575 a larger minority could sign their own names at Montpellier than at Narbonne. At Montpellier, French was in general use by 1490; at Narbonne, not until later.

Even more marked was the linguistic lag between the Rhône Valley and Bas-Languedoc on the one hand and the Massif Central on the other. On the siliceous highlands of the latter region were to be found the veritable sanctuaries of the *langue d'oc*, which remained practically inviolate up to the beginning of the seventeenth century. This was true of the Rouergue, for example, and also the mountains of Saint-Pons. These wretched, backward mountains, the last enclaves of the *langue d'oc* dialect culture, were at the same time (and herein lies the explanation) the last refuge of total illiteracy, being often entirely without schools and schoolmasters. The figures on the frequency of signatures in 1595 as well as in 1643 and 1737, not to mention the earliest statistics on school attendance of the Old Regime, serve to demonstrate the fact conclusively. From this illiteracy there followed the indomitable *occitanisme* of these ancient mountains. Can there be any doubt that mass illiteracy impeded the spread of the French language, which was transmitted through the written word?

It was in this sharply contrasted culture area of the Midi that the second intellectual revolution of the century, the Reformation, took root. It went deeper than the linguistic revolution, penetrating to the level of the popular and peasant conscience. Yet in relation to the latter it offers no significant geographic originality. The distribution of the places of origin of the *émigrés* to Geneva in 1550, the inquest into the crime of heresy launched in the name of the Parlement of Toulouse in 1560, and, finally, the distribution of Huguenots at the time of the civil wars strongly underline permanent features of intellectual geography. The chosen zone of early Protestantism in 1550–60 was the same Rhône–Cévennes–Bas-Languedoc triangle where for a century its coming had been prepared by the privileged penetration of the French language and delimited since long past by the establishment of all manner of cultural exchange. The nerve centers were Romans, Uzès, Alès, Nîmes, and Montpellier. On the left bank of the Rhône it was the valley of the Durance, where the Waldensians, by 1535, were peddling their Bibles and catechisms, "shields of faith, anatomies of dogma and similar books, and above all small psalters ... rhymed, bound, gilded and ruled." On the right bank it was especially the valleys of the Cévennes, and, subjacent to the Cévennes—opposite the Durance—a zone of itinerant ministers, artisans' workshops, and one-room schools: the Haut-Hérault, Vidourle, and, above all, the two Gardons (Gardon d'Alès and Gardon d'Anduze). The lists of foreigners (*estrangiés*) at Geneva and their provenance testify, beginning in 1549, to the presence of veritable clusters of rural Protestantism in the broken foothills of the Cévennes—clusters that ramified as one climbed the *thalwegs*. In this region by 1556 the ministers were preaching openly, baptizing, and celebrating the Holy Communion. Here, in 1560, peasants and craftsmen stormed the convents, cut the monks' copes into doublets and banners, and laid ambushes for the papist commissioners, or *enqueteurs*, while their wives flung sacks of ashes into the eyes of the priors and country priests. It was here, finally, in the large villages that the Protestant nuclei, composed of intellectuals (notaries, judges, and doctors) and artisans (*chaussatiers* who cut the uniforms for Condé's army, surgeons, blacksmiths, and cobblers), embraced the Calvinist faith and propagated it in the surrounding rural parishes. In 1560, for example, 150 armed Huguenots of Gignac, of both sexes and belonging to the above social categories, formed a psalm-singing procession in ranks of three to escort the minister who was to preach a sermon in the nearby village of Saint-André. The petty bourgeois Calvinists strove to win over the peasantry whether by peaceful conversion or by force of arms.

Beyond the Hérault, however, in the whole of western Languedoc, the picture was different. It was quite different, too, in the backward mountains of the Sidobre, the Espinouse, the Montagne Noire, or the Rouergue, which were so dissimilar from the industrious Cévennes to the east. The cultural lethargy evidenced in these regions as far back as 1500 was conducive to religious conservatism, and in the mountains the nuclei of Calvinist artisans—if one excepts the weavers of Castres and the hosiers of Roquecourbe—had little influence on the mass of the peasantry, who rejected the Bible and preferred sorcerers to ministers. In the lowlands the tiny Huguenot communities of Béziers were isolated, and by 1568 they had been literally swallowed up by the papist majority. Finally, in the extreme western part of Languedoc the large city of Toulouse was represented by fewer refugees at Geneva about 1550 than the very small Norman town of Coutances, which was also much farther away. The Huguenot party of Toulouse—composed, I discovered, of wool carders and academics led by a law student named Georges Mignot—was, for its part, easily crushed in the bloody spring of 1562 by much superior Catholic forces (Parlement, nobility, and regular troops, who upended the booksellers' stalls and threw their wares into the street).

An analysis by region, therefore, leads us back irresistibly to the privileged area of the sixteenth-century "enlightenment"—enlightenment with respect to linguistic knowledge and religious innovations, that is. It leads us back, in short, to the great Rhône–Cévennes–Languedoc triangle. It is here, in the neighborhood of the regional capital of Montpellier, and even more in the heart of the Cévennes, that one can attempt to assess the hold of early Calvinism on the peasant masses in the context of the cultural and social crosscurrents of the day.

The Reformation and the civil and religious wars served to make manifest contrasts that had been intensified by the pressures of the century. Let us consider the basic social categories of one busy city and their very different degrees of receptivity to the new ideas.

Religious Reformation and Cultural Receptivity in Town and Country

Montpellier, October, 1552: an attentive young visitor, his regard filled with naïve visions of happiness, casts a curious eye on the city. His first impressions: young noblemen in white tunics promenading through the streets, bombarding the demoiselles with sugar almonds from silver *coquilles*. Next, the winter of 1553 passed in serenading with tambourines, cymbals, fifes, and a trio of lutes—and also with viol and guitar, which were still great novelties. In the homes of the rich bourgeois there were balls right up to Carnival; suppers lasting until dawn; and swinging, wheeling, merry dances by torchlight. At Mardi Gras there were orange fights between youths with sacks of fruit tied to their necks and wicker shields on their arms; in the spring were sea-bathing and excursions to the countryside amid rosemary and bluebells. Félix Platter, our young observer, now settled down in one of the houses of his host, the wealthy Marrano and apothecary, Catelan; he had a room on the first floor, paintings on the wall, a gilded easy chair to study in. Here Platter passed the nights with a fellow student from Basel he had invited to share his bed and help him exorcise the terrors of the dark. The two young men fell asleep munching pralines and playing the lute.

April 4: the university was already out. The distractions multiplied: suppers of partridge, drinking bouts of muscatel and hippocras, masked balls, tender lessons on the lute for Catherine, the daughter of Rondelet. Wardrobe expenses: at Whitsuntide, Félix and his friends wore new, tight-fitting red hose, sometimes leather breeches with green silk embroidery, and shoes that were always new because Vulcain, the cobbler, replaced them every eight days! They watched the nobles, their plumed mounts adorned with multicolored panoplies, tilting at the ring; the defences of academic theses that invariably drew a crowd; the fine autopsies; the popular spectacle of criminals being tortured or executed in public in the presence of young girls and entire families.

Innocent gaiety, cruel pleasures, money, sadism, luxury: Félix Platter describes an art of living practiced by a small group of notables, bourgeois, and nobles in a Mediterranean city in the twilight of a certain Renaissance.

Thanks to the taille registers and the notaries, it is possible to stake out, to delimit, this tiny islet of good fortune about 1555–65. It was located in the Gothic quarter of Saint-Firmin, the residence of the wealthy, of the friends and neighbors of Catelan and Platter. It numbered 160 taille payers—well-to-do citizens for the most part. First, there were the noble lords, or those reputed as such, who paid a taille of £40 to £120. They lent money to the innkeepers of the town and rye to the peasants against reimbursement in *écus*. Their neighbors were often canons who lived, according to the expression then current, *"agréablement dans le siècle"* ("in the comfortable manner of laymen"). Next came the bourgeois and the big rentiers who paid £30 to £80 in taille. They, too, lived off the backs of the peasants, cobblers, and little people with their loans at interest. They also lived off the rents and profits from their lands, gardens, and houses. Next were the group of jurists, registrars, judges, doctors of law, procurators, customs officers, and officers of the gabelle, or salt tax, who were assessed between £20 and £70 each. Below them on the fiscal ladder was an active group whose members were taxed from £10 to £20 composed of merchants, spice dealers, drapers, apothecaries, medical doctors, and university professors. Finally, at the bottom of the hierarchy with an assessment of £5 to £20 were a handful of notaries (the less fortunate), well-to-do shopkeepers, and craftsmen (serving as tradespeople for the above-mentioned gentlemen): booksellers, tailors and dressmakers, pewterers, barbers, cobblers, caterers, and others.

As for the rural plebeian, he was barely represented in the quarter of Saint-Firmin. Out of the 160 taille payers, I count, in fact, just a single peasant. His taille assessment was one *sou*. In a city that was still in large measure agricultural and that lived in part off its loans to the rural classes, these *beaux quartiers* of 1560 were sociological *isolats* that practiced real segregation vis-à-vis the peasants. Yet in 1435, in the darkest days of the urban crisis when Montpellier was reduced to little more than a large village, the quarter of Saint-Firmin still counted twenty-two peasant families. By 1544 this rural plebs had disappeared, leaving only the bourgeois classes. The notables had driven the populace out of their quarter.

Let us quit Saint-Firmin, the pleasant residence of the upper classes and the pinnacle of city life. The rest of the city offers a very different spectacle. It was still impregnated with rural life and encumbered with manure pits, droves of swine, and convoys of mules laden with vats for the vintage that risked poking out the eyes of passers-by in the narrow streets. In these neighborhoods a quarter or a fifth of the taxable inhabitants exercised the trade of *laboureur* (a word translated from the Languedocian *laurador* which here signifies either a simple rural day laborer or a veritable husbandman). Moreover, among the propertyless, untaxable citizens inhabiting these quarters, many were farm workers, or *travailleurs*, by trade who hired out at two in the morning for the wheat, grape, or olive harvests—a rural people with a special consul, the sixth and last on the list, elected by the "*laboreurs* and people of low estate."

About 1554–56 the situation of these town-dwelling peasants, victims of the insoluble contradictions of the advancing sixteenth century, was far from brilliant. They were excluded from the few wealthy sections of the city, but elsewhere, in the popular quarters and in the slums, their numbers multiplied with the demographic inflation. For example, the quarter of Sainte-Croix in Montpellier counted twenty-six *laboureurs* in the *compoix* of 1435 and almost three times as many in the *compoix* of 1544.

They were poor. Their taille amounted to £1, £2, £3, or sometimes only a few *sous*. This was an insignificant sum compared to the £20 to £120 the notables paid. Platter, on the rare occasions when his attention was diverted from the enchanted circle of leading families of his own milieu, noted the precarious situation of the rustics: a diet of chestnuts, sour wine, and black bread; goatherds living on bread crusts; ignorant peasants dressed like the devil himself; raging fevers that killed many people in the bad harvest year of 1555. In fact, the period 1552–57 covered by Platter's account corresponds to a cycle of high grain prices, a time of great distress for the poor; 1552/53 had been a good year, with wheat prices at a cyclical low and a surplus for export, but the harvest of 1554 was poor, and the winter of 1554/55, which the gilded youth passed in dancing, flirting, and supping, was a hard season for the lower classes. In April the price of grain was twice that of 1553. The peasants, singly or in whole groups, came hat in hand seeking loans from the rich bourgeois of Saint-Firmin of fifty or one hundred liters of grain to tide them over until the harvest. The peak of this hunger cycle in 1557/58 coincided with a period of plague and scarcities.

Not all the peasants living in the town and its outskirts found themselves on the wrong side of the social barricades. Side by side with the wretched owners of one mule or one plow were the big tenant farmers, who shared in the swollen profits of the sixteenth century and participated in the exploitation of the wageworkers. From a social point of view, however, a wide gulf separated these well-to-do individuals at the summit of peasant society from the really rich merchants or bourgeois of the towns. Notaries' inventories (unfortunately rare before 1590) offer striking evidence of this cultural segregation—of this continuing contrast—as two typical examples will make clear.

First, let us visit the home of Sauvaire Texier, a merchant draper of Montpellier (who died in 1600). His shop on the ground floor is well stocked with woolen cloth of Languedoc and the north (Meaux and Bourges), 250 bolts in all, as well as bales of wool. A circular staircase leads to seven rooms in the upper stories; there is a reception hall, a kitchen, an attic, and a cellar. Texier's beds have fine wool mattresses. His strongbox is filled with money —two hundred *livres* in ducats, *douzains*, and *ducatons*. He owns gold rings, precious stones, jasper, bracelets, eighteen silver dominoes, a silver chest, a silver chain, and a "vine of gold." There are robes of broadcloth, *goulles*, cloaks to keep the master warm, and, on the floor, a green woolen carpet. There are dozens of chairs, stools and footstools, and banks and benches, all of walnut, the rich man's wood. Texier favored green. His gowns, carpets, and upholstered chairs were all of that color. He had a personal arsenal consisting of a sword, a pistol, an *arcabuse*, and an archer's bow; he also owned a writing desk, nine brass chandeliers, and—reassuring symbols of material security—six dozen towels, four dozen bedsheets, curtains on the windows, and chests full of wheat, rye, and salt pork. Texier had a taste for art objects: a painting in a wooden frame, a painted glass bowl, the *vigne d'or* noted above, and others.

And who was Sauvaire Texier? He came from peasant stock. His sisters married two peasants named Martin and Mathieu. The Texier and Martin families were all petty taille payers—a few *livres* or a few *sous*—in the *compoix* of Mauguio in 1560. This compares to sixty or eighty *compoix* pounds for the big landowners of the locality, who surely looked down their noses at these rural plebeians. But young Sauvaire was a "self-made man,"[1] a man with initiative who quit the country for the town. He made his fortune, and he was able to redeem the farm of Gavot from his father in 1590. He acquired a taste for the luxury of the bourgeois classes with a shade of the exaggeration of the parvenu merchant. In the end he crossed the threshold of real luxury.

Pierre Sallagier was also the son of a peasant. He lived in Sauvaire Texier's native village of Mauguio. He, too, was a success in life, but on the land and as a large-scale tenant farmer. He exploited a rich domain for the Order of Malta just outside Montpellier. He was a rustic rich in chattels; when he died in 1605 he left an inheritance of sixteen pairs of oxen (enough to work 150 hectares), a stable of fifteen horses, ten cows, 340 sheep, twenty-eight pigs, five mules, an array of seven plows, twenty-four *reilles*, and four farm wagons. The *coq de village* Sallagier was well off and never went hungry. But his was a beggarly existence, like that of any peasant, rich or poor. Let us visit the two-room farmhouse where family life unfolded. The scene is one of stark poverty: one bed, one table, two or three chests, a few items of tableware made of tin, six tablecloths, and some towels and bedsheets—no arms, no paintings, no jewelry. There is no hint, in the dwelling of this relatively rich man, of that modicum of luxury, art, or fantasy that was sometimes to be found in the homes of the well-to-do peasants of the eighteenth century. In Sallagier's house, cultural objects, in the traditional meaning of the term, were absent.

The two men, products of the same milieu, were separated by their way of life. Sallagier's only luxury consisted of strutting about in the midst of his vast herds of livestock, the ancient symbol of wealth. Texier, on the contrary, adopted the life style of the city-dweller. A nouveau riche, he endeavored to express with the aid of significant objects—chosen with care if

---

[1] *"Self-made man"* in English in the French editions (tr. note).

not with taste—his membership in a proud and fortunate urban elite. The two men represented two societies, two life styles, and two façades, and they personified, at the same time, the antinomy that opposed bourgeois and peasant, town and country, and—why not?—barbarism and civilization.

Finally, besides its bourgeoisie and its peasants, the city harbored a third force—its artisan class. Textiles, that is, the woolen cloth industry, made rapid strides in the sixteenth century. The *compoix* of 1435 for the Sainte-Croix quarter of Montpellier counted three *cardaires* and two *teisseires* compared to fifteen master carders and six weavers in the *compoix* of 1544. The number had tripled or quintupled in a little over a century. There were structural changes as well. In 1493 a number of Catalan weavers and their families came to settle in the city. Local artisans perfected a whole series of tools for their use: bobbins by the hundreds and a great fulling mill on a millstream with double sluices turning wooden waterwheels fitted with iron rims. Henceforward, the flowered, multicolored broadcloths of Montpellier dominated the regional market. After 1519 the number of carders and weavers in the wool shops swelled without suffering the sort of restraints imposed on the proliferation of the peasants by the shortage of land.

The earliest inventories of the possessions of these weavers (about 1590) testify to their humble daily life. The entire family lived and worked in one or sometimes two rooms in the midst of indescribable congestion two or three looms, a warping frame, and a spinning wheel surrounded by rustic furnishings—a table, a camp bed with a straw mattress, two or three barrels, stools, casks, cases, a *pastière* for kneading bread, and a single oil lamp to work by at night. The carders seem to have been a little better off with two-room living quarters (containing beds, chests, and barrels) and an attic, with four teasel frames and six dozen carding brushes per frame, where the whole family worked. The setting was poor and without a trace of luxury. The jewels, paintings, carpets, curtains, and little mirrors found in every bourgeois home were completely absent here. The cultural milieu, nonetheless, was more stimulating than that of the average peasant, the proof being that the carders knew how to sign their names.

In brief, the three different milieus or three sociocultural classes were, first, the dominant class of landowners, merchants, and office holders; second, the artisan class, particularly the cloth workers; and finally, the peasants and farm laborers. They correspond, in other terms, to the service and direction of society (the tertiary sector), to activities of transformation (the secondary sector), and to the crude production of the soil (the primary sector). The old system of classification was valid long before François Quesnay.

How would these different milieus react—and especially the peasant milieu in relation to the other two—to the cultural shock produced by the Calvinist revolution?

Huguenot Carders and Papist Peasants

The basis of a response is provided by an admirable document, the "roll of those present at the Calvinist assemblies" who were taxed by the Catholic authorities at Montpellier in November, 1560. It supplies the names of 817 individuals and indicates the professions of 561. More than a mere sampling, it constitutes a veritable census. At the head of the list of 561 pioneer Huguenots were members of the artisan class, by far the largest contingent, represented by 132 textile workers. Of these, 42 were wool carders who were the active leaven of the Reformation. A Catholic chronicler stigmatized the sticky-handed carders with penetrating hatred: "The first Calvinist rubbish," he wrote, "succeeded little by little in infecting with that doctrine certain tradesmen, chiefly wool carders and tenterers (*drapeurs-drapans*) encountered in the wineshops, who drunkenly memorized the words and music of the psalms of Bèze and Marot and popularized that new air, 'Lighten thine heart and open thine ears,' etc." After the 42 carders, among the Huguenots in the textile trades came 41 tailors or hosiers, 25 weavers, 5 ropemakers, 5 milliners, 9 cloth shearers, and 4 dyers as well as cotton spinners, dressmakers, tapestry makers, *canabassiers* (hemp weavers), hatters, and so on.

Next in order after textiles came the leather trades (which, as we shall see later, played the role of catalyst among the Huguenot peasantry of the Cévennes). These accounted for 58 names on the Calvinist list of 1560, 33 of whom were cobblers and the rest harness makers, curriers, *blanquiers* (tawers), glovers, furriers, and saddlers. The metal trades—blacksmiths and cutlers—contributed 45 Huguenots to the list. In all, if one includes the other trades, there were 387 craftsmen or shopkeepers among the 561 Huguenots counted and condemned in 1560. It was a classic structure; the perennial sans-culotte dissent of the old urban centers was sometimes heretical, at other times revolutionary, but recruited invariably in the market stalls and workshops.

The artisan contingent were the foot soldiers of the movement. The Huguenot leadership in 1560 came from the ranks of the bourgeois intelligentsia and the petty bourgeoisie, both broadly represented at the assemblies of that year. From the medical and legal professions there were advocates, notaries, apothecaries, registrars, solicitors, bailiffs, and clerks. These learned professions contributed a total of eighty-seven individuals to the statistics of 1560, or 15 percent of all the Huguenots whose occupations are known—a higher proportion, without doubt, than in the population as a whole. The merchants—who were twenty-four in number—and the nobles and the bourgeois of the Saint-Firmin quarter also sent a few dozen delegates to the Calvinist assemblies. Among these rich Huguenots there was more than one Marrano notable, his complex soul prone to multiple abjurations. About 1556–60 old Catelan came out simultaneously—oblivious to the contradictions—in favor of Jewish circumcision, the Catholic cult of the Virgin, and adherence to the Calvinist assemblies!

We have been concerned up to this point with artisans, intellectuals, and notables; that is to say, with the urban structures of Huguenot sociology properly speaking. What of the peasants and farm laborers who constituted over 20 percent of the total population of Montpellier and were so numerous in the outskirts and in the poorer quarters? Their religious behavior set them entirely apart and opposed them to the urban classes, especially to the artisans. The latter were sympathetic to the Reformation almost to a man about 1560. The peasant masses, on the contrary, remained refractory and often hostile to it.

One has only to refer to the list of Protestants of 1560. The number of peasants and farm laborers was insignificant. If they had been won over to the Reformation in the same proportion as the other social groups, there would have been at least 110 or 120 of them among the 561 Huguenots of known occupation because they constituted at least 20 percent of the local population. Now this was not the case at all. I count only 27 cultivators—peasants or day laborers—in the list of 1560, or 4.7 percent of the total. These included tenants of the big farms in the plain—rich, enlightened entrepreneurs who came the closest, in the rural milieu, to sharing the townsman's way of thinking. But such avant-garde peasants were still the exception, a spit in the ocean of peasant conservatism. The rural proletariat, for its part, remained practically impervious to the Reformation. There were but 2 *"travailleurs de terre"* listed among the 817 Huguenots of 1560.

Thus, the ideological choices were radically divergent. In the same town, within the same community, there was a complete divorce between the agricultural element on the one hand and the artisan, intellectual, and bour-

Statistics of Protestants at Montpellier in 1560

PROFESSION	NUMBER	PERCENTAGE
Artisans	387	69
Learned professions	87	15.4
Merchants	24	4.3
Bourgeois	23	4.2
Nobles	13	2.3
Cultivators	27	4.8
Total Huguenots of known profession	561	100
Overall total	817	

geois elements on the other. At Béziers, too, these different structures were fully operative. From a social point of view, the Reformation remained circumscribed to the urban and artisan classes from which it sprang. It did not migrate and did not spill over into the peasant masses, who remained steadfast in their Catholic beliefs.

These figures are confirmed by living history and by popular demonstrations. In 1561 the peasants of Montpellier proclaimed their Catholic faith as a body in opposition to the Calvinist citizenry of working-class or bourgeois stamp. On May 4 and 11 "the cultivators of the land" and their wives formed a procession from the poorer quarters of the city, placing their daughters, whose loosened hair fell to their shoulders (*"le poil descouvert et pendant"*), in the front ranks. The rustics ostensibly were distributing the holy bread, but under their cloaks were hidden daggers and sacks of stones reserved for the Huguenots. There were (the Calvinist historian reported) drunks and prostitutes in the crowd. All were demanding the Mass and the dance and were crying, "We shall dance in spite of the Huguenots." They wanted to celebrate the popular May rites, the ancient *Maïas* of medieval Languedocian folklore, featuring the "Feast of the Ass," burlesque singing, ribald jokes, dances, flowers, and masquerades. The Huguenots, in their already puritanical zeal, had forbidden these festivities and outlawed public dancing. For the peasants of Montpellier the sense of their revolt was clear. It irritated Calvin in his Genevan letters; it would have enchanted Max Weber. Two worlds and two cultures were face to face. On the one hand was an agrarian society, lodged in the city like some foreign body, holding to the old Catholic devotions, and demanding, in its life of poverty and squalor, the right to allow the instincts free reign in dancing and joie de vivre on the traditional feast days; on the other hand was the urban artisan class, Huguenot in faith and already extolling a worldly asceticism, that ethic of self-denial which—thanks to Calvin and later to the Puritans and Jansenists—would little by little come to be accepted as a norm by the petty bourgeoisie of modern times, suppressing and sublimating their primitive instincts.

Between town and country, and especially between peasants and artisans, religious differences from the beginning reveal a cultural and moral opposition which is immediately evident in literacy statistics. As to method: in the records of the sixteenth-century notaries it is possible to distinguish three major categories of signatures. First there are the real signatures, fully spelled out. Sometimes they are fluent, cursive, and with a modern flourish; sometimes they are halting, composed of lowercase letters detached from one another; and in extreme cases they are disjointed capitals, awkwardly juxtaposed—for example, I.VESI (Jean Voisin). There is no question that all of these variants are genuine signatures furnishing men's names in their complete form.

In the second, more primitive category, the signature consists of the person's initials, uppercase capital letters which were normally separated (PV, Pierre Vidal), joined (ℬ, Anthony Bonnet), combined in a bizarre fashion (ᗺ, Loys Belshoms), or reduced to a single initial (M, Pierre Martin). The third category, finally, is the simple sign or mark, which was evidence of complete illiteracy. It might be geometric or a "trade mark"—for an artisan, a rough hammer, for example; for the peasants, a conical plowshare (*reille*) or rake. Very often the mark was a cross or else, at the lowest level, a meaningless scrawl or blob of ink.

Three degrees, then—simple signs, initials, true signatures—marked the transition from complete illiteracy to an elementary level of culture. At Montpellier it was not before 1570–75 that the notaries began to register personal signatures, which were thenceforward affixed to the bottoms of their deeds in meaningful constellations. Let us look at one of these ancient registers dating from 1574–76.

One is immediately struck by the differences between different social milieus. First, for 72 percent of the peasants who came to seek a loan or sign a lease the scribe noted bluntly at the conclusion of the act, *"ne scait signer"* ("can't sign his name"). With respect to the artisans who were clients of the same notary, the figures are reversed: 63 percent signed their names fully (category 1), 11 percent signed with their initials (category 2), and the remaining 26 percent were illiterates who affixed their marks or else were branded with the mention *"ne scait signer,"* forcing the notary to recruit witnesses to sign in their place.

The stonemasons often belonged to the untutored category; the carders, for the most part, were in the group of literate artisans who signed their full names (and we have already seen that they were particularly receptive to heresy, one of the fruits of education). The peasants, on the contrary, were as allergic to culture as they were to the Reformation, and to the rudiments of lay learning as they were to the revival of sacred learning.

These preliminary soundings are fully confirmed by ecclesiastical estate records. Beginning in 1570, all the parties to the canons' contracts signed their names or affixed their marks. These documents teem with agrarian proletarians, who were relatively much more numerous than among the notaries' clientele. A sampling taken here touches the lowest stratum of society. This is what we find, for example, in the region of Béziers and Narbonne between 1575 and 1593, when the registration of signatures was first coming into practice. The acts are peopled by *travailleurs*, reapers or mowers; by peasants, tenants on the large farms; by artisans who doubled as tithe collectors in their spare time; and by the merchants who farmed the revenues of the priories.

The first trial heat reveals the fearsome ignorance of the rural proletariat —their massive lack of culture. Of the farm workers, 90.1 percent signed with a mark in the years 1575–93—sometimes with a cross or *reille*, but more often with a formless scrawl. Witness, for example, the curiously shaky mark of Bernard Bieu, a Narbonnese farm laborer who hired out in 1575 to rake (*enfaysser*) the hay of the plain into windrows: ᗰ ; the fraternal marks of the Nozières brothers, reapers at La Bastide in 1576: ∏∏ ; or the vermicular mark of Doumenge Lafont, who cut hay for the chapter in 1576: ζ .

The efforts of a minority of these day laborers were all the more meritorious; 7 percent of the *travailleurs* mentioned in these registers succeeded (with difficulty) in signing their initials, more or less correctly. For example, Bertrand Teyssier, who helped bring in the hay tithe in the plains in 1575, signed BF (*sic*). Finally, 2.9 percent actually signed their names, if clumsily; Antoine Rech, for example, a farm laborer of Narbonne hired to rake the hay in 1581, signed ARech.

On balance, right in the town of Narbonne nine rural proletarians out of ten were still spiritual strangers to the civilizations of the written word, strangers to the prestige and profits it wrought, and strangers, too, to the new ideas generated in the sixteenth century by the return to the religion of the Scriptures.

Among the cultivators (tenant farmers, sharecroppers, smallholders, farm stewards) illiteracy was less total, but it was still very high. Out of one hundred persons in this group who had dealings with the canons, only 10.4 percent signed their full names. Fewer than a quarter (24.1 percent) used their initials, often clumsily, "dyslexically" inverting the N's or else crossing the I's (or making the two mistakes simultaneously), sticking the letters together, or else scrambling them in rebus, and so on.

Finally, two husbandmen out of three (65.5 percent) made their mark, proof of total illiteracy. The only difference between theirs and those of the rural proletarians was that the true husbandmen's marks were not formless scrawls, but rigidly geometrical and respectable; they were as starched as they were ignorant. Some utilized the rustic cross, like the sharecropper Pierre Villeneuve in 1587, and some the star of David. Yet this particular group, two-thirds of whose members were unlettered, constituted an elite—that of cultivators entrusted with serious responsibilities and tenancies of one hundred hectares by the notables of Narbonne. These farm managers lived near town and frequented the bourgeois classes for business reasons, thereby rubbing shoulders with the tiny privileged world of the written word. This explains the presence in their ranks of a small literate minority. But the moment one leaves the vicinity of the town and penetrates into the countryside and into the mountain districts, the peasants sink wholesale into the crassest ignorance, joining their "poor relations" of the proletariat in their total lack of culture. Thus, in 1579–80, for example, out of eleven peasant consuls of middle rank from different rural parishes of Narbonne and the region of Sault, ten were total illiterates who were unable to sign their own names.

So, between 1550 and 1600 the countryside fiercely rejected the written word. The urban structures, on the other hand, permitted its light to penetrate. In 1575–89, for every hundred artisans of Narbonne and its surroundings having business with the chapter, thirty-four signed their full names, sometimes with a flourish; thirty-three used their initials; and the remaining third, who were illiterate, affixed their marks, purely symbolic graffiti. In other words, two-thirds of the artisans had attained a level of instruction reached by only one-tenth of the rural wageworkers and one-third of the peasant cultivators.

Among the artisan guilds, the most enlightened were those of the butchers and apothecaries, which were very close to the bourgeoisie. But the inn-keepers, the tailors, the carders, and the textile tradesmen also included men with schooling. In the geographical distribution of signatures in the building trades, the opposition between town and country is repeated. The stone-masons of the Narbonnese villages "signed" with a square, a trowel, or a heart; the masons and *gipiers* ("plasterers") of Narbonne itself signed their full names or at least their initials. The same was true of the metal trades: the illiterate village blacksmith made a sign of a hammer as opposed to a whole intellectual elite of urban coppersmiths, *martinayres* ("hammer-men"), *espaziers* ("swordmakers"), pewterers, and halberd makers who signed their full names with a flourish.

A receptivity to culture and a desire to acquire it was what set the active artisan of the urban societies far above the backward peasant. It was what linked him to the bourgeois and the merchants, the best-educated group of all, who were 98 percent literate. This is what in the end distinguished town from country in the hearts of the ancient cities themselves.

To conclude our differential inquiry, the country, rural society—at least in an initial stage—found itself in an impasse. There was a blockage of production which led to the impoverishment of the peasant masses and a blockage of conscience for want of elementary schooling. Schoolmasters, after all, were relatively rare in that peasant milieu, and their classes were not free. Only a minority of cultivators, and even fewer farm workers, sent their children to school on a regular basis. The others abstained, either for lack of money or for lack of ambition. On the land, cultural penury was thus joined to material poverty.

The town, on the other hand, accumulated wealth in movables and over-came, within its narrow circle, the curse of land hunger. It provided profit opportunities, a desire for gain, and a craving for culture. This town was not the town of the peasants, sunk in ignorance and rooted in agrarian folk-ways, but rather the growing city of artisans and merchants who prospered and multiplied and who "provided Calvinism and its offshoots with their natural social base."

In the Cévennes: The Rallying of the Rustics

The opposition between town and country often constituted a decisive and lasting obstacle to the spread of the Reformation. This was true at Béziers and Montpellier in 1560 and again in 1590–1600. Still, the obstacle was not necessarily insurmountable. It represented only a first "moment" or stage in the spread of ideas, and in certain regions it was transcended when the Huguenots of the small towns, the Calvinist artisans, finally broke through to the peasant milieu and succeeded in swinging the rural masses into the Protestant camp. This is what happened in the Cévennes—such an unlikely case that Théodore de Bèze himself marveled at it in relating the evangelization of the region during the reign of Henry II: "It was at this time," he writes, "that the natives of the mountains of the Cévennes (a harsh, inhospitable country if ever there was one in France, and that would seem the least capable of receiving the Gospel on account of the rudeness of spirit of the inhabitants), nevertheless received the Truth with marvelous ardour" to such a point that "almost all the common people" eventually embraced Calvinism. In fact, the "common people" of the Cévennes, artisans and peasants united, manifested such great zeal in felling crosses and burning idols that in 1561 Calvin himself had to censure these mountain Huguenots, who were too revolutionary for his taste.

What had occurred here? How does one explain the creation, by 1530–60, of this ineradicable bastion of heresy in the Cévennes, where Calvinism struck its deepest roots among the French peasantry? How was it that itinerant ministers had become such a familiar sight in the valleys of the Gardons by 1560? It is impossible, in their case, to invoke an ancient heretical tradition, a sort of leaven for the new heresies. Neither the Catharist nor the Waldensian movements played an important role in the mountain valleys of the Cévennes in the Middle Ages.[2] The situation of the living was more important than the weight of the dead. The conversion of the Cévennes was first of all the conversion of the artisans, who were more influential and more numerous there than elsewhere. The social structure worked in favor of an osmosis with the peasant world. The craftsmen, especially the leather workers, planted the seeds of the Huguenot Reformation in the very heart of the countryside.

Let us turn to the lists of refugees at Geneva in the years 1549–60. A large proportion of craftsmen are included in this first wave of French immigrants, with shoemakers in the lead. Among the exiles from the towns of Nîmes, Annonay, and Aubenas, situated at the issues of the valleys of the Cévennes, the cobblers were already the largest of the Huguenot trades. But now let us climb the valleys and penetrate to the very heart of the Calvinist Cévennes—into those regions of Alès and Vigan which would later become

[2] The Waldensianism of the Durance, however, did play a capital role, about 1530, as a relay in the direction of the Cévennes.

Camisard redoubts. Here, the leather trades, and especially the cobblers, were not only the most numerous; in 1549–60 they represented an absolute majority of the local exiles at Geneva. Out of forty-seven refugees from the Cévennes whose professions are known—alongside weavers, hosiers, peasants, doctors, booksellers, and bakers—there were twenty-four members of the leather trades (of whom twenty-two were cobblers), equal to 51 percent of the total.

This phenomenon was peculiar to that triangle of Calvinist highlands formed by Mende, Alès, and Ganges. It is encountered nowhere else. It was artisans and cobblers, the irreplaceable auxiliaries of the Calvinist ministers, who helped sow the seeds of the Reformation in the remote villages of the Cévennes. What is more, their activity could hardly have been more lasting and effective, being based on an avant-garde socioprofessional structure which, in the Cévennes, conferred particular importance on the rural and semirural artisan class. If the Huguenot artisans and cobblers were especially numerous in the first emigration from the Cévennes, that of 1549–60, it was very simply because they formed an active, compact group in the midst of a mountain population with roots deep in the soil.

In the absence of *compoix* let us compare professional structures in 1555–60 in the light of the notaries at Ganges, a large village of the Cévennes already secretly Calvinist, and at Béziers, a community in the plain with a large preponderance of Catholics. The differences are striking. Ganges was a center of industry where 48.6 percent of the notaries' clientele were artisans engaged in the principal trades of transformation—leather, textiles, wood, and iron. The leather trades—tanners and cobblers—were at the head of this group with 23.8 percent, followed by textiles—carders, drapers, weavers, and tailors—constituting 19.9 percent. Iron and wood workers brought up the rear with 4.9 percent. This compact artisan group was clearly dominated by an aristocracy of tanners—Calvinist businessmen with fine Old Testament names who little by little gained control of the hide and leather market from the mountains to the coast. Their seventeenth-century successors, rich curriers with fortunes of £100,000 and more, would send their sons to Paris to study, the supreme mark of social distinction. By the generation of 1560, in any event, the influence of the craftsmen of Ganges over the farm laborers of the outskirts and the peasants of the large tenant farms (together representing 16.8 percent of the notaries' clientele) appears to have been decisive. In 1580 only four Catholic families were left in a community numbering five hundred hearths. In contrast, at Béziers the "secondary" sector—that of the four principal trades of traditional artisan industry (leather, textiles, wood, and iron)—was little developed. Among the notaries' clientele in this same period artisans accounted for only 20.6 percent of the total—much less than priests, nobles, and merchants, whose social influence remained dominant.

Béziers typifies the large centers of the lowlands, where the majority of the populace were traditionalist peasants and notables. Ganges, on the other hand, symbolizes the social structure of the Cévennes, where the artisan class dominated in numbers and influence. Confirmation is furnished by Saint-Jean-du-Gard, a community of two thousand inhabitants deep in the chestnut forests of the Cévennes. In the mid-sixteenth century (1555) 23 percent of the local notary's clientele were cobblers and *coyratiers* ("tanners"), 10 percent were textile tradesmen (hosiers, carders, dressmakers), and 11.3 percent were woodworkers (*fustiers*, or coopers). Only 2 percent of the total were ecclesiastics, whereas for the same year I count canons, priors, and prebendaries as 15.6 percent of the notarial "clientele" of Béziers. Here, too, a revolutionary artisan class held almost undisputed ideological sway over the surrounding peasant masses. It is not surprising, therefore, if the sociology of the Genevan exile mirrors in exaggerated form the socioprofessional structure of this locality; Saint-Jean-du-Gard in 1549–60 was represented by four exiles at Geneva—one peasant and three leather workers.

Thus we come to the end of the social circuit effected by Calvinist ideas. Those ideas spread rapidly from Geneva to Lyons and from Lyons to Languedoc, carried by the ministers, students, Bible peddlers, and mule drivers of the Rhône. They penetrated the workrooms of weavers and wool carders. In the Cévennes, where the cobblers read the Bible at their benches, they germinated amid the filth of the work stalls and the stench of the tanneries and in the shops, too, whence there issued cries of "There goes Jean Blanc" when a priest passed by bearing the Host. In the towns subjacent to the Cévennes, in 1561, the mass of the citizen peasantry was contaminated (while their homologues to the west remained decidedly hostile to Calvin). A last stage remained: the integral permeation of the peasantry. For the Reformation, at the end of its course, reached the gates of the big farmsteads of the Cévennes. It strove, in the shadow of the high-vaulted sheep sheds, to win over the great peasant families. A few rare texts shed light on this last vicissitude.

The hamlet of Lancyre is located at the foot of the fold of the Hortus, a wild outpost of the sierras of the Cévennes. Today it is a farming community, a cluster of farmhouses clinging to a chalky butte. In the sixteenth century, when the demographic expansion just under way had not yet led to its dismemberment, it constituted a single unit, an isolated farmstead, the *mas* of Lancyre inhabited by an extended family group, clan, or *frérèche* by the name of Jean. These Jeans comprised, in 1563, several couples, "pairs with goods in common." Jean Jean, the head of the family, was expressly entrusted with "the rule of the household." Louis Jean, his son or younger brother, could not make a move without first consulting the master.

The Jeans of Lancyre worked a large domain of 314 hectares, of which 264 were sheep runs and 50 were plowlands. They were a well-to-do, prolific, literate peasant family. The family head, Jean Jean, was first on a list of dignitaries (*"prudhommes"*) charged in 1555 with drafting the overall *compoix* of six neighboring villages. The Jeans formed part of the intellectual aristocracy of the peasantry. As late as 1590 they were still engaging in lawsuits. They invested their own labor, and perhaps their profits from the *mas*, in new sheepfolds, hay barns, and pigpens (1558).

Now, about 1560 the members of this well-to-do, enlightened family adhered en bloc, in the words of Louis Jean, "to the true Religion, reformed according to the Word of God and the Holy Gospel." The *frérèche* confronted the capital question of the tithe squarely. In 1563 the prior who came to demand the tithe of Lancyre was refused and driven out. Louis Jean would pay the tithe to the people of the Holy Gospel, he said, and not to the prior "from whom one has never received and does not now receive an edifying doctrine." The collector sued.

The Reformation, propagated at the start by the democratic artisan class of the towns, insinuated itself in its final phase, then, in the authoritarian and patriarchal structures of the outer Cévennes and the valleys below.

Something of this sort also occurred on the great capitalistically run estates in the mountains. By 1555 Calvinist farm managers were putting pressure on their dependents to adopt the reformed worship. And behold, a new dimension of human (or inhuman) relationships of purest Calvinist inspiration was added to those of a professional nature. Olivier de Serres, himself a Huguenot estate manager, has described them in a chapter of his *Théâtre d'agriculture*. He paints the cruel portrait, based on his personal experience and on Calvin's readings (which he himself had followed in Geneva), of the "paterfamilias" gentleman farmer in the Vivarais region of the Cévennes during the period 1560–1600. The "father" is severe with his farmhands because he knows their "perverse character," which is preordained like the "general brutishness which renders them stupid, careless, shameless, and friendless." He is aware of "the natural savagery and perversity" of his hirelings, "full of inconstancy and without honor"; their "general disloyalty"; "the imperfection of the servant class"; "their ancient rebellion and disobedience"; and "the evil caused by their wicked nature." In the name of Calvinist predestination, a doctrine expressly invoked on three occasions and implied in its crudest form in almost every line of text, the agriculturalist of the Cévennes drew up the most terrible indictment against the rural proletarians in his employ: "worthless wretches . . . , leaden spirits in iron bodies," or just simply "whores and thieves," "dregs of society," a bitter draught that one was forced to swallow by necessity. As to be expected, Olivier encountered here and there during his career a few *elect* among these reprobates: "A handful of these poor people are upright and honest, but so few in number! You must even beware of these."

The employer's aggressive and mistrustful conduct was dictated by these pessimistic judgments. He chased "vagabonds, buffoons, and good-for-nothings" off his lands. Every year or every two years he replaced the whole lot of his farmhands. His chief servants were fired for their mistakes; petty underlings were whipped or beaten. He imposed chaste conduct on all and dealt severely with debauchery, which was the vilest of sins. He suppressed the "antekitchen" with its "excess of license" and the playful cries of plow-hands and serving-maids. He ranked himself, on the other hand, among the elect. He delighted in the possession of his wife and his earthly goods, both "gifts of God," with a clear conscience. In his own person he felt the irresistible appeal of a worldly vocation or "calling." Olivier writes that he "exercised the office" or, again, "assumed the burden" imposed by the Lord, of which he proved himself worthy. Was agriculture not "the most holy and the most natural of human occupations, ordained by God's word"? Our man went into agriculture the way others went into religion, and by 1600—before the Puritans—Olivier had developed a thought implicit in Calvin, defining entrepreneurial profits as the earthly criterion of divine election. "Your house being as the house of God, the fear of Him will reside therein, showering it with every blessing, and will prosper you in this world, as is written in the Scriptures." He cites the Old Testament: "If thou shalt harken unto the voice of the Lord, blessed shall be the fruit of thy cattle, blessed shall be thy basket and thy store."[3] This was the source of the "terrifying moral health" of this agronomist and his peers. To increase his profits,

[3] Deut. 28: 1, 4–5.

as God willed, he sold his grain after Christmas at high spring prices, "locking his granaries when the price of grain depreciated, unlocking them again when the price was reasonable." He paid his workers, in his own words, "as meanly as possible" without remorse and without cynicism. He even withheld a portion of their wages to keep them from quitting. The good conscience of a certain business Calvinism is linked to the depressed state of wages about 1590–1600, and it arrived just in time to serve as a justification.

In default of decent wages the paterfamilias attended, without illusions, to his people's salvation. Bible in hand, he exhorted them "to fear God, to practice virtue, to avoid vice." By force of homilies and hard bread he inculcated the bourgeois thrift and worldly asceticism that led to social advancement.

One would search in vain for similar precepts and behavior among the Parisian, Italian, or Catalan agronomists. Compared to them, Olivier was a radical innovator, for he generalized from a social, religious, and human experience without precedent in the Latin countries. The nineteen editions of the *Théâtre d'agriculture*, published between 1600 and 1675, acquainted the rest of France with the astonishing "model," formed in the Cévennes and the Vivarais, of a farmer entrepreneur initiated, thanks to the Huguenot ethic, to the earliest spirit of capitalism.

In the Calvinist Cévennes—among the artisan class of the towns, the farming, wine-growing democracies of the outskirts, the peasant or capitalistic oligarchies of the isolated farmsteads, and the rural proletariat—the conquest of souls by force or persuasion was already completed by about 1570–90. By the close of the century, in many parishes there remained no more than one or two Catholic families. The peasant personality itself was affected by this mass conversion. In communities like Ganges (1570–1600) ministers and elders organized the police of morals in a pitiless manner (in imitation of Calvin's Geneva), with informers, fines, admonitions, and humiliating public confessions and reparations. The consistories, peopled with artisans "with grimy mechanic's hands," posted spies on the ramparts. They poked into gardens, barnyards, and private chambers. The very bedposts had ears. In the deliberations of these consistories, the same monotonous denunciations were endlessly repeated. A certain man had "debauched, fornicated, slept in the bed" of a certain woman. The sexual taboos multiplied. The guilty made honorable public amends. The "village whores" were set upon. The Mass, dancing, laughter, bowling and card playing, too long or too intimate betrothals, the debaucheries of serving-girls, abortion, feminine vanities and masculine quarrels, prenuptial pregnancies, and gypsy witchcraft all were proscribed without distinction, warily in the case of nobles, savagely in the case of the rural populace. Only usury and human exploitation—both flourishing in the Cévennes at the close of the century— were spared the thunderbolts of the consistory. Not once in fifteen years did the consistory of Ganges censure a usurer, a tanner entrepreneur, or a farm manager for being too greedy with his debtors or workers.

One can debate the social theories of Calvinism forever. Its historical practice in the south of France about 1590 leaves no room for doubt. It was the formal restriction of pleasure and the tacit tolerance of usury; it was asceticism by proclamation and capitalism by preterition. And it was the creation of a new kind of man with a remodeled personality.

The Cévenol of 1500—a ribald, hearty fellow who loved to dance, a superstitious papist, and a sorcerer—was lost to memory, relegated to the depths of the subconscious. A new man had emerged from the Huguenot crucible; his religion was purged of magical rites, his libido was repressed, and he was a believer in bourgeois thrift and Christian liberty. This cheerless but free people would survive, true to its own nature, well beyond the Camisards in the peasant histories of André Chamson and the novels of Émile Zola. (One remembers the personnage of the old governess from the Cévennes armed with her terrible Bible with its iron ornaments in *Madeleine Férat*.) It calls to mind the more far-reaching but very similar story that led from Merrie Old England to the Puritan Commonwealth.

2

The Huguenot Offensive and the Lands of the Priests

The heresy spread and often triumphed. It was guided in its peregrinations by cultural lines of force. It was propagated by intellectuals and by plebians of the artisan class. By 1550–60 the rest of society—the rural bourgeoisie, the patriarchal family, the peasantry—had been infected. Huguenot concepts, which were purely religious in origin and principle, became charged in transit—in the process of "penetrating the masses"—with an active force, an affective and revolutionary potential. Did they exert an influence or suggest a direction in regard to social problems and the agrarian question which were aggravated by the secular trend?

The Coveters of the Goods of the Church

March–April, 1560: at Nîmes and Annonay, situated in a region lying just below the Cévennes that was seriously infected with heresy, the first Calvinist insurrections broke out, sparking forty years of religious warfare. At a single stroke in a lay society starved for land and quite incapable of raising its yields per hectare, where assarters, land engrossers, and extended peasant families had been contending over the new assarts and the last scraps of arable for the past sixty years, the problem of the Church's lands was posed: Who was to get the "temporalities" of the clergy?

Here, as in every preindustrial society, the land question was at the heart of the revolutionary process. And the temporalities constituted a perfect target for the hard-pressed treasury and the rancors of the landless. From 1500, in fact, the Church enjoyed a fortunate stability of real income, in the form of rents and tithes in kind, which was not eroded by price inflation. Her accumulated savings were converted into landed capital and preserved from eventual dismemberment by the institution of mortmain. This led to a perceptible pattern of land concentration. At Béziers, for example, the list of land purchases by the cathedral chapter between 1500 and 1550 is impressive for its continuity, if not for its extent.

Hence there germinated, side by side with the temptations of Calvinism, the determination to seize the lands of the clergy. The project was close to the hearts of the bourgeoisie; it also responded to the studied reflections of the jurists, because the king's finances were in a shambles with the fall of the Grand Parti of Lyons[1] and the royal bankruptcy. Why not make the Church bear the costs of the financial restoration? One could sell off the Church's possessions to the highest bidders—to the rich—and turn the proceeds over to the treasury. One could follow the example of Henry VIII, who had confiscated the lands of the English monasteries.

The question was raised at the Estates of Languedoc sitting at Montpellier in March, 1561. The pivot of debate was the goods of the Church. True, the royal commissioners hesitated on this point, and their proposals were mitigated in substance. If the goods of the clergy must be confiscated, let it not be all of them, the commissioners said, but only enough to redeem the king's domain, the royal aids, and the salt tax, which had been mortgaged to private financiers by the empty treasury.

Also, if the king's proposals were ratified by the Estates, the populace would assume its share of the national deficit side by side with the clergy through the classic French expedient of taxes on consumption, for the price of salt would be raised and a tax would be levied on wine. In short, tax the clergy and tax the people—a blow to the right and a blow to the left.

These royal projects had the effect of splitting the provincial assembly of 1561. The clergy, for its part, accepted, hoping thereby to cut its losses. It would be willing to redeem the aids, gabelles, and domains through the forced sale of part of its lands for the benefit of the treasury. But it was outflanked by the covetous bourgeoisie.

As soon as the audition of the king's letters was concluded, Claude Terlon, a celebrated advocate of Toulouse and leader of the Third Estate of Languedoc who was vaguely sympathetic to the Reformation, took the floor. He demanded that the Third Estate meet separately to deliberate in freedom without the other two orders. In these separate sittings of the regional Third Estate, some revolutionary motions were adopted. The

---

[1] Grand Parti: a consortium of royal financiers bankrupted in the late years of the reign of Henry II (tr. note).

timid concessions of the clergy encountered the total intransigence of the bourgeoisie. Through the mouth of Terlon, the Third Estate "concludes and decrees that the king must make the Church sell its temporalities," with the sole exception of the "principal residence" of the prelates and other ecclesiastics. The exception was of no great importance in view of the fact that the Church's benefices—the better part of its revenues—consisted of tithes and rents on farms far from the "home office."

The bourgeois and revolutionary nature of Terlon's projects was clearly evident in his second proposal, which was also ratified by the Third Estate. In actual fact, it would have raised the merchants and bourgeois of the *bonnes villes* to the ranks of lords and paymasters of the Church of France. Terlon envisaged the municipal subsidy of religious cults and the transformation of the beneficed ecclesiastics into salaried officeholders appointed by the urban consulates. He anticipated a sort of "communal constitution of the clergy."

In his plan for the expropriation of the goods of the Church, Terlon relied on the support of various social forces, and first on the Huguenot faction of the Third Estate whose elected spokesman at the Estates of Languedoc in 1561 was the advocate Chabot, of Nîmes. Chabot backed Terlon; he attacked the priests for their ignorance and corruption, and he demanded that they be made to shoulder the fiscal burden to compensate the people for the evil "that they have caused by their vices." He mirrored the impatience of the common people of Nîmes who had chosen him as their delegate—the carders, cobblers, weavers, and day laborers who, in the cahiers of 1561, were already demanding the confiscation of a part of the lands of the Church. Chabot also made use of street demonstrations; while he was addressing the Estates at Montpellier, an orderly crowd was waiting outside ready to intervene in his support. When, having finished speaking, he left the hall, "these people quietly dispersed."

At the same time, a fraction of the nobility backed Terlon because it wanted its part of the quarry. Terlon, in fact, expressly reserved a share of the Church's goods for the privileged classes in order to gain their support for his project. This support had already materialized at the Estates of Orleans (1540), where Third Estate and noblesse formed a common front over the question of church lands. At the provincial Estates of Montpellier in 1561, Crussol, duke of Uzès, rallied to the cause of Terlon and Chabot, offering to submit the recommendations finally adopted by the Estates to the court and to the queen; to wit, the sale of the lands of the clergy and tolerance for the new heresy. The duke of Uzés was not forgetting his own interests in this whole affair. A few years later some fine ecclesiastical lordships, purchased dirt cheap, would round out his estates and reward his zeal as a neophyte Huguenot.

Chabot, Terlon, Crussol: Huguenots, jurists, and gentlemen formed an alliance to plunder the Church, speculating on the king's need of money and sustained by popular sentiment. In Languedoc this alliance was more energetic and more radical than in the rest of France. The Paris bourgeoisie and the Third Estate of Picardy were considerably more cautious than these Languedocian notables who were mounting a daring attack against the lands of the Lord. True, at Abbeville and at Paris the Third Estate in 1560–61 demanded a partial levy on clerical wealth, but they dared not demand its total expropriation.

At the Estates of Pontoise (August, 1561), Languedocian enthusiasm prevailed over Parisian prudence. Terlon's project, formulated at Montpellier in March, was endorsed almost intact by the whole of the French Third Estate. Naïvely delighted—"joyous to accept the temporalities of the Church"—the delegates of the Third Estate at Pontoise proposed the alienation of the goods of the clergy and the creation of Terlon's municipal budgets for religious cults with capital provided by the surplus proceeds from the sale of clerical properties, once the state's debts had been extinguished. These funds, in turn, would be lent to the bourgeois "at a reasonable interest and return." The advantage was double; the interest would serve to pay the priests' salaries, and the borrowed capital, injected into the economy, "would increase the business activity and mercantile traffic of the kingdom."

Thus, to mobilize the market in land, buried in the slumber of mortmain; to mobilize savings and at the same time reduce the interest on capital to a "reasonable" figure; and, in the final analysis, to revive trade and commerce —this in essence was the revolutionary bourgeois order of the Terlon project first formulated by an advocate from the Midi and then cheerfully endorsed by the Third Estate on a national scale. But the monarchy was not bold enough to accept such a plan as it stood. It limited itself to ordering, in 1563, the forced sale for the benefit of the treasury of a quarter of the capital wealth of the great benefices of the kingdom. Other partial expropriations would follow in 1568, 1574, and 1576. This activity now remains to be studied in the perspective of a social history of the land.

A Typology of Land Buyers

The first sales of church property, beginning in 1563, were attended, at least in the south, by a realignment of social forces. Henceforth, the mass of the artisans—the Huguenot democracy of the cities—was relegated to the background, barred from the land auctions in the same way it was ejected from the "political councils of the Huguenot church." The sale of the lands of the Roman church brought the wealthy classes to the forefront—merchants, magistrates, and nobles who were sometimes Calvinist and sometimes Catholic, lured by their common appetite for land. Heroic heresy found itself sharing the stage with business Calvinism.

At Nîmes and Uzès, two citadels of the Reformation, one can readily detect the rise of the group of notables who resolved the land question to their personal advantage. Here, the artisans and even the landless farm laborers at the assemblies of 1561 had demanded, with a passion born of bitterness and hope, the expropriation of church property. In reality, they were the unwitting instruments of people richer than themselves.

Who was it, then, in actual fact, who turned up at the bidding in the diocese of Uzès when the great sale of church lands opened in 1563? Let us attempt to define the land buyers in sociological terms by taking specific examples. At the head of the list is Guillaume Calvière, who purchased for a pittance (£145) the mills and fief of the great prior of Saint-Gilles. Calvière was a bourgeois and an implacable militant of the Reformation. As magistrate and lord of Saint-Césaire, he would participate in 1567 in the Michelade, the massacre of the Catholics of Nîmes, some of whom were put to the sword and others of whom were buried alive in a well. The same year (1567) Calvière would also direct the Council of Twenty-One (thirteen officers of justice and eight captains) who ruled Nîmes "as a republic" and confiscated the remaining possessions of the Church. In 1569 Calvière would be condemned to death for the Michelade by the Parlement of Toulouse. He would be captured by the Catholics on his return from conducting negotiations with the German Protestants. Thanks to a truce, however, he would be exchanged, "freed and let go."

The bourgeois and nobles who bought up the *"biens nationaux"* of the sixteenth century were militants and often soldiers. Valentin Grille was a Provençal captain and Protestant. In 1563, for the sum of £1,537 he purchased the land of Saint-Maurice "with a castle, rents, dues, lands, vines, oil presses." Grille, a fighting man, would later defend his faith and his lands tooth and nail. Between 1563 and 1568 he participated in all the major actions—at one time vanquished by Joyeuse, at another victorious over the Catholics and a killer of peasants. He ended up as seneschal of Beaucaire after having also participated in the Nîmes massacre of 1567.

In the diocese of Nîmes, the land offensive of the Calvinist notables was even more spectacular. Here one encounters some old acquaintances: those condemned to death in 1569, all of whom possessed what would be known much later as *"biens nationaux."* Let us confine ourselves to a few typical examples.

As early as 1546 the Barrières, a family of petty magistrates from Nîmes, were casting covetous eyes on lands and lordships. In that year the advocate Jean Barrière was busy buying up olive orchards. In 1553 this same Jean Barrière became a seigneur ("lord") of an oil press by purchase. In 1561 the family was Calvinist, and the "squire" François Barrière signed his name at the head of a list of inhabitants of Nîmes who demanded the expropriation of the temporalities of the Church. In 1563, putting his theories into practice, he purchased the lands of a church chaplaincy.

Huguenot land buyers, like the Cambises of Alès, also acquired lordship over forges and coal mines. Jean de Cambis, *sieur* of Soustelle, with a small band of men organized the Michelade at Nîmes in 1567. The same individual four years earlier had paid one thousand *livres* for "archdeaconate" lands as well as the ecclesiastical lordship of Cendras in the heart of the coal fields.

Robert Le Blanc, lord of La Rouvière, was jurist, Huguenot, soldier, and land buyer. In 1562 he laid siege to Bourg-Saint-Andéol with Crussol and three hundred men. In 1563 he paid £2,157 for ecclesiastical lands and lordships in the diocese of Nîmes. He was one of the lot condemned to death in 1569 for their part in the Michelade.

An educated businessman, Jacques Poldo d'Albenas had left his native mountains about 1530 determined to make his fortune. After completing his university studies, he became a commissary officer. In January, 1543, he advanced money to some citizens of Nîmes to supply grain to the galleys of Marseilles. He died a squire after the classic *cursus honorum*: money, land, offices, and the nobiliary particle. His son, Vidal d'Albenas, a Protestant, was one of the big land buyers at Nîmes in 1563, paying out £4,250 for former episcopal lands and lordships. He would be among those condemned to death in 1569 for the Michelade.

Last and richest on the list of land buyers at Nîmes was a persevering individual by the name of François de Pavée. In 1561 he signed the petition of the inhabitants of Nîmes demanding the expropriation of the goods of the clergy, especially the lordships, because it is scandalous, he said, to let one-self be ruled by priests. His interest was not platonic. In 1563 he himself made off with two lordships besides a rich grange, formerly of the canons of Nîmes, that went for the sum of £15,125! He, too, would be implicated in the Michelade and condemned to death in 1569, but he dropped from sight, apparently none the worse off for his death sentence.

The Nîmes land buyers of 1563 constituted, on the whole, a clearly defined group or clan—almost a private club. They were bourgeois or magistrates aspiring to noble status, or more often nobles of recent coinage, authentic or not. In brief, two-thirds of the land buyers in the diocese of Nîmes in 1563 (twenty-four out of thirty-six) are identified as "nobles" or "lords" of some manor. Whether already nobles or as yet still bourgeois—the frontier was easily crossed—these people were joined together by their Calvinist faith and by intermarriage. With their money, connections, and influence, they dominated the great land auctions. They shouldered aside not only Catholics of every sort, but also the Huguenot rank and file, the cobblers and weavers. As good Protestants, they did not forget their private interests in their prayers. They were sometimes learned men, often businessmen, and, when the occasion demanded, also military men. The Michelade four years later would seal them in a pact of blood guilt.

In the diocese of Montpellier, at the auction of church properties of 1563, one big buyer accounted for half the purchases. Out of £26,000 in accepted bids, his alone amounted to £12,500. The person in question was Simon Fizes, counsellor to the king and secretary of finances who, on September 16, 1563, with these £12,500, acquired the barony of Sauve, formerly the property of the bishop of Montpellier. He was a curious fellow, this Fizes. His brand new barony, carved out of the Church's patrimony, did not suffice to erase the memory of his humble origins. "The said Fizes," an anonymous text of 1576 informs us, "calls himself Monsieur de Sauve. Some allege that his family is so little known that he had been a lackey in his youth." Fizes did, in fact, come from a family of poor, illiterate peasants. He "succeeded" thanks to his native ability, but also thanks to the patronage of his compatriot, the Languedocian Bertrand, keeper of the seals, who first employed him as a lackey and later as a private secretary. The Guises became his protectors and arranged his marriage (to what end?) to Charlotte de Beaune, lady-in-waiting to the queen. Fizes was a discreet husband, or rather a cover, because the ambitious Charlotte, with her delicate lips and pert little nose, was the mistress of Charles IX, Henry of Navarre, and the duke d'Alençon. Born a peasant, a minister at his death, Fizes the former lackey passed for a man of parts—and made a career as the obliging husband. The purchase of a church property, the barony of Sauve, in 1563 represented a landmark in his rising fortunes. Henceforth, Fizes and the beautiful Charlotte were Monsieur and Madame de Sauve. In 1564 they were hosts to Charles IX in their Montpellier town house, the *hôtel* Jacques Cœur. Monsieur de Sauve entered the Estates of Languedoc in 1570, and three years later, without abandoning his career at Paris, he had himself named governor of Montpellier. His sisters, born penniless, became the first ladies of the town and were joined in marriage to Calvinist leaders and Protestants themselves. From Paris, where he made his residence, Fizes, the protégé of the Guises, was nonetheless the protector and secret sympathizer of the Huguenots of his native region, whom he alerted to the impending massacre of Saint Bartholomew's Day.

Jean de Bouques was another of the land buyers of Montpellier in 1563. The son of a merchant, he was a militant Huguenot become a gentleman of the robe. He acquired a property for £230 and some customary rights for another £155 at the auction of 1563. He was already implicated in Calvinist disorders the same year. In 1568 he was the moving spirit behind a sort of committee of public safety. Accused of having pillaged the home of Joyeuse and the cathedral of Montpellier, he was purged from the magistrature by the Catholics when they returned to power. He would be arrested and condemned to death by the Parlement in 1568 and decapitated at Toulouse.

The Languedocian endeavor to liquidate the church lands formed part of a widespread venture affecting Germany, England, and France. In the south of France, the immediate results of the offensive were disappointing. The total sales in 1563 for the combined dioceses of Agde and Montpellier amounted to only £36,000, or roughly the value of three or four big village priories in a region that counted more than a hundred. It was a far cry from the disposal of church lands in 1790 that profoundly altered patterns of landownership.

The ecclesiastical land sales, which were staggered from 1563 to 1591, were nevertheless significant. They help to clarify the aspirations of a particular social group—that of the land buyers delineated above in a series of short, converging biographies.

It was a group composed of notables. Even more than in 1790, artisans, peasants, and people of low estate were excluded from its ranks. Although swarming with self-styled nobles, it was not recruited from among the genuine nobility. It did not constitute a bourgeoisie either, at least in the classic sense of the term; it was related rather—Calvinism aside—to certain urban elites of the Italian Renaissance. Patricians rubbed shoulders with parvenus, the latter led by a former lackey. The members of the group devoted themselves to bourgeois activities, to trade and legal pettifogging, but the noble values, especially those relating to warfare, were by no means foreign to their mentality. The lands of the Church—like public offices and the magistrate's robe—were, for these people, a means of enrichment and an occasion for social promotion, their supreme ideal being to accede to the noble life and to the vanity of a lordship. In the last analysis, the episode of 1563 helped to set in motion a process that would lead, in the course of the seventeenth and eighteenth centuries, to the concentration of a certain fraction of the countryside in the hands of the urban notables of Languedoc.

3

The Tithe: Reform or Revolution?

For the rebels of 1560, and for rural society in general, the question of the Church's tenth of the harvest fruits was second only to the question of the Church's lands. Should the tithe be eliminated by a pure and simple revolution, or should it be taken away from the clergy and transferred to another group, to another church? The question was at the heart of social contention. In an economy incapable of true growth and unfitted to "maximize" its aggregate product, it is problems of distribution that naturally tend to take a front seat and preoccupy the public mind.

The Calvinists Confiscate the Tithe

The first solution—the transfer of tithe income—was favored by the Huguenot leaders. In December, 1562, the question was raised in the Protestant Estates sitting at Nîmes. The nobles sent delegates, but the bourgeoisie managed to double its representation, thanks on the one hand to the urban consuls and on the other hand to the delegates of the Protestant consistories—nearly all of them commoners—who replaced the late "order" of the clergy. What amounted to a doubling of the Third Estate imposed bourgeois solutions. The Estates of Nîmes decided on the complete expropriation (and not the partial expropriation favored by the monarchy) of the temporalities, the better part of which (in Languedoc) were, in fact, represented by the tithe. The Huguenot circles—ministers and soldiers, military staffs and consistories—would appropriate the tithe income themselves. And, as in the days of the papists, the farmers who had placed the winning bids would collect the tithes, deduct a modest profit, and hand over the rest, the "rente," to the organization of the reformed churches.

The bidding began at once. The stakes were high. For the single diocese of Montpellier the tithable priories "plundered" by the Protestants in 1562 represented, all told, a capital of one million *livres* (thirty thousand *livres* in tithe income). Up to 1560 this patrimony, composed of a few dozen benefices, had been let out to various tithe farmers by the Church. Two years later in the countryside of Montpellier and other Protestant areas the system changed titleholders. On the one hand, the Protestant collectivity affirmed its determination to collect the tithe in the place of the papists. On the other hand, the Huguenot bourgeoisie took an option on the tithe farms. The great majority of the new tithe farmers were drawn from its ranks. It eliminated the Catholic bourgeois bidders by intrigue or by force. It also thrust aside, in the last "round" of bidding, the rank and file of the Huguenot artisans—militant Calvinists from the outset, but too poor to compete successfully against their wealthy coreligionists.

A breakdown of the Huguenot tithe farms of priories in the diocese of Montpellier in 1562 reveals that twenty-one out of the eighty-five successful bidders (25 percent) were merchants. This group included the classic type of bourgeois soldier. Antoine Verchand was a rich merchant who became a captain in the civil war and adjutant to baron des Adrets. Together with the baron, he captured four hundred sheep belonging to the Catholic forces at Lattes; the soldiers who were guarding the sheep were killed or driven into a nearby waterhole, where they drowned. His fighting days over, the former soldier Verchand became a tithe farmer. He leased tithes and lands formerly belonging to the Church for the sum of £527 per year. He was implicated in the troubles at Montpellier in 1569 and condemned to death in absentia at the Parlement of Toulouse, but he survived to become consul of Montpellier, and it was finally the plague that killed him in 1579.

Some of the Huguenot merchants who farmed the Protestant tithes were also local political figures, consuls of Montpellier in 1562. Others in the same group were militant Calvinist activists. The merchant Pierre Raymond, who farmed the benefice of the Aresquiers at the end of 1562, was one of the five strong men of Montpellier the same year, a member of the revolutionary pentarchy (merchants, a magistrate, and a surgeon) who prepared the city's defenses against the papists and had the suburbs razed.

Militants and merchants, these men readily agreed to farm the secularized tithes, because the nature of their affairs had already familiarized them with agricultural matters. The trading class of Montpellier in 1552–62 was composed almost entirely of country merchants. They bought up the wool crop of the sheepherders and village butchers. They bought olive oil from the hillside parishes and wood from the communities of the *garrigue*. They sold the woolen cloth of the Aude to the peasants of the Cévennes, and they advanced grain to the rustics who ran short before harvest time. These rural merchants, therefore, found themselves in their natural element as tithe farmers.

Side by side with the merchants were a certain number of tithe farmers drawn from the group of magistrates, rentier landlords, and well-to-do bourgeois, including a few Marrano converts to Calvinism whose families had passed from the countinghouse to the magistrature without losing their taste for tithe profits. One also encounters tax registrars and Huguenot notaries with a little capital who farmed the fat tithes on the fields and vineyards of the plains region; Nicolas Talard for example, a wealthy and indefatigable militant of the Reformation, led a deputation in 1560 to Geneva to bring back a frightened minister of the Gospel. In 1562 he contracted for several tithable priories, including that of Montels, for £1,150 per year. In 1567 the Parlement of Toulouse sentenced him to death. Other Huguenot tithe farmers of 1562, this time from the financial and legal professions, included a tax collector, a *procureur aux aides*, and some legal advocates.

Besides the merchants (in the majority), the magistrates, and other bourgeois (who were less numerous), the group of Huguenot tithe farmers of 1562 counted a few authentic or self-styled noblemen attracted to this activity by their nose for business or their Protestant zeal—men like Vincent Manni, scion of an enobled Italian merchant family (and lender of grain to the peasants), or Bertrand de Sobeyras, another companion of baron des Adrets and a butcherer of Catholic sheepherders. Sobeyras farmed the big benefice of Fabrègues for £450.

Some of these Huguenot tithe farmers were even former ecclesiastics. Jean Teulet, who took a lease for five hundred *livres* per year on the tithes of a big priory in the *garrigue*, was a notorious defrocked former canon, as was Jean Lebas, or so it seems. The pious and erudite historian Louise Guiraud stoutly maintains that the latter remained faithful to the Church, but I am not so sure. If that is the case, what was he doing collecting tithes for the Protestants in 1562?

Thus, at Montpellier, as at Nîmes, a group of notables scrambled after the land profits suddenly made available through the struggle against the Church. The upstart nobles and the bourgeois magistrates staked out their claims to the lands of the priests. The merchants, for their part, being experienced in agricultural affairs, tended to specialize in tithe farms. In this way a coalition of merchants and magistrates monopolized both land and tithes. By 1562–63, in their pursuit of land and profits they had turned the generous impulses of the Calvinist artisan class (still so vigorous in 1561) to selfish account.

Thirty years later at the end of the century, when the Church tried to recover its lost riches it came up against Protestant businessmen who were still monopolizing the ecclesiastical "benefices" with the complicity of the municipal authorities. In 1589 the prelates complained to the provincial Estates sitting at Béziers: "The consuls of the towns which are in the hands of those of the false religion claim to have preference in the farming of the benefices in their districts; seizing the revenues of the Church, they make their own ministers share in them."

Moreover, when the Church refused to surrender the tithe in good grace, the Protestant leaders seized it by force. At Montpellier in 1595, at the height of the harvest, and to the great outrage of the canons who were preparing to garner the tithe, some masked Huguenots on horseback attacked the peasants and seized the carts laden with sheaves. The priests denounced the deed, but it was a waste of time. Nobody was talking and no one in town seemed to know who the culprits might be.

The Tithe Payers Go on Strike

The Huguenot bourgeoisie appropriated the tithe by consent or by force. But the peasants did not willingly surrender the tenth sheaf to the new master, who was just as rapacious as the old. They wanted to eliminate the tithe completely, not transfer it to other hands, for these villagers were often oppressed by poverty, and they were "Huguenots" when it came to paying the tithe even before becoming Huguenots in matters of faith. They drew revolutionary inferences from the Reformation. They tried to abolish the tithe, for them the principal burden—much heavier than manorial dues, heavier even than the royal taille. Thus, all the tithe collectors, yesterday's or today's, papists or Huguenots, encountered sullen if not savage resistance on the part of the peasants.

Beginning in the early sixteenth century, it is fairly easy to follow the southward progress of the idea of an antitithe revolt. One center of origin was located in the Rhineland regions of Switzerland and Alsace, where the Bundschuch, by 1502–1505—long before the outbreak of the Peasants' War—was already busy indoctrinating the peasants to refuse the tithe and to abominate the possessions of the Church. In France the idea spread from its Alsatian bases southward along the Saône and the Rhône. By 1524

Francis I was bemoaning the multiplication of Lutheran sectarians in the countryside of Lyons, where "some people who have strayed from the Holy Church have conspired to stop paying the tithe at the sound of the tocsin." In 1529 some insurgents of Lyons "mutinied against the payment of any tithes at all." By way of the Rhône, the *idée-force* of an antitithe strike had reached the Midi as far as Nîmes by 1540.

In the Cévennes the first signs of agitation were registered as early as 1550. In that year an inhabitant of Saint-Martin-de-Ligujac refused to pay the surtithes to his prior and justified his refusal with the usual arguments of Huguenot propaganda—the prior resided elsewhere, therefore he could not administer the last sacraments to the sick, who were left to die like dumb beasts; he was never there to ring the church bells to warn of an approaching storm; and so on.

In 1560 the antitithe epidemic infected the Midi from the Rhône to the Atlantic. Two kinds of strike made their appearance. One was the purely religious kind, the reasonable strike, in which the peasant, having passed to the Calvinist camp, nevertheless agreed to pay the tenth sheaf, but only to pastors of the new religion.

Such exemplary reasonableness was not universal. For many peasants, and not just Calvinist peasants, the refusal was unconditional, a sort of wildcat strike against paying tithes to anyone at all. The rustics believed the word of the "big merchants and bourgeois" who in Languedoc attracted many people to the Reformation with the promise "that they would be free and exempt from paying tithes." In the summer of 1560 they made bonfires of registers and charters: the *coq rouge*.[1] Their design was clear, whatever their faith—to pay no more tithes whatever, whether to Rome or to Geneva.

The strike movement spread westward like a contagion toward the region of Agen, where "since before the civil war the tithes were no longer paid," and toward Guyenne and Périgord, where the Catholic peasants themselves stopped paying. In Calvinist country the movement was at the expense of priests or at the expense of ministers, whichever the case might be, as a Huguenot tithe farmer by the name of Pierre Rafinesque learned to his sorrow. In April, 1564, not far from Montpellier, he came to collect the tenth of the lamb crop on behalf of the synod. The peasants eluded his request, or signified their refusal, letting their wives speak for them: Claude Prunet declared "that he was sick with the gout" and unable to pay for the moment;

[1] *Coq rouge*: the firing of manor houses and manorial registers during the Russian peasant revolts (tr. note).

Jean Euset "was not at home," but his wife and niece turned Rafinesque out of the house.

The problem is not so much to describe the antitithe strikes for their own sake as to measure their economic and social repercussions. In the twentieth century, workers' strikes cost employers millions of workdays every year. In the same way, after 1560 the antitithe strikes cost the clergy dearly and lightened the burden of the rural classes. Is it possible to measure, even approximately, the financial losses they entailed? On this point the scattered texts are of little help. The world of the peasant was for the most part beyond the pale of the written word, and his strikes, save for a few notable episodes, have left almost no traces in the archives of the period—more especially since they were usually a question of insidious forms of sabotage, of intermittent resistance, and of prosaic actions overlooked by history but nonetheless extremely pernicious for clerical finances. It is only in the tithe records and capitulary accounts that the effects are clearly perceptible. Let us take two cases: the tithes in grain and the tithes farmed out for a sum of money.

At Saliès and at Creissan, the tithe deliveries in grain in the period 1560–1600 (or to be more exact, 1572–93) were lower by far than at any other time in the 270 years between 1480 and 1750. There were analogous movements at Cuxac and Narbonne and in the dioceses of Agde and Béziers, where the Huguenots, as it happens, constituted only a small minority. Finally, at Gaillac, where the League was in control—as it was in the Narbonne region —the peasants showed the same lack of zeal, and around 1580 the tithes in grain sank to their lowest level in this area.

The tithes in money, for their part, permit us to generalize—to universalize, if one prefers—for hundreds of parishes the results suggested by their homologues in kind, which are limited to a handful of localities. At Narbonne (Catholic country) and at Aiguesmortes (semi-Protestant) we possess a record of the tithe farms in money for three-year or five-year periods for every parish, or priory, dependent on the *mense* of the chapter. The two median curves synthesize, for each of the two chapters, dozens of individual parish curves.

Despite the different sources and different local conditions, the various curves of tithe income, based on the abstract medians of lease contracts or on the actual total cash receipts, are convergent. In "normal" times (before 1560 or after 1600) they rise (or fall) in nominal value at the same secular rhythm as wheat prices. This signifies, in all probability, the stability of agricultural production and most assuredly the stability of real tithe income. But between 1560 and 1600 the behavior of these same curves is abnormal. Their movement expressed in nominal values is distinct from the movement of prices. At a time when nominal prices were climbing steeply, nominal tithe income was making little progress. Prices took the elevator; tithes in money took the stairs.

The case was exceptional during the course of the two centuries under study. It was characteristic of the age of the Wars of Religion. The disassociation of tithe income and prices signifies simply that actual tithe deliveries (combining grain, wine, olive oil, wool and so on) had collapsed. The conclusions to be drawn from the curves expressed in monetary terms thus confirm the data on tithes in kind.

Is this disassociation to be explained as the result of a kind of oversight, of intellectual laziness on the part of the canons who "forgot" to adjust their income to the cost-of-living index when the lease contracts came up for renewal? No, the priests were not all that naïve. It is true that inflation eroded fixed money income, like perpetual quitrents, but it did not affect the tithes, which were let for short terms and constantly varying amounts. For that matter, up to 1560—and again from 1620 to 1650—the canons, in farming out their priories every three or five years, were careful to adjust the rent as a function of the rise in prices. Their instincts did not betray them, because tithe incomes rose as prices rose, and sometimes even a little faster. In reality, the two curves diverge only at the moment of the Calvinist insurrection (1560), and they follow independent paths for a period that coincides exactly with the civil war.

Did the tithes decline, then, as the result of a depression in agricultural production provoked by the war? No doubt in part; the insecurity, the seizure of plow animals, the devastation, the villages "put to the sword" (in the exaggerated words of the chroniclers)—all these calamities were incompatible with a smooth-running agricultural economy and the tidy yields of periods of peace.

But in the last analysis, the tithe was not just another war casualty. To begin with, the fighting was interrupted by truces. For example, peace reigned almost undisturbed in Languedoc from June, 1563 (from which date the pacification edict of March was loyally observed), to September, 1567, when the entire southern rim of the Massif Central erupted in violence in response to the appeal of Condé's emissaries. In this case, the province enjoyed five fortunate and assuredly peaceful harvests in succession (1563–

67), and Charles IX, amid acclamations, showers of sweets, and a hail of sugar almonds, rendered an uneventful visit to his lands of the Midi. The plowing, harvesting, and threshing were carried out without hindrance or disturbance on the part of the soldiery. Despite all this, tithe deliveries were disappointing. At Béziers and elsewhere the canons had never garnered so little in grain tithes as during that peaceful five-year period.

It was not the harvest that was found wanting for five years running; it was the tithe itself. Production was not off; the producer was in hiding. The antistrike proclamations of the provincial Estates (1564–71) find their justification in the plunging curves of the tithe farms. The strike against the tithe, in the form of sabotage or open resistance, was raging in Languedoc in 1563–67 just as it was during these same years in the Paris Basin.

Semiclandestine but obstinate, the antitithe strike had a pernicious effect on priestly finances and was more to be feared than spectacular aggressions like the sacking of churches or the theft of chalices. The case of the chapter of Béziers is typical in this respect. A study of its accounts shows that its financial losses as a result of the crisis in tithe income were extremely heavy and in the end disastrous. In the year 1558 the chapter was at the height of its financial fortunes. Forgetting for a moment its income in grain from five granges (350 hectares in all), which was considerable, and from the "great tithe" of Béziers itself, let us confine ourselves to the receipts collected directly in money that were entirely rural in origin, resulting for the most part from the farming of the tithes of twenty parishes or "priories." These twenty priories, in an average year, were worth eight thousand *livres* to the chapter. In truth, the tithe was in a healthy state in 1558, only two years before the great shipwreck. It was securely pegged to the cost-of-living index. The canons were hardly to be pitied; Their budget of 1558 was bursting with health, and there was no question of their having to borrow. The "loans" entries under "extraordinary receipts" amounted to barely seventy-five *livres* in 1558! People did not pity the canons; they envied them; they wanted them dead.

Then the "events" of 1560–63 intervened. At Béziers the danger was great, but the canons, armed to the teeth and supplied with arquebuses and powder, escaped massacre, and soon the fugitive traces of Calvinism had been completely obliterated in the region. Peace and security returned. All would have gone well for the local clergy had it not been for the devilish problem of the tithes. After their brush with Huguenot propaganda, the peasants of the Béziers region remained good Catholics, but alas, they became poor tithe payers. The golden days when the price of the tithe farm was automatically pegged to the cost of living were at an end. One can judge for oneself—between 1558 and 1590 the annual receipts from the farming of the tithable priories went from £7,923 to £10,550, but in the same interval the price of a *setier* of wheat more than doubled. As a result, and in the space of just one generation, the canons' real income from the tithes had dropped precipitously. The goose that laid the golden eggs was very sick indeed.

The affliction was not fatal, but the time had come for clerical austerity. For want of money the priests and canons were forced to reduce their outlays for prebends, church reparations, choir boys' gowns, and legal wrangling. The ceremonies became less pompous and the lawsuits less numerous; the benefice holders drew in their belts. Even then, since spendthrift habits are hard to break, the chapter went steadily into debt. At Béziers the "loans" entries, which were insignificant in the prewar accounts, suddenly became swollen in the time of troubles. As early as 1575 the ordinary receipts (from the tithes), which amounted to £9,000, were supplemented by a loan from a merchant of Béziers for £3,000. Beginning in 1580, the tithes were in a critical state, and the financial administration panicked; annual borrowing almost equaled normal annual income. For 1590 I calculate £10,550 in ordinary receipts compared to £22,534 in new loans, of which £15,626 were set aside for the reimbursement of pressing debts with the rest going to current expenditures.

In this manner the refusal of the peasants to pay the tithe proved advantageous to the creditors of the impoverished, debt-ridden chapter. These creditors were merchants, advocates, lay lords, or notaries like Raymond de Rocolles, who in twenty-five years of activity (1579–1604) succeeded in assembling five large notes against the chapter for a total of £4,201. Finally, some creditors were mercenary captains of the civil war like the "Roman gentleman" who lent eight hundred *écus* to the chapter in 1587. The interest was high, from 10 to 11 percent per year, and the capital was not much eroded by inflation, because in Languedoc, as in Saintonge and the Dauphiné, the dizzying rise in prices was over by 1580. Up to 1600, therefore, debt charges were a heavy item in the budgets of the churchmen, who had become a favorite prey of the moneylenders. The canons could not go on indefinitely borrowing money. They were finally forced to sell certain landed properties. The outcome was unforeseen but logical. Coming in the wake of the expropriation of church properties, a deep-rooted peasant resistance to the tithe ultimately forced the clergy to surrender a supplementary portion of its lands.

At Béziers in the summer of 1570 the canons had notices put up announcing the sale of lands to pay their debts ("notices will be affixed to make known to whoever should want to purchase them that the fields the chapter has in the said locality will be sold to pay the debts of the chapter"). There followed the sale of a green meadow and a noble fief to a merchant for £2,500. This did not suffice. In the fall of 1571 there were new debts and new sales. This time, the canons sold off some grainfields and a large olive orchard. In 1576 an entire lordship went on the auction block—as usual, to service the debt. Monsieur de Maureillan, forever in the market for church property, got it for £6,500. His descendants would not retrocede this land to the chapter before 1643, at the time of the clerical and land reaction.

Side by side with the goods of the church sold by constraint on behalf of the king there existed, then, a second category—that of clerical land sold by its masters of their own free will at the time of the civil wars to extinguish debts arising from the crisis in tithe income. In this case, too, the land transfers profited the bourgeoisie and the well-to-do. In all, if one adds up the two categories of alienated goods it turns out that more than £26,000 in lands, farms, "customs," and dwellings, in a total of thirty-eight lots, were alienated by the chapter of Béziers between 1557 and 1589 in successive blocks to various bourgeois and nobles. It was only at this price that the chapter managed to escape total bankruptcy and was able to cope successively with the Protestant offensive, with the secularizations required by the treasury, and, finally, with the tithe debacle that threatened to wreck its finances. One discovers the equivalent of this vast land transfer just about everywhere—in every region and in every canton. At Montpellier, for example, the bishop Subjet, ruined by the tithe "discounts" and gone deep into debt to support, even so, "his small suite," was forced to sell the counsellor Griffi his castle, land, and lordship of Murviel for two thousand *écus*. As a minor consolation, the prelate retained the right to visit the castle and to have his people climb the tower and shout three times at the top of their lungs, "Long live his lordship the bishop." In addition, Griffi promised to present Subjet once each year with a pair of gold-plated spurs provided with velvet straps.

4

Struggle and Action of the "Lower Classes"

Peasant action made the tithes run dry and ruined the clergy. At the same time, it ended by enriching the notables, lay lords, and bourgeois, since it facilitated their engrossing activities with regard to the lands the debt-ridden Church was forced to part with at cut-rate prices.

Despite this primitive working alliance, peasants and notables were a long way from always acting in concert. In a short time, divisions appeared in their ranks, for their objectives did not coincide. The Huguenot leaders confiscated the tithe on behalf of their synods or "colloquies." The peasants, on the other hand, would have abolished it outright, and some of them wanted at the same time to do away with—or at least reduce—royal taxes and manorial dues as well. The ultimate, more or less conscious goal of these rebels was to lighten their burdens, increase their income, and assert their dignity.

Such pretentions were intolerable to members of the Huguenot bourgeoisie because they feared the unleashed fury of the populace and were themselves infatuated with noble titles, offices, and legality. They wanted to deny their commoners' condition and join the ranks of the nobility, and as a landed class they had a vested interest in peasant submissiveness. Finally, they needed the political support, however dubious, of the great nobles who helped them raise their armies and backed them in their seizure of the lands of the clergy. Hence, the bourgeoisie reached a compromise with the Huguenot nobility and later, in 1574, with Montmorency and the Catholic nobility of "*politiques*"[1]—a compromise that in the final analysis ignored peasant demands and sacrificed their interests. The bourgeois, in fact, united with the nobles against the villages. In 1561 they were in a panic over the jacquerie of Agen and the murder of baron de Fumel, who was butch-

---

[1] *Politiques*: the moderate Catholic faction (tr. note).

ered by his own peasants. They shared the anguish of the lords of Agen who had taken refuge in Toulouse after their castles were put to the torch. In 1562 the Huguenot delegates of the towns and the consistories meeting at Nîmes approved the "plaint of the Messieurs of the Nobility" and castigated a certain rebellious peasantry that thought the Holy Gospel contained a principle of social liberation. The Nîmes delegates were indignant: "In certain localities some totally perverse people believe that the Gospels promise them land freedom and enfranchisement." And they warned: "For this reason, the assembly particularly exhorts the judges to conduct inquests against these people and to punish them as fomenters of sedition, both for their scandalous discourses and for their refusal to pay their manorial or feudal dues, obligations or quitrents, and also the tithes to the farmers or holders of benefices, and to make and administer prompt and proper justice." Thus, by 1562 the notables had formed a united front against "land freedom." Meanwhile, among the peasants an independent combativeness asserted itself, and this new, extremely complex awareness on their part is one of the outstanding facts of social psychology in the second half of the sixteenth century.

Prior to 1550, in fact, peasant uprisings in the south of France were still limited in character—often little more than tax riots. It was the salt tax and the taille, and these alone, that were attacked by the *pétaults* of Guyenne in 1548. They criticized neither the tithe nor manorial obligations. After the middle of the century these taboos were removed. The tithe, as we have seen, became the principal stake in the struggle. At the time of the jacquerie of Agen (1560–61), the peasants "in certain localities stopped paying the tithes and bragged that they would also stop paying tailles (to the king) or dues to the lord." The crucial questions were now being attacked head on by the rustics, and their active struggle against the tithe was completed by an antitax and antimanorial program. At the same time, the revolts assumed symbolic meanings that make them easier to analyze than in the past.

Carnival at Romans

Around 1580, on both banks of the Rhône—in Languedoc and Dauphiné (the provincial frontiers are of no importance in this connection)—a colorful and impassioned peasant insurrection flared up. It was ignited by hardship and misery and the price of bread: "In that same year, 1580, and since the year 1579, a great multitude of starving poor, more than four thousand men, women and little children came here from the Vivarais country weep-ing and wailing" and so hungry they were devouring the beans in the fields. Hunger and revolt were brewing everywhere in the Rhône region, from the Languedocian Vivarais—the movement's point of departure—to the countryside of Romans in the Dauphiné, an old Huguenot stronghold where the uprising would reach its climax. In this region of the middle Rhône—where for twenty years the authorities had been denouncing the contagious influence of the Swiss leagues and even certain infiltrations of revolutionary Anabaptism—the parochial youth societies in charge of the popular festivals, or *reynages*, were the active cells of the insurrection. The revolt was first "sworn" in a few Protestant villages, and its initial objectives were modest: to force the soldiers and brigands to respect the peace and to reduce the taille that left the taxpayers with nothing to their names but "rocks and clay." But soon both the base and the program of the movement were broadened. A working alliance was concluded between the peasants ("the village faction") and the artisans of Romans, "an infinity of carders and other mechanical people," led by a local athlete, king of the arquebus, the "wicked draper" Jean Serve, better known as Paulmier ("Handballer"), who was "a coarse and clownish fellow." Serve was so "insolent" that he refused in 1579 to kneel before Catherine de Médicis, who was visiting Romans. The insurgent peasants of the "communes," encouraged by these urban reinforcements, raised their demands, declaring "that they did not wish to pay anything at all," that in 1579 "they had won the tailles and part of the tithes and that the said year following they would win the rest of the said tithes and the quitrents and rights that they owed the lords." Tithe, quitrents, and taille, the three pillars of the traditional order, were being called into question. The peasants grew bolder. They occupied Châteaudouble, a bandit hideout, where we see them "inflated with vainglory" and "threatening the gentlefolk" with dirty and wicked words to "turn their houses upside down." Châteaux and manorial registers went up in flames, "and there was not a yokel who did not behave as if he were as great a lord as his lord." Simultaneously, the project of social inversion which would give the Rhône rebellion its ultimate meaning began to take form.

The episode began as a popular revolution; it ended as an Elizabethan tragedy arrayed in the bright colors of the Renaissance. In the winter of 1580, in fact, excitement began to mount at Romans, which had become the nerve center of the whole movement. The artisans and peasants, incited by the approach of Carnival, acted out their revolt in the streets of the city.

"They organized several great feasts, street dances and masquerades, and throughout the week in their dances and masquerades they proclaimed that the rich of their town had grown rich at the expense of the poor people." This popular ballet expresses better than words the latent motivations of the rebels. Certain dancers with Swiss drums and bells on their feet brandished naked swords; others flourished rakes, brooms, threshing flails, and death shrouds (the massacre of the rich by flogging them to death —a simple fantasy or sometimes actually perpetrated—would remain a significant theme of agrarian revolt up to the Spanish Civil War).

And so these flail bearers cried at the top of their voices that "before three days are out Christian flesh will be selling at six *deniers* the pound." These words alone struck terror into people's hearts, and the judge Guérin, our probable narrator, scarcely dared repeat them. Paulmier, for his part— dressed in a bearskin like Spartacus, a detail which seems to have terrified the bourgeois—seized possession of the seat of the consulate, whence he expelled the representatives of the ruling classes. It was an upside-down world in which a pound of rancid tuna and wormy wine cost twenty to twenty-five *sous*, while "partridge *à l'orange* and roast woodcock" and the most exquisite dishes (not to mention Christian flesh) cost only four or five *deniers*, at least according to a long, ludicrous, and *carnavalesque* "price list" composed by the "gentlefolk" and intended to hold Paulmier up to ridicule. It was precisely these "gentlefolk" who, for their part, seized the occasion of Carnival to trick themselves out in tinsel, which symbolized their appetite for power, ostentation, and intimidation and at the same time their desire to forge an alliance with the brutal forces of a virile repression, Turkish style, against the "Scythian" barbarism of the rebels. The members of the "law and order" party, therefore, disguised themselves as king, chancellor, archbishop, high judge, arquebusiers, Swiss, and turbaned Turks. Returning from the Mass, their procession intersected one of the popular party, already dressed in mourning for the people they regarded as their oppressors. The herald of Paulmier's men was disguised as death's messenger in red and blue (the mourning colors) and mounted on an ass, and his followers were crying over and over, "Christian flesh for six (or four) *deniers*." The rich interpreted this scandalous slogan as the expression of cannibalistic intentions in their regard. Nobles, magistrates, bourgeois, and merchants credited the crowd of artisans and peasants with a horrible design to kill them all, if not to eat them, on the day of Mardi Gras in order to marry their wives and divide up their property—a shadowy motive in various revolts. The whole thing was seen as a heinous conspiracy, a Feast of Fools, a bloody buffoonery of a Mardi Gras (or *Gradimars*) which would literally turn the world upside down and confound the meanings of words and the sense of things.

Justified or not, what had become a deep-rooted fear incited the gentlefolk of Romans to take punitive action. They chose as their leader a certain Laroche, the bosom friend of Jean Serve and his comrade in arms during the civil wars, who would become, as sometimes happens, his mortal enemy. The city divided into hostile factions corresponding to the different quarters, rich or poor, and to the animal totems which constituted the prizes in their respective folk festivals—the sheep, hare, and capon parties (the peasants and craftsmen led by Jean Serve), and the cock, eagle, and partridge parties (of the gentlefolk). Laroche was invited, metaphorically, to "embrace" the partridge.

It will be observed that the animals chosen by the poor—contrary to those in the bestiary of the rich, which were delicate or rare (the partridge) or more often virile (the cock, the eagle)—were weak and emasculated, or "bad omens," as the notary Eustache Piémond, who was nevertheless sympathetic to the rebels, remarked. The insurgents did not seem exactly determined to win at all costs. The mourning rites they employed (the psychological significance of which is quite obscure, as far as that is concerned) indicate that they experienced a certain regret (mixed with hatred, of course) at the eventual demise of their masters. In fact, it was they, the downtrodden, who, on the day of the massacre following the death of Paulmier, let themselves be overpowered and slaughtered by the nobles without offering resistance "like a bunch of pigs."

Carnival, in any case, preserved its rights (the final butchery would not take place until a little later by the light of Mardi Gras candles brandished in the hands of children), and it constituted for the two parties an inspired pretext for theatrical exaggeration. Both sides organized jousts, tilting at the ring, balls, and marvelously ordered banquets, whence there issued reciprocal letters of defiance and challenges. All these festivities were a prelude to the bloody combat in which the factions finally fell upon one another to the strains of music. The occasion for the massacre was furnished the night preceding Mardi Gras by the last parade of the partisans of the partridge, with gamboling, masquerades, and a procession of four kings and a queen so richly dressed "that she was all aglitter." Did those of the capon faction try to attack this queen and pillage the procession? Whatever the case, the gentlewomen at the masked ball of the partridge faction were seized by panic. A band of Mardi Gras sword wielders, armed by the infuriated rich, left the ball, and at dawn the same day (February 15, 1588) they felled Paulmier, who was taken by surprise, with the blow of a pickax to the face. The other leaders of the popular faction were forced to scale the walls with ropes or swim for their lives in the icy waters of the Isère. Fifteen hundred peasants of the surrounding countryside, alerted by the sound of the tocsin, hurried to the aid of the artisans, but they were too late. Inside the sealed ramparts of Romans, the massacre lasted three days, and it was thus that the gentlefolk were "liberated from the tyranny of the peasants and the Leaguers." The butcher La Fleur and eight other ringleaders were hung. The cadaver of Paulmier, "too putrefied and stinking" to be strung up, was cast into the city dump. The gentlemen finally took their revenge on the rebels, "whom they butchered like hogs." In this way the Carnival of Romans, an abortive episode of social inversion, came to an end. Everything was set right side up again; the dominant classes, for a moment topsy-turvy, landed back on their feet. The better to affirm the return of order, the judges had an effigy of Jean Serve, the rebel chief, hung upside down by the heels.

The bloody Carnival of Romans, a long series of symbolic demonstrations, was a sort of psychological drama or tragic ballet whose actors danced and acted out their revolt instead of discoursing about it in manifestos. The whole was composed like a work of art, giving immediate access to the creations of the unconscious. Since it lacked an interposed ideological screen of the sort that filters and obscures, it was capable of revealing, in the insurrection and in its repression—in the swordplay of reciprocal fears—a certain unformulated content which, in the case of ordinary and less expressive revolts, remained masked from view.

At the same time, thanks to the very richness of its themes and their precise articulation, the Rhône revolt justifies a comparative, thematic study of other medieval and postmedieval revolts that also occurred in the Languedocian, Provençal, and Franco-Provençal region. For example, the public sale of human and Christian flesh, the undeniable cannibalistic fantasies, and the related theme of wife exchange that one meets with at Romans in the anxieties of the rich for a certainty, and probably also in the threats of the poor, are already encountered at the time of the Tuchins, during the Montpellier revolts of 1380, in much the same order and in almost the same sacrilegious terms. "The fomenters of sedition," according to one account, "quartered the bodies of the king's officers with knives and ate the *baptized flesh* like savage animals or threw it to the beasts."[2] Not content with devouring the flesh of the husbands, these rebels, too, were accused of wanting to possess the bodies of the wives. The poor of Béziers in 1381, according to a chronicler, planned to murder their own spouses in order to replace them with the beautiful consorts of the rich. Even if they are exaggerated, such accusations represent a significant element in the accounts of these revolts and, consequently, in the obsessions of the narrators who served as the spokesmen of their age. In fact, the abduction of rich ladies and noble maids by the poor is a constant and recurring theme in the popular revolts of the past as late as the uprisings of lower Brittany in 1675. Young Karl Marx saw in this the peculiar mark of a then outdated primitive communism.

In regard to the related theme of sacrilegious cannibalism by men and beasts—a theme sometimes connected to hysterical episodes of castration—it is attested to not only at Romans and Montpellier, as we have seen, but also during the Huguenot sack of Lodève in 1573 and in the revolt of the boatmen of Agen in 1635—not to mention the popular saturnalia that accompanied the quartering of Ravaillac in 1610.

A new psychohistory will someday have to elucidate the various symptoms of "identification" that crop up in the threats, in the anxieties, and sometimes in the actual deeds attending these plebeian and peasant uprisings.[3] For us, the important thing is to underscore, thanks to the fascinating example of Romans, the enormous emotional charge released in the southern revolts of the second half of the sixteenth century. These rebellions were extremely audacious. They called into question, as we shall see later, institutions that earlier insurrections respected. But if they were more daring from a social point of view, both revolts and repressions also seem to have been more ferocious. Their political objectives were more far-reaching, but at the same time they awakened the most deep-seated impulses of the human psyche.

[2] One will not fail to note the remarkable similarity of the two expressions (the indication of a psychological synchronism): "baptized flesh" at Montpellier and "Christian flesh" at Romans two centuries later.

[3] With regard to one of these symptoms, a psychoanalytical study of cannibalistic fears and fantasies in the history of European societies will be found in the works of Devereux (who links the phenomenon to certain very specific childhood regressions and anxieties). In general, the symptoms of inversion and identification are nowhere more evident than among the Tafurs, who were millenaristic insurgents who took part in the First Crusade. The Tafurs, led by their king, ate the flesh of the Turks, decked themselves out in the luxurious dress of their victims, and raped the latters' wives.

The Croquants of Languedoc and Central France

Furthermore, the peasant movement was far from dead after the bloody Mardi Gras of 1580. No sooner had it been crushed in the Rhône region than it started up again in the mountain districts of Languedoc, the Auvergne, and the Limousin in the Massif Central. These were all regions that had been ravaged since 1560 by war, brigands, and guerrillas. They suffered much more than the plains districts from the terrible effects of famines like that of 1586. On this point, Gamon, a bourgeois of Annonay, confirms the report of a poor mountain woman of the Lozère who was forced to subsist on carrion and bracken bread. He speaks of the "unheard-of sterility" of the harvest year 1585/86 in the Vivarais, of grain unobtainable at any price, and of country folk "forced to eat acorns, wild roots, bracken, marc and grape seeds dried in the oven and ground into flour—not to mention pine bark and the bark of other trees, walnut and almond shells, broken tiles and bricks mixed with a few handfuls of barley, oats or bran flour." As often happens, famine bred plague, and that of 1586 left grim reminders in the mountain records. Jean Burel watched as the plague-stricken made their wills—one perched on a stepladder, another standing in an open field, and still another from his window (precautions taken to keep from contaminating the notary). Eustache Piémond, for his part, counted eight hundred dead in his native Saint-Antoine and saw his maidservant, his two grown daughters, his brother, his sister-in-law, and their four children all die of the plague. Stricken himself, he took refuge in a granary. He survived, however, by God's mercy, together with four of his children. "But the cost was great."

It was in this climate of disaster and often of warfare and bloodshed in the Massif Central that the peasant revolts of the end of the century would break out. For ten years beginning in 1582, a tax revolt raged in the Haute-Uzège. The archers sent out by the tax collectors were beaten to death by the inhabitants. In the Espérou in 1587 some arquebusiers hidden in the woods threatened to cut the ears off the sergeants of the tailles.

In the 1590's a steep cycle of rising prices in a period of declining gross product set off a new wave of tax strikes. In 1593–95 the entire southern part of the central plateau was affected. The Vivarais and the Gévaudan, where the League was not in control, refused the taille to the royalists. The collectors sent in mounted troops and assigned soldiers to harass the recalcitrant; constrained them by "devastations, imprisonment and the seizure of stock"; committed horrible deeds; and confiscated roofing tiles, doors and windows, plow animals, and clothes. In League country, in the extreme north of Languedoc (Velay), it was exactly the same, and the peasants there showed the same lack of zeal in paying the taille to Joyeuse as their neighbors to the south showed to Henry IV. It is true that Burel, of Le Puy, would rather "devour wife and children" than surrender to Henry IV, but he was not insensitive to the general distress and to the reactions of the impoverished masses. In 1593 at Le Puy, he writes, the books of the taille were trampled in the mud; the women attacked the porters bearing the registers and threatened to pull the first consul's beard out by the roots. The *pinatelles*, vellon coins that infested the south of France, provoked the people's wrath in the Velay as they did at Narbonne. In 1592 the consul of Le Puy ordered the peasants to accept these coins, by force if necessary, in payment for their produce at the market. At this the rustics attacked the minters of *pinatelles* with murderous intent.

These episodes were complicated by subsistence crises and high prices. Thus, in the famine year 1595 some country folk came to Le Puy to work on the ramparts and vainly begged bread of the consuls: "For the love of God, let me take home a loaf of bread or a half *carton* of grain to feed my poor children. We come to work on your moats. Yet shan't we have a single loaf?" To these misfortunes were added the terrible cruelties inflicted by the soldiery. Burel, an eyewitness, writes indignantly: "Never did the Jews do any worse to Our Lord than is done to our poor peasants. They imprison them, they nail them down by their outstretched arms and hands; others force their mouths open and inflate them until they burst, hanging them by the feet. Oh, poor peasants. Be consoled in your misery. Help us to bear the cross of Our Lord."

The resignation preached by Burel was not the only attitude possible. In 1595 some bands of Croquants appeared in the north of Languedoc. Homologues of the Norman Gautiers, the Francs-Museaux, the Chateaux-verts, and the Lipans of the Perche, they were the comrades in arms of the Croquants of the Limousin, Quercy, and Périgord (1594), whose platform has been described by Jean Tarde and other witnesses. It embraced struggle against the nobility who treated the rustics like slaves, doubling or tripling their rents; the motto "liberty"; solidarity of the rustic third estate regardless of religion; refusal, if possible, to pay tithes, tailles, and rents; repression of League and royalist rogues who had "stolen the oxen and raped the girls"; defense of the country folk against the urban bourgeoisie, who set high prices on their wares and demanded high rents for fields and farms purchased for a song; resistance to the tax agents who ransomed the country districts to line their own pockets; and, to conclude—a form of agitation peculiar to the working class—strikes and the posting of pickets in gentlemen's vineyards. These multiple initiatives do not possess the character of a systematic "program." They are, on the contrary, empirical and unsystematic. Some could have sprung spontaneously from the peasant consciousness. At other times they seem to have been inspired by village intellectuals like the advocate Porquery and the procurator Pauillac, a poorly dressed, dirty little fellow.

As for the Languedocian Croquants of 1595, they were just as determined when it came to action, but their program seems to have been less daring. Burel watched five hundred of them "who did not want to pay any taille whatever" pass beneath the ramparts of Le Puy on Good Friday, and then again on the eve of the harvest, twelve hundred more "summoned the villages to come over to their party, not wanting to pay any taille at all, ruining and pillaging all those who refused." These rebels of Languedoc were obsessed by the fisc, but apart from taxes they were little inclined to question the established order. For that matter, they quickly fell under the dominance of the royalist nobility, who used them as auxiliaries against the League. And finally, one fine day, Chevrières, who ruled the Velay on behalf of Henry IV, grown weary of these cumbersome allies, surprised, massacred, and dispersed them.

The "Campanères" Militants

In the southwest corner of Languedoc during the 1590's the peasant movement presented analogous traits. The action was lively, but the objectives were restricted, being limited to a demand for peace and a call to arms against the fisc. This, for example, was the program of the *campanères* leagues or conferences organized in the Comminges beginning in 1591. The origin of these leagues was a common resistance to the taille, and it was this resistance that served to crystallize the hostility of the notables of the Estates of Muret against these militant countryfolk. The rural leagues of the Comminges also exercised police functions and endeavored to clear the region of brigands.

Directed against the taille, brigandage, and war, the *campanères* confederations of the Pyrenees region of Languedoc represented an original (but limited) creation of peasant militants, no doubt less "enlightened" than the petty magistrates who had assumed the leadership of the Croquant movement in the west-central area. In the lists of participants in the federal assemblies from the Comminges, there was not, in fact, a single noble or a single magistrate—no one but rustics, village consuls, or syndics, for the most part illiterate. There was, however, one noncultivator, a country merchant, village delegate, and chief of the moderate faction named Jean Désirat.

Indeed, two currents emerged in the *campanère* movement. The more radical peasant-based faction persisted in its refusal to pay the taille up to the spring of 1594. These extremists seem to have been mixed up in Huguenot agitation. In November, 1593, "three or four hundred armed men calling themselves Croquants from the (*campanère*) Conference" participated in the seizure (by the Huguenots) of the churches of Comminges and in the looting of church property.

However, a second, conciliatory faction appeared which tended to rally the peasant league directly to the banner of the Holy League and to place it under the orders of the most Catholic of all parties. The spokesman for this current was Désirat. In 1593, under his influence, the *campanère* league joined the Estates of Muret, and the Estates, which had long shied away from it, now made it welcome. Still urged on by Désirat, the confederates promised to respect the Church as well as the rights of the *seigneurs justiciers*[4] and to pay their taxes faithfully. Finally, the "associated villages" furnished foot soldiers to the Leaguers of the Bigorre. From then on, the peasant league was wrapped in the mantle of the Holy League, just as elsewhere the Croquants wore the royalist colors. What sprang originally from peasant initiative had fallen into the hands of the nobility, the towns, and the local clergy.

Nevertheless, Désirat and his *campanères* friends did not entirely abandon their demands and confrontations after 1593. They continued to clamor, before the notables of Muret, for a reduction of the tailles and the signing of a truce with the Huguenots (March, 1594) or, failing that, the confiscation of the Church's revenues with which to engage the indispensable soldiers.

This, in outline, was the course of the peasant movement in Languedoc and its border regions, and more generally in the south of France, in the sixteenth century. The general tendencies seem to have been common to the whole of the Midi—Guyenne, Périgord, Languedoc, and the Dauphiné—and the rebels cared not the least about provincial frontiers. Rural unrest

---

[4] *Seigneurs justiciers*: lords possessing, among other prerogatives, the right to dispense justice (tr. note).

in the years 1525–60 was born of fiscal discontent and the struggle against the tithe. It found its justification and its point of honor in Calvinist propaganda. It later blossomed in the revolutionary praxis of the years 1560–94, at which time it mounted an assault on the whole established order, becoming by degrees—without system and with varying intensity—antitax, antitithe, and antimanorial all at the same time, and sometimes even antibourgeois. The peasants formed alliances with the urban artisan class—the Rhône uprising of 1580 and the Croquant movement of 1594 marking a veritable climax—and at moments the communards of Romans seem to storm the gates of Heaven, while the Croquants prefigure 1789.

But there was no eighteenth-century enlightenment to give a rational direction to these primitive movements. Growing popular awareness was attended by outbursts of barbarism, and it was not even of a lasting nature, for it very soon subsided. The conflict continued, but bogged down little by little into a struggle for limited objectives. After 1595 and especially after 1600 at the time of the celebrated popular revolts that preceded the Fronde, the attacks against the tithe and against the privileges and social order of the Old Regime, with rare exceptions, ceased. The only issue—a violent issue it is true—was royal taxation. The great objectives of 1560–95 were abandoned, and revolutionary passion settled back into the rut of antitax agitation. Jaurès gave way to Poujade.

5
Witches' Sabbaths and Revolts

The peasant consciousness expressed itself in popular uprisings that were savagely emotive down to the final reverse. But it also turned out in mythical dress—in the chimerical and fantastic revolt of the witches' Sabbath, an attempt at demonic forms of escape. In fact, entire regions of the south of France were affected by a wave of satanism and witchcraft at the end of the sixteenth century—the Pyrenees, the Rouergue, the *langue d'oc*–speaking parts of the Massif Central, and as far as the Alps and the Jura. In these mountain districts, especially in the Vivarais and the Pyrenees of Languedoc, the witches' Sabbaths were concurrent with the popular revolts.

Let us briefly recall the most significant episodes in the history and geography of satanism in the Midi, going back to the closing years of the fifteenth century. Around 1490 the Cévennes, like the Vivarais and the Queyras, were bewitched mountains teeming with dozens of witches, many of them issued from specialized witches' clans. The best known of them, Martiale, passed for a baby poisoner, wine thief, and caster of spells. She had sworn "servile" homage of the Devil. All of these women were accused of celebrating the cult of the Satanic he-goat, a stinking, lustful beast, with his customary rites—the anal kiss, the frigid embrace, wild dancing, offerings of black candles, the trampling under foot of the cross, and insults to the Virgin, who was nicknamed "the Red."

The witches were tortured and reduced to ashes at the stake in 1493. Then the epidemic subsided, and a lasting period of peace ensued, at least in the Cévennes, which would abjure Satan when it embraced the Reformation. Here, at least, the Huguenots succeeded—like Zwingli's disciples in Switzerland—in destroying the web of demonic superstitions and in taking the peasant consciousness in hand. By about 1590 the days of witches' Sabbaths were definitely over in this region. The Calvinist consistories of the Cévennes had only to censure affairs of a benign sort—loaves marked with cabalistic symbols, magic dealings with the gypsies, and so on. The Reformation brought a more lucid, more humane, and more comforting religion, and it effectively cured anxiety (or displaced it).

But this victory was incomplete and precarious. It was incomplete because if Satan had been driven from the Cévennes, he was still defending some strongholds farther to the north in the Vivarais. There, in 1490, Louise Fumat, a peasant woman, was hung for having trampled the Host, prostituted her body, murdered her husband, and participated in a witches' Sabbath. A generation later (1519–30), the Vachonne du Roux, Catherine Las Hermes, and others were burned at the stake, accused of sowing discord between husbands and wives, profaning the Host, bewitching the swine, and dancing a jig around the he-goat.

It was a precarious victory, because after 1550 witchcraft, which had momentarily abated, picked up new momentum in a mounting wave that broke over the entire Midi and culminated in the great witch burnings of 1577–1600. There is nothing more striking, in this connection, than a comparison between the narratives of the two Platter brothers, Félix and Thomas, composed forty years apart. In the Montpellier region, the Satanic malady was still benign in 1556; it had grown pathological by 1596.

Under the reign of Henry II, Félix Platter, the elder brother—himself a superstitious and timorous soul—mentions witches and sorcerers only in passing. Forty years later, his young brother Thomas encountered infinitely greater anxiety and fear of Satan. In the first place, there was the obsession with the *aiguillette*, the universal dread of Satanic castration that Thomas describes for us in detail. At the moment the priest solemnizes a marriage, a witch slips up behind the spouses, ties a knot in a string, and casts a piece of money to the ground, at the same time invoking the Devil.[1] If the piece of money disappears, the marriage will be unhappy, sterile, and adulterous: "There is no doubt but that it is the Devil himself who makes off with the coin and keeps it until the Last Judgment." About 1595 Platter encountered a veritable ligature psychosis, and his recital, because of its very exaggeration, gives a good measure of the degree of dread engendered by the witches:

---

[1] The ritual is a symbolic castration in imitation of the technique of the pig castrator, in which a ligature of strong thread or cord is tied around the testicles, which then drop to the ground, leaving the bursas ("purses") empty—hence the allusion to the piece of money (G. Maugard). For that matter, the diabolical *aiguillette* is called *ligatura* in the Church Latin of Languedoc in 1609. On the castration complex, one would have to cite numerous passages from Freud.

"In Languedoc, not ten marriages in one hundred are celebrated publicly in church. The couples, accompanied by their relatives, go in secret to the neighboring village to receive the marriage blessing." Only then can the newlyweds return home free of anxiety, partake of the wedding banquet, prepare their bed, and take leave of each of their guests with a kiss on the mouth. Platter, a sober-minded doctor, concludes with a grave shake of his head that the panic was so great that there was a danger of local depopulation for fear of the *aiguillette* and because of fewer marriages!

The complex of castration by ligature was inseparable from the obsession of impotence on the husband's part and, in certain cases, of frigidity on the part of the wife—the "coldness" that the peasants of Languedoc, around 1600, associated in a curious way with infertility. This theme would only lose its malefic content little by little. It still survived in the folklore of Roussillon and Catalonia after it had disappeared in Languedoc, and in the more backward regions of Europe such as Sicily and southern Italy, propitiatory rites directly related to castration continue to be employed by newlyweds right up to our own day. The remedies would differ, but the basic anxiety would remain the same as that among the people of Languedoc at the close of the sixteenth century.

It was precisely the leading minds of Languedoc, the people most highly placed, who believed in satanism and were sometimes themselves dangerous sorcerers. Augier, the provost of Languedoc, poisoned beautiful ladies with a gold ring wherein there dwelt a *spiritus familiaris*.

Beginning in 1580 with the famous witchcraft epidemics (well attested in the Franche-Comté and the Basque provinces, where there were more than five hundred witch burnings), the whole chain of bewitched mountains began to stir once more, the chimneys of these great factories of mass delirium started to smoke, and lines of force of demonic influence spread from the Pyrenees to the Jura across the *langue d'oc*–speaking heights of the Massif Central. In the Languedocian Pyrenees, a region of dreadful adjurations, local historians would still call attention, on the eve of the Fronde, to trials of witches accused of the "bewitchment of stock, the loss of babes in the cradle, general damage to the harvest fruits" and, as a consequence, to the hanging, burning, cudgeling and banishment of the guilty. Farther north, the Rouergue was seriously infected. Around 1595 sorcerers reigned unchecked in the region, thanks to the crass ignorance of the natives. These coarse, ungodly mountain folk were ignorant of the Bible, and because they lived in isolated farmsteads or hamlets far from any church,

they did not go to Mass and were easy prey to every sort of demonic obsession. Not far away, in the country of Saint-Pons, a den of astrologers and
hotbed of superstition, the Devil was equally at home. He haunted priests
and notaries, whose anxieties have been handed down to us in their records
of 1590–1600, and he tugged at the feet of the body of Suzanne Rességuière,
who had hung herself from the bars of her window, with the force of six
men. It seems to have been common, about 1605, for specters to make the
journey from Rouergue to Saint-Pons and return, across the passes of the
Montagne Noire, sweeping the snow from their path along the way.

Towards the east, the Huguenot Cévennes, as we have seen, henceforth
experienced only benign forms of the disease. The veritable witches' highroad now passed farther north. It left the Rouergue, detoured around the
Calvinist Gévaudan, and converged on the Vivarais, where the stakes
flamed up again in 1581 following a lull of fifty years. In 1582 some consuls,
doctors, and apothecaries of Annonay attacked the witches' Sabbaths of
the mountain districts with the whole arsenal of exorcisms and tortures
practiced by the parochial churches of the town. We may cite, among others,
the procedure used on Catherine Boyaronne, a fifty-year-old peasant woman
of Saint-Symphorien. Some notables of known integrity "scorched her like
a pig" and poured boiling fat into her ears and over other parts of her body—
cooked her alive, in short—to make her confess that she had taken her
daughter to the witches' Sabbath. Finally, from the Vivarais the magic
chain of satanism rejoined Savoy and the Jura (by way of Lyons), where
witchcraft was rife in the age of Master Boguet.[2]

These were the facts: a surge of obscurantism, a crisis of the occult at the
end of the century, and a wave of rural satanism, especially in the mountain
districts. How is one to account for all this when, at the same time, the Reformation seems to imply the progress of enlightenment? Thomas Platter,
in 1595, proposed a geographical explanation. After his travels in the French
Midi he asked himself where these witches' villages were located, and his
answer was: in areas of dispersed settlement where the nature of the terrain,
and so on, prevented the peasants from frequenting the Catholic masses or
the Calvinist temples, where pastoral visits were rare and difficult, and
where the ignorant rustics had no access to the Scriptures. Here, entrenched
in their remote farmsteads, a perfect prey for the Devil, the peasants secreted
the agrarian ideology par excellence—witchcraft. Thus, the spiritual wastes

---

[2] Master Boguet: judge of the County of Burgundy and notorious persecutor of rural
sorcerers at the end of the sixteenth century (tr. note).

of the Rouergue and the mountain of Saint-Pons were veritable hornets' nests of sorcerers. It was a witchcraft of the isolated backwaters.

This explanation is doubtless too static, but one can breathe life into it by considering it in the context of other sixteenth-century developments. The rise of witchcraft was not solely a function of immutable geographical conditions. It can be dated with precision. It proclaims the failings and the mounting crisis of religious organization. In this connection, certain sociological analyses formulated in quite a different context are capable, mutatis mutandis, of offering some useful suggestions. The demographic advance of the sixteenth century resulted in the relative overcrowding of population in the ancient parishes, in the outskirts of the towns, and on the assarted mountainsides. Now, the local clergy, no more than the civil authorities, neither foresaw nor understood nor even seemed to notice this phenomenon, and no special measures were taken to cope with it. It was only in the seventeenth century that the bishops in their pastoral rounds would become concerned about the dying, who, alone in the remote settlements of recent colonization, far from their churches, were denied all spiritual consolation.

After 1560 the civil wars still further aggravated this situation of abandonment. Some priests were massacred; others sought safety in flight. Many ecclesiastics abandoned their flocks, picked up an arquebus, and transformed themselves into soldiers of the League. The clerical organization, therefore, was inadequate to its tasks. What was especially distressing was the spiritual dereliction of the mountain districts—areas of guerrilla activity, brigandage, and terrorism. Far from their priests, the peasants found themselves alone with their anxieties and their primordial fears—and abandoned themselves to Satan.

Patterns of Inversion

Does it not, however, impoverish our analysis to reduce the epidemic of satanism to a simple question of spiritual deprivation, darkened consciousness, or the shortcomings of religious organization? Beyond this "negativism," the sturdy character of a full-fledged, authentically rural ideological essence, springing from the depths of time and the depths of the psyche, has to be restored to the phenomenon of witchcraft. Then it no longer appears as the simple expression of a spiritual void, but rather as a lively reaction of a peasant consciousness disillusioned with the ideologies of urban origin, brutalized after 1560 by war, and haunted by the specters of misery and death—and often by fears of sexual failure (the *aiguillette* and the castration complex). The peasant consciousness suddenly broke loose from its moorings, fell prey to the ancient deliriums, and abandoned itself to all its demons. In default of a veritable liberation it embarked upon the adventure of a Satanic revolt.

Between these frenzied uprisings and the authentic popular revolts which also reached their climax in the same mountains about 1580–1600, there existed a series of geographical, chronological, and sometimes family coincidences. But above all there was a certain deep-seated kinship between witches' Sabbaths and popular revolts at the level of mental structures and the unconscious psyche. We have already mentioned, apropos of the *aiguillette*, certain characteristic anxieties. But the narrative mechanisms themselves also reveal some remarkable traits in common. In the two phenomena, insurrection and witchcraft, one in fact encounters, from time to time, the fantasy of inversion—that fictitious reversal of the real world so frequent in myth and in "primitive thought." There is nothing surprising in the fact that this inversion is associated with certain types of revolt, both chimerical and real—if often hopeless. For to turn the world upside down is not the same as to revolutionize it, or even to transform it in a true sense. It is, nevertheless, in an elementary way, to contest, to deny, to proclaim one's disaccord with the world as it is. The witchcraft of 1600, like the revolts and popular festivals, bears the systematic imprint of such a tendency.

Typical of this obsessive desire for permutation is the testimony of a young sorcerer of the south, a fifteen-year-old adolescent of Saint-Jean-de-Luz, describing the Black Mass just as he claims to have seen it celebrated "six or seven times" in 1609 by the priest Jean Souhardibels in the locality of Cohandia (in the region of Labourd):

> At this Mass, Souhardibels performed the elevation with a black Host, while raised off the ground, his feet up and his head inverted facing the Devil; and he remained in this posture during the elevation, the time it took to say a *credo*; and the witness placed himself before us in the same position the better to show us how it was done (for Satan teaches them the most horrible acts one has ever seen). And he spoke of more besides and of things that he could hardly find words for; the priest's body was entirely off the ground so that, although his body was inverted with his head down and his feet in the air, nevertheless, performing that elevation, he said, the body and arms of the priest were in proportion to those of our priests when they perform the true elevation of the Host in the Church of God, because (the wit-

ness added) the Devil at the *sabbat* makes everything appear upside down in a manner that seems altogether impossible to men, but not to him. [Lancre, 1612, pp. 464–65.]

Precious testimony, for in the utterly absurd picture it paints of a priest saying Mass with his legs in the air and his head upside down it marks the stubborn, and in the end perfectly explicit, pretention of a certain mythical thought to permute institutions—the fanatical desire to turn the world head over heels. Two years later, in 1611, another witness repeated the same idea in a form more consistent with the law of gravity. "The priests of the Labourd," he declared, celebrate the Black Mass not according to the normal rites, "but all backwards." For example, they officiated with their faces turned toward the people and not toward the altar, as in the true Mass. Also, in the place of a white Host they consecrated a black rape—again, a painstaking perversion and inversion of normal relationships.

These themes of an "upside-down world" were not specific to the Basque mountains, a melancholy land of sorcerers. They are also encountered under different guises in Catalan witchcraft: Latin prayers recited backwards and demons with upside-down bodies whose faces peer out from where their bellies ought to be (in the demonic paintings of the Catalan school conserved in the museum of Perpignan). The same themes are encountered in the whole Mediterranean Midi, from Narbonne to Antibes, no longer in the drama of witches' Sabbaths and Black Masses, but under the preposterous cloak of the Feast of Fools, of the saturnalia of the Church, and of the Mass-bouffe and the Mass-farce celebrated by a carnival abbot who gaily intones the burlesque hymn, *"Memento David sans truffe."*

Among those who aped the Mass and the church hierarchy, the passion of inversion was carried to extremes. Not long afterwards, Naudé would describe one of these "offices" of Mediterranean folklore by the Cordeliers (Gray Friars) of Antibes. During the Feast of Fools, the lay brothers, scullions, and gardeners occupied the choir stalls in place of the priests. The priestly trappings were rent and turned inside out, and the holy books were read upside down and backwards with eyeglasses that had orange peels for lenses. The Mass and the psalms were a babble of confused little cries.

Now, these themes of inversion, so painstakingly formulated, are met with not only in the saturnalia of the witches' Sabbath and the Feast of Fools, but also in those great social saturnalia—the popular revolts of the past. In default of any real chance of success, it was very difficult to elaborate an effective plan for the revolutionary transformation of society. Once the rebels went beyond their immediate demands, they were seized by savage, sometimes millenaristic longings for the permutation of ranks, rites, and the real: "the first shall be last." Reading the holy books backwards and upside down was a grotesque farce for the lay brothers of Antibes, but it was also, one hundred leagues distant, a serious act of social defiance invented independently by the Anabaptists of Saxony when they wanted to glorify the poor and illiterate.

Closer to home, in the Rhône region of the Midi, the whole artisan and rural revolt that culminated in the bloody masquerades of the Carnival at Romans was interpreted, in the popular and bourgeois psyches, in terms of inversion—the permutation envisaged between rich and poor and, to the point of absurdity, the permutation of rank and condition, of goods, and of wives, not to mention the prices of all commodities.

Thus, the new states of consciousness of the closing sixteenth century sometimes seemed to miscarry by abandoning their objectives or else by slipping savagely into the irrational. The reasonable confrontations—those involving tithes, land rents, lordships, privileges, inequitable land distribution, and the established disorder—were not as yet the work of an enlightened elite, bearers of the "light of reason" and a modern conception of man. The still primitive struggles remained mired in obscurantism. The peasant insurgent was groping in a world of shadows that thickened toward the end of the century. The increase in population, as we have seen, was not attended by a harmonious growth of wealth, and this social failure had its equivalent at the level of peasant consciousness, agrarian struggle, and unconscious impulse. For rural freedom did not win the day. The old anxieties returned in force together with the old frenzies, and one witnesses in the behavior of the popular masses the recurrence of a *pensée sauvage.*

PART THREE

The Rent Offensive

The contradictions of the sixteenth century—the same later formulated as abstract models by Malthus and Ricardo—survived the Wars of Religion. They cast their pall over much of the seventeenth century as population, after 1600, continued to grow at a more rapid rate than aggregate real income. There were many signs, to be sure, that the demographic engine was running out of steam and that poverty was acting as a check and restraint on natural increase. In those villages still affected by population growth, the number of persons subject to the taille (see Part I, chapter 2, above) increased, in most cases, a bare 2 or 3 percent per decade, compared to 10 percent per decade in the exuberant sixteenth century. In a minority of cases, the rising cycle was actually reversed by the plague of 1630, which decimated a quarter to a third of the inhabitants of certain parishes. The essential fact remains, however, that despite occasional outbreaks of the plague and despite a slower rate of increase, the population of rural Languedoc continued to grow under Henry IV and Louis XIII. Not until 1680 or later did the movement entirely subside.

Society was suffering, in short, from a surplus of people, who were outrunning their means of subsistence. In fact, agricultural production after 1600, as measured by the tithes and the cadastres, failed to keep abreast of the growth of population. To be sure, some conspicuous successes were posted; between 1600 and 1655 the approaches to the Gulf of Lion were planted with new vineyards producing for the Genoese market, and silk culture and the mulberry tree were introduced in the Cévennes and the Comtat Venaissin. And if we turn from these privileged sectors to the overall production of such basic commodities as cereals, pastoral products, and olive oil, the picture, at first glance, is far from somber. There are indications in the first half of the century of a healthy recovery and a rise in agricultural output, but closer analysis suggests that this development had little to do with genuine economic growth. It represents, rather, a supreme effort to make good an earlier setback. In the period between 1600 and 1640–60 aggregate real income from agriculture, which had declined during the civil wars, barely managed to climb back to the level of Francis I's reign. In the interval, however (between about 1550 and 1650), population, in

These pages, dealing with the period 1600–50, constitute a résumé of pages 415–508 in the original version of the present study (Paris: S.E.V.P.E.N., 1966).

spite of everything, kept on growing. From the Renaissance to the baroque
period, and up to about 1650–55, the maledictions of the sixteenth century
worked their evil effects. The economic cake was being cut into smaller and
smaller portions. The familiar factors of pauperization, already encountered
in the post-1500 period (see Part I, chapter 3, above), continued operating
from the Edict of Nantes until the Revocation, as seen especially in the
persistent subdivision of landholdings. In view of the fact that the latter
process was not accompanied by a permanent rise in yields per hectare, it
could only result in progressive impoverishment. Once again it is the *compoix* that attest to this relentless pulverization of rural property, which continued up to about 1680.

In one respect, however, the first sixty years of the *grand siècle* mark a
significant break with the previous phase studied in Part One of this book.
With the advent of Henry IV or Louis XIII we perceive for the first time,
in fact, the characteristic lift-off of land rents and increased exactions of
every sort being siphoned off the gross product by the "propertied classes."
The rent paid to the landowner by the tenant farmer was leading the pack.
It was stimulated, evidently, by the rise in population, which led in turn to
an increase in the number of prospective tenants and to growing land
hunger (for want of a corresponding increase in the acreage under cultivation). This boom in land rents took place in a modified context; farm wages
—stabilized at rock bottom in the wake of the general impoverishment of
the sixteenth century—henceforth constituted an irreducible constant. Thus,
it was the tenant's profit that was curtailed by the "inflation" of land rents.
The working farmer, so prosperous in the age of the Renaissance, found it
increasingly difficult to make ends meet in the century of Louis XIII.

The state's share, in the form of direct and indirect taxes, remained fairly
stationary from the days of good king Louis XII to the early reign of Louis
XIII. But Richelieu changed all that. With characteristic vigor he tightened
the fiscal screws in order to finance the war and consolidate the absolutist
monarchy, touching off riots and revolts in the process. The peasant, that
"workhorse of the State" and the principal payer of tailles and gabelles, was
the first to suffer the effects of the cardinal's turn of the vise. The Catholic
Church, meanwhile, was busy collecting its tenth of everything the land
produced. The lean years of the Huguenot successes and the resistance to
the tithe (1560–95) were succeeded by the fat years of the Counter-Refor-
mation and the baroque period. Churches, episcopal palaces, convents, and
seminaries, built with the treasure of the tenth sheaf (which the peasants,

forgetting their earlier resistance, acquitted without a murmur), sprang up on all sides. Finally, in addition to this threefold drain on the gross product—the landlord's in the form of rent, the state's in the form of taxes, and the Church's in the form of tithes—there were the interest payments and reimbursements that filled the coffers of the moneylenders, whose miserable, rustic clientele had become so numerous. The claims outstanding (which constituted the usurer's capital) and income from *rentes constituées*[1] were largely spared the eroding effects of inflation after 1600 because, despite temporary upswings and brief, if violent, fluctuations, the price revolution was definitely over by the last decade of the sixteenth century. The debt-ridden peasant could no longer hope for relief from a runaway inflation and was now more than ever at the mercy of the moneylender. The seventeenth century was the golden age of Monsieur Dimanche, the loan shark.

Thus, for the first two generations of the hundred years under discussion, agrarian society in Languedoc was increasingly rich in human resources but poor in goods; it was condemned to the progressive fragmentation of a fixed compass of cultivable land and victimized by high land rents and all manner of levies against the gross product. The latter filled the coffers of the thriving "propertied classes" (as Quesnay was to call them a century later): the Crown, the landowners, the Church, and others whose swollen profits ate into the agricultural producer's income. The situation was rife with social tensions.

Matters came to a head after 1625, when the disinherited segment of society, conscious of its own distress, occasionally rose up in bloody revolt (at Agen in 1635, in the Rouergue in 1643, at Montpellier in 1645, and in other places). The hated taxes served as a pretext for these "popular emotions" (or tumults), but behind the antitax slogans lay atavistic motivations of the collective unconscious. The insurgents of Agen in 1635, by simply allowing their primordial instincts free play, spontaneously resuscitated the castrating, cannibalistic exploits dear to the heroes of the Iliad and the primitive rebels of the Middle Ages.

The third generation of traditional peasant society in Languedoc, having reached a stage of demographic maturity, retained its vigor but was beset at the same time by insoluble frustrations and contradictions. Trapped between impassioned demographic energies seeking release on the one hand and Malthusian and Ricardian checks and restraints on the other, it was

---

[1] *Rentes constituées*: money loans between individuals at legal, fixed rates of interest (tr. note).

moving steadily in the direction of a negative denouement and toward a reversal of the conjuncture. The economic expansion that had lasted almost two centuries reached its painful culmination and was succeeded, in the reign of Louis XIV, by a violent contraction. We shall now attempt to determine its chronology.

PART FOUR

The Depression

In the harvest year 1653/54 wheat prices on the *mercuriale* of Béziers climbed to ten *livres* and six *sous* per *setier*, their high point of the century. Then began an irremediable downhill slide to the shoals of Colbertism and the quagmire of the Revocation. Phase B of the nominal price curve at Béziers, which lasted from 1654 to 1690, prefigured (as was also the case in Italy) a similar movement in the north of France and in northern Europe in general. To cite several markets for which figures exist, Milan seems to have felt the effects of the depression before Aix and Béziers, Béziers before Paris, and Paris before Danzig. Is it a question of monetary shock waves originating in the Mediterranean epicenter and reverberating northward to the distant shores of the Baltic? The dates speak for themselves; at Milan the decline set in in 1637, at Béziers in 1654, at Paris and Beauvais in 1662, and at Danzig not until 1663.

But harvest fluctuations also help to explain some of these discrepancies. Phase B was about to be ushered in at Paris, it appears, as early as the decade of the 1650's, when the harvest failure of 1661/62 intervened, rocketing that year's cereal prices to record highs for the century. In the capital Louis XIV might celebrate his accession with appropriate pomp and circumstance, but in a "red belt" extending from Blois to Boulogne the poor were dying of hunger, subsisting on a diet of cabbage stalks and bran mash soaked in codfish water—wretched, spiritless creatures dragging out their last miserable days.

Nothing of the kind happened in the semiarid south, which was spared the pouring rains and blight that ruined the harvest of Louis's accession in the north. It was southern wheat, paradoxically from Languedoc and Gascony by way of Bordeaux, that helped feed Paris and Normandy in the famine year 1662. A perceptible rise in cereal prices was registered on the markets of the Midi, but it was insignificant compared to the battering they took at the time of the Fronde. And the downward drift was not interrupted at Béziers (as it was at Beauvais) by the misfortunes of the early 1660's. The cereal price curve remained depressed and sluggish up to 1673. Here we have phase B of Colbertism in its pristine state; prices were low, money was "scarce," and harvests, which were often bountiful (as we shall see from our indices of productive activity), rotted in the barns for want of a market.

Trade was "strangely dormant." The overall cost of working the land was greater than the return. The crisis affected the whole of Europe; the slump in the grain trade of Languedoc and Burgundy mirrored a similar situation in the Baltic region, where the two-hundred-year boom in cereal exports from Poland, Prussia, and the Livonian estates of the Knights of the Sword temporarily subsided about 1650.

International misfortunes stem from international causes. In the Estates, the bishops of Languedoc were wont to blame the depression in the grain and wine trades on the depredations of Barbary pirates or on the tribute levied on river traffic by the customs farmers, whose vessels patrolled the Rhône. These were doubtless contributing factors, but they were limited in their effects. In reality there were several underlying reasons for the drop in prices of the 1660's which transcended the frontiers of a particular region or even of a particular nation. These included a falling off in demand attributable to major demographic declines in Spain, Italy, northern France at the time of the Fronde, Germany, and Poland—the last two completely devastated, it will be remembered, between 1635 and 1665 by the armies of Sweden and her allies. Cash demand, meanwhile, had also declined, primarily as a result of the much-discussed "monetary famine"; that is to say, the shortage of circulating coin.

Finally, there is a lesser-known fact emphasized in some recent studies: despite the contraction of demand, production held up, at least for a time, and the supply side of the ledger showed a certain inelasticity. This was the case, for example, in England and Brittany thanks to a sunny cycle of bumper harvests and also, no doubt, to redoubled efforts on the part of the producers. In the south, Italian and Gascon maize continued to reach the market in quantity, and in Languedoc itself agricultural production, as seen from the tithes, with the sole exception of wine, remained steady and even posted occasional gains up to about 1670.

A contraction of international demand but not of international supply (rather the contrary)—is this the secret of the decline of farm prices? Is this how we explain phase B of Colbert's ministry? The south, where the break in nominal prices (phase B) first occurred, also showed unmistakable signs of recovery earlier than the Paris Basin. In the first place, the cyclical upswings of 1678 and 1684 were decidedly more pronounced at Béziers and Aix than at Paris and Beauvais. It seems reasonable to assume that the south was in some way better insulated against the effects of the depression than the north. But once again, local, strictly "cyclical" factors were at work. In

Provence and Languedoc, for example, the higher prices of the 1680's were the result of poor harvests, while in the north, with its cooler, more humid climate, the harvests naturally did not suffer to the same degree from the scorching droughts of those years.

The year 1690, or thereabouts, was the great turning point. At Béziers the nominal prices of cereals, wine, and olive oil skyrocketed, matching the records set during the Fronde between 1690 and 1700 and surpassing them about 1709–15 and from 1718 on. The reasons for a Europe-wide rise in prices at this time were complex. Northern Europe, in the decade of the 1690's, suffered from a succession of severe winters, cool, damp summers, and poor harvests. But the winds of inflation were also blowing. The governments of France and England were at war, stockpiling supplies and imposing new taxes which were immediately translated into higher prices. Most important of all, perhaps, the major powers financed their budget deficits by borrowing and in the end by devaluation. These combined factors doubtless contributed more to the buoyancy of nominal prices in the period 1690–1700 than the as yet insignificant influx of Brazilian gold.

It was, in other words, an unhealthy kind of inflation symptomatic of hard times, food shortages, and black marketecring. In France it coincided with the agrarian disasters of the closing years of the reign. Yet it also served to revive "currents of production and profit" in certain sectors of the economy by creating contradictions, compensations, and "price scissors." For example, in Languedoc around 1700 agriculture collapsed, but the woolen textile industry began to boom; at a time when land was going out of cultivation, ships laden with bales of cloth were setting sail from Marseilles in increasing numbers bound for the markets of the Levant.

The behavior of the *nominal* price curves, with their jagged peaks and deep valleys, their breaking slope towards the end of the century, is in sharp contrast to that of *metallic* prices,[1] which follow an unmistakable, if rather cheerless, secular decline. If we convert the prices quoted on the grain market of Béziers into gold or silver prices, we obtain for the period 1650–1730 a gently descending curve that soars and dips and is bent but not broken by the various projections of 1690 and 1710. The decline of gold and silver prices continued for some eighty years—a sign, in all probability, of monetary scarcities and economic contraction or the two combined. Certain chronological discrepancies emerge when we compare the two curves. Phase B on the nominal price curve was relatively short-lived; it coincided,

[1] Prices calculated in grams of pure silver (tr. note).

more or less, with Colbert's ministry. Phase B on the metallic price curve, on the other hand, covers the entire period from Fouquet to Fleury (ca. 1655 to ca. 1730). In short, the two systems of notation, nominal and metallic, are in disaccord. Must we reject the first in favor of the second and sacrifice the substance for the shadow of reality?

In fact, the contradiction cannot be resolved in a sterile debate over grams of silver and *livres tournois* or between the platitudes of pure quantitavism as opposed to the paradoxes of a moneyless economy. What is required is a real solution based on concrete facts. For this we must examine, starting with the tithes, the more meaningful series underlying the ambiguous price data: production curves and gross income curves, both nominal and real (that is, converted into measures of grain). From these indices of productive activity we shall turn to data on population and thence to a spectral analysis of distribution. In this way, not only is one able to discover what lies behind price movements, whether nominal or metallic, but one is also in a better position to interpret them and to fit them into their social and economic context.

1

The Vicissitudes of the Gross Product

Wine

The first symptoms of malaise in agricultural production appeared in viticulture. About 1670 Intendant d'Aguesseau appraised the state of the industry in his native Languedoc. He could admire certain capitalistic successes (such as a wine grower of Béziers, from a family of cloth merchants, with a cellar for ten thousand hectoliters). He describes the distant—but not too distant—markets for the wines of Bas-Languedoc, which were exported to Italy (Rome and Genoa) by sea; to the southeast of France (Marseilles) and to Grenoble, Geneva, and Lyons via the Rhône; and to the wine-drinking fringes of the Massif Central (the Vivarais, Gévaudan, and above all Mende, a city of hard drinkers) by mule train. This traffic seems on the whole quite provincial when compared to that of the French wines of the Atlantic coast that were shipped as far off as England, Holland, and the Baltic. The only wine of the Midi that was known abroad in this period was the muscatel of Frontignan.

On the one hand there was a limited export market (according to d'Aguesseau); on the other were mediocre wine tithes (according to my own research). At Béziers, Agde, and Narbonne, the production of the large, well-situated maritime vineyards began to decline in 1645-50, collapsing under Colbert to half the record pre-Fronde levels. Thereafter, wine production stabilized at this "floor" until 1710 (when our curves and documentation are interrupted). At Gaillac about 1700 the wine tithe was noticeably lower than it had been under Louis XIII and two times less than it was at the time of the Fronde. There were timid signs of recovery beginning in 1725-30, but the movement was first held in check by a break in wine prices and was then effectively blocked, in 1730, by the prohibitions against planting vines. The advance of viticulture at Gaillac would not truly resume until

1734 and especially 1740, when these prohibitions fell into disuse. The record
levels of the Fronde were not equalled on a regular basis until after 1751–
52. They were not really bettered before Turgot, in 1779. Here, then, is a
series that provides food for thought in appraising the successes of viticulture in the first half of the seventeenth century and the importance of the
subsequent decline under Colbert and Louis XIV.

The interest of these wine tithes resides, first of all, in the fact that they
serve to refute a certain canal mythology popular with some historians, who
maintain that it was in fact Paul Riquet, the Two-seas Canal, and the port
of Sète that launched the production of wine for a mass market in the Midi.
This happens to be incorrect. Agde and Béziers were located right on the
waterway, yet their vintages had never been so mediocre as in the half
century following the completion of Riquet's great undertaking (1680–
1730). The canal would bear its late fruits during the economic recovery
that arrived with the second generation of the eighteenth century, not
before.

The collapse of the tithes at Gaillac under Louis XIV was indicative of
a broad malaise affecting the whole Aquitanian wine industry. The winegrowers of the southwest under Colbert were crying poverty. In 1678 John
Locke soberly questioned one of them; this man, his wife, and three children
subsisted on rye bread and water. They ate no meat except for animals'
entrails on feast days. For outside work the husband earned the very modest
sum of seven *sous* per day, the wife barely three *sous*. Their vineyard was
small and unprofitable. The farm expenses, costs of wine barrels, and land
rent were very heavy. The taille ate up all the profit. "Their house . . . was
poor, one room and one story open to the tiles, without windows." They
were fleeced by the tax collector, who seized their crockery and skillet for
nonpayment of the taille.

What was the source of these difficulties in viticulture and the decline in
tithed wine production after 1650–60? Prices or, more exactly, the price
structure had ceased, by this time, to be remunerative. Not even the spring
freezes served to buoy up wine prices. The price of new wine at Béziers between 1655 and 1690 declined 50 percent from forty *livres* to twenty *livres*
per *muid*; this compares to a 25 percent decline in the price of wheat. Wine
was the most seriously affected of all the major crops by the depression. It
declined much farther in price than olive oil and mutton, and much farther
also than wages and taxes. The burden of charges became unbearable, and
a once-prosperous viticulture went into the red. The winegrower in the end

stopped planting and tending his vines. He was the principal victim of Colbertism.

The crisis of the southern vintages between 1655 and 1690 was at the same time deeper and more protracted than, for example, the famous crisis in viticulture of 1778–85. It lasted one whole generation; it compounded the effects of the collapse of prices by a decline in production and ended with an appalling contraction in the wine trade. In the face of this disaster, all the wine-growing villages, large and small, reacted in the same way, as attested by dozens of documents. They shut themselves off from the outside world, refusing entry to their neighbors' wine or grapes. They consumed barrels of local *piquette* in their homes and in the taverns "until the price should rise," as the inhabitants of Nègrepelisse wrote in 1666. The great vineyard of Languedoc split up into a multitude of small cells, stubbornly barred and bolted from the inside. The efforts of each group to shelter itself from the effects of the crisis only made matters worse for all concerned.

The strong surge of wine prices, which linked up with cereal prices again after 1690, did not succeed in reanimating the wine industry. The tithes remained depressed and lethargic during the whole later reign of Louis XIV and even under the Regency. Prices were powerless to revive production, it seems, for various structural reasons; taxes were too heavy, the market was too restricted, and wine drinkers, between 1690 and 1715, declined both in numbers and in purchasing power. In a general way, the winegrowers of the end of the reign were dispirited. They lacked the heart to plant. One has to wait until 1720, 1735, or 1740 for the economic and psychological climate to change, thus permitting the wine tithes to "take off" for new and record heights.

But in 1700–15 a defeatist mentality still prevailed, and a provincial inquest on abandoned holdings in 1714 revealed, as do the *compoix*, a quantity of *vignasses*—ruined vineyards lying fallow because of inability to pay expenses and at the same time reward the producer for his labor.

In these circumstances the grape growers and wine merchants sought to adapt themselves to hard times, from Colbert on, by prospecting the new market for brandy. In what was to become the classic solution to the problem of surplus production, the excess wine was "recycled"—distilled into spirits. Up until 1660 brandy was hardly produced at all in the French Midi. It was still an Atlantic affair of Dutch sailors, hard drinkers of Brittany, winegrowers of the Gironde, and Basque fishermen who stank so of spirits and tobacco that their wives turned them out of bed. Still, about 1615 there were ships at Marseilles loading casks of brandy for the Canaries, and a few years later, for Saint-Malo. The sea is the bearer of new techniques. But at Montpellier under Louis XIII, brandy was still little more than an apothecary's preparation.

Then, quite suddenly, about 1663–64—when the crisis in viticulture was already in full swing—some new signs appeared. In 1663 at Béziers we find the first mention of a draught of brandy in the wine harvesters' meal ration. The following year at Lunel, at the time of the vintage, complaints were raised against a new type of industrialist heretofore unknown in the region —the distiller. People said that their furnaces drove up the price of wood, that their distilleries discharged noxious waters, and so on. The protests were in vain. There was no standing in the way of progress. The same year, 1664 (April 10, to be exact), "spoiled wine for making brandy" is quoted for the first time in the century on that economic recorder of infinite precision that was the *mercuriale* of Béziers. From that moment on it was quoted regularly in each new price list. The date is worth remembering. It opens a new chapter in economic history—starting at the bottom of a depression in viticulture—that of the brandies of the French Midi. The beginnings were slow, however. In 1670 d'Aguesseau, in an extremely knowledgeable report, did not as yet mention any exports of brandy from Languedoc. But Basville, in 1698, already assigned it an important place in the export trade.

Thus, the crisis in wine growing and the slump in the wine trade had the effect, under Louis XIV—and in broad regions of France—of stimulating drunkenness. Brandy-based alcoholism annexed itself to the wine-based alcoholism of the age of Louis XIII. Brandy, wine, and tobacco largely replaced the devaluated stimulants of the Middle Ages—pepper and other spices. By the reign of Louis XIV, drinkers in the west of France were downing spirits of perry and cider, predecessors of the terrible calvados that would one day destroy whole peasant generations. In the towns, the rich, with their marc brandy, no longer held a monopoly on drunkenness. By 1675 the workers, too, were sampling eau-de-vie and walnut brandy in small doses. In the streets, hawkers were selling spirits in tin cups on tables or stools protected by portable oilcloth screens. By 1680 even in the sober Midi the bishops were fulminating against the village tavern that was the ruination of the countryside.

Sète at this time began to develop into a center of liquor exports. In 1676–84 a group of financiers—treasurers of France, collectors of the salt tax and tailles who had grown fat off the king's bounty—founded at Sète an ephemeral Levant Company, which shipped its casks of brandy as far as Amsterdam. Later, in 1699, a copious vintage threatened to drive prices down. The immediate reaction was distillation. Forty-five thousand hectoliters of wine passed through the port of Sète. But another 45,000 hectoliters were distilled and transmuted into 10,000 hectoliters of brandy for export.

At the end of the century, during the brutal crises of Louis XIV's reign, brandy would be the salvation of the wine-growing industry. Beginning in 1690–93, it contributed (with the help of a few poor vintages) to the pegging of wine prices to wheat prices for the first time in thirty-five years. But this salvage operation did not constitute a cure. The tithes on wine would not really pick up again until about 1735–40, when the markets revived and the best Languedocian vintages were loaded at Sète for shipment "as far as England, Holland and, ultimately, Russia."

Grain

After wine comes grain. Evidence comes from a dozen villages scattered from Aquitaine to the Camargue. Let us consider for a moment the graphic representation of these data. First, in three villages there was a "break" in grain production beginning in 1635. The decline in grain tithe deliveries, modest at first, became frankly alarming after 1675, by which time it matched the decline in the olive oil and wine tithes in the same districts. It serves to confirm, therefore, a general decline in agricultural production in the last quarter of the century.

At Cuxac, in the Narbonne region, there were also signs of a certain malaise beginning in the years 1630–35. But in the case of this village, the situation returned to normal (if just barely) under Colbert. The real decline did not get under way until 1682. From that date until 1740, when our documentation comes to an end, the curve remained constantly depressed.

In summary, grain production in the four villages showed no signs of faltering under Colbert. It preserved, in that period, a solid and sometimes prosperous position. The brutal plunge did not begin until about 1675–85; it lasted half a century and was concomitant with that of wine. In reality (despite a slight animation around 1700–1705), the grain tithes would not actually link up with the "eighteenth-century" growth cycle before 1730. It seems, in fact, that in the cases just cited one is in the presence of a characteristic set of curves, at least for the part of the Midi stretching approximately from the Rhône to the Garonne; one notes the decline of 1675–85 and the "floor" of 1680–1720—the latter a period of stagnation marked by the end of land reclamation, by the death of the pioneer spirit, and by a general retreat of arable. This is precisely the evolution that one encounters in the extensive tithe records of the Camargue, which supplied Arles with its grain for export. The mass of tithe revenues at Arles in a normal year rose from 2,160 *setiers* to 2,500 *setiers* between 1613 and 1665; it fell to 1,640 *setiers* in 1687–91 and then to 1,370 *setiers* around 1712. The last quarter of the seventeenth century was a turning point, and the decline was permanent.

It is now necessary to try to characterize this crisis in grain production, which was almost everywhere in evidence beginning about 1675–80. First, it was a real crisis—not semifictitious, as was the case one hundred years earlier at the time of the antitithe strikes. In the 1680's, the decade of the Revocation, the tithes were faithfully handed over, and if they declined they did so because of the failure of production, not the sabotage of the producer. It was a grave crisis. The tithes in some instances fell below their sixteenth-century and even their fifteenth-century levels.

It was a complex crisis. In the beginning, around 1680, the decline was provoked by an unlucky series of poor harvests. The terrible droughts of 1680 and the following years carved deep notches in the curves. However, the drought passed but the depression in the curves of cereal production persisted. The accidents of climate, therefore, as often happens, only served to provoke the crisis; they brought into play deep-seated, human causes more lasting than themselves.

Finally, the crisis was late in coming. Wine production collapsed beginning about 1650–60. The production of cereals in half the known villages resisted for almost another twenty years; it did not begin to slump generally before 1675. A similar disparity evidently reflects distortions in the price structure. If the volume of the vintages collapsed well before that of the harvests, it was because the price of wine declined earlier and above all because it declined much farther than the price of grain. Compared to the winegrower, the pariah of the Colbertian deflation, it was natural that the wheat grower—less sorely tried by declining prices—should cut a better figure at least for a certain time.

But it was not just a question of the *mercuriales*. In this region, wine and grain belonged not only to two different price systems but also to two different stages of economic development. Wine, in the seventeenth century, was already quite intimately involved in a certain market economy. It was therefore affected, like today's products, by all the caprices of the marketplace. For the winegrower the decline in prices spelled disaster.

On the contrary, in the Mediterranean Midi, a lean, dry region that was sometimes a cereal exporter but more often a cereal importer, grain was still ensnared to a greater extent in a traditional subsistence economy of local autoconsumption. The French Midi was not Brie or Poland. It is enough to read d'Aguesseau; in 1670 the wheat or rye of Languedoc was little traveled —"It was consumed at home." There were cases of local transfers from mountain district to mountain district or from the plains to the mountains. A little grain was exported by way of Bordeaux. But, as the intendant notes, the essential was still local consumption within the borders of each diocese. The great circuits of cereal exports (Toulouse-Bordeaux-Antilles, Toulouse-Narbonne-Barcelona) were not set up until the eighteenth century.

Under these conditions, to study the tithe in grain in the seventeenth century is to take a deep sounding in the calm waters of subsistence agriculture. This sector of the economy resisted the Colbertian price decline for a considerable time, which indeed is what one would expect, since a large portion of grain production never reached the market at all. Such a salutary inertia could continue for twenty years or more, but in the long run the persistent absence of profitability, the burden of fixed charges and expenses, and, finally, the repercussions of the demographic regression just beginning brought about, in their turn, the collapse of the family economy based on cereal production.

In short, the decay of wine growing was an early reflection of market stagnation. The decay of grain growing, beginning in 1680, was followed, or accompanied, by a much more serious phenomenon: the declining trend in population.

Olive Oil

The price of olive oil was sheltered from the forces of deflation after 1660. It held up better than the price of grain and much better than the price of wine. The purchasing power of the olive grower under Colbert was revalued in terms of bread, wine, and meat. This price was steady because olive oil, besides being a major item of local consumption, was also disposed of through select and, it seems, stable outlets. Even more widely traveled than wine, it was being marketed, around 1670, a good distance to the north. The oil of Uzès was shipped as far as Lyons and Paris by road and via the Rhône; the oil of Agde went overland by cart to Toulouse and from there by canal boat down the Garonne to Bordeaux, whence it was shipped by sea to England, Holland, or the Paris trade network. Thanks to market stimuli, the decade of the 1660's was prosperous for the olive, as evidenced by the olive oil tithes from six different villages. A common upsurge beginning in 1630–35 raised all six curves to a low maximum for olive oil production situated in the period 1660–70. It was a "low" summit because in reality it barely equalled or sometimes just surpassed certain earlier maxima already obtained on the long production curves of the sixteenth century. Such as it was, this low maximum of olive oil production during the first decade of Colbertism was not without significance. It attests to a sustained local demand—for cooking, soapmaking, and cloth manufacture—and to a certain foreign demand as well. This happy age culminated in 1670 with a bumper olive harvest, one of the best of the entire multisecular series.

But then, following the high point of 1670–72, something went haywire. A sort of lethargy set in—a listlessness (already noted in the case of wine and cereals). The olive oil curves level off and slowly decline. After 1680 the decline became accentuated in most of the olive-growing regions, and it continued right up to the bad years of the decade of 1700.

Certain events rendered this decadence irreversible. The freezes of the decade of the 1690's had already ravaged the orchards and contributed to a rise in prices. The winter of 1709 completely destroyed the olive plantations of Languedoc. By a fortuitous mischance, an intense cold wave in late January descended on trees which were gorged with water from the heavy rains of the previous months. All the trees died, impaled on spears of ice. It was a perfect example of a superdetermined catastrophe, an extremely rare conjuncture of independent causal series such as occurs once every two or three centuries. The olive oil tithes, in any case, had never since 1480 registered a similar disaster. In 1709 all the curves are interrupted, and for almost the space of a generation there were no further tithe collections. The new olive trees—saplings or graftings on the crippled trunks—would not begin producing until 1723 (and then only a few jars) and sometimes not until 1740. The renewed olive oil curves limped along at deplorably low levels which about 1740–80 were still well below those of the sixteenth and seventeenth centuries.

The worst thing was that for some twenty or thirty years (1709–35) the olive plantations of Mediterranean France ceased to exist. Now, in that interval structures shifted, new positions were staked out, and markets were lost. The olive oil of Cadiz, the Levant, the Morea, and Crete invaded the kitchens and soapworks of Provence. This time the olive plantations of Languedoc would never recover their former splendor.

Thus, the wine, grain, and olive oil harvests all tended to decline. The movement was general after 1680, and about 1700–10 the entire range of food crop production collapsed at once, like a geological formation. Did a similar disaster overtake livestock production, that is, stock raising?

Livestock

The *carnencs* (tithes on livestock—above all, sheep) disclose two distinct types of evolution, one rural and the other suburban. First, let us examine the rural type: at Moussan (in rolling, hilly country) and in other villages stock raising, after experiencing important fluctuations, attained a sort of maximum around 1657–60 and then abruptly collapsed. The nominal curves of the *carnencs*, which were farmed out for a money rent, were plunging, up to 1685, much more steeply than the price curves for dressed meat. This was the sign of a serious reduction of herds.

What brought on the crisis was an economic malaise and above all the epizootic diseases of 1676 (pox) and 1682 (plague). The ravaged and decimated herds produced considerably less manure, and this deficiency of fertilizer helps to explain, in turn, the drop in food crop production (olive oil and grain) at Moussan around 1675.

Later, the village herds were reconstituted, and about 1700 the curves of the *carnencs* at Moussan began to mount once more. It was a modest rise measured in real prices. In fact, the number of sheep in the eighteenth century just managed to match the figures for the reign of Louis XIII, and at best it remained well below the ceilings established during the reigns of Louis XII and Francis I, which were the golden age of stock raising in the south of France.

What were the reasons, in the midst of the universal Malthusianism, for this particular crisis in stock farming during the middle and late reign of Louis XIV? One perceives causes of various sorts; meat prices (largely pegged to grain prices between 1650 and 1720) were not sufficiently remunerative to meet fixed charges (taxes, salt for the stock, and so on), but above all, livestock, the ancient symbol of agrarian wealth, fell victim to the logic of poverty. After 1660 indebtedness was the scourge of the reign; creditors, first off, seized the stock, a four-footed forfeit that was easy to take and easy to sell (witness the repeated interdictions that were vainly renewed against the practice). In a general way, the debt-ridden late-seventeenth-century peasant's lack of capital and savings was translated into a shortage of stock. To "capitalize" meant to increase one's "chattels" (livestock). In addition, the demographic regression and the crisis in living standards in the last decades of the reign (1690–1710) would restrict the outlets for meat and for the stock raisers.

The second trend or type of evolution was quite different. Side by side with the unhealthy livestock industry that we have just touched on there also existed, paradoxically, under Louis XIV and the Regency, an extremely healthy one. It flourished in those middle-sized towns of Languedoc which managed, in the midst of the general contraction, to avoid the demographic decline and to preserve bourgeois wealth and the old standard of living. At Béziers, Narbonne, and also at Arles, the herds had already grown in size under Louis XIII. The process continued, despite brief arrests and passing difficulties, under Louis XIV, with some impressive rates of increase. The early sixteenth-century records were actually bettered in these territories in the first half of the eighteenth century. For the first time in these privileged centers, the herds burst the Malthusian bonds that had contained their growth for over a century and a half.

The behavior of the towns, in short, was atypical. At the same time that sheep farming in the rural countryside stagnated or regressed, the urban herds, coagulated around the chief towns, multiplied. It was a particular sort of evolution dependant on the specific wealth of the towns of this period, which were avid for good meat and ringed with slaughter pens. The town butchers were monopolists who bought up the livestock of the countryside for leagues around. The rise of urban stock farming is to be attributed to these favorable but exceptional structures, altogether nonexistent in the purely rural districts. Interesting though it was, the success of that one sector could neither mask nor compensate for the overall regression of agricultural income as reflected in the general movement of the money tithes beginning in 1675–80.

Real Aggregate Income: Final Decline, Tendential Inertia

With the money tithes, which are true indices of aggregate income, we finally dispose of the capital source for the reigns of Louis XIV and Louis XV—the source that serves to integrate all the others and that recapitulates, in the overall evolution of agricultural income, the different price and harvest movements and the data on stock farming, wine growing, cereal culture, and so on. What we actually possess, in this case, is a complete description of the trend of agricultural production, a weighted price index in that it simultaneously concerns the portion of the harvests that reached the market and the portion retained by the peasants, farm laborers, and landowners in the giant fund reserved for sowing seed and family consumption.

Let us therefore consider the charts of this gross nominal income. Let us convert the latter into gross real income at constant prices—for example, by means of its conversion into the pilot value of wheat. What does the operation tell us?[1] First, there was a fairly lively rise in the real product up to Colbert's ministry. In the first half of the seventeenth century, agricultural production (measured in wheat) mounted very slowly. Quite suddenly, beginning in 1655, some of the old records began to fall. The difficulties of the Fronde were forgotten. The last five years of Mazarin's ministry—the Fouquet years—were a period of vigorous growth. About 1660–65, at the latest, a sort of ceiling was reached—a relatively high ceiling, in fact. Compared to the early seventeenth century, tithed agricultural production had increased between 50 and 80 percent (but compared to the early sixteenth century, the increase was considerably less).

In other words, for the first time in 150 years the gross income curve (nominal) broke through the ceiling of nominal prices. For the first time in that fortunate decade the global income in real terms of five hundred villages scattered from Narbonne to Nîmes exceeded by a significant figure (from 30 to 40 percent, depending on the diocese) the records set a century earlier under Francis I or Henry II. Had the more-than-a-century-old Malthusian cycle been broken? If so, the real meaning of Riquet's canal project and Colbert's labors becomes clear.

The momentary increase in production of this brief period of expansion was very favorable to living standards, particularly in the case of autoconsumption at the family level, but it was not attended by a rise in productivity or by the diversification of crops (on the contrary, wine growing decayed). The increased supply up to about 1670 of the traditional farm products (grain, olive oil, and sometimes sheep) therefore weighed heavily on agricultural prices, which were already depressed, without any corresponding diminution in costs. For this reason the profits from agricultural enterprise vanished (as we shall see) in the decade of the 1670's.

---

[1] Cf. Joseph Goy and Emmanuel Le Roy Ladurie, *Les Fluctuations du produit de la Dîme: Conjoncture décimale et domaniale de la fin du Moyen Age au XVIIIᵉ siècle* (Paris, 1972).

The structures destined to play host to this expansion, in other words, remained Malthusian in character. The cultivators, in order to protect their income, could not indefinitely compensate for the decline in prices by an increase in production. They soon found themselves faced with ruin. The forces of stagnation and, finally, of regression prevailed.

Let us turn again to questions of production; the high levels attained about 1660–65 lasted for some ten or fifteen years (thanks to which, with local exceptions, it was a period without food scarcities), but the factors of progress had already ceased to function. Production leveled off after 1665 because the producers stopped investing in a significant way or because new investments were characterized by declining profitability, or none at all.

Then, beginning in 1680, came the irremissible decline of the gross product. The major, all-inclusive curves of the money tithes serve to confirm, in this respect, the fragmentary data of the tithes in kind studied previously. The decline was especially severe in the villages of the Narbonne and Béziers countrysides. After an impressive drop in the decades of the 1680's and 1690's, which was followed by a brief improvement in 1700–1705, the tithes of these rural priories in the period 1710–15—during the darkest hours of Louis XIV's reign—fell to 50 percent of their real value in the age of Colbert. This was even lower than in the days of Henry IV and Louis XIII. It is not to be wondered at. The diocese of Narbonne—I will return to this subject later—was one of the hardest hit by rural desertions in the early eighteenth century.

The decline was less severe, if still very pronounced, in the countryside of Montpellier and Nîmes. In this case, one is forced to invoke a geographic inequality of economic decline. The regions of Nîmes and Montpellier boasted woolen and silk industries and, thanks to this fact, disposed of supplementary income, of compensatory activities, and of stabilizing counterweights, whereas in the purely rural countryside of Narbonne and Béziers these cushioning factors were absent, and the agrarian crisis ran its full course with nothing to offset it.

In terms of the secular movement, the dominant tendency of the seventeenth century and up to 1720, despite some broad fluctuations, was one of inertia in agricultural production. The regression of the closing years of the reign reduced the gross product (after the brief Colbertian upswing) to its starting level of the seventeenth century or the sixteenth century or even earlier. Vauban leads us back to Sully. Was it a return to a golden age? No, more like a descent into hell, because in a hundred years population, costs, and needs had all increased. The decline of the gross product—its return to the depressed level of an earlier age—implies, due to the structural changes that had occurred in the interval, the buildup of certain intolerable pressures. These could only be relieved by a deflation of population, by a "good" bleeding that would restore the equilibrium.

For a shorter, intrasecular interval, the retreat of the gross product (1675–1720) serves to define a chronology thanks to which it is possible, at least in the case of one region, to settle an old dispute—Voltaire versus Vauban, Voltaire versus Boisguillebert. The *Détail de la France* and the *Dîme royale* fix 1660 as the critical date that marked the beginning of the decline in land income (by 500 million) and also of mass underconsumption, as registered at the market fairs, the wine shops, and the butcher shops. Voltaire rejected this thesis. "Boisguillebert," he said in so many words, "is nothing but a fool to claim that everything was in a state of decadence after 1660. Just the opposite is true. France had never been so prosperous as she was from the death of Mazarin to the war of 1689. As for mass poverty, it was caused by the war and the heavy taxes after 1690."

When all is said and done, Voltaire was not wrong in correcting Boisguillebert and in attributing a certain vitality to France under Colbert. In the Midi, at least, the rise in production largely compensated for the decline in prices in the first period of Colbertism. The *real* decline in farm income did not actually begin before about 1675, fifteen years later than the date assigned by Boisguillebert but fifteen years earlier than Voltaire imagined.

Could the correct date not be the one suggested in a text of 1684 by the Venetian ambassador who had visited the provinces? "Since the beginning of the last war, land values have declined more than one-third through the impoverishment and the defection of the population, aggravated by the vexations practiced in expelling the Calvinists." The point of inflection indicated by the Venetian diplomat was the year 1672. Our curves (quinquennial) give 1675; the maritime provinces of Brittany and Guyenne, which were so vulnerable to negative trade fluctuations, rose in revolt in 1674–75. These concordances are suggestive. They fix a chronology and indicate, in passing, the provocative role of the Dutch war, which was disastrous for trade, in sparking the recession of the gross product. The war with Holland caused the decline of French exports and accentuated the preexisting monetary famine.

For all that, our chronological compromise is valid above all for the southern regions. In certain provinces of the north, the real decline of agriculture could have begun much earlier—by 1650–60 and perhaps even with the Fronde or the Thirty Years War. The tithe series for the north, once exploited, will supply the exact dates. For the south one must insist on this massive decline in overall production beginning in 1675–80. A similar diminution in the quantities produced was very probably attended by a decline in the quantities bought and sold, that is, by a fall in the *volume* of transactions. Otherwise, how does one explain the general regression at the close of the century of cash crops like wine, olive oil, and silk?

In all likelihood, the *number* of transactions and the velocity of monetary circulation also diminished. In this connection, we dispose of a series of registers, the *contrôles des actes* of the notaries. I have been able to inspect such records for several important registry offices extending from the Cévennes to the sea. These offices inventory, between 1691 and 1789, more than 800,000 notaries' acts, including wills and marriage agreements but also and above all loan contracts and transactions involving personal and real property. The annual or triennial curves constructed from the data provided by these registers begin a little late but give us the trend nevertheless. There was a fall in the number of transactions from 1690 to 1709, a minimal "floor" from 1709 to 1717, and a slow reascent thereafter from Law to Turgot.

The years 1709–17, in short, were the bottom of the depression—the tragic decade when in the farming regions the quantities produced, the quantities marketed, and the number of transactions all fell to their lowest levels.

Terres Mortes

If agricultural production regressed at the end of the seventeenth century, it was first of all because yields were falling off once again. About 1660–70, at the height of a grain cycle, wheat returned four or five for one and much more (six, seven, or eight for one) on good land, according to the exhaustive Languedocian inquest of Intendant d'Aguesseau. Fifteen years later, in the midst of the agrarian debacle (1683–87), the good land of Coussergues (in the region of Béziers) returned less than four for one. It was a regression that set the cultivators of the region back one hundred years, with yields that were not much better than those of the miserable civil war harvests (not even three for one about 1580–85).

How is one to explain this decline in productivity? The cause was probably not so much the poverty of the land as the poverty of the cultivators, who lacked working capital, credit, and livestock, and therefore also manure, as the land engrossers sometimes learned to their sorrow. In 1706, for example, a parish priest by the name of Albouze acquired a property near Narbonne. The expert who later appraised it for him reported that the land was worked out and infertile "because it had not been manured for a very long time."

It was not only fertilizer that was lacking. In fact, the entire cycle of agricultural labors was sabotaged in the decade of the 1680's for want of cash. Take the example (one out of a dozen) of the tenant farmer Grangeant at Maurin in 1681. He neglected to have his wheat fields weeded, dispensing only sixty *livres* for this purpose instead of the four hundred or five hundred *livres* required. As a result the fields were invaded by weeds which would seed and multiply the following year. The same Grangeant "forgot" a plowing in 1681 for lack of money to pay his farmhands. In 1682 he "forgot" to thresh his grain. One encounters similar behavior on the part of most of the impoverished tenant farmers of the end of the century who were irascible in regard to their landlords and without means and without conscience in regard to their fields. It is not surprising, in these circumstances, that yields, harvests, and tithes all declined to ridiculously low levels.

Today's neglected arable is tomorrow's waste. At the same time that the tithes were plunging and that the *Roi-Soleil* was growing old, the evidence of abandoned holdings multiplied.

The actual signal for the wholesale retreat of cultivation was the scorching drought of 1680 and the following years. The harvests burned up, but because of grain imports from Aquitaine, the Levant, and the Maghreb, prices were little affected. This was more than enough to ruin the farmers caught in a squeeze between poor harvests and low prices, who were also incapable, for lack of capital and above all for lack of incentive, of reconverting to a profitless viticulture. This time, the examples of deserted holdings are almost beyond counting.

The locality called Les Claux, situated on the slopes of the Gard in a region of rolling hills, is well documented in the *compoix*. It was virgin land (or land that had recovered its virginity) at the end of the fifteenth-century wave of desertions. Between 1500 and 1610 the zone was reclaimed through *rompudes*—broad wheat fields, low dividing walls of stone, and cleared forest land. Numerous vines were planted there under Louis XIII. Now, in the *compoix* of 1682 Les Claux had begun to return to its former state, and *hermes* insinuated themselves between the vines and the stone walls. The long process, which was to culminate in today's total abandonment of these marginal soils, was under way.

The true center of destruction in the decade of the 1680's was farther to the east in the dioceses of Béziers, Saint-Pons, Agde, and, above all, Narbonne and Albi. Ravaged by drought and heavily in debt, these zones failed to pay two-thirds of their tailles in 1680 and more than half, equal to £253,000, in 1681. Debts and arrears accumulated, and the debt-ridden taxpayers preferred to abandon their holdings and decamp. The scenario was much the same all over the province. The taxes owed on abandoned properties, "which were increasing day by day" in 1701–1702, were paid, paradoxically, by the body of taxpayers who remained active. The productive land paid for the nonproductive. The dead clung to the living. A cumulative process of desertion was set in motion, because the added tax burden led to further peasant indebtedness and new abandonments. Subsidiary factors—the military call-ups, the emigration of Protestant landowners, and the agitation of the *"fanatiques"* (1702–1705)—hastened certain desertions. But let us not forget that notwithstanding the misfortunes of the Huguenots it was the Catholic dioceses (Narbonne)—economically the most depressed—that were the hardest hit.

In 1708–16 (with the curves of production and transactions at their lowest levels) a critical point seems to have been reached; there was a shortage of money, land income was eroded away by heavy tailles inequitably assessed, and insolvent village collectors went cheerfully off to gaol at the first summons from the tax officials. Entire communities prepared to abandon their lands, sometimes as a form of simple blackmail but sometimes in actual fact. In the mountain districts—the Vivarais in 1711 and the diocese of Castres in 1714—new red patches of land invaded by waste appeared on the map.

Finally, in 1715 came the slow thaw of the Regency and of Fleury's ministry. The movement of desertion subsided, and the wounds began to heal. The abandoned land was recovered. The last mentions of deserted holdings were—depending on the diocese—in 1728, 1732–33, and 1739–41, at the latest. The farming frontier began to advance again, and the *Wüstungen* that had excited the public mind between 1690 and 1720 were forgotten.

CHAPTER

2

The New Demographic Depression

Land desertion was an evil associated with the decline of the gross product, but it was also a symptom of something else. If a diocese like Albi counted a quantity of "abandoned lands," it was because the villages had been "reduced to a few inhabitants . . . by affliction and mortalities." Was it death itself, then, that created and extended the red zones of deserted holdings? Was the demographic conjuncture, the depopulation of the rural communities, what lay behind the movement of abandonment? It is necessary to reconsider the statistical history of population.

Parish Registers and Easter Communicants

First, we have the aggregate statistics on Easter communicants which permit us to situate the more refined series of data from the parish registers in their proper context. (These I shall consider subsequently.) Approximately every ten years the bishop of Montpellier, like all his colleagues, made the rounds of his diocese. In every parish he asked the priest the capital question of religious sociology: "How many communicants do you have here?" The answers—150, 820, 982, or whatever—are of no great interest in themselves, but the succession of answers forms a time series running from 1657 to 1772 for a hundred-odd parishes. Thanks to this massive sampling, it is possible to delineate the inflections of a secular trend of rising and declining population.

First, the question of method: in calculating the final averages, one must eliminate a certain number of villages with a majority or a large minority of Protestants—the pseudoconversions of the late seventeenth century tend to vitiate the statistics. This leaves the Catholic villages, where the figures do have a demographic significance. In the rural areas, in fact, in the period under study, religious observance, or at least Easter communion—barring a

few scandalous exceptions—was all but universal. The noncommunicant
was quickly tracked down and denounced by village vigilantes. As a rule,
he was not a strong character but a simple soul, a marginal case, the village
idiot. In reality, as far as the priest was concerned, a genuine noncommunicant was inconceivable. Leaving aside Huguenots, Jews, and new converts,
anyone who had attained the age of reason (at seven to ten years of age) was
ipso facto a communicant for the record, even in the extremely rare case of
one who in fact missed Easter communion. "About fifty communicants;
all have satisfied their pascal obligation save one," a village priest noted
in 1741. Such statistics are sweeping but demographically exhaustive.

I have composed a table of the priests' responses to their bishops' inquiries
concerning the number of communicants.[1] Reading down are the names of
the villages in the diocese of Montpellier (ninety-eight in number, not
counting those of the Huguenots). Reading across are the successive dates of
the thirteen documented pastoral visitations between 1657 and 1772. Each
figure (number of communicants) in the table refers to a given village and
a given year. The ideal would be to add up, for each of the thirteen years, the
number of communicants in all the villages taken together. One would obtain from the successive totals a statistical series over a century long covering ninety-eight villages. But such a simple procedure is impossible. For
each of these years, certain villages are missing from the list. The bishops, in
their annual rounds, visited only a portion of their parishes. The chronological cross-sections are never complete.

We must therefore forget about absolute totals and limit ourselves to
isolating the trend by calculating indices and averages. One problem is what
year to assign the index 100. In any given year of pastoral visits chosen arbitrarily for this purpose, no matter how complete, some villages are necessarily absent. Let us agree, then, that the index 100 be applied in each case to
that year of the "seventeenth century" (the documented interval from 1657
to 1711) in which the maximum number of communicants were recorded
in relation to the visits preceding and those following. The peak might
occur in 1657 in one village, in 1677 in another, in 1704 in still another, and
so on. The diocesan average of all the village indices, by year of pastoral
visit (1657, 1665, and so on up to 1772), will indicate, for all the known
parishes taken together, the relative distance from the demographic "seventeenth-century" maximum for the diocese on a rising or falling scale. This
diocesan maximum, which approaches the index 100 but always falls short,

[1] See the original French edition, Volume II, *annexe* 18, pp. 773–74.

will itself correspond to the year of a pastoral visit in which the largest number of villages attain an index of 100 and in which the diocesan average of all these indices is, for this reason, at its highest point. Thanks to these various calculations, one obtains for the period 1657–1772 a series of successive indices for the diocese which can be tabulated as follows:

	AVERAGE DIOCESAN INDEX OF THE NUMBER OF EASTER COMMUNICANTS	NUMBER OF "OLD CATHOLIC" VILLAGES VISITED
1657	81	37
1665	81	29
1671	89	22
1677	90	89
1687	87	25
1690	86	90
1699	82	85
1704	86	40
1708	83	15
1711	80	52
1741	74	76
1756	77	26
1772	89	48

The first essential point of inflection to be noted on this curve is the summit in 1677 coming at the end of a rise. There follows a more or less continuous decline, interrupted by a brief upturn in 1704, which leads step by step (1687, 1690, 1699, 1711) to the unmistakable trough of 1741. Thereafter, the curve picks up again and almost returns to the maximum of 1677 by 1772.

The cardinal fact is the secular minimum of 1741. The number of communicants had declined by 18 percent since 1677. One inhabitant out of five in the Catholic countryside had disappeared.

In general, the demographic decline began in 1677, especially in the coastal areas. Between 1677 and 1687–90, forty-one parishes reported a decline in the number of Easter communicants, while thirteen showed no change. On the other hand, in this same interval thirty parishes continued, under Louvois, the demographic advance registered under Colbert; it was only beginning in 1690—even in 1700 or 1710 in certain cases—that these thirty were swept up in the general decline, sinking to a low point in the middle of the eighteenth century like the rest. These slight chronological discrepancies are not without significance. Compared to the clear, sharp, abrupt nature of the economic decline beginning in 1675–80, the population decline was hesitant and confused. It was often under way by 1680, but sometimes not until ten or twenty years later. In viewing these two different types of movement, one is probably justified in distinguishing the inductive element (the state of the economy) from the effect induced (the demographic decline). This naturally does not preclude the possibility of reciprocal causality, mutual repercussions, and interrelations.

Does the overall curve for the diocese, with its characteristic highs in 1677 and lows in the years 1730–40, reflect a more general trend? As a matter of fact it does happen to parallel the movement of population in neighboring Catalonia and Provence quite closely. In Catalonia, beginning precisely in 1677, a new agrarian phase opened. Droughts multiplied. Grasshoppers devoured the crops. The population was ravaged by epidemics, famine, and, finally, war. These losses would not be made good until the great demographic leap of the Enlightenment. In Provence, too, the population curve describes a slightly negative fluctuation about 1690–1725. Catalonia, Provence, and Languedoc, then, shared the same fate, and a demographic chronology emerges which was common to all the regions bordering the Gulf of Lion.

The curves of Easter communicants not only confirm and accord with earlier and parallel studies, but also furnish certain precisions of capital importance concerning the economy itself. The communicant was at the same time an adult worker, or at any rate a working child of ten or more, good for heavy tasks at low pay. The decrease in the number of communicants corresponds essentially, therefore, to the decline of the *active* population, of the number of potential workers, in other words. Such a decline struck an additional blow at production. The preexisting economic crisis was aggravated by the demographic crisis which it engendered and by the growing shortage of labor. The effect reacted upon the cause.

The Declining Trend: Parish Registers

A number of local curves, based on parish registers, serve to confirm the overall tendency traced by the curve of pascal communicants and at the same time suggest certain shades of difference. We shall confine ourselves, in the present abridged edition, to two topical and typical examples.

Montpeyroux was a village of olive growers and mule drivers—rhubarb dealers who in the eighteenth century obtained their supplies at Lorient or

Nantes and retailed them at Marseilles. At Montpeyroux baptisms and marriages began to mount with Henry IV, culminating in the years 1674–90 (when there were fifty to sixty baptisms and ten to fifteen marriages each year). In the decade of the 1690's death intervened in force, setting off a demographic decline. The low-water mark of baptisms and marriages was registered in the years 1735–50. There followed at last a new advance under Louis XVI; marriages and births were more numerous, and burials were rarer. At Viols-le-Fort it was the same, with a long decline in marriages after 1700 down to a minimum in 1747.

Poles of Resistance: The Towns

Certain wealthy villages and certain active sectors seem to have been inoculated against depopulation. These immunized zones included the suburban countryside. The villages that successfully resisted the movement were often close to an important town like Montpellier, whose own demographic vitality kept them alive and vigorous. The fortunate villagers carted wood to the town or found work there. Their wives did the townswomen's wash or nursed their infants. Their modest earnings from these activities helped tide the rural classes over until the harvest and enabled the village population to weather the demographic crisis.

The towns themselves managed to do quite well during the period of adversity. The large port village of Sète had passed from zero to three thousand inhabitants by 1735. The growth of Montpellier continued up to 1720, then leveled off until about 1750. These happy urban exceptions are to be found all along the Gulf of Lion, where the phenomenon sometimes assumed considerable importance. Barcelona and Marseilles, practically untouched by the agricultural depression, were also spared the demographic recession after 1680, thanks, no doubt, to the rural exodus which replenished their numbers.

Gross Product and Rural Population

Let us ignore these exceptions for the moment and return to the question of the overall tendencies. The two main facts, in order of time, were the decline of the gross product by the late 1670's and the decay of rural population beginning in 1685, 1690, or 1700. Does the time lag signify that an accommodation was taking place? In fact, it looks very much as if population was adjusting painfully to the conditions of a contracting economy. The basic problem, from the present point of view, is that of the actual mechanisms involved. How does one pass empirically, and concretely, from agriculture to demography, from the gross product to rural population? The mediator was, quite simply, death. At Montpeyroux and Cessenon, the phases of population decline (in the late seventeenth and early eighteenth centuries) were characterized by severe epidemics and broken by years of scarcity when deaths exceeded births.

What did people die of, or, more exactly, what did people die of in excess? In extreme cases, of hunger, but more often of malnutrition or dietary deficiencies. This type of death seems to have been frequent in the bad harvest years among the poorest classes (farm laborers and textile workers). This was the case in 1680 and 1694 during the two famine years that provoked and initiated the depopulation of Languedoc. Again in 1709–10 many people perished. The poor of Languedoc who managed to survive subsisted on millet, turnips, spring vegetables (beans), and, in the most desperate cases, grass—bread made of couch grass and sheep's entrails.

It seems reasonable to speak of a return of the specter of hunger beginning in the decade of the 1680's. This was the case in the north and center of the realm, where the famines of 1694 and 1709 ended thirty years of relative abundance. In the Midi the chronology of hunger, despite shades of difference, reveals a similar trend. It was the long decline of the gross product which, among other factors, explains the growing crisis of subsistence. The effects of poor harvests are benign when agriculture is in a prosperous state. They are devastating when farm production is chronically depressed even in normal years.

But hunger does not explain everything—far from it. People also die, if more subtly, of contagious diseases which flourish in famine years. The undernourished make good germ carriers because their resistance to pathogenic organisms is low. Subsistence crises are almost always endowed with an epidemic multiplier, as arbitrary as it is unpredictable.

A priest in the region of Narbonne described this fatal concatenation of famine and disease in 1693–94. Nature, he noted on August 3, 1694, has been sick for the past seven or eight years because of the wars, crop failures, and contagions. In the year 1694, "It is hunger that has caused the most havoc." The inhabitants endured it in their homes until the death of their father, mother, or children. Then they abandoned their accursed village, their Massif Central or their Rouergue. They were "like skeletons or specters" who wandered far from their parishes, seeking the means to prolong their listless lives, thanks to the charity of good-hearted people. They carried disease wherever they went, especially the *purpre*, which "spreads like wild-fire," invades all the houses, "frequently infecting everybody who dwells therein," and causes much death and many miscarriages which kill simul-taneously "the mother and her fruit."

History, then, has more than one trick in its bag when it comes to adjust-ing population to declining resources. The depopulation, which affected a majority of parishes impoverished by the depression, was a complex phe-nomenon: it was dominated by high mortality; it was induced, secondarily, by late marriages and even in a few marginal cases by contraception; and it was aggravated, finally, by emigration to the towns from the decaying rural localities—or to the army.

In this case, depopulation was late—later in general than in Alsace or Bur-gundy, the region of Beauvais, or the Loire Valley, where the plagues of 1630, the horrors of the Thirty Years War or the Fronde, and the famine of 1661 often emptied the villages of their last inhabitants prematurely.

The demographic decline was, as a rule, of quite moderate proportions (18 percent in the rural districts on the average in two generations, 1677–1741). In certain situations, however—in the villages or districts the most cruelly afflicted—the human losses were much more serious. They were se-rious enough in extreme cases (a severe epidemic accompanied by large-scale emigration) to wipe some villages and hamlets completely off the map.

3

From Land Subdivision to Land Concentration

From demography in a strict sense—the demography of disappearing hamlets and nondisappearing villages—we must now pass to cadastral demography as a first approach to problems relating to the diverse apportionment of aggregate income.

Cadastral Demography: The Decrease in the Number of Taille Payers

How did the number of taille payers—that is, property owners—evolve during the downward part of the cycle beginning, approximately, in 1675–80? Did it generally parallel the number of people as it had done in the preceding period? Once again, we shall let the figures speak for themselves, both during the period of contraction and also, for the sake of comparison, during the subsequent upturn of the eighteenth century. The data in question come from thirty-two different villages.[1]

There exist, within this group, wide divergences in the respective trends due to local conditions and also to the insufficient chronological continuity of the series, which are arbitrarily interrupted for the various localities according to the random survival of their tax records. Still, over the long run it is clear that these different series all belong to the same family. They testify to a deceleration, then, at the end of the seventeenth century and to a decline of the taxpaying populations which begins in 1670, 1680, 1690, 1700, or 1710, depending on the village (and leaving aside certain precursors like Souabès, where the collapse occurred as early as 1630–40).

The number of taille payers, which had generally been growing very slowly since Henry IV or Louis XII, leveled off about 1680–90. Thereafter, at best it stagnated, and at worst it collapsed. The demography of the tax-

---

[1] See the table published in the original French edition, page 567.

paying population, in the present case, does nothing more than confirm and reflect, with a time lag of ten to twenty years, the effects of plain demography. Turning to the parish registers for verification, one finds that the decline suggested by the cadastral data is, in fact, borne out by the demographic statistics based on civil status and the number of communicants.

But the cadastres and books of the taille are more than a simple control. They also help us to enlarge and develop the conclusions that emerge from our purely demographic studies. In the first place, these studies can now be seen in their proper perspective, in their secular context. In fact, in the light of the *compoix*, which stretch far into the past, one perceives that the significance of the demographic regression which began about 1680 lies well outside itself, well outside its strict chronological limits.

It marked the end of an era—the end of a powerful, mounting wave of population which had originated under Louis XII and which would culminate and recede under Louis XIV. Graph 1 on page 317 summarizes the tax census figures for various villages from the fifteenth century to the eighteenth century—figures derived from *compoix*, books of the taille, and master land-tax registers. It gives the true measure of that long tide of taxpayers which, beginning at low water in the fifteenth century, mounted rapidly in the sixteenth century up to about 1570; continued to rise, but at a less lively rate, thereafter; was almost slack in the early reign of Louis XIV; receded slowly from the period 1680–1700 up to about 1750; and reversed itself again in 1770, beginning a powerful new rise which was destined to continue without interruption up to about 1870.

Between these two major demographic advances—the first lasting with diminishing force from the Renaissance to the Revocation and the second covering the nineteenth century from Turgot to Gambetta—the period 1680–1750 sometimes resembles a platform, often a trough, and at the very least a demographic pause. True, cadastral population did not plunge to the depths as it had at the end of the Middle Ages, but a negative fluctuation is nevertheless perceptible in the curves. It marked the end of a great cycle of demographic agrarian expansion which had persisted, with varying fortunes, for over a century and a half (from about 1500 to about 1680). The overall process is described by the ballistic arc of a series of curves. These curves, springing from the depths of the fifteenth century, stormed the Malthusian heights, leveled off, and, beginning in 1680–1700, curved downward as if drawn by an invisible magnet.

Reinforcing the Front Ranks

On the other hand, this broad chronology accords with a certain number of sociological facts. Thanks to the *compoix* and the books of the taille, one passes directly from the enumeration of people to the distribution of property—from the demographic trend to the shifting reality of land structures. In this domain, what was new, from the end of the seventeenth century, was a shift toward the bottom of the tables of landed property. From 1500 up to 1630, sometimes, and often up to 1680, the shift was toward the top, toward the microlandholdings. A persistent subdivision of property accompanied the more or less spirited rise in the peasant population.

After 1680, give or take a few years, one witnesses, in most cases, a reversal of this ancient, almost two-centuries-old tendency. The irresistible evolution shown in the tables was toward a reinforcement at the bottom. The petty properties were shipwrecked. The smallholders' plots were swallowed up by the middle taille payer and often, too, by the great or the very great. The reduction in the number of landowners worked to the detriment of the petty landlord and to the advantage of the more important by a sort of natural selection, which, from a statistical point of view, eliminated the weakest and the least endowed in the struggle for subsistence and profit.

Here we shall consider a single but perfectly typical example, the village of Saint-André-de-Sangonis, which possesses a superb series of data (see Table 3).[2] A master *compoix* of about 1636 gave birth to a whole progeny of successive taille rolls, excellent records which served to keep the master *compoix* up to date, which assigned to each taille payer his proper portion, and which reflected any changes in landownership without altering the aggregate assessment of 1636 (this remained fixed at a total figure of 1,307 cadastral pounds). These serviceable documents include a *brevette* of 1690, a "transcription of the *compoix*" dated 1726, and every year a new roll of the taille.

I have opted, in the case of this complete series, where such a choice is possible, for two chronological vantage points, one on the heights and one in the valley. The first is the year 1690, when the maximum local taille-paying population of 893 was recorded, and the second is the year 1749, when the number of taille payers (697, of whom 563 were natives) dropped

---

[2] See the numerous concordant examples (twenty-three in all) presented in the original French edition of this work, pages 571–81.

to its lowest level immediately prior to the upswing of the second half of the eighteenth century.

How were the 1,307 cadastral pounds—which constituted the total assessment of the *compoix* of Saint-André since its composition in 1636—distributed at these two turning points? In 1690, at the height of land subdivision, the table of landownership shows a shift toward the top compared to our previous set of statistics (1665). In 1749, on the contrary, there was a shift toward the bottom, toward concentration, in relation to 1690. The critical threshold, defined as usual by a comparison of the different columns, corresponds to landholdings with an individual assessed value of three *livres*.

Three *livres*, then, represents an upper limit in measuring the decline of the smallholder. Toward the top of the table there were 774 holdings valued at less than three *livres* in 1690 but only 555 in 1749. Two hundred nineteen *microfundia* had been swept away by the depression. But three *livres* also represents a lower limit with respect to the land ambitions of the better favored. Toward the bottom of the table, including that figure, there were 119 middle and big taille payers in 1690. Two generations later in 1749 their number had grown to 142. The 219 missing smallholds, therefore, had left room for the creation of 23 larger estates. Nine petty properties had produced one big property. The village, in short, was teeming with land engrossers in the middle of the eighteenth century.

They were of quite diverse sorts, depending on the hamlet in question. In the settlement of Cambous it was the notables—the local lord and the bailiff Léotard—who enlarged their domains between 1690 and 1749. The peasant proprietors, for their part, declined in numbers without, however, rounding out their holdings. Their number had contracted, but their properties had not been consolidated. Finally, the farm laborers, who were often part-time potters like the Cannet family, dwindled and disappeared from the cadastre. In the hamlet of Sainte-Brigitte the engrossers sprang from the people. Here it was the peasants and their cousins the teamsters (both of whom were cousins to the artisans) who consolidated the ragged land plots of the farm laborers. In other words, as is also demonstrated with monotonous regularity for other villages, the promoters of consolidation were socially diverse, but the phenomenon itself was characteristic—the common denominator of the period.

Finally, then, at the end of our series of monographs we are confronted with the problem of land concentration and its modern corollary—the appropriation of the land by the urban classes. From this viewpoint, the evolution of about 1700 did not exactly parallel that of the fifteenth century, during the previous great rural depression. At that time, from 1350 to 1450, land concentration was purely and simply the effect of the demographic collapse. Its results were sometimes even more striking than was later the case under Louis XIV. It led to the constitution of important estates, but the majority of these remained strictly in the hands of the rural classes: gentleman farmers or country priests, big peasants, "yeomen,"[3] or *frérèches*.

The land concentration of the late seventeenth century, which continued into the eighteenth, has some traits in common with the homologous episode of the waning Middle Ages, since it, too, was stimulated by a decline in the rural population (although less marked under Louis XIV than in the fifteenth century). But the comparison breaks down at this point. If some of the causes were the same, the social effects were quite different. The medieval episode was attended by a precipitous return to the land. The modern one was inseparable from the fortunate promotion of the urban patriciate—nobility, gentlemen of the robe, and bourgeoisie—who had embarked upon the conquest of the countryside. It was a lasting conquest, which, despite certain reversals, would leave its indelible imprint in the cadastres right up to the twentieth century.

[3] *Yeomen* in English in the French editions (tr. note).

CHAPTER

4

The Land Is No Longer Profitable

I have been describing up to this point a certain number of important, probably interrelated phenomena which were touched off successively or simultaneously: the decline of nominal prices, continued by that of metallic prices; the decline, much later, of the gross agricultural product; the retreat of population; and the decline of the peasant smallhold and the correlative rise of the large consolidated holding.

How does one explain this recession all along the line? The inquiry into determinants and processes involves a detailed analysis capable of elucidating changes in the vertical distribution of the gross product by superimposed levels of income. Once again, we shall have to speak of profits, rents, wages, and charges—and of the more or less corresponding social categories.

The task is difficult and more awkward than for the preceding periods because in the case of certain basic variables—entrepreneurial profit and agricultural wages—our sources, although suggestive and concrete, are now incomplete. The long series—which have served us so well—of direct farm leases, of mixed wages, and of wages in kind practically come to an end in 1660. Things become easier to describe but sometimes impossible to quantify. Certain facts, nevertheless, emerge clearly, first of all in the key domain of profit.

1665–72: The Death of Profit

After 1660, and especially after 1670, the agricultural product was still rising (for the time being), but its heart was not in the effort because profit was dead. This, at least, is what can be inferred from the long series of account books.

Take the budgets of the canons of Béziers and Montpellier. Receipts consisted essentially of tithes in money and hence of agricultural income in a

251

broad, representative, and weighted form. Expenditures went for church luxuries as well as private luxuries, salaries, fiscal charges (ecclesiastical tithes, the salt tax, the taille on nonchurch properties), and interest on loans. Under Louis XIII and still under Mazarin receipts exceeded expenditures one year out of two or two out of three. Year in, year out during the more or less fortunate seventeenth century the canons usually managed to turn a profit. This normal period came to an end in 1663 at Montpellier and in 1671 at Béziers. From that time until the close of the century the canons' budgets refused to balance, just like Colbert's and his successors'. It was a financial impasse—a continuing, regular deficit every year without exception. The canons' accounts did not show regular budget surpluses again until 1720—surpluses which would continue, incidentally, to the very end of the prosperous eighteenth century.

The reasons for this death of profit under Colbert and after Colbert are not always easy to elucidate (I shall return to the problem later), but the consequences were evident. For want of profits and lack of savings the spendthrift landowners went hopelessly into debt. A poor harvest drove them to the wall because, lacking reserves, they were suddenly unable to meet their current obligations. The history of agricultural enterprise—tenant farmers of the ecclesiastical estates, big peasant cultivators who were the titularies par excellence of farm profits and farm deficits—is no less revealing in this connection for its chronology of failures between the post-Fronde period and the Revocation.

1680: The Shipwreck of the Tenant Farmers

The first portents of the crisis in tenant farming began to appear about 1670–74. Vanishing profits (just noted in the ecclesiastical accounts) also affected the tenant farmers, some of whom lost their possessions and went to prison in these years.

The year 1679, and above all 1680, was the moment of truth for the insolvent, debt-ridden cultivators, whose ruin was consummated by a severe drought that would have been supportable had it not devastated an already impoverished countryside. In the reduced framework of this edition, three examples will have to suffice.

The first is the estate of Le Viala. A tenant, three-quarters illiterate, one Pierre Arribat, had held the lease since 1676. He was poor, reduced to borrowing, "and he disposed of funds without surety." In 1680 a twin disaster supervened: his ruin was consummated by the drought, and he himself died. The canons anxiously followed his last illness: Arribat is dying, Arribat is dead. His widow, Marguerite, a complete illiterate, took the helm. The chapter, moved by her misfortune, wrote off part of her debts. She agreed to keep the tenancy "as a good farmwife and paterfamilias [*sic*]." She was aided by her son-in-law Tapié (who boasted a fine signature). But Marguerite did not succeed. She did not pay her rent for the farm or the rest of her debts. In 1684 she was distrained. She defended herself as best she could and tried to keep her harvest. The owners were forced to post a lookout at the farm day and night in order to prevail over the widow and save the grain that constituted, in this case, their rent for the tenancy. Months thus passed in skirmishing between the lady tenant and her masters, backed by all the other creditors. Finally, in the summer of 1685 the battle was joined. Tapié, the son-in-law, called out the rest of the clan and, with a cousin, broke down the gates of his own farm and carted off the grain that had been seized by the chapter. Tapié was caught, distrained, and imprisoned, but no one else offered to take over the lease and practice the profitless trade of tenant farmer in his place. Le Viala, a booming grain factory in the sixteenth century, was now a twisted wreck of a place that the canons could only hope to salvage by assuming the responsibilities of direct management.

At Maurin, a vast estate with twenty-five pairs of oxen, sowing seed worth four thousand *livres*, and livestock valued at ten thousand *livres*, the serious difficulties also began in 1680 when the poverty of the unhappy tenant was suddenly exposed by the drought: persistent debts; land unworked; litigation in the courts of Toulouse; lack of capital, cash, credit, oxen, plows; short seeding; neglected, unweeded, worn-out land—all through the fault of the tenant Pierre Grangeant, who was forced to abandon his lease in 1683 for lack of funds. (He would struggle along with his debts and his lawsuits until 1689, at which date he was condemned by the courts.)

In 1683, then, Maurin changed farmers, the rent having been reduced to attract the new tenant, a certain Régis. The latter's reign was quickly beset by new disasters. In 1684, lacking money for reapers and for wagons to cart the sheaves, Régis bungled his harvesting and threshing. In the spring of 1686 he was unable to pay his female weeders, and before long his fields and furrows were overrun with weeds. In the summer of 1686 his grain was impounded for nonpayment of the canons' prebends. Régis, literally beseiged by his creditors, no longer so much as dared to take his teams out of the barn; the marquis de Graves had them seized on the highroad for unpaid debts. In the fall there was not enough money to pay the farmhands (the "high" wages of 1686—to which I shall return later—were one of the causes of the tenant farmers' ruin).

The canons tried to get rid of Régis, but to no avail. Nobody wanted to take his place. In 1687 Maurin went from bad to worse—still no money in the farmer's purse, no weeding, a poor crop. Finally, as a last resort, Régis was reduced in rank from tenant farmer to sharecropper, a typical case of social demotion in a period of economic distress.

At the farmstead of Saint-Pierre, the tenant Thomas Lagarde, an illiterate (who made this mark: ⴲ), also found himself in difficult straits in 1680. The drought of that year ruined his harvest and left him owing his landlords one thousand *livres*, a sum he was incapable of reimbursing in view of his poverty. In 1686 he still owed the thousand *livres*, and his relations with the canons, whom he insulted profusely and whose carting he refused to do, were envenomed. Lagarde, although sick, irascible, and penniless, managed nevertheless to hold his lease until his death in 1692.

The relations between lord and tenant were further embittered with Vézinet, Lagarde's successor as leaseholder at Saint-Pierre. The new tenant, burdened with a cruel lease and oppressive rents, was quickly unmasked (in the eyes of his landlords, the canons) as an insolvent and odious personage. His livestock browsed the chapter's mulberries, and he diverted its share of the grain from the threshing floor. By 1696 the canons were sending out an "inspector" to sequester his crops. A pack of creditors descended on Vézinet, robbing him even of the keys to his granaries. It was only a question, in 1696–97, of who would be the one to seize his grain and have him summoned before the Parlement of Toulouse. Vézinet countered, like Largarde before him, by refusing to do any carting for the canons (like the other tenants of that time, his lease contract obliged him to haul a certain number of cartloads of produce for his masters, a condition that recalls the medieval corvées). The problem, at bottom, was always the same. It was that this Vézinet did not have a cent to his name; that he made no profits; and that he was incapable, in 1697, of paying his workers and meeting his rent in grain or in straw.

In October, 1697, Vézinet seems to have come to the end of his rope. He had, he said, no sowing seed; his grain had been seized. But this tough and rather malicious tenant, who returned blow for blow, refused to put his neck in the noose without a struggle. His riposte to confiscation was theft. He reaped part of his grain before it was mature and sold it to the mule drivers and wagoners of the town. In June, 1698, he furtively sold off his harvest still in sheaves. By July he was frankly committed to agrarian sabotage. He refused to thresh, neglected to plow the fallow, and carried off the sheaves by night to sell for his own profit, although he owed the chapter three thousand *livres*. In the end, he, too, played on the solidarity of the peasant clan; in 1699 some of his cousins, who were farm laborers, threshed his grain for him and dissembled the part set aside for rent.

In 1700 comes the epilogue. Vézinet was led away to prison in Narbonne in the custody of eight guards. He was freed after a month and returned to his farm, where one fine day (October 5, 1700) he put the key under the door and disappeared without leaving an address. The wretched and cunning Vézinet was probably, for some ten years, more oppressed by rent and less spoiled by profit than any other tenant of Saint-Pierre in the course of two centuries.

In short, the cultivators of around 1680–90 were having a very difficult time of it. They were debt-ridden and broke. Even the better off fell into the habit of paying for everything in kind, not excepting prostitutes, or *grisettes*, whose only recompense was the right to go gleaning in their clients' wheat fields. Our tenant farmers were constantly on the verge of bankruptcy, when it did not actually overtake them. Consequently, they were filled with anxiety, sick with worry, depressed, or irascible, as the case might be.

On the whole, it was without question precisely the farmer class, the big tenant farmers as a group, that was ruined (not forever, to be sure) beginning in 1680. Let us take a count; of the thirteen leased-out estates for which long series of contracts have been preserved, ten experienced insurmountable difficulties between 1680 and 1695. Husbandry, temporarily, had ceased to be profitable.

It is difficult to say under exactly what conditions farm profits disappeared, because the tenants' account books for this period have been lost. Certain observations are, however, a matter of common sense, and first of all the following: at a certain moment, for the tenants as well as for the canons, expenses—that is, costs—must have exceeded income. The former resisted decline while farm prices crumbled. Profits and savings were throttled, exposing the defenseless cultivators to all the hazards of climate. This explains the provocative (but not in itself decisive) role of the droughts of 1680 and the following years.

The Stickiness of Wages

Which are the "sticky" charges that one can properly incriminate? First, there was indebtedness, to which we shall return later; next were wages, a major charge capable, as we have seen, of devouring a large portion of the big farmer's gross income. Unfortunately, in this period we no longer have at our disposal sources on wages in kind. But money wages or the monetary fraction of mixed wages paid to farm workers are sometimes known and furnish suggestive references, which are briefly as follows: between 1658 and 1680 the wages of farm laborers, as a general rule, held up quite well. A similar phenomenon, in a regime of stable productivity, tended necessarily to reduce profit margins, since the prices of wheat or wine declined faster than labor costs.

In regard to the annual cash salaries of plow-hands and carters, of whom there were four or five on a normal grange, constituting the specialized labor force of agriculture, these increased spectacularly (in *livres tournois*) between the period 1640–55 and 1686. The rise amounted to as much as 30 percent, whereas the price of wheat diminished or stagnated during the same period.

On the whole, *real* wages were rising under Fouquet and, above all, under Colbert. This rise, at least up to 1675, was not compensated for by a decline in employment. Rural employment, on the contrary (despite a certain "hard-core" joblessness), remained at a maximum up to the end of the third quarter of the century because agricultural production was rising or stable without an increase in productivity.

The rise, or the stability, of nominal labor costs while nominal prices declined constituted, therefore, one of the factors in the extinction of profit which led rapidly in turn to the collapse of agriculture. A pure deduction? No, an actual fact. In the fatal decade of the 1680's, the peasant entrepreneurs who left their keys under the door were acknowledging their real inability to pay their workers, as well as their reapers, female weeders, and carters, at the agreed wage rates. Wages, therefore, were among the charges that consumed the farmer's profits and contributed to his downfall. This does not in the least signify that farm workers were now living like princes, but simply that a process of pauperization, which had been generating entrepreneurial profits since the Renaissance, was finally checked during phase B of the Colbert period. The agricultural employers finally had to bear the cost of this resistance on the part of their salaried workers.

Sagging Land Rent

The rigidity of charges induced a decline in farm profits which often ended in disaster. But this decline soon reacted in its turn on such charges as proved to be relatively flexible. In particular, it provoked the deterioration of land rent, because the impoverished tenants were incapable of enriching their landlords to the same extent as in the past. The regime of high rents, as established under Louis XIII and Mazarin, was no longer tenable after Colbert. The texts suggest and the diagrams confirm the regression of farm rents. John Locke (at Montpellier for a cure) noted this phenomenon and blamed it on peasant poverty and the monetary famine. "Land rents in France," he wrote on May 1, 1676, "have diminished by more than half in the past few years on account of the poverty of the people and the lack of money."

It was in Languedoc that Locke first entertained this idea. I encounter the same stereotyped notion fifteen years later, in 1691, in the deliberations of the canons of Béziers, who declared that they could not pay their debts out of current income, "rents having diminished in recent years by more than half."

My diagrams fully confirm these suggestions. Moreover, since they are based on rents in grain, they prove that the decline of land rent was real and not just nominal. The fourteen scattered estates of Languedoc which furnish this information present a variety of curves, but I note that after Colbert there were only two cases in which there was a continuing rise in real rent expressed in grain—a rise that by way of exception prolonged the balmy first half of the seventeenth century. Elsewhere, in more than 80 percent of the cases (twelve estates out of fourteen), the climb of land rent was arrested after 1650–60, or 1675–80 at the latest. The curve first leveled off and then declined. The tenant farmers were delivering 20 to 50 percent fewer sacks of grain to the landlords' granaries. The percentage varies, but the sense of the movement is unmistakable. About 1700 the rentier landlords were not doing well at all.

It is now possible to sketch in a plausible chronology. The decline in prices (since 1655) was succeeded—despite a momentary animation of production —by a crisis in profits which, even in the case of tenants who kept careless accounts, is manifest in the disappearance of farm earnings and savings (about 1665–72). This movement was attended by a decline in land rent and prolonged, after 1680, by the griefs of farm management on even the biggest estates. A chain of misfortunes, a deficit ending in bankruptcy—it is this process that explains the discouragement and helplessness of the producers and, as a consequence, the fatal plunge of the indices of economic activity—the curves of tithe income and the production charts—in the period after 1675–80.

At this point the *general* problem of costs—and not just in the case of the big tenant farms considered heretofore—suddenly became acute. As prices fell (beginning in the decade of the 1660's) inflexible costs contributed, in fact, first to the shrinkage and ultimately to the death of profit. After 1675–80, when they began to weigh on a declining farm production, these charges—even if stabilized—could become insupportable in certain cases. For *even without any change at all*, by virtue of the simple increase in their relative importance vis-à-vis a contracted gross product, they acquired an additional, an excessive, capacity for destruction.

Deflation versus Agriculture

I do not include in these costs only—or even primarily—those previously studied, which were the particular burden of the big tenant farmers: land rent and wages. I have in mind the general charges affecting every kind of agricultural production, whether it involved family farm units, scattered holdings, or capitalistic estates; namely, debts and usury on the one hand and taxes on the other.

First, the debts. Under Colbert, contrary to a famous saying, it was the franc that ruined agriculture.[1] Never, in fact, were creditors better off, nor their capital more secure, than in the period 1650–80. *All* agricultural prices experienced a long nominal depression. All obligations contracted prior to 1653 and still outstanding were automatically revaluated by this deflation. A debt contracted under Louis XIII would have lost a part of its real value calculated in wheat under Mazarin through price inflation. Now, under Colbert, thanks to the inverse effects of deflation, the same debt was rejuvenated. It completely recovered the purchasing power it represented at the

---

[1] *L'épi sauvera le franc*: "agriculture will save the currency," a slogan from the depression years of the 1930's (tr. note).

time of Richelieu. The capitalist who had the happy idea of lending money during the Fronde, in the midst of rising prices, was counting his blessings during the subsequent price deflation. His capital, calculated in wheat, increased of its own accord between 1650 and 1670. Monsieur Dimanche was not to be pitied, and Don Juan would have been the last to say so.

This was more especially the case because seventeenth-century debts were long lived. I have discovered among the canons' papers one debt of record longevity dating back 107 years; contracted in 1598, it was still unpaid in 1705, although the interest by that time amounted to four or five times the original principal. Good old faithful debt.

Could one imagine, in our century of runaway inflations, still having to pay—even having to face the process server—for the debts or follies of a great-great-grandfather? Yet this is just what happened in the seventeenth century, as is shown by the edifying story of the Lalle debt that remained active for eighty-four years. In 1611, Antoine de Lalle and his son Henri, respectively landowner and procurator at Béziers, borrowed three thousand *livres* at interest from the chapter of that city in Spanish doubloons and quarter *écus*. Henri, who assumed the obligation, was in no hurry to settle. From 1618 to 1647 he constantly postponed repayment and stinted on the interest. In order to molify his ecclesiastical creditors he had given up one of his sons as a canon to the chapter by 1618, but there was no hint of reimbursement. In 1669 Henri died without paying. That was his mistake, for the price deflation under Colbert was reinflating his obligation. His son Jacques, also a procurator, after various distraints decided to pay back three hundred of the original three thousand *livres*.

In 1689 the balance, £2,700, was still outstanding, still unpaid, and Lalle and the canons were in litigation. In 1695 four generations had passed. Now it was Jacques's daughter Marguerite who had shouldered the ancestral liability. Marguerite had yet to pay back any of the £2,700, and she was forced to sell an entire sharecrop farm to discharge the debt of her great-grandfather—a debt which had succeeded, therefore, after nearly a century in destroying the family's landed fortune. The dead had foreclosed on the living.

A similar tragedy of indebtedness would be unthinkable in periods of rapid inflation (the sixteenth or the twentieth century). It is comprehensible, however, in the seventeenth century, when prices were flagging and when long periods of deflation injected new life into the most venerable of debts. The peasant communities were among the most sorely tried. At the time of the plague of 1630 and during the Fronde they had borrowed right and left. The price decline that supervened in 1653–55 reduced them to pretty much the same cruel straits as those of the American farmers of the 1930's who had gone into debt during the Coolidge prosperity and found themselves obliged to pay for fertilizers and tractors (purchased on credit) with wheat or cotton worth half as much as before the crash.

It was the same for the villages of Languedoc after 1655. The municipalities had gone into debt, sometimes for serious and sometimes for frivolous reasons—war, plague, lawsuits, gifts to some important personage. Bagnols had £80,000 of debts, Gignac £105,000, and the least of villages proportionate amounts. These sums had to be reimbursed at par at a time when wheat, wine, olive oil, and livestock—the basic sources of village wealth—had lost one-third to one-half their nominal value. Municipal indebtedness remained chronic, and the great administrative inquest of the Intendance in 1686–91—unfortunately incomplete—revealed that all the villages were saddled with heavy debt charges. The rural community up to John Law's day remained the moneylender's favorite milch cow.

By the end of the seventeenth century, however, certain compensating factors had begun to come discretely into play. First, Colbert was dead and war was approaching; then, in 1689, one ventured at last to tamper with the money—to devaluate the *livre tournois*. The unpaid creditors were the losers —and it was about time. Simultaneously, and doubtless correlatively, nominal prices slowly began to rise. At a single stroke, between 1690 and 1720 debt capital calculated in grain lost a round 20 percent of its value, and the debtor was relieved of one-fifth of his obligation.

The best was yet to come. In 1716–20 John Law, the liberator of the debt-ridden, appeared on the scene. Law's "system" killed indebtedness thanks to the abundance of money and thanks to the decline in interest rates—not only in the north, where the relieved countryside could better give itself up to drink, but also in Languedoc, where the peasants declared that "one must take advantage of the times" and issued their ultimatum to the moneylenders: "agree to lower interest to 3 percent or 2 percent or else we shall borrow the money we need elsewhere at that rate and pay you back out of the proceeds." The village archives and the Estates around 1720 abound with demands of this sort, which generally had the desired results.

At last one witnesses the painless decease of the ancient debts of Colbert's time. They had dragged on deplorably for forty years, reimbursed almost twice over in terms of interest but with their principal still intact. All at once Law's inflated bank notes permitted the debtors, or the sons of debtors, to discharge their old debts, if necessary by contracting new ones at very low rates. Thus, for example, in 1720 in the archives of the Narbonne chapter one finds traces of the reimbursement by different individuals, "in thousand-pound notes," of £55,000 in loans all dating back to the same period of generalized indebtedness; that is, to 1658, 1666, 1669, 1674, and 1676.

The revolution represented by Law's system had some lasting results. The rate of interest actually specified in the Languedocian contracts fell, not-withstanding certain fluctuations, to 3 percent in the interval 1720–60. Money remained cheap for forty years. It was the end of a sort of golden age of rent and of hard times for borrowers.

During this period of low interest rates, *nominal* prices were rising. The latter movement, which began, as we have seen, about 1690, continued almost without interruption up to 1770. Its effect was to considerably allevi-ate the burden of debts. Thus, for example, a long-term loan calculated in wheat lost half its value between Louvois and Turgot. To the delight of the debtor, above all if he was an agricultural producer, interest rates were fall-ing and capital values were shrinking. For these two reasons the financial situation of the peasant communities slowly improved in the seventeenth century in contrast to their debt-ridden condition at the time of Colbert and the Revocation.

On balance, if one combines on the one hand the nominal price curves for wheat (which serve as an index of the real value of capital) and on the other hand the curves of interest rates, it is possible to distinguish two distinct periods. The first was very hard on debtors, with prices stagnant and interest still high. It was in full swing up to about 1680–90. The second, especially the phase lasting from about 1720 to 1760, was much more favorable to the same category. Was it purely by chance that the collapse of agricultural pro-duction occurred at the end of the first period, when inflexible interest rates were combined with stagnant prices to help break the movement of expan-sion? Inversely—by a familiar dialectic that one also encounters in 1930–35—this slump in production, in its turn, reduced the peasant debtors to a sit-uation of even greater insolvency and contributed, beginning in the 1680's, to the paralysis of farm credit and of the spirit of enterprise.

From this point of view, Law's system—the New Deal of the Regency—represented, in a more or less conscious way, an attempt at "feedback" into the economic body. It relieved the debt-ridden and revived certain basic circuits of rural production.

The Ill-timed Attack of the Tax Collector

Taxation, too, like the exactions of the rentier landlords, struck an inopportune blow at the economy. Comparing the different graphs, one is able to distinguish two main phases of fiscal policy in Languedoc under Louis XIV. The Colbertian phase lasted up to about 1675. The Languedocian taille was stabilized in nominal value. An analogous stabilization obtained in the case of indirect taxes (such as that on salt). One is inclined to congratulate Colbert for his fiscal restraint. Is the chorus of praise justified? Perhaps, but not without a certain number of reservations. In fact, while taxes were stagnating in this fashion agricultural prices were falling. Therefore, the taille and the price of salt, despite their nominal immobility, were in practice revaluated. In the 1660's the government was in the black and could purchase bread, wine, and meat for the army—or, for that matter, begin work on Versailles and the Canal du Midi—at bargain prices. Colbert was aware of this happy state of affairs and rejoiced about it on more than one occasion.

The incidence of taxation, therefore, remained high. In the absence of surviving account books, let us turn to the testimony collected by Locke in the neighborhood of Montpellier in 1676. According to his figures, direct taxes consumed a round 10 percent of the gross agricultural product, 25 percent of the marketed gross product, and 40 percent of land rent or net income. This was sufficient, in marginal cases, to compromise the profitability of land and to sometimes justify antitax revolts (for example, that in the Vivarais in 1670).

For all that, up until 1675 nothing had been lost as yet, and one would have been wrong to despair. True, taxation was heavy, and since 1655 nominal prices had declined more than nominal taxes, but the decisive comparison as far as the trend is concerned is not between prices and taxes but between real taxes and real income. From 1650 to 1675 it was unquestionably real income that was the more dynamic and the faster growing of the two. Taxation was one of the charges that compromised farm profits, but it was slowly outdistanced by production. A certain optimism was still permissible. One last effort, and gross product could take the prize.

It was a pious hope; the effort was doomed. As we already know, the front-runner was winded—"fagged out." Production would collapse and give up the contest at the last moment.

The second phase opened in 1675–80. In regard to taxes there was little

change at first. The taille remained stable for a dozen years. Then, beginning in 1690 and up to 1715, it increased very rapidly in *nominal* value. This
increase was justified, in part, by the general rise in prices. The *real* increase
in the taille, assuming constant prices, was provoked by the growing demands of foreign policy and the war. It was less marked, in reality, than the
nominal increase. Calculated in wheat, the purchasing power of the taille
did, however, grow noticeably between 1690 and 1715. To this particular
surcharge one must add the supplementary burden of the poll tax, which
was levied beginning in 1695–1701.

For a dynamic, expanding economy, exactions of this nature—a wartime
surtax and a new poll tax—would have been painful but supportable and
in certain cases stimulating. Commissariat purchases, as is well known, re-
inject a portion of the tax monies back into the economy and can serve to
buoy up the grain and cattle markets, as happened on occasion in Languedoc, for example, in 1694, 1695, and 1701. The difficulty was that the new
taxation decreed by Louis XIV and his ministers from the close of the
century came at a bad moment because it affected an agriculture in decline.

Let us return to our comparison of the movements of real taxes and real
income: on the one hand we have aggregate production (whether destined
for sale or for autoconsumption) measured and weighted by the tithe, and
on the other hand the overall amount siphoned off in direct taxes—the two
variables converted into measures of wheat.

In the early Colbert period, despite the grumbling about taxes, income
held the advantage, at least in Languedoc, where it grew faster than direct
taxation up to about 1675. From the period 1675–80 to the end of the reign
just the contrary was true; the scissors opened, but in the bad sense. Income
weakened by fits and starts. But taxes out of income were unyielding at
first and then increased substantially between the League of Augsburg and
the king's death. This was unfortunate. It was not that the tax collector was
so much more wicked than before; it was that the taxpayers were producing
less and getting poorer. If they were fleeced under Colbert, they were flayed
under Chamillart. By 1686–88 the taille payers were just about at the end of
their rope. In 1688, according to Montbel, the general secretary of the Estates, 95 percent of the villages of Languedoc were served by forced collectors, poor peasants or farm laborers without resources of any kind who were
forever in and out of gaol like the decurions of the late Roman Empire.

At the end of the reign, when the tax-income scissors were opened their widest, there is massive evidence of the abandonment of insolvent lands, a movement which culminated in about 1715–20.

Taxation was not the only nor even the primary factor responsible for the decline of agriculture—far from it. It was only one variable among others. But just as before the Fronde, simplifying minds decided that it was the big culprit. Antitax agitation remained at the heart of certain popular uprisings, which were dramatic manifestations of mass psychology.

CHAPTER

5

The Savage Rebellions

"Long Live the King, Fie on the Elect"[1]

In November, 1669, an elderly bishop from that marginal region of Languedoc that is the Vivarais pointed out the symptoms of an agrarian malaise that was more serious and no doubt more precocious than elsewhere because of the specific poverty of the mountain districts. The former abundance, he reported, has given way to scarcity; the poor people of the countryside are starving; the more well-to-do inhabitants of the towns are in difficult straits; and the heavy public outlays—royal aids, the Canal du Midi, debt retirement—have driven the taxpaying landowners to the wall, for "the tailles mount faster than their income from the land."

In April, 1670, the malaise in the Vivarais was exacerbated by a series of disasters. A very cold winter killed the fig trees and caused a sudden leap in the price of coal in the region of Saint-Étienne. The blacksmiths, to the outrage of the farm workers, immediately raised the prices of pickaxes and sickles. In general, everyone was complaining: "The crushing subsidies [taxes], the special taxes" were eating into income which was already depressed. The populace was seized by a sort of panic recurrent in the Midi in the seventeenth century. People believed that the authorities were about to introduce the capitation, a tax on persons, on top of the tax on real property (the taille). As early as 1627 it was rumored at Villefranche-de-Rouergue that the king was going to tax every newborn infant and every jug of water drawn at the fountain. On April 30, 1670, the town of Aubenas was gripped by the same anxieties; henceforth, said the gossipmongers, there would be a tax of one *sou* per day for every farm worker, ten *livres* for the birth of a male child, five *livres* for the birth of a daughter, three *livres* for a new suit, five *sous* for a hat or a shirt, three *sous* for a pair of shoes, and one

[1] Elect: officers of the taille (tr. note).

265

denier for a pound of bread. It was an insane tax schedule, a caricature of the poll tax. (Nevertheless, in retrospect it contained a certain grain of truth. A quarter of a century later, at the urging of the intendant of Languedoc, Basville, who was impressed by the insufficiencies of the tax on real property, a personal tax, the capitation, would actually be instituted in the kingdom).

At Aubenas in the midst of this panic a tax collector by the name of Casse, ignorant of what was going on, appeared on the scene. He had farmed the tax of two *écus* on every hack and eight *livres* for every tavernkeeper. He innocently posted notices announcing his forthcoming collection. The common women, supported by a few laborers, were in a rage. Casse was spit upon and beaten up. The mutineers, their appetite whetted, then went off to create an uproar before the notables of the town council.

The agitation set off by this incident lasted several weeks. At the head of the citizen mutineers were the usual, often well-to-do members of the artisan class. I count, among the leaders condemned to death at the time of the repression, a cobbler, a hatter, a tavernkeeper, a coppersmith, a distiller of brandy, a carder, and some peasants. The rebels were opposed by the gentlemen and the rich bourgeois of Aubenas—by the honest folk, whether papist or Huguenot. These good people, who were partisans of law and order feeding off royal finances and sinecures, fearful that their homes would be sacked, would have been the last to join in a violent tax revolt. For that matter, they believed the mutineers were inspired by the Devil, and they interpreted the uprising in terms of collective guilt—as a manifestation of divine justice "to turn us from the paths of sin."

The revolt itself was unquestionably animated by vague democratic aspirations of prophetic or evangelic origin ("the last shall be first"). The anonymous author of a manuscript account of the uprising cites certain words of the mutineers to that effect: "The gentlemen and the honest folk were regarded as inferiors [by the rebels] destined, in their thinking, to become servants in their turn. They said that the age of prophecy had come; that the kettle would be smitten by the earthen pot."

This prophetic tendency is repeatedly encountered in the Midi revolts of the modern period (in particular, at Romans in 1580 and in the Rouergue in 1627). It rested on biblical reminiscences, on vague longings for social inversion, on the frustrations of the nonprivileged, and, finally, on a certain antagonism between the common people and the nobility—an antagonism also attested by John Locke at Montpellier in 1676. One should not, however, overestimate these rather nebulous democratic cravings of the insurgents of Aubenas. The phenomenon was much less manifest here than among the insurgents of Brittany in 1674, whose program included various explicit measures for the humbling of the privileged classes. In the Vivarais of 1670, resentment against the nobles cropped up in drunken tavern talk. It did not lead to action. In the context of day-to-day agitation, of actual battle cries, the rebels of the Vivarais remained prudent, royalist, and, as often was the case in the seventeenth century, strictly antitax. The mutineers of Aubenas did not shout "Down with the nobles" and not even "Long live the Third Estate" like the Croquants of 1590. They did not brandish demands against the privileged classes but confined themselves to reviving the old antitax, monarchist slogan ("Long live the king without taille and gabelles") in a different form: "Long live the king, fie on the elect."

This revolt of the town-dwellers spread to the neighboring countryside. The peasants revolted, to the strains of a *Mazarinade*, against the royal financiers and tax farmers. They lacked a leader and naturally went to look for one among the wealthiest nobles. Theirs was a common reflex among the rustic rebels of the Old Regime. The Red Hats of Brittany forced the nobles to become their leaders after making them change into peasant dress. In the Vivarais, Antoine du Roure made an ideal chief of the villagers in revolt. If he refused the role, no matter; he had no choice. A crowd of peasants and laborers invaded his home. Their leader, the sheepherder Laroze, slapped Roure and called him a coward. Stung by these "friendly insults," Roure resigned himself to assuming command of his revilers.

The two protagonists of this scene, Roure and Laroze, possess a symbolic significance. Laroze embodies unbridled popular violence, complicated in his case by sadistic tendencies (during the massacres of Aubenas he strutted about with the "intestines" of a notable, accused of having admitted the royal troops into town, strung around his neck). Roure, on the other hand, symbolized above all, in the rebels' eyes, military competence and respectability. The question of his real personality, it is true, is much debated. His biographer, Raoul de Vissac, in a swashbuckling account, makes him out to be a sort of knight-errant, an authentic nobleman, a paladin straight out of the Middle Ages of belfries and gargoyles. Inversely, the Languedocian authorities who finally subdued Roure and had him drawn and quartered always refused him the nobiliary particle and described him as a "peasant."

Antoine du Roure does not deserve the highest aristocratic honors, but neither does he merit the "indignity" of being classed as a commoner by

enemies intent on humbling him. In reality, Roure was a notable, a rural
bourgeois, a well-to-do gentleman farmer, the proprietor of "ten thousand
écus of property" centered on a farmstead called La Rande, pompously re-
baptized "Château de la Rande." The family included well-to-do peasants
and prosperous bourgeois as far back as the end of the sixteenth century.
Antoine's father, Guillaume du Roure, yearned for social advancement and
promotion to the nobility "either by office or by land," as he put it himself.
In 1651 he succeeded, after a long quest, in acquiring a noble domain. The
family was indisputably en route to the nobility even if it had not yet
arrived.

Antoine du Roure was an educated man and a good Catholic. In his youth
he had served in the royal army (another reason why the rebels chose him
to lead them, he being a "general" with battlefield experience). Wealthy
landowner, fervent Christian, former officer, and husband to a noblewoman,
Roure was no stranger to the system of heroic, religious, theological, and
military values that gave meaning to life and death for the French ruling
orders under Louis XIV. The democratic messianism of certain plebeians of
Aubenas, on the other hand, was very far from his normal preoccupations.
Roure fixed on the antitax aspect of the revolt, which was the common
rallying point of the discontented and evoked a sympathetic response even
among the privileged classes. The rebels shouted, "Down with the elect.
Death to bloodsuckers of the people," and Roure joined in the chorus. In his
letter of June 20 he proposed "to exterminate the *elect* who are starving us
to death." It was on this platform that he rallied his partisans to battle. The
latter were poor devils, but also grange tenants, silk growers, and "a quantity of honest peasants won over to the rebellion," sometimes under the
threat of seeing their crops set afire if they remained loyal to established
authority.

The end of the tale is well known. Aubenas was sacked; then the mutineers were defeated. At this point for Roure, as for Jean Cavalier in 1704
and Marcelin Albert (the chief of rebel winegrowers) in 1907, there remained but one solution consistent with a loyalist, monarchist mentality—
to go throw oneself at the feet of the king (in 1907, at the feet of the pres-
ident). At least Clemenceau, for his part, would receive Marcelin Albert
(and mockingly pay his return ticket to Narbonne out of his own pocket),
but at Versailles, where he betook himself, Roure was turned away at the
gates. Determined at this point to flee the country in order to implore a
different king—the most Catholic king of Spain—he was surprised and cap-

tured at Saint-Jean-Pied-de-Port while having a last glass of wine, his pistols just out of reach. He would later die on the wheel.

The revolt of the Vivarais was typical of a certain mass psychology and of a more instinctive than rational reaction to the rural crisis. In reality, this revolt affected a society suffering material distress but psychologically integrated; any developed concept of a struggle between classes or orders was foreign to these people, even if their actions—their tactics—at times appear as a kind of groping toward revolution. For this reason, the only conceivable common enemy—the only possible scapegoat—was not the king, who was still adored ("If the king only knew"), but distant, abstract "Authority," especially the royal tax collector, who was alien to local society and whose demands, apparently, implied no reciprocity.

The rebels ignored the worst of local evils, neither attacking them nor seeking redress. They allowed the *real* cancers of usury, rentes, and the tithe to devour the peasants' substance and directed their violence solely against taxes. Sometimes those taxes were real, but in certain absurd but highly provocative cases they were nonexistant, potential, or perfectly fictitious— strange hobgoblins like the hat tax, the shirt tax, or the tax on unborn infants, which had never existed except in the fantasies of those who revolted against them.

The Fanatics of the Cévennes

After 1680, with the economy collapsing and the Revocation drawing near, the revolts changed sides and significance. Henceforth, the regions with Catholic majorities remained calm for the most part. Brittany was quiescent after 1675, Bordeaux after 1676, and the region of Boulogne after 1663. This prudent behavior would continue, despite hard times, up to the end of the reign. In Languedoc itself, the leading role passed from one mountain range to the next—from the papist Vivarais to the Huguenot Cévennes.

What was the source of this Catholic tranquility? Certain reasons, which were at the same time political and religious, cannot be excluded. Take the notary Borrély, a petty bourgeois of Nîmes and a typical average Catholic of the end of the seventeenth century. About 1685–90 he was losing money year after year and so afraid of ending up in the workhouse that he would permit himself only shabby, secondhand wigs. He knew that the suppression of Protestantism contributed to his own ruin and to that of his native city on account of the exodus of the moneyed class and the flight of capital.

But little matter; he was above all else a faithful believer, and for that reason he was captivated by the divine surprise of the Revocation, by that mass conversion of the Huguenot communities (which he knew, however, to be insincere). "Whatever people say," Borrély noted in his private journal in this connection, "there is something of a divine miracle in this." This Catholic believer, filled with wonder at the religious success of his king when the Protestant coalition was threatening in 1689, became an unhappy but exemplary taxpayer whose mind was on anything but revolt. "The distress is great, but our great king has so many affairs to handle it is proper to make a sacrifice," he wrote when the time came to hand over his share of the six million in taxes for the province.

French Catholicism had been politically restive since the League. Everything suggests that in 1685, dazzled by the Revocation, the Catholics returned to the ranks. The natural counterpart of growing Catholic moderation was the Huguenot uprisings. The Protestants had not stirred since the wars of Rohan. They had remained calm in 1632, in 1650, and during the revolt of the Vivarais. At the close of the century, for obvious reasons, they became bellicose again.

The Protestant peasants, like everybody else, suffered from the economic depression, the disruption of trade—"so deadly in the Cévennes"—and the epidemics. In 1685, the very year of the Revocation, the Hautes-Cévennes were short of chestnuts and wheat, and people were forced to subsist on acorns and grass. For the Huguenots these misfortunes were aggravated by religious oppression. This special oppression in their regard was, from the beginning, more than just an affair of state. It also incarnated the spirit of revenge of a Languedocian Church, triumphant and exalted in the Century of Saints and enriched, up to the time of Colbert, by the increase of the gross product and the correlative rise in tithe income. The persecution of the Huguenots was encouraged by Versailles, but it was directed on the spot by the powerful bishops' "lobby" that turned the provincial assembly into a war machine against the Calvinists. The Estates of Languedoc, between 1661 and 1680, multiplied anti-Protestant pressures and measures: they hounded "P.R." consuls from the fiscal assemblies of the civil dioceses;[2] they demanded "that one smash the head and tear out the heart" of the Huguenot monster by expelling the last of the Protestants from Privas; they commanded that the city consuls and professional syndics be 100 percent

---

[2] "P.R.": *prétendus réformés*, or self-styled reformed Protestants (tr. note).

Catholic, even in "R.P.R." country;[3] they petitioned the king (with success) to absorb the "chamber of the Edict," the last judicial safeguard of the Calvinists, into the all-Catholic bosom of the Parlement of Toulouse; they demanded the suppression of the Protestant academy, already transferred to Puylaurens; they succeeded in having several temples razed to the ground; they harassed the ministers; and finally, with the Revocation and the destruction of heresy, they voted, as a mark of their gratitude to the king, the erection of an equestrian statue weighing 450 hundredweight.

The Huguenots, then, were face-to-face with a concerted campaign of unlimited oppression engineered by the central authorities and the local clergy, by the intendant and the Estates, and by the royal administration and the hierarchical society of the three orders embodied in the provincial assembly. Impoverished to the same extent as the papists by the crisis and by taxes and tormented by the tithe that they were forced to pay against their will—whereas the Catholic peasants had by now resigned themselves to this particular charge, heavy though it was—they were, in addition, the target of a special campaign aimed at eradicating Calvinism.

Now, in the Huguenot Cévennes the reformed religion represented culture. To destroy the one, as was done in 1685, was to compromise the other, and it meant seriously disturbing the psychic and emotional equilibrium and the daily life of the population. The all-embracing character of Calvinism in the Cévennes, as it has seeped down into the daily life of the people, is a phenomenon that has not escaped the attention of modern observers.

The religious conversion in the case of the Cévennes was so complete that it succeeded in entirely uprooting the ancient folklore, something unique in France. In that region, as Charles Bost has pointed out, one no longer hears any of the old folk songs. They have disappeared in favor of the psalms that the old people sing to babes in their cradles. This was an old story in a region where the psalter of Marot and Théodore de Bèze was the local source of a second culture, popular and musical in nature. By 1659 (a bishop noted) in towns with a large number of Calvinists one heard the resounding strains of Marot's psalms in the mouths of artisans and, in the country districts, in the mouths of the peasants, whereas the Catholics remained mute or sang only ribald drinking songs.

French *langue d'oil* culture itself penetrated the *langue d'oc* region of the Cévennes in the seventeenth century from the peasant's earliest childhood,

---

[3] "R.P.R.": *religion prétendue réformée*, or self-styled reformed religion (tr. note).

almost exclusively through the agency of the Bible and the Protestant texts—
The ABC of Christians (a sort of biblical and liturgical abecedary), the
Catechisms of Calvin and of Bèze, and *Mirror of Youth*, which children had
to learn by heart. It was a strange land where French, in contrast to the
maternal *langue d'oc*, was regarded almost as a holy tongue and, in extreme
cases, as proof of divine inspiration. The religious mystics of the Cévennes,
when they spoke *en langues*—that is, in a foreign tongue under the inspiration of the Holy Spirit—expressed themselves fluently *in French*, to the
wonder of the dialect-speaking populace.

In a milieu such as this, the Revocation, the attempt to uproot Protestantism entirely—its preachings, its psalms, and its Bibles—amounted to forced
"deculturation." We all know of the traumatic shock and bloody consequences that normally result from similar undertakings, especially in the
twentieth century. The Protestant Cévennes of the seventeenth century was
no exception to the rule. The traumatism of a people deprived of its ministers and its spiritual leadership, tormented by a sense of guilt (for having
accepted the Revocation and temporarily repudiated its faith), and oppressed, in the bargain, by hard times and taxes was so severe that it engendered authentic cases of anxiety, neurosis, and even hysteria, which would
turn into bloody fanaticism. All of these effects stupefied the authorities, and
especially Basville (who would have made a wretched psychiatrist). A devout Catholic and at the same time a strict rationalist, he had not anticipated
anything like this implacable dialectic—Revocation, sense of guilt, fanaticism—when he unleashed his dragoons.

I shall now attempt to describe this concatenation. Such a description is
indispensable for an understanding of certain peasant mental processes and
for shedding light on the course taken by the final uprisings, so different
from the old-fashioned antitax revolts—and at the same time so similar to
them in some respects.

The Huguenot riposte began to develop in 1688–89; it culminated with
the Camisards. From the beginning it was more than a purely religious
struggle, for it was also attended by certain political and social overtones.
Thus, the program of Miremont, who anticipated the insurrection of the
Cévennes as early as 1689, was aimed at exploiting not only the Protestants'
despair but also "the universal discontent" of subjects of both faiths, the
classic antitax reflex. Miremont, the rebel marquis, talked like one of Antoine du Roure's disciples. He demanded "the abolition of stamped paper
and intolerable taxes" and the destruction of customs bureaus and tax of-

fices. In this he summed up the recriminations, at the same time liberal and retrograde, formulated the same year in a pro-Huguenot pamphlet entitled *Sighs of an Enslaved France*: "The splendor of the nobility has been tarnished, the authority of the Parlements cast down, the Three Estates abolished" by the odious tyranny of Louis XIV. It was a popular program with the Protestants (despite certain reactionary features) because it vindicated the ancient right of revolt against tyranny. In the Calvinist songs of the Gévaudan, by 1686, the pope was a rogue but Louis XIV was a tyrant.

Still, it was not Miremont but Jurieu whose vigorous thought would animate the rebellions of Languedoc. He, too, dwelt on political themes. In his *Pastoral Letters* he accepts a sort of social contract, a right of peoples over kings, a legitimate recourse to insurrection. But Jurieu, Paul Hazard to the contrary, was in no sense a modern thinker. He was a prophet, the repository of a very ancient message. This prolix exile, combative as a Lenin, was the continuator of the great millenarians of the Middle Ages and the Reformation—Eudes de l'Étoile, Joachim of Fiore, Thomas Muntzer, and the Revolutionary of the Haut-Rhin.

The Apocalypse According to Jurieu

If one is to believe Jurieu, the coming revolution had to conform to the ancient visions of the Book of Daniel and the successive stages of the Apocalypse: first, a great bloodletting and the persecution of the righteous; once the ordeal was over, the coming of God's regeneration of the human species; the final casting down of Babylon and Rome—the harlot arrayed in purple and scarlet; and, finally, the world would bloom again, more beautiful than before. All the signs, and first among them the Revocation itself, convinced Jurieu that in 1685 France was still in the first phase but that the rest was sure to follow.

From his Dutch exile he courageously addressed himself, then, to apocalyptic problems at precisely the point where the minor pseudo-Joachimite prophets of the twelfth century had left off. He sought to interpret the prophetic cipher 1,260, which marked, as to date and duration, the Woman's retreat to the wilderness; the prophecies and death of the two Witnesses; and the reign of the Beast in chapters 11, 12, and 13 of the Apocalypse. He trifled with the millenia and extracted their square roots. He manipulated the prophecies of Usher, the archbishop of Armagh, and the dossiers of his own ancestor, Du Moulin, the author of *Fulfillment of the Prophecies*. After carrying out these calculations, Jurieu placed "a great hope" in the precise year 1689 and prophesied the end of papism between 1710 and 1720, followed by the Second Coming and "*a thousand years* of peace and righteousness on earth under the reign of Christ." Our author, however—a fanatic but also a bourgeois—was careful to reassure worldly interests; true, the millenium dear to his heart would institute the community of goods as prophesied in the Scriptures, but it would also respect private property (?).

Humbug? Perhaps. But these prophecies, published in 1686, and a few others in the same style (*Enlightenment on the Apocalypse, Balm of Gilead,* and so on) were "more common than almanacs" in Huguenot Languedoc. The police seized copies in the remotest farmsteads of the Cévennes. Their natural credulity made the populace receptive beforehand; the weavers of Béziers became infatuated with Nostradamus. In the neighborhood of Nîmes, Huguenots of both sexes discussed Jurieu and chapter 11 of the Apocalypse at the bakeoven and at the mill. As early as Christmas, 1686, at a secret assembly attended by many carders, the predicant Serein preached on chapter 16 of the same book: "The Chastisement of Babylon and of the Beast." In 1689 another predicant by the name of Roman, undergoing interrogation by Broglie, who had seized him by the hair, cried in his captor's face, "Follower of the Beast!" The language of the Apocalypse had assumed the force of law.

These popular predicants of Bas-Languedoc, most of them, in Basville's words, "miserable wool carders and peasants" who had replaced the refugee preachers after the Revocation, were dominated from on high by the only intellectuals in their group, the schoolmaster Vivent and the lawyer Brousson. Now, these two men were faithful disciples of Jurieu. If they returned to France at the risk of martyrdom in 1689 it was because the Amsterdam theologian had expressly prophesied for that very year the "great hope" of the revelation of Saint John at Patmos. Both of them, later on, as they were being hunted down like wild beasts, would remain right up to the moment of their martyrdom "fanatics of the Apocalypse."

François Vivent deserved the epithet for the hate and execration he dedicated to the Church of Rome: "a devils' lair, a nest of repugnant winged creatures." Claude Brousson, for his part, was a gentle, talented apostle of the apocalypse filled with superstitious wonder. Hostile to rationalism and science, an enemy of Descartes, convinced with the Bible and against Galileo that the sun revolved around the earth, Brousson also decided, beginning in 1686–87, to try his hand at prophecy. His prophecies (which he naively distributed to the Roman Catholics) on the future destruction of the Anti-Christ—the pope—and on the imminent Second Coming of Jesus Christ were lifted straight out of Jurieu's commentary on the Apocalypse. So, too, was his fine sermon, the "Mystic Dove," delivered in the Cévennes and copied endlessly by the Calvinists: " 'My dove,' spoke the Lord, 'that hide yourself in the clefts of the rock and the mountain caves . . . my dove, show me your face and let me hear your voice, for your voice is sweet and your face is comely. Rise up, my love, and come away, for the winter is past and the flowers are budding and the time for singing is at hand. Don't you hear the turtledove? Rise up, my love, my fair one, and come away with me.' " In a manuscript text, Brousson identifies this "dove" hidden in the rocks and caves (the theme is from the Song of Songs) with the Woman of the Apocalypse, the spouse of Jesus Christ forced by the Devil to retreat momentarily to the wilderness.

The clownishness of Jurieu, who was forced to revise his prophecies after every new deception, failed to discourage his zealots in Languedoc. The apocalyptic mentality, which transforms the worst misfortunes into an antechamber of supreme joy, was far too reassuring as a system of interpretation for that. Brousson's attitude was typical; in 1694–98 he clearly perceived in his clandestine wanderings the economic and demographic crisis we have studied in this book. He saw a province shorn of young men, of sheepherders, and of peasants to till the land. He saw a people defeated and dispirited, towns almost ruined for want of trade, and highways filled with poor folk who importuned travelers for half a league. Having taken note of these everyday phenomena, Brousson, like Daniel before Nebuchadnezzar, applied his system of interpretation. He rationalized, after his fashion, and deciphered these woes as premonitions of the approaching chastisement. It was God, he affirmed, who was punishing the sinful France of the Revocation by visiting these misfortunes upon her. "The heavens are all aflame" against Louis XIV. The bottomless pit was about to swallow up the king's armies. Finally, following these ordeals, everything would be set right once more; God's light would descend upon the Roman Catholics; He would create "a new people to sing his divine praises."

The revolt of the Camisards (1702) would reveal how profoundly the rebels (who were almost all peasants and village artisans) were imbued with this mentality. Abraham Mazel, whose murder of Abbot Du Chayla set off the war, had prophesied, as early as 1701, the destruction of the Empire of the Beast. In the fall of 1702 Abbot de La Pize, prior of Saint-Martin-de-Bobaux, received the visit of a band of Camisards who reproached him "for remaining in a Church which is the Babylon and the prostitute described by Saint John in the Apocalypse." They felled him with three musket shots in the stomach and finished him off with their swords. In 1703, following an engagement at La Calmette, an officer discovered the body of a soldier, his face disfigured. He had been a predicant, and the text of a sermon was found in his pocket. From beginning to end it was a long exposé of a prophecy from the Apocalypse ("Apoclice" or "Pocalice"). The text, supported by citations, announced that after buckets of blood had been spilled, *in 1705* France and Louis XIV would rally to Protestantism in a body and by royal decree and would beg the Huguenots' forgiveness.

Convulsive and Prophetic Hysteria

The Apocalypse was not all. The Camisard revolt, born of misery and persecution, was without question exalted by the millenarianism of a Jurieu, but it would have been equally inconceivable in the absence of another element frequently found up to the present century in the socio-religious movements of oppressed peoples—convulsive and prophetic hysteria. Michelet, a passionate reader of the *Sacred Theatre of the Cévennes*, had pointed it out, and Charles Bost, in turn, reacted in a healthy way in the 1920's against the current excesses of a prosaic, rationalistic historiography. As the discoverer of unpublished documents which substantiated Michelet's intuitions, Bost confirms the words of Borgès that erudition is sometimes the most modern form of the imaginary.

At the origin of the movement of visionaries who were to become the leaders of the Camisards was a young shepherdess of sixteen, Isabeau Vincent, of Saou (in the Dauphiné), who talked in her sleep, exhorting the Huguenots to remain true to their faith. Once in prison, Isabeau, in the words of the Catholic historian Brueys, "did not react like birds that stop singing when one puts them in a cage"; on the contrary, she kept "chirping" more and more of her revelations.

In any event, the little shepherdess' imprisonment came too late. By the summer of 1688 Isabeau had her imitators, and a host of petty or "sleeping" prophets were soon propagating "the divine, bewitching malady." One of these was a young peasant by the name of Gabriel Astier, who brought the "fanaticism" to the Languedocian side of the Rhône—into that "wild, poor" country that was the Huguenot part of the Vivarais.

Isabeau, in the midst of her delirium, remained superficially calm. But

Astier introduced the convulsive style to the Vivarais—a great seizure in successive stages à la Charcot: fainting, then convulsions, then a sort of paralysis which left him "stiff as an iron rod," and finally the declaration of repentence. Astier's local imitators, the disseminators of frenetic camp meetings, were legion, and the Huguenot peasants "left off tilling the soil" and set up rustic *théâtres*, the better to see these young prophets fanaticize. It is not impossible that scenes of sexual exhibitionism occurred at such gatherings: "... the prophets having had the insolence to perform lewd acts in view of their assemblies," as wrote one scandalized Huguenot—Brousson.

The "convulsionaries" of this region in 1688–89 were awaiting the coming of the hero liberator, of the "Messiah" in the broad sense given the term in today's sociology of religion. The Messiah, in a sermon preached in the Vivarais early in 1689, was none other than the Prince of Orange, whom an angel was to go and fetch back to France by the hair with an army of one hundred thousand men. (The Catholics, on the other hand, were so frightened of this prince that at the news of his supposed death students of the Jesuit colleges disguised as demons dragged his lacerated effigy through the streets.)

This initial blaze of messianism came to a tragic end. Like many prophets of the oppressed (like Thomas Muntzer stopping cannonballs with the outspread sleeves of his robe, and, in another context, like Epikilipikili, the Congolese miracle worker, immunizing his disciples against European bullets), the visionaries of the Vivarais, protected by angels white as snow and no bigger than one's finger, believed themselves invulnerable. Besides, they were nonviolent; shouting "Tartara, back Satan," they opened their jerkins to the soldiers' muskets and left three hundred dead on the field at the Assembly of the Serre de la Salle, where some thousands of persons were gathered (February 19, 1689). This massacre did not destroy messianism in Languedoc, but for a decade thereafter it remained dormant, confined to tiny, secret cults.

The second outbreak, that of the Camisards, began in the summer of 1700. It had been smoldering in the messianic Vivarais, and it was there, not far from Vals, that it finally flared up, inspired by the visions of a certain Marie la Boîteuse, who wept tears of blood. From the Vivarais—and this was decisive—the epidemic spread for the first time southward to the Cévennes and Bas-Languedoc. Daniel Raoux, an illiterate peasant, was propagating messianic fanaticism in secret cults in the diocese of Uzès at the start of 1701. There were scenes of hysteria on May 22 of the same year against the priests who came to collect the tithes. That summer the valleys of the two Gardons were contaminated, and in the fall it was the turn of the Lozère range of the Hautes-Cévennes, which would become the principal center of the movement. Paradoxically, the royal routes staked out by Basville—for the religious repression and for the passage of cannon—facilitated the spread of the "cultural" influences of the visionaries of Vals and Uzès deep into these rugged mountains.

The "convulsionaries" of Languedoc, who would constitute the soul of the Camisard insurrection, had finally established a stronghold, and it is possible from now on to describe their behavior on the basis of numerous concordant, independent sources. Camisard sympathizers had furnished the first accounts by 1707 in the *Sacred Theatre of the Cévennes*. The *Mémoires* of Villars and the reports of the provincial police—the latter not exhumed from the archives of the intendance until the twentieth century—contain descriptions that are convergent with the texts of the *Sacred Theatre*, even though they come from the hostile camp this time and are sometimes furnished by the bitterest enemies of messianism. Their enemies invariably treat the convulsionaries as fanatics, but never as imposters. Finally, the *Mémoires* of Marion and Mazel, published in 1931, provide for the first time direct autobiographical material.

Let us cite at random one of a dozen descriptions of these scenes of messianism (this one, as it happens, from the *Sacred Theatre of the Cévennes*):

> The prophets said that their seizures partook of the miraculous and the divine; that they began with chills and dizziness, as if fever-ridden, which caused them to stretch and yawn several times before they fell . . . they clapped their hands . . . they flung themselves backward on the ground; they closed their eyes; their bellies swelled up; they drowsed in this state for several moments; afterwards, waking with a start, they rattled off anything that came into their heads. They said that they saw the heavens part; that they saw the angels, Heaven and Hell.

The other sources corroborate, on the whole, this lively description from the *Sacred Theatre*. It was generally possible to distinguish three stages: the fall to the ground; the convulsions or contortions, which were sometimes frightening to behold; and the discourses inspired by the Holy Spirit, at times incomprehensible, but at times more or less coherent prophecies on the destruction of the empire of the Devil, the Beast, and the False Prophet. Élie Marion, who dwells on his own case in a text until recently unpublished, is the most careful in describing the symptoms. His attacks, he writes, were attended by chills and preceded by high fever. His eyes closed, his body began to shake, and he was agitated by mighty sighs and sobs and "extremely violent tremors," the whole lasting a quarter of an hour without a word being uttered. Then came the final stage, the prophetic moment: "the Spirit formed words in his mouth," agitating his whole body with strange motions accompanied by anguish.

Certain cases can be explained away as simulation, possibly pathological in nature, but this could not entirely account for attitudes that the visionaries sustained against all comers, for they were seen to "fanaticize" in the face of every conceivable punishment—despite their parents' entreaties and the threats of the authorities. Esprit Séguier demonstrated this extraordinary capacity for escape from reality right on the torture rack. Certain symptoms of hysteria are frequently mentioned as accompanying the development of these seizures: insensibility to blows and pincers; loss of memory; and glossolalia, interminable discourse in a language not one's own (people who in their daily life spoke nothing but *langue d'oc* dialects set to reciting the Bible or the Psalms in French during the prophetic phase). Sometimes, too, inhuman howling has been noted. Esprit Séguier barked while at Pont-de-Montvert; Isabeau Cipeyre, in the midst of a seizure, crowed like a cock or howled like a dog. Finally, on several occasions one encounters the symptom of the "hysteric ball." The prophet Rouergas declared to the bishop Fléchier (who interrogated him on November 5, 1701) that when the Holy Ghost entered his body he felt something like a stone in his stomach. Certain descriptions succeed in evoking the celebrated arctic hysteria encountered on numerous occasions by ethnologists of the twentieth century. A participant in a secret assembly falls into a two-foot snowbank as if he were having an epileptic seizure, and then with his eyes tightly shut he begins preaching and prophesying.

Some of these scenes are almost solitary affairs, taking place, for example, in prison under the eyes of a guard, a judge, or, for that matter, a torturer. But more often they are quite in the nature of a public spectacle performed to the metric beat of the members of a clandestine cult, who embrace, weep, pant, shake, howl, groan, and beat their breasts, the whole forming a sort of witches' Sabbath while the prophet is having his own seizure and announcing with a frothing at the mouth, to whoever cares to listen, that the world is coming to an end. The levelheaded Villars, after witnessing such a scene, sighed with consternation, "These people are all lunatics."

That there existed among the visionaries some who were really feeble-minded congenital idiots is beyond question. The *Sacred Theater* describes the seizures of a certain Pierre Bernard, a sheepherder of the Cévennes who was a "poor imbecile." He "dropped like a dead man", and then his body became very agitated, leaping and tossing as if it were being shaken by a giant hand. At last, filled with remorse, Bernard opened his mouth "to say that he had been tormented in this way on account of his sins," and the Languedocian shepherd recited passages from the Scriptures in French as if he knew the Bible by heart. The pastor Dubois cites four other examples, besides that of Bernard, of feebleminded persons who became visionaries, among them "a woman half-wit who was transformed into a great preacher."

These were marginal cases. Five simpletons or pseudosimpletons out of almost a hundred Camisard visionaries whose names have come down to us is a significant but not a decisive number. In reality, one also encounters among the hundred some perfectly normal personalities afflicted only by a passing disorder—people like Jean Cavalier, for example.

Jean Cavalier, a poor peasant who became a rebel chief and Villars's inter-locutor, was in fact one of these inspired convulsionaries. Later he would resume a normal psychic, social, and sexual life. He would be Pimpette's lover and the governor of Jersey, and he would converse with Voltaire. In his *Mémoires* he would gloss over his old neurosis, publicly censure his prophetic years, and rationalize the revolt he had lived through, depicting himself simply as a former figher for a just cause, that of freedom of con-science (which was exact, but only part of the story). But numerous other witnesses speak in his stead. They tell of the dream he had when he was twelve in which he saw himself as his brothers' liberator and which resolved him on a prophetic career. Arnassan, Marion, Pimpette's mother, and the *Sacred Theatre*, independently of one another, describe Cavalier's trances during the war of the Camisards—"the strange agitation" that lifted up his body and shook it violently, making the bed quake, after which the Holy Ghost dictated his conduct and tactics, ordering him to engage in a certain battle or to kill a certain traitor. Villars himself was induced to negotiate with Louis XIV by one of Cavalier's visions, in which a voice said to him, "You shall speak to the king."

The "divine madman" Cavalier was not the only member of his species. Quite the contrary, he was a typical representative of a certain faction of the Huguenot younger generation around 1700, and he did not hesitate to pose as the champion of sons betrayed by culpable and turncoat fathers. The young rebel (who at the same time showed a tender attachment to his mother) declared, in fact, that he had been "designated by the grace of God to watch over the conduct of the flock in order to defend the cause of the Law that our fathers have unfortunately forsaken out of cowardice." The same invectives, addressed to a merciful God against "the cowardice of our fathers," issued from the pen of Rolland, a wool comber and pig castrator become a *maquisard* of the Cévennes. In the case of these young, sometimes adolescent youths, whose still impressionable and poorly integrated personalities readily lent themselves to manifestations of hysteria, a violent oedipal conflict found its sacred justification in contemporary circumstances.

How many were there of these young prophets? The Catholic chronicler Brueys, almost surely exaggerating, speaks of hundreds and even of thousands of visionaries in the Vivarais and the Dauphiné beginning in 1688–89. Élie Marion, himself a convulsionary, made up two lists from memory in his *Mémoires*. First, he names the fourteen "inspired ones" active in the Cévennes and Bas-Languedoc in the years 1700–1704. Almost all of them were from the class of poor peasants and village artisans. There were wool combers, but also a farm worker, a baker, a pig castrator, a weaver, a cowherd, and a mason. There was not one veritable bourgeois or intellectual, that is, not one gentleman, in the lot. The great Camisard leaders Mazel, Rolland, and Cavalier were included in the fourteen.

In addition, Marion furnishes a list (which he claims is incomplete) of eighty persons, sixty-three men (including the fourteen "inspired" previously named) and seventeen women, "who, when the war came, received the gift of preaching." None of those, incidently, whom Marion qualifies as "not inspired" among the principal Camisards (he names only five who lacked the spark) figure among these eighty vessels of the Holy Ghost. In short, there were probably about one hundred true prophets in all. It was from that phalanx, one learns, that the military chiefs were chosen, essentially because of their visions since in the beginning "these leaders knew nothing of warfare," and it was the Holy Ghost that had to inform them, in a fatherly way, which battle to wage, which sentinel to post, and which priest to assassinate.

Here we touch on the essential difference between the Camisards and their brother fanatics of English-speaking Protestantism. The apocalyptic Muggletonians of the seventeenth century, and also the quakers and shakers of every species, were generally pacifistic and nonviolent. On the contrary, the "shakers" and convulsionaries of the Cévennes were heralds of war, not peace.

This warmongering tendency was not immediately apparent. For a long time, from 1688 to 1701, the individual or collective crises of hysteria of the persecuted Huguenot peasants were attended (a fact in no wise in contradiction with the most recent observations) by a crushing masochistic guilt complex. They were dominated by an obsession with sin, by remorse for the collective apostasy committed in 1685, and by a throbbing desire for repentance. "Have mercy on our souls! Repent of your sins!" cried the wandering child prophets of the Uzège and the Gardons in 1701 in the midst of clamoring multitudes.

Then in 1701–1702 a new tendency began to emerge. On January 16, 1702, Françoise Brès told her persecutor Du Chayla from the gallows that his turn to perish would come. Four months later (May 8 and May 19, 1702), and for the first time in a long while in the secret assemblies of the Hautes-Cévennes, the king came under personal attack, and the predicant-prophet Mandagout issued the first call to arms: "Tear down the churches, kill all the Catholics."

Historians rightly date the actual cycle of Huguenot violence, in response to the violence of their enemies, from the assassination of Du Chayla—"the disagreeable adventure of the abbot Du Chayla," as Basville calls it. For a long time scholars have limited themselves to establishing a sort of a equivalence between the crime and the punishment; the abbot had probably tortured, and he had surely condemned to death, and so he was assassinated in his turn. If that was not equitable, it was at least rational and logical—an eye for an eye, a tooth for a tooth. "It was the law of retaliation, a wise and reasonable law," as a recent historian of the Camisards remarks bizarrely, evoking in support of this "idea" Oradour and the atom bomb.[4]

Such a "commercial" view of matters is not entirely inexact, and it might satisfy some minds, but it empties the opening act of the war of much of its human, emotive, and irrational content. One must read the *Mémoires* of Abraham Mazel, who was the chief person responsible for the murder, in order to understand in what a frenzied and hallucinatory context, in the midst of what fits of delirium, the assassination of the priest was plotted and carried out.

---

[4] Oradour-sur-Glane: A French village where in June, 1944, German soldiers murdered over six hundred men, women, and children in reprisal for the death of an SS captain (tr. note).

Abraham Mazel, born in 1677, was the son of a Huguenot peasant of Saint-Jean-du-Gard. His mother was a native of the Hautes-Cévennes. In October, 1701, he had his first revelation at an assembly near his village led by the visionary Cabrit. In the spring or early summer of 1702 he had a dream: some fat, black steers were devouring the cabbages in the garden with impunity; the dreamer drove them out. Mazel, like his contemporaries, predicants or Camisards—like Brousson and Cavalier—was very attentive to the interpretation of dreams, which he regarded as signs and portents. In fact, a few days later a vision revealed the meaning of his own dream; the garden was the church of Jesus Christ, and he himself, Abraham Mazel, was the chosen of God to drive the intruders from the divine cabbage patch by force. Who, then, were these intruders, the fat, black steers? The color black in Camisard texts is always identified with sin; as for the ghostly beeves, these could have had, strangely enough, a demonic significance. For Mazel, in any case, there was no question about it. The black steers that must be driven out and quickly destroyed—or in any event restored to their true "bovine" vocation as celebates and eunuchs—were, as he states expressly, the Catholic priests. Beginning with this dream, it was in fact open season on priests by fire and sword, as subsequent events would demonstrate.

Mazel joined a band of prophets who had taken refuge in the maquis near Barre-des-Cévennes some months earlier. Among them was the wool carder Esprit Séguier, a dried-up, swarthy, toothless, heroic—and neurotic—personnage condemned in his youth for the rape of a little girl. It was he who, after his capture, "would fanaticize in all its forms" on the torture rack. Condemned to be burned at the stake, he declared, "My soul is a garden of shade and fountains"; on the stake itself, his hand half severed from his body by the executioner, he tore it the rest of the way off with his teeth.

It was in the midst of these men, at the assemblies of the mountain of Le Bougès, that Mazel would have the decisive convulsions that would lead to the Du Chayla affair. On July 22, 1702, he relates, "the Holy Ghost came upon me in such a terrible manner that the convulsions visited upon my body inspired fear and terror in the souls of the beholders . . . ; finally, my mouth was opened and quite a long discourse issued forth." (The personality split in this case was complete, and Mazel's mouth functioned independently of its normal user as a "God box," to borrow the expression of certain visionaries of the twentieth century.) Following this discourse, "the Holy Ghost commanded us to deliver up our brothers who were imprisoned at Pont-de-Montvert," where Du Chayla was playing the role of jailer.

Thereupon, the troop of prophets, swelled by peasant adherents, set off, obedient to Mazel's visions, to attack the house of the abbot. From start to finish, the "Holy Ghost," which expressed itself through the successive revelations of Mazel and Séguier, dictated every detail of the order of march and of attack, the tactics of combat, and the ultimate decision to murder the abbot (July 23, 1702).

The bloody expedition concluded with an episode that is less well known but very revealing. The troop of prophets went to Saint-André-de-Lancize on July 27, 1702, writes Mazel, to "execute another order pronounced by my lips." His men killed the priest Boissonnade, destroyed the *marmousets* (idols or images of the saints) found in the church, and "inflicted wounds" on another priest, Parent by name, who served as schoolmaster at Saint-André.

What kind of "wounds"? Mazel does not say, and Rampon, another visionary who participated in the affair, was equally vague in his own memoirs composed late in life. He noted simply that the insurgents wanted to "kill the concubine" of the two priests if they could have found her. But the Catholic chroniclers had no reason for any such reticence or for any such significant omissions. Two of them, Louvreleuil and Mingaud—the latter the priest of a neighboring village who entrusted Parent to the care of a surgeon—declared on the one hand, with regard to the priest Boissonnade, that in taking his life the insurgents had cut off his ears and nose, and on the other hand, with regard to Parent, the schoolmaster-priest, that he had been castrated, which led to his death nine days later.

Such was the incident that touched off the war: a dream, a convulsive delirium, murder, castration. The sequence clearly shows that Mazel would do anything to fulfill his dream and drive the priests out of the earthly paradise. In this case, he and his friends steadfastly let their obsessions determine their actions. They would persevere in this path, moreover, during the whole course of the war, which they waged—not without success—by force of hysteric visions accompanied from time to time by a proper miracle, ordeal, or firewalking.

Such impulses depended in very large part on irrational motivations which would require the elucidation of the phenomenon of prophetic hysteria and in extreme cases—among the most highly inflamed or frankly neurotic—an analysis of the unconscious. Analysis would be difficult, to say the least. Cavalier and Mazel cannot be invited to stretch out on the couch of some hypothetical historian-psychoanalyst. One can only note certain obvious traits that are generally encountered in similar cases of hysteria (conversion hysteria)—among them infantilism, theatricality, and sexual frustration.

This last point, to conclude, deserves a brief comment. The Camisards themselves were conscious of it. In the case of young prophetesses, they report that the visions disappeared when they married and lost their virginity —after the end of a phase of sexual inhibition, in other words. In a more general way, is it not remarkable that the two great attacks of convulsionary fever in the first half of the seventeenth century in France occurred in the two sectors of religious life where sexual morals were the most demanding, the most ascetic, *and the most interiorized*? One sector was among those puritans of the French Midi, the Huguenot peasants of the Cévennes, and the other occurred some thirty years later in the bosom of Parisian Jansenism among the convulsionaries of Saint-Médard.

The Taxpayers' Resentment

In the last analysis, the Camisard episode is amenable to a multiple interpretation. The traditional one—that it represents a righteous struggle for freedom of conscience—is exact but a long way from exhaustive. It leaves certain essential aspects in shadow. We have noted, in the wake of other authors, the prophetic character of the movement. But it contained another much more down-to-earth element, one that was subordinate but far from negligible. This was the old fight against taxes—the resentment of the taxpayers.

The Huguenot villagers listened to the prophets, but they were not forgetting the new and detestable poll tax which oppressed a countryside already impoverished by the economic depression. In October, 1702, the bishop of Alès, spiritual head of the Cévennes diocese, wrote the minister of war that "the capitation is as much involved as religion in their seditious enterprises." The example of the Huguenot areas of the Vivarais, which had been stirred up by Cavalier's emissaries, is no less conclusive; there, too, the antitax strike was intimately involved with the religious insurrection and prophetic illuminism. On June 17, 1703, Montrevel predicted "a general movement in the Vivarais . . . fomented by the Consistory," and added, "It is certain that the people have been extremely agitated for several days . . . to the point that in several localities of the Vivarais they have refused to pay the capitation." These antitax strikes unquestionably had important consequences. In 1703 in the province of Languedoc, 70 percent of the first installment of the poll tax was still unpaid, and some enormous accumulated back taxes would be owed by the end of the Huguenot uprising in 1705.

The insurrection in the Cévennes, the last peasant war of the Old Regime, marks the end of an era. More than any of the earlier civil wars, it takes account—after its fashion—of the original traits of the society that engendered it. It was a society impoverished by the crisis and traumatized by the Revocation. The Camisard uprising reveals itself, therefore, with its particular logic, as an explosive mixture of prophetic neurosis and antitax ferment.

Conclusion

A Great Agrarian Cycle

Witches' black magic at the end of the sixteenth century; prophets' white magic at the beginning of the eighteenth century—the radical antithesis in mythical content must not be allowed to obscure the affinities of certain mental structures or the long persistence, in the modern period, of a capacity for anxiety and for wonder, of a faith in miracles, which today is lost. Is this one sign, among scores of others, of a certain cultural continuum between 1500 and 1700—itself resting on the social continuum and the specific unity of a great agrarian cycle?

Periodization

I have endeavored in the present book to observe, at various levels, the long-term movements of an economy and of a society—base and super-structure, material life and cultural life, sociological evolution and collective psychology, the whole within the framework of a rural world which remained very largely traditional in nature. More particularly, I have attempted to analyze, in their multiple aspects, successive phases of growth and decline. These phases, taken together in chronological sequence (lift-off, rise, maturity, and decline), imply a unity and serve to describe a major, organized, secular rural fluctuation spanning eight generations.

To put it more simply, my book's protagonist is a great agrarian cycle, lasting from the end of the fifteenth century to the beginning of the eighteenth, studied in its entirety. I have been able to delineate and to characterize it thanks, naturally, to the price curves, but more particularly thanks to demographic studies (of taxpayers and of total population), to indices of production and business activity, and to the series of charts reflecting land, wealth, and income distribution.

The major tendency of the modern cycle thus defined is not the "*être de*

289

raison," the abstract universal raised to a fetish with its explanatory but inexplicable virtues criticized by Pierre Jeannin. Happily, a solid documentation, rich in diverse, continuous, indicative series of data, has made it possible to dissociate in a fruitful manner "the elements and components" of the long-term movement. These sources have divulged its internal connections, "its significance, modalities, and chronology." The complete cycle can be broken down into several distinct phases.

First phase: the low-water mark (preconditions of growth). People were scarce (because the demographic structure had collapsed at the end of the previous—medieval—long-term cycle, which was also secular, spanning the period from the eleventh century to the fifteenth century). Arable land and even forests were once again abundant, constituting reserves of unemployed resources available for a resumption of expansion. Landed property was consolidated into large holdings, and families into powerful clans. Low land rent tended little by little to stimulate the activities of assarters, farm operators, and peasants. Food was more plentiful, and people were better nourished, healthier, and in other respects less vulnerable to the plague microbe after a good hundred years of selective slaughter. All of these things helped set the stage for a new period of advance.

Second phase: the advance. This period came about, as has been seen, essentially of its own accord, fueled by the simple accumulation of endogenous factors. The combustible material had been piling up for a long time, and the slightest spark (a series of good harvests, a supplementary injection of precious metals into the monetary circulation, the influence of new circuits of trade or of new poles of urban growth, or simply a period of peace and prosperity) was sufficient to ignite the fires of expansion.

The expansion—a rapid mutation at the end of a period of silent gestation —thus made its local debut quite abruptly about 1490–1500. It was population that got off to a fast start; the economy itself made little headway at first. For this reason, by 1530 a serious contradiction developed. On the one hand was the dynamic elasticity of population; on the other was the stubborn inelasticity of agricultural production. Was the latter, which has been widely noted elsewhere in western Europe—in the north as well as in the south—the "fruit" of technical conservatism, lack of capital, and the absence of a spirit of initiative and innovation? In all events, it brought in its wake signs of austerity—forms of "rationing": wage rationing through the reduction of real wages and the pauperization of hired hands and day laborers, and land rationing through the accelerated subdivision of tenures. Impoverishment proceeded at the same time from a sort of "iron law" of wages and from the breakup of landholdings without any increase in yields per hectare. Malthus and Ricardo had joined forces.

A disparate, discordant development of this sort is incapable, notwithstanding a rise in entrepreneurial profits, of secreting agrarian capitalism on a large scale. True growth, which would have raised the average gross product per capita, remained, under these conditions, an impossible goal situated far over the horizon.

Contemporaries—the notables no less than the people—were only confusedly aware of the real situation. Should one be surprised at their relative insensibility? No, there is nothing at all shocking about it if one reflects carefully on the mentality of the period. The people of that age had other things on their minds besides the gross product. The most representative among them—and this was one of the strongest and most typical traits of traditional society—were preoccupied to the point of self-immolation with religious questions. The civil war combatants, whether Huguenot or papist, were possessed by a bloody obsession with heavenly salvation. After 1560 they threw themselves body and soul into the religious struggle.

It is true that in Protestant circles the sacred combat dissembled certain social goals which raised the question of church land, of the tithe and taxes, and even of the three orders of society. Such projects tended, in an obscure and piecemeal fashion, to mitigate the deficiencies of social development.

But the results were mediocre. The social agitation of the end of the century degenerated into an antitax movement, if not into the madness of the witches' Sabbaths that turned the world upside down but did nothing to transform it.

Third phase: after 1600, maturity. The Malthusian and Ricardian checks tended to become veritable social stumbling blocks. Thus, from the point of view of population—for reasons connected with the deterioration of living standards—the death rate drew dangerously close to the birth rate. To be sure, in Languedoc (as in Provence, the Loire valley, the Beauvais region, Holland, and England) population continued to grow after 1600, and the French Midi—like many regions of continental Europe to the north—had thus far escaped the long, premature retreat of population that affected Castile and certain parts of Italy beginning in 1600. Nevertheless, as far as

Languedoc is concerned, a demographic deceleration is clearly perceptible after 1600. The general curve of population had been climbing steeply under Francis I and Henry II. Between 1570 and 1650 it gradually leveled off.

New parasitic phenomena were superimposed on the cases of "rationing" and austerity observed in the second phase (which continued into the third) : rente in all its forms—interest on loans, rent from land, tithes to the Church, and taxes to the state—"took off." The rentier mentality prevailed over the spirit of enterprise. Gentlemen farmers were transformed into parasitic landlords. In certain respects, society tended to sink into a state of social conservatism, the paralyzing consequences of which aggravated the Malthusian effects of an immemorial technical conservatism.

During this third phase, an enormous increase in taxation reflected in its way the temptations of prestige and of state power embodied in the policies of Richelieu. The state, which had consolidated its forces at the end of the previous phase of expansion, embarked on far-ranging wars, the costs of which were too heavy for society to bear.

This third phase of so-called maturity in agrarian development, which preceded a certain decline, was therefore quite different from the phase of the same name described by theoreticians of modern economic growth. It was not the "healthy" maturity of industrial societies, or at least of the most favored among them. On the contrary, it was a period filled with pitfalls and beset with growing difficulties and accumulated obstacles—a period in which the gross product, in the long run, persisted in marking time; in which the demographic advance, for this reason, was held in check; and in which capital was diverted toward rente.

Granting this, is it correct in connection with such a period to employ catchall phrases like "the crisis of the seventeenth century" or to speak of the "reversal of the conjuncture" beginning in the early decades of the century? Such expressions are perfectly valid in regard to the Spanish co-lonial conjuncture, to Latin America, prematurely stricken by the silver famine and above all by the debacle of the indigenous population. They are equally valid in regard to Castile and Italy, and a few decades later they could be applied to Germany and neighboring Burgundy devastated by the Thirty Years War. But outside these geographical limits, vast as they are, simple extrapolation is impossible. One cannot even assert that the "Med-iterranean conjuncture," as a whole, supports the thesis of a change of di-rection around 1620: some violent short-lived crises, yes; a demographic slowdown (attested to beginning in the last third of the sixteenth century), without a doubt; but a universal secular depression, no—at least not yet— because Provence, Languedoc, and Catalonia, all of the considerable Mediterranean littoral of the Gulf of Lion from Tarragona to Toulon, escaped that radical reversal of the economic conjuncture which henceforth assumed a southern, peninsular, and—from a European point of view—almost marginal character.

On the northernmost shores of the Mediterranean, the conjuncture subsided, changed pace, and grew *sluggish*, but it did not yet *reverse itself*. The "chronological disparity" and "permanent opposition" in 1694 that Pierre Jeannin called attention to established itself along a frontier passing far to the south—a frontier that served to isolate the Spanish colonial and "Italo-Castilian" conjuncture condemned to a long decline beginning in 1620. North of this line, in numerous regions of continental Europe and the New World, in the huge area extending from Mediterranean France and Catalonia to the North Sea and to the Puritan countries of the Atlantic seaboard, the populations knew nothing yet, nor would they know for some time to come, of that malady of long-term decline that afflicted Italians, Castilians, and Spain's American subjects.

In Languedoc, in any event, agricultural production, although sluggish, did not collapse. Quite the contrary, after 1620 certain sectors, like viticulture, were even fairly lively. The demographic advance continued, if at a much slower pace, and numerous categories of rentiers prospered, redoubling their outlays on prestige, piety, power, and conspicuous consumption and multiplying their châteaus and churches.

The "carefree prosperity" of the sixteenth century was evidently at an end. Signs of sclerosis and social and demographic maturity multiplied, and it is here that one discovers an analogy with the infinitely more serious scleroses affecting Castile and Italy; but it is here alone, for, local exceptions aside, the gross product and population for the most part held firm.

The tragedy of Languedoc, in the third phase, was not the collapse but only the inelasticity and rigidity of agricultural production—not its decline, but its failure to grow significantly. Let us accept, for the sake of argument, the most favorable (counterfactual) hypothesis—that the gross product had increased substantially under Richelieu and Mazarin. In that case it would have sustained the continuing demographic advance, the resulting subdivision of tenures, and the increased exactions of the rentier classes without difficulty and without sacrificing the standard of living. It would have financed the wars and ambitions of the cardinal ministers with Napoleonic good cheer.

Nothing of the sort occurred. The gross agricultural product from Francis I to the Fronde remained, in the long run, practically stationary, with only a slight tendency to rise. This was the reason for so much misfortune, even if the conjuncture did not "turn around" and even if its complete reversal—marking the tragic climax of a difficult time—did not, in fact, occur until later, in the final phase of the great agrarian cycle that I have termed "the recession."

Under Colbert the obduracy of production seemed for a moment exorcised. The gross product increased, and for a period of ten or fifteen years it broke through the secular ceiling. Unfortunately, the production of wine, which was the most profitable crop of the region in normal times, did not rise; indeed, it declined during this brief period of prosperity. The contradiction is not without significance, for society in the age of Colbert was not equipped, materially or psychologically, to receive and continue this partial and precarious rise of the gross product. The increase in supply, resulting automatically from the rise in production, occurred in the midst of falling prices, which it served only to accentuate.

Farm profits were wiped out by 1665–70. Production itself finally collapsed in the disastrous decade of the 1680's, affecting the peasant smallhold no less than the great ecclesiastical estate.

We are now well into the *fourth phase, the long period of recession.* Aggregate agricultural production declined without, however, falling excessively low. The movement was limited essentially to wiping out the temporary increase registered in the days of Fouquet and Colbert. Production simply retreated more or less to the permanent, basic depressed level it had been unable to rise above in the sixteenth and first half of the seventeenth centuries.

This return to Louis XIII, to Henry II, and indeed to Francis I at the very end of the reign of Louis XIV had depressing consequences for peasant society. For a long time—up to 1650—the low level of production had been compatible with the continuation, increasingly slow and difficult, of the demographic advance and the process of land subdivision. It was even compatible with the institution of increasingly heavy rents and charges. People exerted themselves a bit more and tightened their belts, and society managed somehow to make ends meet. After 1650 the momentary upsurge of production (between 1655 and 1675) had granted peasant society a new lease on life. The demographic advance, land subdivision, and onerous exactions could continue for a while longer.

But the return to a depressed level of production after 1675–80 necessitated, in the last analysis, a readjustment, a social reassessment, a sort of cheerless process of rationalization. In which domain? There was no question, for reasons of high politics, of the government curtailing its demands in the face of a declining gross product. Quite the opposite: taxation would increase at the end of the reign contrary to all economic logic but in harmony with the grandiose designs of the Sun King, served by a ruthless bureaucracy.

The readjustment and reordering, therefore, would have to be in other directions. First, since nothing could be done about public exactions, certain private exactions contracted a bit. Land rent showed unmistakable signs of decline in real terms at the close of the century. But the chief victim of social readjustment was population. Society's solution to the contraction of the gross product and its return to the secular status quo were of the cruelest sort. It reduced the number of mouths to feed—the size of the potential work force—by brutally amputating a fraction of its human complement. It handed over a pound of its own flesh. After 1680, in fact, all demographic growth, no matter how modest, was arrested. Here we come to the capital fact, the truly unprecedented event; population, for the first time in two centuries, entered upon a long-term decline, a decline provoked not so much by the repeated famines—which were perhaps less serious than in the center and in the north of France—as by joblessness and poverty; by chronic undernourishment; by the low standard of living which favored the spread of epidemics; by the primitive sanitary conditions of the poor; and—very accessorily—by emigration, late marriages, and even a little birth control. A natural corollary to the decline in numbers of the poorer classes was the downfall of the smallhold tenant. Land subdivision, which had been raging since the Renaissance, was finally arrested, and a phase of consolidation, to the advantage of the land engrossers, set in.

It was no longer a question, as it had been in the first half of the seventeenth century, of the simple abatement of a particularly lively conjuncture, but rather—from 1675–80—of its complete turnabout, a turnabout reflected as clearly as one could hope to see in population statistics and in the cadastres. The almost two-century-old movement of rising population and land subdivision had lasted since 1500. Extremely animated during the better part of the sixteenth century, in the seventeenth century it showed obvious signs of maturity, sclerosis, and fatigue. Finally, in 1680 it disappeared, giving way to a movement in the opposite sense. This was a perfect illustration (at least in the regional case of the French Midi—elsewhere the timing might be different) of the reversal of the conjuncture. It was the critical juncture that historians almost everywhere are rightly struggling to date in the exhausted Europe of the seventeenth century.

Technical Impasses and Cultural Stumbling Blocks

Throughout the present book, and in particular in the last part devoted to the "recession"—the interrupted development and contraction of an ancient rural society—I have tried to situate the determinants and to assign the actual responsibilities by establishing an accurate chronology. From this point of view, at least, one connection seems solidly established. It was the technological weakness of this society, its inability to raise productivity, its incapacity to increase production lastingly and definitively, which created the barrier that interrupted the almost two-century-long advance in population and peasant smallholdings at the end of this period.

One is truly in the presence of that "preindustrial society characterized by slow technical change" where the "processes of growth and decline" were still dominated "by the play between demographic expansion and limited resources" (Vilar, 1960, p. 51). From beginning to end of the great agrarian cycle of 1500–1700, the gross product ran the show—for that matter, in a most passive manner, by sheer weight of inertia. It was the gross product that progressively bent the population curve inward (its ballisticlike trajectory evokes this braking action on society to perfection). It was the gross product that induced phenomena of pauperization in the second and third phases; through its incapacity to grow, it rendered the increased exactions of the third phase (exactions that a dynamic production, on the contrary, would have sustained without difficulty) intolerable. Finally, in the fourth phase the retrogression—or, to be exact, the return to a state of inertia following a momentary upswing of the gross product—provoked the final decline of population, of smallholdings, and of land development. This denouement was logical and inevitable. The Malthusian scissors between production and population could not go on opening forever.

Under these circumstances, is one forced to reject the classic explanation which imputes the difficulties of the seventeenth century and its terminal crisis to the "monetary famine"? By no means. Even if somewhat outmoded, the quantity theory of money does not deserve such a summary execution, but it can no longer pretend to the absolutely central role it once enjoyed. It must be integrated into a unified system of explanation at once more sweeping and more flexible.

If, following the lively advance of the previous period, certain European economies, populations, and societies, like those of Languedoc, leveled off and finally declined during the course of the seventeenth century, it was not only because the Spanish-American colonizers had worked out the best gold and silver mines and depleted the ranks of the mining proletariat of the Andes. A monetary impasse really existed, but it was not the only obstacle to expansion. It formed part of a whole structure of interrelated impasses: the land impasse, the lack of unlimited reserves of fertile, easy-to-work, profitable land; and, more important—dissembled, so to speak, behind the phenomenon of land hunger—the technological impasse, which constituted the essential impediment.

The most striking evidence in the latter domain is the average Languedocian wheat yield, which, according to first-hand sources, remained stabilized at a low figure (from 3 to 4.5 for 1) from the sixteenth century (our earliest data) to 1730–40. The only improvement, and it was not lasting, was registered in the age of Colbert. Yields did not really begin to rise, and then very sluggishly, as far as that is concerned, until 1750.

In other words, if society contracted and the economy lost momentum and finally fell back to its base level at the end of the seventeenth century, it was because the economy was incapable either of increasing or renewing its stocks—its stock of precious metals, to be sure, but also its stock of good land, which was limited by definition, and, failing this, its "stock" of technical progress, which was so ridiculously modest in the sixteenth and seventeenth centuries. Let us pursue one of our earlier hypotheses. If grain yields had risen a few points between 1500 and 1700 (as would occur later), or if one had succeeded in planting vines on a massive scale and a continuing basis (as would be the case almost uninterruptedly between 1760 and 1870) or else in introducing widespread irrigation (as the Catalans did beginning in 1720), Languedocian society, through the simple increase in income per land unit, could have coped with the rise in population and the headlong subdivision of landholdings as well as the growing burden of charges of all sorts. The fragmentation of peasant tenures proved excessive and the increased charges intolerable because production and productivity remained stabilized at centuries-old levels.

In fact, this technological immobility was the fruit of a whole series of cultural stumbling blocks. Some have spoken of a *natural* ceiling on productive resources. But "nature" in this case is actually culture; it is the customs, the way of life, the mentality of the people; it is a whole formed by technical knowledge and a system of values, by the means employed and the ends pursued. The forces that first deflected the expansion, then checked it, and ultimately broke it were not only economic in a narrow sense but also cultural in a broad sense, and even, in a certain measure, spiritual. In this last category, above all, their actual impact is impossible to measure but their power of constraint is obvious.

Despite a certain evolution, of which we shall speak in a moment, Lanquedocian society, as far as its ruling elites were concerned, remained theological and military at least to the same degree as French society as a whole, and under Louis XIV the sons of the petty bourgeoisie, just like the sons of the nobility, were, whenever possible, still intended for the army or the church. For the most gifted minds of that age, the salvation of souls was more important than the improvement of techniques. The pragmatic, "disenchanted," and profoundly nonreligious universe in which we live was scarcely conceivable, at least for the masses of the people, before 1700.

In the sixteenth century, for example, in a society which was nevertheless very dynamic, the capital of human energy accumulated since the Renaissance was not invested in the economy or consecrated to the safeguard of a minimum level of well-being. It was dissipated wholesale in the fire and flame of the religious struggle. It was only as a second thought and on the rebound, so to speak, that the Protestants of the civil wars advanced certain social demands—timid demands for that matter—such as the redistribution of land and the reform of the tithe.

After 1600 the victory of Catholicism became more and more inseparable from a certain revival of "feudal" society ("feudal" not in the narrow, institutional sense of the medievalists but in the broad sense in which the philosophers of the eighteenth century used the term). The comparative failure of the agronomists and Protestant leaders is a reflection of this revival. Serres, Laffemas, and Sully, who were concerned, each in his own fashion and sometimes in contradition to one another, with questions of economic expansion in agriculture or manufacturing, had no significant following after 1620. The nation, with Richelieu, would prefer war, and with Louis XIV, despite the Colbertian interlude, it would prefer glory. The aristocratic ideal of prowess and the Catholic ideal of salvation would determine the conduct of the ruling classes.

During what I have termed the phase of maturity (the third phase), rent exacted its heavy tribute from a sluggish production, and this golden age of rent was inseparable from a certain number of styles or ways of life which aimed, as the case might be, at ostentation or security—styles of life reflected in the bourgeoisie's passion for offices or land, the clergy's investments in monasteries of baroque architecture, and the libertine or military pursuits of the nobility or of those who aspired to the nobility. These modes of life signified relative wealth; they did little to stimulate expansion.

In the fourth phase ("recession") the policies pursued by the state, with the assent of a large portion of the elite, were aimed at assuring at whatever cost the resplendent glory of one man and his lineage, the war-making and territorial power of the realm, and the absolute monopoly of the Church. Such policies are the perfectly logical consequence of a certain system of values (aberrant values in our eyes), but they ran directly counter to the recovery of a contracted economy. Versailles and the army—the military and sumptuary budgets—increased the pressure of taxation, and taxes inopportunely amputated a gross product already in full retreat.

As for the Revocation—another striking aspect of these global policies—it revealed, in the person of Basville, its principal promoter in Languedoc, an exacerbated concern for a combined religious and political monism. For the intendant of Languedoc the unity of the faith was an absolute good which had the added merit of guaranteeing the unanimity of the French people in their obedience to the Very Christian King.

Such an attitude was not absurd if one only places oneself in the specious perspective of its promoters. But it was costly, and it furnishes the remarkable example of a culture that was destructive of its own economic foundations. Doubtless the Revocation was neither the first nor the principal cause of French economic decadence at the close of the reign. In 1685, nevertheless, it came at a very bad moment for a Midi swarming with Huguenots and in the early stages of an economic decline (under way since 1675–80). In Languedoc, at least in the Protestant cantons, the Revocation accentuated the existing stagnation. It consummated for a time the ruin of the silk industry of the Cévennes and subjacent regions. It provoked the flight of capital from Nîmes.

Catholic contemporaries were conscious of these misfortunes. "Misery is very widespread since the change of religion," the notary Borrély wrote at the conclusion of some notations on the subject. Nevertheless, the same Borrely had accepted in advance and would justify a posteriori the decree of 1685, for he saw in it a supreme sign of grace, a divine miracle, the work of God. Besides, Borrely was convinced that the Protestants—those "ill-intentioned devils," those monsters, those fanatics—fully deserved their bitter fate. No matter if they dragged their Catholic contemporaries down to ruin in an epidemic of bankruptcies. That was the price that had to be paid. From a certain point of view, therefore, responsible men of that age acted out their own history and consummated their own misfortunes without illusions. It was a question of the stakes; religious unity, for many of them, represented a higher value in itself than the rescue, at any price, of profits or material well-being.

By the same token, the rebels who rose up against different kinds of oppression did not always adopt a line of conduct that was—according to our own criteria—perfectly rational and capable of putting an end to their suffering. For a very long time they confined themselves to fighting the tax collector, whereas the real source of their difficulties lay in the social organization itself and was much more general. A single revolt in eighteenth-century France sought explicitly (at the direct instigation of English exiles influenced by their own revolution) to raise the issue of equal rights and representative government. The daring program drawn up by the Ormée at Bordeaux intrigued, for a time, the princes of the Fronde, but it did not awaken a lasting echo among the population, and this attempted graft of Anglo-Saxon political thought onto the French rebel consciousness was destined to wither on the limb. The eighteenth century of the philosophes, whose activities would eventually prepare the way for the reception of political programs from across the channel, still lay ahead. In the seventeenth century the French and English cultural areas were at variance. To have spoken to a French rebel of those days, whether pre-Fronde or post-Fronde, of the actual abolition of privilege and of a national elected assembly would have been a little, mutatis mutandis, like preaching socialism to an African native in 1850 or 1900. But if one could have talked to that Frenchman of 1640 or 1670 about the taille or the salt tax, he would have seen red, even if taxes were only one of the many sources of his difficulties.

In another domain, that of religious oppression, the natives of the Cévennes during the course of the Camisard insurrection departed from what—according to our possibly subjective criteria—should have represented the rationale of such a revolt. They did not confine themselves to advocating freedom of conscience or even to simple Protestant proselytizing, but adopted, as a line of conduct, the hysterical trance inspired by the convulsions of the visionaries and the imminence of the Second Coming. Such behavior was highly appreciated and, wherever possible, imitated by the Camisards' Protestant contemporaries, but in our culture of today, and even at the time among devout Catholic rationalists like Fléchier and Basville, it was considered aberrant and neurotic.

In this perspective, the study of cultural impediments ought to be pursued beyond the limits of "culture," in the narrow sense of the term, to the farthest reaches of the unconscious psyche; the *aiguillette* rites, so widespread and so terrifying, and the forms of behavior encountered during the popular revolts and "emotions" have disclosed, on several occasions, the existence of extremely well characterized anxieties, impulses, and fantasies which were expressed in a symbolic "language" of frightening obviousness, the likes of which are no longer to be found in our contemporary culture.[1]

A long monograph on the Camisard peasants has permitted us to elucidate in a different connection—starting with the convulsive seizures—the symptoms of hysterical "conversion," that deep-seated enthnological neurosis of traditional societies which today is in the process of disappearing in the more advanced countries. Thanks to these symptoms, there emerged the underlying role of a severe sexual repression inculcated from earliest childhood in the Cévennes by the Huguenot ethic and inculcated elsewhere

[1] The revolts of the Old Regime and the "lower classes" involved in them have inspired, as is known, a whole series of important studies. Some seek to relate the uprisings to a finality which transcends the immediate and even the conscious interests of the rebels themselves: the "objective" struggle against manorialism or absolutism, the intrigues of aristocrats or bourgeois who openly or "underhandedly" incited to riot, and apocalyptic objectives. Other authors emphasize, among the motivations of these "primitive rebels," the instinct of self-preservation and the hunger drive—the basic tendencies of the human ego, in other words. These different analyses, all of which have proven fruitful, are by no means mutually exclusive. Our own studies of popular uprisings serve to confirm and complete them at many points. But ours also evoke, for the interpretation of the most deviant and aberrant phenomena which are inexplicable in rational terms, certain impulses underlying not only supraindividual motivations but the conscious ego itself. Such impulses could only originate in the oldest and deepest recesses of the human psyche—the id. In a general way, only this appeal to the unconscious, to the intervention of deep-seated impulses, is in measure to explain the ferocious, desperate, irrational energies that were released in the old-style popular revolt. It was not just a violent means to a justifiable end; it was also the savage expression of a long-repressed resentment. In its most stupifying forms of aggression it represents a *passage à l'acte*.

—in Languedoc or at Paris—by the Jansenist ethic, which steadily gained ascendency under Louis XIV and the young Louis XV.

Jansenist or Huguenot, profound psychological motivations conformed, in this case, to the imperatives of the social structure and more precisely to the basic demographic facts of that age which implied, for the majority of young people, a long period of sexual inhibition prior to marriage and justified a severe repression of the biological instincts.[2]

Materially impoverished and sexually repressed, traditional society at the end of our period, as far as the popular classes are concerned, seems to have been characterized by a double series of frustrations and deficiencies which mutually reinforced and conditioned one another.

The material aspects of the great agrarian cycle were, in a word, inseparable from its cultural aspects properly speaking. One sustained and fortified the other. The economy stagnated, society remained intractable, and population—following its early triumphs—retreated, because society, population, and the economy lacked the progressive technology of true growth. But they also lacked—at least as yet and at least to a sufficient degree among the ruling classes and among the people—the conscience, the culture, the morals, the politics, the education, the reformist spirit, and the unfettered longing for success which would have stimulated technological initiative and the spirit of enterprise and permitted an economic "takeoff."

Seeds of True Growth

The picture, however, must not be blackened excessively. I have been speaking of a secular rural fluctuation or, more simply, of a great agrarian cycle. Let no one be misled by my use of this convenient expression. It was not at all a question of a sort of eternal return, of a two- or three-century-

---

[2] The existence of such a period of sexual inhibition, which lasted much longer and was much more rigorous than that of our contemporary culture, can be gathered from a certain series of facts (brought to light by the studies of Goubert [1960] and, for Languedoc, those of Godechot and Moncassin [1964]), namely:

a. *The absence or the minor importance of contraception* before 1730 in Languedoc as well as in the Beauvaisis.

b. *The extremely low percentage of premarital conceptions and illegitimate births* (0.5 percent in Languedoc throughout the eighteenth century). If premarital sexual relations had been really important, they would have resulted—because of the ignorance of contraception—in a great many births of this sort. This was not the case.

c. *The constant practice of late marriage* (at twenty-five years for women and twenty-nine years for men in Languedoc between 1700 and 1789). The period of sexual inhibition, determined by the above two factors, was thereby automatically extended.

long swing of the pendulum which, following a phase of expansion, brought society back to its point of departure, to the "zero degree" from which it started. Such a conception would be absurd and, for that matter, inadequate in light of the known facts. In reality, even if the contagion of true growth had not yet broken out at the close of the seventeenth century—far from it— there existed by this time, within Languedocian society, some isolated factors of real growth, shining like incandescent particles in the darkest hours of Louis XIV's reign. They portend, but as yet no more than that, a modern type of development based on an increase of individual wealth which was slow but unlimited.

First, in the case of agriculture; vine cultivation (for wine and spirits) and silk culture, despite their difficulties at the end of the period, were much more widespread in 1700–10 than in the sixteenth century, as the figures cited by Basville and the *compoix* clearly show. Progress in this domain, despite partial setbacks, was irreversible. Viticulture took two steps forward from Henry IV to Mazarin and one step back under Louis XIV. It was still one step ahead.

Furthermore, it is indisputable that at the end of the seventeenth century the agricultural sector lost its nearly exclusive preponderance. A manufacturing sector was developing, not without difficulty. For a long time Colbert had been preaching to deaf ears. That effective but unpopular minister (for him, as for Jules Ferry, *les roses poussent en dedans*) was largely unsuccessful in seducing the Estates of Languedoc, and when the members of that august assembly did at last agree to the minister's projects—Riquet's canal and the new manufactures—it was in their eyes a sort of bargaining counter conceded to the court in the hope of obtaining new anti-Protestant measures from the king: "We will give you the canal if you will hand over the Huguenots."

But little by little, beginning in 1670–72, the first seeds of an industrial mentality began to spread among the local population. The provincial Estates accorded the "pistole per piece" premium on woolen cloth exports readily and without being coaxed. Languedocian cloth manufacturing became a subsidized industry. By 1685–1700 it was competing successfully in the Levant with the Dutch, and trade figures for Marseilles, the obligatory port of exit, begin to swell from the moment statistical series become available in 1700. This progress would continue, despite temporary setbacks, in the decades that followed.

The Languedocian cloth industry, then, first began to prosper about 1680–

1715 at the very time that agricultural production was collapsing. The two curves—agriculture and woolen manufactures—crossed paths. The retreat of agriculture was very partially compensated for by the advance of textiles, where growth factors were undeniably present.

This is a book of rural history. It is not our purpose here to study the details of manufacturing in Languedoc, a subject that merits a book of its own. We should only point out that the present example of an antithetic development—where the decay of agriculture did not prevent certain seeds of "maritime," industrial, and commercial progress from taking root—was not unique in late seventeenth- and early eighteenth-century Europe. One encounters other examples in Provence, in Catalonia, and, much farther afield, on the shores of the Baltic and the North Sea. In fact, the northern plains of the European continent in the years 1680–1720 witnessed the consummation of an impressive slump of the rural economy. The production and trade in cereals, flax, and hemp regressed just like those of wheat, wine, and olive oil in Languedoc in the same period. This contraction of supply induced in the north of Europe, as it did in the French Midi, the upward movement of agricultural prices and a general series of unhealthy, speculative cyclical upswings—black-market phenomena which caused the *mercuriales* to spiral upward in the second half of Louis XIV's reign. Nevertheless, the wholesale decline of a vast agricultural sector did not drag all the other segments of the northern European economy down in its wake. The English export industries were spared to a degree, and they actually picked up quite briskly in the 1710's, a decade fatal, in many instances, to agriculture. The case resembles that of the Languedocian woolen textile industry on a much larger scale.

Thus, despite the agrarian tragedy, the economy possessed stabilizing forces—industrial and commercial counterweights which acted to check the decline. They represented limited growth sectors, they constituted elements of feedback, and they helped forestall a total collapse, an uncontrollable chain reaction like the one which afflicted various regions in the late Middle Ages. They enhanced the approaching chances of recovery.

The Question of Illiteracy

In the intellectual domain, too, despite some cultural stumbling blocks and despite the economic and social regression of the late seventeenth century, an irreversible process was under way, and certain advances, if still extremely modest, did nevertheless reach "a point of no return."

The determining factor was the slow diffusion of some kind of elementary instruction. Let us try to take its measure from a single typical example. At Aniane, an important rural parish in the valley of the Hérault, the registers of the political council (the equivalent, more or less, of a municipal council) have been carefully conserved for the period 1571–1715. On important occasions all the councillors (who were merchants, artisans, peasants, and sometimes farm laborers) signed the register. Among these individuals, representative for the most part of the more fortunate fraction of rural society, some were illiterate and some were literate; the percentage varied.

How did this percentage evolve the length of a diachronic series covering a century and a half? In the beginning, about 1570–1625, the figures testify to a fearsome rate of rural illiteracy. In this circle of village councillors, which was not one of grinding poverty, one individual in three, and sometimes one in two, was a complete illiterate who signed with a mark (in the form of a cross, a trowel, a hammer, or such), thereby demonstrating his inability not only to write but even to use his simple initials.

The generation of councillors who took their seats around 1620–30 (a generation that probably grew up under the worst conditions during the difficult years of the war and the League, about 1580–1600) broke all records for basic ignorance. Montmorency, who in his senseless revolt of 1632 often relied on the support of the municipalities, did not find it difficult to lead these illiterates around by the nose.

Beginning in 1630, on the contrary, progress was rapid and almost continuous, although it is still possible to distinguish two stages. Around 1660–70 the council included no more than 10 to 20 percent complete illiterates who signed with a mark. In the following period, 1670–1710, the proportion declined still further, falling to practically zero. This does not mean that the entire village, especially the majority, which consisted of women, manual laborers, and poor peasants, now knew how to read, write, and count. Very far from it. But the minority of petty bourgeois, the plebeian elite of artisans and peasants represented on the council, henceforth included a high proportion of individuals with some schooling who disposed of the rudiments of reading, writing, and perhaps arithmetic.

Maggiolo's literacy maps of about 1685–90 do not in reality contradict this point of view. It is true that with the "two sexes united" they reveal a state of crass ignorance as compared to northeastern France, but if male literacy alone is taken into account it can be seen that the Gard (a *département* that was in part Protestant and better schooled) and even the Hérault counted a creditable percentage of adult males able to sign their own names.

These respectable results were due to the efforts of the Protestant schools (in the Gard), but also, in Catholic country (the greater part of the Hérault), to the perseverance of the Roman clergy. The diffusion of a certain amount of learning was, in fact, inseparable from instruction in the rudiments of Christian doctrine; and the naming of a schoolmaster to teach the ABC's and the catechism was the Church's business.

The bishops, during the course of their pastoral visits, never forgot to inspect the village schools. They worried about the schoolmaster. (Was he meeting his classes? Did he, unmindful of his duty, collect fees from the poor? Did he sing in the choir?) They were aggrieved over the absenteeism of students who had to mind the stock or tend the cherry trees. The episcopate, if one substitutes the principle of secular instruction for miter and crook, was acting as a body of elementary school inspectors.

At the end of the century this activity of the prelates began to bear fruit. In the diocese of Montpellier it was conducted by the bishop Colbert, who was meticulous like his uncle, a Jansenist, and a fervent partisan of the elementary schools (*les petites écoles*) in the manner of Port-Royal. Thanks to him, all the villages that still lacked schoolmasters in 1677 were provided with them by 1704. In the latter year in thirty-seven villages (comprising 4,082 families) 1,887 children, including 1,247 boys, were attending class. The lesson of these old educational statistics is that every second household, without exception, had a child in school. The proportion was low by present-day standards, above all when one considers the poor quality of instruction, but it was not, however, negligible. An enormous reservoir of ignorance still subsisted in the rural areas, but the Church, in the manner of the Huguenots, had assumed, by the reign of Louis XIV, the task of cultural uplift in the south of France. The clergy had its own reasons, but the results were significant, and progress was steady if slow.

This effort was all the more remarkable in that it was carried out at the height of the economic debacle between 1680 and 1720. Here again, the two curves, the descending curve of the gross product and the mounting curve of popular instruction, cross. In this case, it was not economics that determined culture, for in that case one would have seen a decline in popular instruction. It was, on the contrary, culture which, in the midst of a slump in production, anticipated the future development of the economy and the resumption of economic growth beginning in 1720.

Culture anticipated and, one might even add, determined developments. Beginning in the very first decade of the century of the Enlightenment, it was one of the factors that helped lay the foundations and prepare the conditions of the coming economic recovery. The diffusion of elementary instruction, limited though it might be, in fact improved the comportment of economic man even in the most isolated villages. Thus, the large-scale tenant farmers, who as a class were still illiterate at the end of the sixteenth century, were often able to read and write at the end of the seventeenth and beginning of the eighteenth centuries, as a comparison between the numbers of marks and signatures affixed to the bottom of the lease contracts clearly indicates. The farmers now knew a little reading, writing, and arithmetic and could thus market their produce in the most favorable circumstances. Now, as is well known, a good farmer is not just someone who knows how to farm. He must also, when the proper time comes, know how to sell.

Similarly, when the great noble and ecclesiastical landowners, prodded by the crisis, made up their minds between 1690 and 1720 to take over the management of their properties and to invest their own capital in the enterprise or risk insolvency, they did not confine themselves to repeating—unknowingly—the "anticrisis" responses of their predecessors and ancestors of the fifteenth century, who had been forced to assume the role of gentlemen farmers in somewhat analogous circumstances. For these landowners of 1700 were no longer dealing with clumsy, unlettered rustics exclusively. Thanks to limited but real progress in primary instruction, they could recruit their bailiffs, their foremen, and their farm managers from a stratum of already literate peasants, some of whom were capable of writing French and of adding up columns of figures. These competent individuals made effective and productive collaborators.

Changes in Patterns of Behavior

Finally, the progress of elementary instruction was inseparable, even among the people, from a certain psychological transfiguration and a general improvement in behavior. Dr. Puech, at the end of the nineteenth century, worked through the judicial archives of the Présidial of Nîmes for the years 1620–1720. As he approached the end of this period, the good doctor—just like Boutelet and Chaunu in an analogous study of Normandy—observed some significant changes in comportment. The following are the anthropological conclusions of Puech's crime statistics: "Man did not remain immutable. His behavior improved. He mastered his anger better and was less prone to violence." The virtue of self-control, so highly esteemed by the modern world, made considerable progress. Duels, sword fights, and knife fights grew rare in this region of the Gard in the early eighteenth century. Fencing masters were forsaken for dancing masters and musicians, the latter already in vogue by 1650–60. The *papegay*, a sort of folkloristic target range, formerly a school for firearms, became a simple pretext for uproar and debauchery to such a point that it was suppressed. Violent sports, *paume* and *ballon*, were abandoned in favor of the taverns and the bawdy houses. Duels and brawls gave way to gambling, debauchery, and swindles. In general, aggression began to take on various disguises; one passed "from foul play to stealing." The lions were transformed into foxes, at least in the vicinity of the towns and in the more civilized lowlands, for in the mountain districts, and especially in the Vivarais of Roure and his rebels, fatal stabbings were still common occurrences and aggression continued to express itself in physical violence.

One encounters the same phenomena of selective attenuation in the domain of religious fanaticism, or simply in religious feeling. In the Cévennes, as we have seen, this *phanatisme* survived intact, still capable of degenerating into bloody forms of exaltation. But near the towns, the hold of religion was clearly weakening by the end of the seventeenth century. John Locke and Basville noted this development for Montpellier and for Nîmes, respectively, apropos of both religions. In 1704–11 the bishop Colbert despaired of Celleneuve and Juvignac, two villages close to Montpellier, whereas elsewhere, in the distant countryside far from the towns, he was satisfied by the perfect assiduity at mass, by the unanimity of the Easter communicants, and by the popular faith in miracles performed in the local sanctuaries to the Virgin. Now, in those two suburban villages, free of Huguenots but infected by the nearby town, most of the men had forsaken the mass, there was dancing at the very doors of the church, and the taverns were packed during the holy services. A certain urban indifference, in other words, was beginning to rub off on the rustics of the surrounding neighborhood.

The picture, then, is full of contrasts. A great mass of people, especially mountain-dwellers, remained mostly illiterate (for example, in the region of Saint-Pons, despite some progress) and prey to primitive violence (as in the Vivarais) or to religious fanatacism with neurotic symptoms (as in the Cévennes). But the towns, and with them the neighboring lowlands, were slowly becoming literate and beginning to repudiate, in part, individual violence. If the people did not abandon religion, it no longer occupied the preeminent position of former times. Do these different traits, still nebulous and embryonic, represent the germs of a new psychology more intellectual than emotional, more cunning than aggressive, and more practical than mystical? Such changes, in any case, are not irrelevant to economic history. Formed in greater numbers, it was the educated and competent, the practical-minded, composed individuals, who would one day be responsible for solid cases of economic growth.

Malthus Would Be Too Late

That day was no longer very far away. In the five-year period 1715–20 in Languedoc (as in neighboring Catalonia), the long slump of the gross agricultural product, which had lasted—on the French side of the Pyrenees—since 1675–80, was finally surmounted. The recessionary wave that marked the conclusion of a secular fluctuation slackened. Some original symptoms appeared. They were characteristic not simply of a normal, ordinary advance or a *recovery*, but of a new age of growth to the measure of the incoming century—and one not entirely unworthy of our own. The forces of transformation—wine growing and manufacturing, competent farm management, and new mental attitudes—were now sufficiently powerful to tilt the old balance. They lent the inevitable upturn a character which was more than one of simple economic, monetary, and demographic recovery, conferring upon it certain innovating aspects that were a far cry from the pauperizing processes of the sixteenth century.

Between 1720 and the end of the century the rural landscape grew more diversified, and certain sectors of production "took off." Wine growing extended its hegemony and multiplied its returns per hectare. Maize, alfalfa, and beans were planted on the fallow. Wheat yields, which had remained stationary since the time of Francis I, improved slightly beginning in 1750. There was only one serious shortcoming—irrigation was little practiced in Languedoc at the very time that the Catalans were resorting to it more and more widely.

Progress also affected roads, canals, ports, and manufacturing (woolen, silk, and cotton textiles; hosiery; and mining and metallurgy) from Law to Necker. The curve that has been published for the woolen cloth industry suggests that one is in the presence of an almost continuous rise which shattered all the mediocre records of Colbertism. Nîmes, with fifty thousand inhabitants, had become one of the great manufacturing towns of France by the end of the century. The Protestants, above all those in the Cévennes—

still subject to harassment but less and less to outright persecution at the hands of the authorities—were cured of their fanaticism thanks to the reasonable preachings of Antoine Court. They could devote themselves wholeheartedly to business in conformity with their ancient and profitable vocation of secular asceticism.

The indices of economic activity, tithes in kind and in money, confirm the fact that the gross product had become the determining factor. It was agricultural production that first showed signs of life. It had begun to advance by 1715–20, before prices and before population. For the space of a generation (1715–45) the rise in the gross product and in real income (nominal income increasing faster than prices) bestowed its still-modest benefits on a declining or stationary rural population. As a result, gross per capita income rose.

Beginning in 1740–50, it was the turn of the demographic sector, which was shaken from its lethargy by economic animation, by the growth in wealth of society as a whole, and by the modest if by no means negligible rise in people's living standards—that is, in the final analysis by the decline in the death rate that resulted and which can be perceived in the parish registers and in the statistics of the provincial administration. Population began to advance, and once again the race was on between population on the one hand and food supplies and the gross product on the other.

It is impossible to describe the vicissitudes of that contest within the compass of the present book. Suffice it to say that according to our charts the outcome was never in doubt. In the sixteenth century agricultural production was completely out of the race. After 1750, on the contrary, the rise of the gross farm product matched and sometimes perhaps outdistanced the rise in rural population. The average living standard was still quite low, but the threat of a general Malthusian kind of impoverishment had disappeared.

All the elements are in agreement, for it seems in fact that wages during the course of the eighteenth century, as was also the case in Catalonia, paralleled or very slowly overtook grain and bread prices. Here again, the evolution was radically different from the one encountered during the sixteenth-century price revolution. The wageworkers were still poor and perhaps even more acutely conscious of their poverty, but the process of pauperization had been banished, and this was in itself a fact of capital importance.

Land pauperization was checked in the same way as the deterioration of wages. It is true that the subdivision of holdings grew rife again beginning in 1750 or 1770—a bit earlier or a bit later depending on the village. The advance in rural population, once under way, imposed its own laws, and, as in the sixteenth century, it forced the multiplying peasants to dismember and divide up their tenements among their more and more numerous heirs. The process recommenced at the end of the reign of Louis XV, when the long phase of land consolidation which had lasted approximately from 1680 to 1750 came to a close. It continued under Louis XVI, traversed the Revolution without faltering, and persisted under all the subsequent regimes up to the time of the phylloxera epidemic. The *compoix* and books of the taille, the cadastres, and the land tax rolls all attest, one series after another, to the progress of land subdivision from 1770 to 1870.

The movement appears to be of the same nature as the analogous process of the sixteenth century. Yet its significance is different, for it was a far less serious matter to carve up the family holding when income per hectare was rising and when the vine was invading every village, as it did from Louis XV to Napoleon III. The rise in earnings per unit compensated for the reduced size of the allotted holdings. The new generations of winegrowers, even if they were more cramped for space, were not necessarily poorer—far from it—than their fathers and grandfathers, who plowed and sowed.

The overall impression is that society after 1715–20—after Louis XIV— was no longer held in check, blocked, and ultimately bowed by the perfect rigidity of the gross product. It was, on the contrary, the gross product itself which, during the entire course of a growth cycle lasting more than a century (up to 1873) and principally affecting viticulture, determined the progress of society, population, and the standard of living.

The Malthusian curse had fallen on Languedoc in the sixteenth and seventeenth centuries just as it has fallen in very different circumstances on certain peoples of today's Third World. In the modern period (and no doubt also in the preceding medieval period) it had invested a great agrarian cycle, after a vigorous starting phase, with the character of an inexorable fluctuation. But the curse was slowly lifted in the eighteenth century even before it had been formulated, in 1798, by the man whose name it bears. Malthus was a clear-headed theoretician of traditional societies, but he was a prophet of the past; he was born too late in a world too new.

Tables and Graphs

The Compoix

The tables on the following pages permit one to trace in two stages, thanks to the *compoix*, the "diachronic" evolution of landed property. I had intended to present the statistical data contained in these tables in the form of graphs, frequency polygons, or histograms. On these histograms, the different categories of property, from the smallest to the largest, would have been ranged graphically from left to right. This solution raised some typographical difficulties and in the end had to be rejected. In any case, the tables in question are perfectly intelligible. The properties are ranged in order of increasing size, reading from top to bottom. In the columns reserved for the "tendency," the accumulation of plus signs on the upper part of the column signifies an increase in the number of smallholdings and therefore of land subdivision. Inversely, minus signs predominating in their place suggest a propensity toward consolidation. The crossbars in the form of horizontal brackets indicate the positions of the "critical thresholds."

TABLE 1. Saint-Thibéry

A. Categories of landholdings in tenths of a *setérée* (first 0, holdings too poor to be taxed; second 0, from 0 to 10 tenths; 10, from 10 to 25 tenths, etc.).*
B. Number of landholdings in each category in 1460.
C. Total land area of all holdings in each category in 1460.
D. Number of landholdings in each category in 1690 (cf. B).
E. Total land area of all holdings in each category in 1690 (cf. C).
F. Tendencies.

A	1460		1690		F
	B	C	D	E	
0	8		39		+
0	3	23	34	235	+
10	22	398	59	1 017	+
25	35	1 446	58	2 076	+
50	28	2 920	85	6 142	+
100	12	1 585	17	2 153	+
150	10	1 765	19	3 292	+
200	15	3 478	10	2 200	—
250	9	2 445	5	1 429	—
300	8	2 594	6	1 930	+
350	7	2 684	1	387	+
400	6	2 618	1	408	—
450	5	2 384	3	1 418	—
500	6	3 188	5	2 176	—
550			1	573	+
600	3	1 898			—
650	1	662			—
700			2	1 414	+
750	1	784			—
800	1	812			—
850					
900					
1 000	3	3 296	5	5 323	+
1 250	3	4 207			—
1 500			5	8 713	+
2 000	1	2 225			—
2 500	2	5 180	2	8 337	+
3 000					
TOTAL	189	45 692	357	49 223	

* In the same way, in column A of the next two tables the line £1 corresponds to landholdings assessed at between £1 and £1 10s., and so on.

TABLE 2. Montagnac

A. Categories of taxation in 1520.

C. Categories of landed properties in 1660. (The total tax being £380 in 1520 and the total land assessment £7,600 in 1660, the line-by-line comparisons between A and C are possible only in percentages; for example, the line "£30" in A and "£600" in C both represent 8 percent of the respective totals.)

B and D. Number of landholdings by category.

E. Tendencies.

A		1520 B	C	1660 D	1660 / 1520 E
£	s		£		
0		82	0	212	+
	5	69	5	135	+
	10	41	10	47	+
	15	26	15	28	+
1		33	20	29	−
1	10	26	30	16	−
2		11	40	10	−
2	10	2	50	10	+
3		11	60	4	−
3	10	3	70	3	=
4		5	80		−
4	10	2	90		−
5		3	100	2	−
6		5	120	1	−
8		1	160	1	−
10			200		
12		2	240		−
15		1	300		−
20			400		
25			500		
30			600	1	+
TOTAL		323		499	

TABLE 3. Saint-André-de-Sangonis

A. Categories of landholdings, in cadastral pounds. (The total land assessment of the master *compoix*, composed in 1636, is £1,307; the comparisons are between homogeneous cadastral pounds.)

B, C, E. Number of landholdings in 1665 (*"département des dettes"*) and in 1690 and 1749 (rolls of the taille).

D and F. Tendencies.

A		1665	1690	1690/1665	1749	1749/1690
		B	C	D	E	F
£	s					
0		17	18	+	18	=
1		186	218	+	120	—
5		161	191	+	127	—
10		136	132	—	141	+
1		67	102	+	63	—
1	10	51	53	+	43	—
2		28	37	+	23	—
2	10	32	23	—	20	—
3		51	36	—	39	+
4		24	21	—	31	+
5		16	19	+	14	—
6		18	20	+	24	+
8		15	15	=	23	+
12		4	4	=	8	+
16		2	1	—	1	=
20		2	3	+	2	—
20		1		—		
TOTAL		811	893		697	

The following graphs were prepared by the Laboratoire de Cartographie of the École Pratique des Hautes Études, VIᵉ Section.

GRAPH 1. The Long-term Tendency of the Cadastral Population.

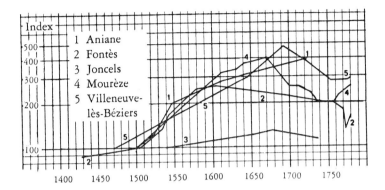

GRAPH 2. Number of Communicants in the
Catholic Villages of the Diocese of Montpellier.

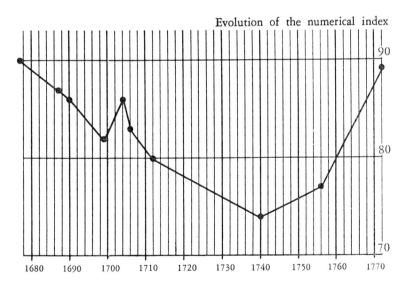

GRAPH 3. Grain Tithes (in hundreds of *setiers*).

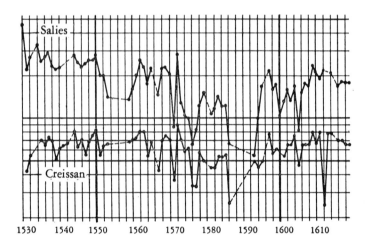

GRAPH 4. Wages as a Percentage of the Harvest at Narbonne.

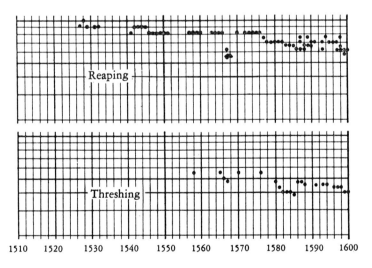

NOTE: At the start of the series, about 1480–1500, the reapers' wages were about 10 percent of the harvest.

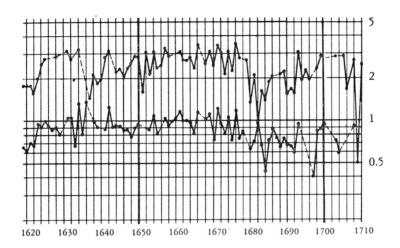

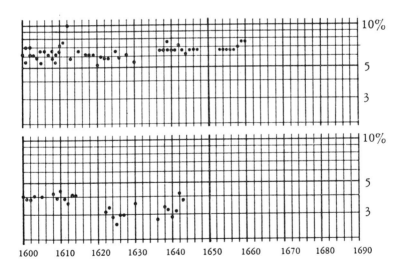

GRAPH 5. The Taille at Montpellier (in *livres tournois*).

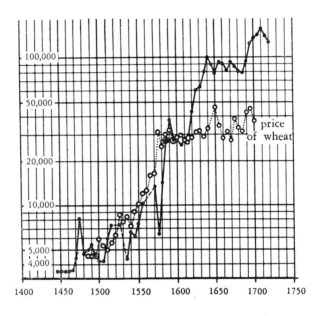

GRAPH 6. Price of Salt at Castelnaudary (in *sous* per quintal).

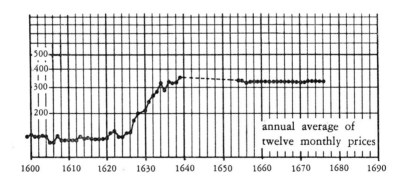

GRAPH 7. Illiteracy and Social Groups in the Sixteenth Century.

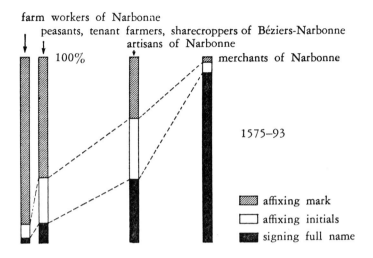

GRAPH 8. Percentage of Marks out of Total Number of
Signatures at the Political Council of Aniane.

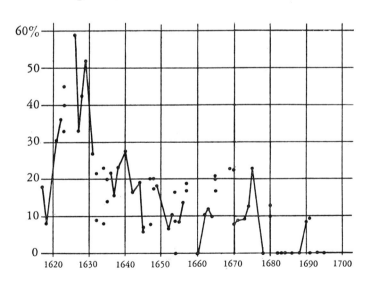

AC	communal archives
AD	departmental archives
ADH	Departmental Archives of the Hérault
Annales	*Annales: economies, sociétés, civilisations*
B.A.G.F.	*Bulletin de l'Association de géographes français*
B.S.H.M.	*Bulletin de la Société d'histoire moderne*
B.S.L.G.	*Bulletin de la Société languedocienne de géographie*
E.N.A.M.	École nationale d'agriculture de Montpellier
R.H.E.S.	*Revue d'histoire économique et sociale*
R.H.M.C.	*Reue d'histoire moderne et contemporaine*

Principal Manuscript Sources

1. COMMUNAL ARCHIVES

The chief sources in the communal archives are the subseries BB, CC, GG, and FF—deliberations, *compoix* and tailles, population, the police of the vintages, and so on. I have explored the collections of a certain number of communes, a list of which follows accompanied by information on the fiscal sources (subseries CC) for those parishes which are the richest in poorly cataloged or uncataloged archives.

Agonés

Compoix of 1558 (a portion of the general *compoix* of the Val de Montferrand —AC Les Matelles).

Compoix of 1644.

Argelliers

Compoix of 1531, 1664.

Bassan

Compoix of a little before 1580.

Transcription of 1700 of the *compoix* of 1613 (CC 1).

Taille rolls of 1670, 1696.

Land tax of 1791, *an* VI, 1818.

Bédarieux

Lost *compoix* of 1605.

Compoix of 1632 (CC 1), 1646 (CC 2), 1660 (CC 3), 1664 (CC 4), 1685 (CC 6), 1788 (CC 10).

Bessan

Compoix of 1502, which served up to 1553.

Taille rolls of 1523, 1526, 1527, 1534, 1535, 1538, 1539, 1544, 1554, 1558, 1559, 1563, 1567, 1570, 1575, 1576, 1582, 1583, 1587, 1588, 1590, 1592, 1595, 1596, 1600, 1611, 1652, 1690.

Transcription dated 1717 of an earlier *compoix*, now lost.

Taille roll of 1775.

Land tax roll of 1791.

Candillargues

Compoix of the first half of the sixteenth century (before 1554).
Compoix of after 1573 (CC 1).
Compoix of 1638 (CC 3).
Compoix of 1755 (CC 4).

Caux

Compoix of 1615, 1756.

Ceilhes and Rocozels

Compoix of the second half of the sixteenth century (CC 1).
Compoix of 1658 (CC 2), mistakenly dated 1630.
Compoix of 1681 (CC 3).

Cessenon-sur-Orb

Compoix of 1560 (CC 1, CC 2).
Compoix of 1634 (CC 3, CC 4).
Compoix of 1688 (CC 5, CC 6).
Brevette, eighteenth century (CC 7).

Fabrègues (unshelved)

Compoix of 1593.
Brevette of 1600 (CC 7).
Compoix of 1693.
Taille roll of 1698.
Capitation of 1702 (CC 9).
Compoix of 1778.
Brevette of 1778.

Faugères

Compoix of 1589 (CC 1).
Transcription, 1711, of the *compoix* of 1589 (CC 2).
Taille roll of 1722.

Fontès (subseries CC unclassified)

Taille rolls of 1406, 1427, 1483.
Taille roll of 1504.
Progeny of a lost *compoix* of 1504: taille rolls of 1505, 1533, 1539.
Progeny of a lost *compoix* composed about 1540: transcription in very poor condition; taille rolls of 1543, ca. 1570, 1581.
Compoix of 1604.
Taille roll (nonresidents) of 1675.
Brevette of 1695.
Taille rolls of 1742, 1746, 1772, and almost yearly thereafter.
Compoix of 1775 and its progeny of taille rolls.
Matrix of 1791.
Land tax rolls of 1793, 1818, and almost yearly for the nineteenth century.

Frontignan

Compoix of 1525 (CC 1).

Compoix of 1570 (CC 4, Vol. 1, and CC 2, Vol. 2).

Transcription, before 1585, of the *compoix* of 1570 (CC 3).

Compoix of 1622 (CC 5).

Compoix of 1730 (CC 10 to CC 12).

Gabian

Compoix of 1656, 1722.

Copy, 1778, of the *compoix* of 1766 (ADH, B 1067).

Gallargues-le-Petit

Compoix of 1672 (CC 1).

Compoix of 1790 (CC 2).

Garrigues

Compoix of 1627 (CC 1).

Compoix of 1683 (CC 2).

Gignac

See the printed catalog of the AC Hérault.

Joncels

Compoix of 1537 (ADH, B 9901).

Compoix of 1651 (CC 1).

Excellent copy of the *compoix* of 1651 (ADH, B 1065).

Brevettes of 1651, 1676, 1737 (CC 2).

Lagmas (AC Gignac)

Compoix of 1552.

Copy of the *compoix* of 1552 comprising only taxpayers residing in Gignac (CC 7).

Compoix of 1601 (CC 15).

Taille rolls of the eighteenth century listing taxpayers originating from Gignac (CC 38ff.).

Lansargues

Compoix of 1602 (CC 1, CC 2).

Compoix of 1653 (CC 3 to CC 6).

Brevette of 1703.

Brevette of 1787 (CC 7, CC 8).

Lauroux

Taille rolls of 1579, 1580, 1581, 1592, 1593, 1597, 1600, 1601.

Lost *compoix* of the beginning of the seventeenth century.

Taille rolls of 1610, 1620, 1621, 1624, 1626, 1628, 1630, 1631, 1632, 1634, 1635, 1640, 1642, 1647, 1648, 1655, 1663, 1664.

Compoix of before 1675.

Taille rolls of 1685, 1692, 1697, 1706, 1712, 1720, 1722, 1731, 1733, 1735, 1738,

1741, 1745, 1747, 1748, 1749, 1750, 1752, 1753, 1755, 1758, 1760, 1764, 1765, 1766, 1767, 1771, 1778, 1783.

Le Bosc

Compoix of 1670.

Taille rolls of 1732, 1742, 1752, 1767, 1781, 1787.

Lespignan

Compoix of the fifteenth, sixteenth, and seventeenth centuries (series B and Municipal Archives, shelved in part. Cf. *Inventaire imprimé*).

Les Plans

Compoix of the early sixteenth century (incomplete).

Compoix of 1604.

Taille rolls of 1631, 1635.

Compoix of 1644.

Taille rolls of 1648, 1649, 1651, 1671, 1673, 1705, 1706, 1709, 1712, 1713, 1714, 1726, 1738, 1759, 1763, 1766, 1770, 1775, 1778, 1780, 1785, 1790.

Lunel

Compoix of about 1300.

Taille rolls (without shelf marks) of 1396, 1403, 1415, 1421, 1427, 1435, 1462, 1518, 1528, 1575.

Compoix of 1594 and almost yearly series of taille rolls, seventeenth and eighteenth centuries (CC 31 to CC 46).

Maraussan

Compoix (incomplete) of the end of the sixteenth century.

Compoix of 1645.

Taille roll of 1655.

Transcription of 1685 of the *compoix* of 1645.

Taille rolls of 1693, 1694, 1723, 1724.

Compoix of 1728.

Taille rolls of 1773, 1775, 1776, 1790.

Margon

Compoix of before 1577.

Taille rolls of 1605, 1606, 1607, 1608.

Marsillargues

Compoix of 1718 (CC 1 to CC 5).

Taille rolls 1568 to 1738, annual series (CC 7 to CC 12).

Mauguio

Compoix of before 1595.

Compoix of 1653 (two copies).

Brevette of 1750.

Compoix of 1770.

Mèze

Compoix of 1595.
Compoix of 1769.
Brevette based on the *compoix* of 1769 (CC 12).
Matrix of 1791.
Land tax rolls of *an* VIII and of 1822.

Montagnac

Taille roll of 1520.
Compoix prior to 1547 (transcription of a lost *compoix* of before 1520).
Compoix prior to 1570 (a second transcription later than the above).
Compoix of 1605 (third transcription).
Compoix of 1621, complete in three volumes, composed by Martin Revel.
Compoix dated 1600, in reality a copy of the *compoix* of 1620.
Compoix of 1630, incomplete.
Compoix of 1659–63, original in one volume, copy in three volumes.
Compoix of 1786.

Montpeyroux

Compoix of about 1500 (CC 6).
Copy of the *compoix* of about 1500 dating from the eighteenth century, of no interest (CC 1).
Compoix of 1586 in good condition (CC 2, CC 3).
Compoix of 1652 (CC 7 to CC 9).
Brevette of 1790 (CC 11).
compoix of industry (CC 17).

Mourèze

Compoix of the end of the fifteenth century (CC 1).
Compoix of 1611 (CC 2).
Compoix of 1646 (CC 3).
Tailles rolls of 1631, 1642, 1647, 1659, 1665, 1670 (CC 4).
Taille rolls of 1702, 1707, 1712, 1715, 1717, 1724, 1728, 1729, 1733–35, 1736, 1737, 1738, 1741, 1745, 1746, 1750, 1751, 1756, 1757, 1759, 1762, 1763, 1764, 1769, 1772, 1773, 1774, 1783 (CC 5).

Murviel-lès-Béziers

Compoix of 1546.
Compoix of 1734.

Neffiès

Taille roll and extract of *compoix* of 1535.
Taille rolls of 1624, 1632.
Taille roll (nonresidents) of 1646.
Taille rolls of 1654, 1662.

Nézignan-l'Évêque

Taille rolls of 1610 and 1618 (*"Compoix des herbages"*).

Taille rolls of 1621, 1624, 1625, 1628, 1629, 1641, 1646, 1655, 1658, 1667, 1675, 1677, 1682, 1687, 1688.

Pignan (unshelved)

Compoix of before 1558 (CC 1).

Compoix of 1594 (CC 2).

Brevette of 1655 (CC 8).

Compoix of 1750–62 (CC 3, CC 4).

Portiragnes

Fragment of *compoix* of before 1577.

Taille rolls of 1600, 1601, 1604, 1605, 1606, 1608, 1609, 1618.

Compoix of 1619.

Taille rolls of 1620, 1625, 1626, 1627, 1630, 1632, 1639, 1641, 1645, 1647, 1648, 1670, 1671, 1686, 1702, 1708, 1730, 1741, 1744, 1751, 1756, 1757, 1769, 1770, 1775, 1776, 1777, 1778, 1780, 1782, 1783, 1789.

Compoix cabalistes of 1746, 1747, 1757, 1758, 1764, 1767, 1768, 1769, 1772, 1777.

Puéchabon

Series CC.

Taille rolls of 1617, 1631, 1635, 1636, 1637, 1638, 1639, 1640, 1641, 1642, 1643, 1644, 1645, 1654, 1658.

Brevette of 1684 (CC 2).

Taille rolls of 1754, 1760, 1762, 1763.

Roquebrun

Rubric of the *compoix* of 1601 (CC 1).

Compoix of 1658 (CC 1).

Taille roll of 1677.

Statement of land values (anonymous) of 1745, 1746, 1749, 1775.

Roujan

Compoix called that of 1480, in fact, simply of sometime before 1525.

Taille roll of 1525.

Compoix of 1540.

Taille roll of 1605.

Compoix of 1637 (original, AC Roujan; copy, ADH, B 1175).

Compoix of 1715.

Compoix of 1779.

Saint-André-de-Sangonis

Compoix of 1636 (CC 1), misdated 1654 in the catalog (CC 2 to CC 11), rendered unusable by abundance of cancellations and corrections.

"Département des dettes" on the *compoix* of 1665 (CC 19).

Brevette of 1690 (CC 12).

Almost yearly series of taille rolls from 1700 to 1789 (CC 22 to CC 35).

Saint-Apollinaire-de-Rias (Ardèche)

Taille roll of 1574 (ADH, B 38537).

Taille roll of 1618 (ADH, B 37365).

Saint-Georges-d'Orques

Compoix. See the *Inventaire imprimé.*

Taille rolls of 1746, 1747, 1748, 1750, 1752, 1753, 1754, 1755, 1756, 1757, 1758, 1759, 1760, 1761, 1770 (CC 5, CC 6), etc. (almost yearly).

Saint-Guiraud

Compoix of 1600 (CC 1).

Taille rolls of 1641, 1645, 1646, 1649, 1665.

Compoix of 1664.

Taille rolls of 1725, 1727, 1734, 1739, 1741, 1748, 1749, 1750, 1751, 1754, 1756, 1761, 1773, 1774, 1776, 1779, 1781, 1784, 1790.

Saint-Jean-de-la-Blaquière

Taille rolls of 1751, 1769, 1783, 1785.

Saint-Mathieu-de-Tréviers, see **Tréviers**

Saint-Saturnin

Compoix of 1600 (CC 1, CC 2).

Almost yearly series of taille rolls from 1692 to 1789 (CC 3, CC 4).

Saint-Thibéry

Compoix of 1460, 1469; *compoix* of the middle of the seventeenth century (two volumes); transcription of the latter dated 1690 (two volumes).

Sérignan

Taille rolls of 1453 (copied in a register of trial proceedings in the communal archives).

Compoix of 1521.

Compoix of 1550.

Compoix of 1603.

Transcription of the *compoix* of 1603, of a little before 1665.

"Département des dettes" on the *compoix* of 1670.

Taille rolls of 1737, 1738, 1742, 1747, 1748, 1749, 1750, 1751, 1757, 1760, 1762, 1763, 1764, 1766, 1768, 1775, 1776, 1777.

Compoix of 1778. See the *Inventaire imprimé* of the ADH, series B (*in fine*).

Taille rolls of 1779, 1780, 1782, 1785, 1786, 1790, 1791.

Soubès

Compoix. See the *Inventaire imprimé.*

Taille rolls of 1604, 1626, 1629, 1648, 1655, 1659, 1664, 1667, 1669, 1676, 1678, 1687, 1693, 1697, 1698, 1699, 1701, 1703, 1704, 1705, 1742, 1743, 1745, 1749, 1750, 1752.

Thézan

    Compoix of 1638.

    Compoix of 1685.

Tréviers

    Compoix in the register of the *compoix* of the Val de Montferrand of before 1558 (AC Les Matelles).

    Compoix of 1637 (CC 1, AC Saint-Mathieu-de-Tréviers).

Vaillan

    Compoix of 1637.

    Compoix of 1774, and almost yearly taille rolls.

Valros

    Taille roll of 1636.

    Compoix of 1664, 1674, 1675, 1679.

    Taille rolls of 1686, 1774, 1779, 1786, 1787, 1788.

Villemagne-L'Argentière

    Compoix of 1624.

    Taille roll of about 1586.

    Taille rolls of 1593, 1597, 1601, 1604, 1607, 1610, 1620, 1623, 1627, 1678, 1717.

Villeneuve-lès-Béziers

    Taille roll of 1490.

    Fragment of a *compoix* of before 1603.

    Compoix of 1644 (ADH, B 1120).

    "Calculs des compoix" of 1644.

    Statement of land values of 1692, 1695.

    Taille rolls of 1722, 1756, 1775, 1778, 1779.

In addition, I have worked extensively in the Communal Archives of Montpellier and Narbonne. They contain, paradoxically, a considerable body of material concerning various aspects of rural life.

Montpellier

The *Inventaire imprimé* is divided, curiously, by armoires. I have constructed certain series from armoires A and B (*compoix* of Montpellier), armoire C (deliberations, accounts, *mercuriales*), armoire D, which contains the records of the commanderies (expenditures, data on daily wages in the sixteenth century, nurses' wages, and so on) as well as the accounts of the *claverie* (taille receipts). I have also put to use the registers of the subseries FF, which are not listed in the catalogs of the various armoires.

Narbonne

Subseries BB 1 to BB 54 are communal deliberations; BB 55 to BB 73 are acts and contracts of the consular administration.

2. DEPARTMENTAL ARCHIVES

Ardèche

Mazon collection.

Aude

G 29 to G 58—contracts, together with accounts of the chapters Saint-Just and Saint-Pasteur of Narbonne (fundamental source for the tables and graphs concerning land rents, tithes, agricultural income, farm management, mixed wages and wages in kind, interest rates, and so on).

Aveyron

ET 64 (Trézières collection)—Molineri inquest (1643).

Gard

C 1335 to C 1852—diocesan *compoix* of the dioceses of Nîmes and of Uzès (mid-sixteenth century).

G 130 to G 744—documents of the cathedral chapter of Nîmes, especially G 586 to G 739 (accounts).

G 1088 to G 1100—lease contracts and accounts of the collegiate chapter of Aiguesmortes.

E 371 to E 1220—notaries (I have confined my researches chiefly to the notaries of Nîmes and of Saint-Jean-du-Gard).

Haute-Garonne

B 1 to B 1921—registers of the Parlement of Toulouse.

C 2276 to C 2431—minutes of the meetings of the Estates of Languedoc.

To these sources, conserved in the AD Haute-Garonne, should be added the "Report d'Aguesseau" (Ms. 603 of the Municipal Library of Toulouse), used extensively in this book.

Hérault

B 1 to B 44—registers of the *cour des comptes* of Montpellier (gabelle leases, fiscal problems).

B 881 to B 11297—fiscal matters of the communities and copies of the *compoix* (in poor condition). These documents have been given a new set of numbers, from B 1000 to B 43000, in the *Inventaire imprimé*, Series B, vol. IV.

B 11301 to B 22246—accounts of the dioceses (especially for lists of communities).

B 22251 to B 22804—war accounts, tithe accounts, and such (according to the new system of numbering in the *Inventaire imprimé*).

Series C. (Intendance of Languedoc)

C 7 to C 39—the population movement in the *généralité* of Languedoc, 1770 to 1789.

C 1114—inquest of Intendant Le Nain (register devoted to the parishes of the diocese of Montpellier).

C 3018 to C 3031—indebtedness of various communities.

C (unnumbered registers)—verification of the *compoix*, especially in the diocese of Montpellier, in 1734.

IV C—1 to 2377.

D 138 to D 172 (collection of the royal society of sciences of Montpellier)—meteorology; observations of Bon, Badon, Mouret, and others; epidemiology.

II E (notaries)—I have studied those of Agde, Béziers, Cournonterral, Frontignan, Ganges, Lansargues, Marsillargues, Montpellier (notaries Cornier, Billotte, Bizeray, Hébrart, Navarre, and Jonquet, notably for postmortem inventories), La Salvetat, and Saint-Pons. I have also consulted the notarial archives of the clergy of Montpellier (conserved in the ADH) and especially the registers concerning Chapter Saint-Pierre (notaries Darles, 1566–1602, and Rosselly, 1603–32).

III E (civil status)—copy of the registers of baptisms, marriages, and burials after 1737.

Series G. Chapter Saint-Nazaire of Béziers

G 67 to G 136—deliberations of the chapter (information concerning the affairs of the estates, the tithes, and such; sometimes quantitative data on the leasing of the estates or of the tithes, notably at the end of the seventeenth century).

G 147 to G 212 and G 446 to G 450—lease contracts (a fundamental source, like AD Aude, G 29 to G 58).

G 337 to G 348—"tithes" (some quantitative data, but much less rewarding than the preceding from this point of view).

G 497 to G 500—extracts of the *compoix* for the chapter's properties.

G 529 to G 786—some data, sometimes quantitative, on the priories and the estates.

G 818 to G 821—Rocolles documents (cf. G 837 and G 901).

G 829 to G 1049—accounts in money and in kind, state of oil supplies, and the like (a capital quantitative source, like G 147 to G 212, for the study of income, receipts in money and in kind, expenditures, prices, and money wages and for information on interest rates).

Bishopric of Montpellier

G 1146 to G 1168—pastoral visits in the diocese of Montpellier.

Chapter Saint-Pierre of Montpellier

G 1735 to G 1764—deliberations of the chapter (same observations as for G 67 to G 136).

G 1765 to G 1782—deeds and lease contracts.

G 2398 to G 2633—accounts of the chapter (receipts, expenditures, estates; a fundamental source).

Chapter of Agde

The leases and farm contracts of the tithing priories and landed domains are found in the minutes of the notaries of Agde, ADH, II E, *étude* no. 2, except for the years 1664 and 1665 (*étude* no. 1).

Tarn. *Collegiate Chapter Saint-Michel of Gaillac*

G 477 to G 488—"deliberations" (these registers, especially for the end of the sixteenth century and for the seventeenth century, contain numerous statistical data on the farming of the tithes).

G 535 to G 559—accounts of the chapter (more statistical data which serve to complete the above).

Vaucluse

Collection Chobaut (papers of Hyacinthe Chobaut) conserved in the library of the Calvet Museum of Avignon (an essential source for the history of plants and the dates of the vintage).

3. NATIONAL ARCHIVES

I made use of the National Archives only occasionally, because the quantitative sources of the Old Regime essential to my undertaking are, as a general rule, buried in the communal or departmental archives. One chapter of the book, however, is based on an important document in the National Archives—the minutes of the sales of the goods of the Church (G^8, reg. 1336, dated 1563 and the years following). I have also done some work with the *doléances* of the Estates of Languedoc (H 748^{108}, and so on).

4. NATIONAL LIBRARY (MANUSCRIPTS)

For the study of the revolt of the Vivarais (1670), I used Mss. Fonds Languedoc-Bénédictins, vol. 95, and the Clérambaut collection, vol. 791.

5. PRIVATE ARCHIVES

Thanks to the kindness of the present owners of the domain de Coussergues (Hérault), I have been given access to the archives of the Sarret family (accounts, property inventories, and so on, for the sixteenth through eighteenth centuries).

6. HOSPITAL ARCHIVES

I employed the collection of the general hospital of Montpellier (deposited in the ADH), especially series E (registers of family expenditures), F (admittances), and G (matters concerning vagabonds).

Bibliography

Abel (W.), *Die Wüstungen des ausgehenden Mittelalters*, Stuttgart, 1955.

Adher (J.), "Le diocèse de Rieux au xviiie siècle," *Annales du Midi*, 1909.

Agriel (H.), "Le Causse de Sauveterre," *B.S.L.G.*, 1919.

L'Agronome ou dictionnaire portatif du cultivateur, Paris, 1764.

Aigrefeuille (Ch. d'), *Histoire de Montpellier*, Montpellier, 1885.

Aimes (A.), "Guy de Chauliac," *Monspeliensis Hippocrates*, winter, 1962.

Albigny (P. d'), "Les calamités dan le Vivarais," *Revue du Vivarais*, 1912.

Albiousse (C. d'), *Histoire de la ville d'Uzès*, Uzès, 1903.

Album des vins de France, Montpellier, 1937.

Alméras (Ch.), *La révolte des Camisards*, Paris, 1960.

Alphandéry (P.) and Dupront (A.), *La Chrétienté et l'idée de Croisade*, Paris, 1954.

[Amblard], "Les notes Amblard, notaires à Saint-Pons, 1590–1665," *Revue d'histoire du diocèse de Montpellier*, III, 1911–1912.

Anatole (C.), "Conti, Molière et quelques autres," *Communication au congrès occitan de Montpellier*, 1962.

Anglade (J.), *Les troubadours*, Paris, 1908.

Angot (A.), "Étude sur les vendanges en France," *Annales du Bureau central météorologique de France*, 1883.

Appolis (E.), *Manuel des études héraultaises*, Valence, 1943.

————, "Les compoix diocésains en Languedoc," *Cahiers d'Histoire et d'Archéologie*, 1946.

————, *Le diocèse civil de Lodève*, Albi, 1951.

————, *Le jansénisme dans le diocèse de Lodève au xviiie siècle*, Albi, 1952.

————, *Entre jansénistes et zelanti, le "Tiers parti" catholique au xviiie siècle*, Paris, 1960.

Ariès (Ph.), *Histoire des populations françaises et de leurs attitudes devant la vie depuis le xviiie siècle*, Paris, 1948.

Armengaud (A.), *Les populations de l'Est-Aquitain au début de l'époque contemporaine*, Paris, 1961.

Arnaud (E.), *Histoire des protestants du Velay*, Paris, 1888.

Arnould (M. A.), *Les dénombrements de foyers dans le comté de Hainaut* (xive–xvie *siècles*), Brussels, n.d.

Atger, (E.), *Le paludisme dans la région languedocienne autrefois et aujourd'hui*, Montpellier, 1931.

Aubenas (R.), "Le contrat d'*affrairamentum* dans le droit provençal du Moyen Âge," *Revue d'histoire du Droit*, 1933.

Audigier (P.), *Histoire d'Auvergne*, Clermont-Ferrand, 1894.

Augusti (Fra Michel), *Llibre dels secrets de agricultura*, Barcelona, 1617.

Auzias, *L'Aquitaine carolingienne*, Toulouse, 1937.

Avenel (G. d'), *Histoire économique de la propriété, des salaires, des denrées et de tous les prix*, Paris, 1894.

Aymard (A.) and Auboyer (J.), *L'Orient et la Grèce antique*, Paris, 1953.

Azzi (G.), *Le climat du blé*, Rome, 1927.

Baehrel (R.), *Une croissance: la Basse-Provence rurale*, Paris, 1961.

Balandier (G.), *Afrique ambiguë*, Paris, 1957.

Baldung (H.), *Hexenbilder*, Stuttgart, 1961 edn.

Balso, "Le Biterrois," *B.S.L.G.*, 1954.

Baratier (E.), *La démographie provençale du* xiiie *siècle au* xvie *siècle*, Paris, 1961.

Barbut (G.), *Historique de la culture des céréales dans l'Aude*, Carcassonne, 1900.

Bardon (A.), *Histoire d'Alès, 1341–1461*, Nîmes, 1896.

———, *L'exploitation du bassin houiller d'Alès sous l'Ancien Régime*, Nîmes, 1898.

Baret (Commandant), "Vente des biens du Clergé au diocèse de Béziers," *Cahiers d'Histoire*, 1934.

Barrière-Flavy (C.), *La chronique criminelle du Languedoc an* xviie *siècle*, Paris, 1926.

Barry (J. P.), "Cartographie parcellaire de Boissières (Gard)," *Atlas de la cartographie parcellaire*, Laboratoire d'écologie du Muséum national d'histoire naturelle, 1952 (mimeographed copy).

———, "La végétation des garrigues de Nîmes," *L'année biologique*, 1960.

——— and Le Roy Ladurie (E.), "Histoire agricole et phytogéographie," *Annales*, 1962.

Barthes (R.), *Mythologies*, Paris, 1957.

Basville, *Mémoires pour servir à l'histoire de Languedoc*, Amsterdam, 1734.

Baulant (M.) and Meuvret (J.), *Prix des céréales extraits de la mercuriale de Paris*, Paris, 1960, 1962.

Bautier (R. H.), "Feux et population à Carpentras," *Annales*, 1959.

Beauquis (A.), *Histoire de la soie*, Grenoble, 1910.

Bellaud-Dessalles (M.), *La Grange-des-Prés et les gouverneurs de Languedoc*, Montpellier, 1917.

Beloch (J.), "Die Bevölkerung Europas zur Zeit der Renaissance," *Zeitschrift für sozial Wissenschaft*, 1900.

Bénédict (R.), *Patterns of Cult.. .*, New York, 1960 edn.

[Benjamin de Tudèle], *Voyages de Benjamin de Tudèle*, Paris, 1830 edn.

Bennassar (B.), "En Vieille Castille: ventes de rentes perpétuelles," *Annales*, 1960.

———, "L'alimentation d'une ville espagnole au xvie siècle," *Annales*, 1961.

Benoit (F.), *La Provence et le Comtat Venaissin*, Paris, 1949.

Béral (P.), *Histoire de l'hôpital de la Charité de Montpellier (1646–1682)*, Montpellier, 1899.

Bercé (Y. M.), *Recherches sur les soulèvements populaires du Sud-Ouest pendant la guerre de Trente ans*, to appear.

Beresford (M.), *The Lost Villages of England*, New York, London, 1954.

Berlie (P.), "La région de Rians," *B.S.L.G.*, 1922.

Bernard (A.), "Le *dry farming* et l'Afrique du Nord," *Annales de géographie*, 1911.

Bernardy (A.), *Euzet, mon pays*, Uzès, 1958.

———, *Remontons la Gardonenque*, Uzès, 1961.

Bertier de Sauvigny (G. de), *La Restauration*, Paris, 1955.

Besançon (A.), "Histoire et psychanalyse," *Annales*, 1964.

Bézard (Y.), *La vie rurale dans le sud de la Région parisienne de 1450 à 1560*, Paris, 1929.

Bigot (abbé), *Histoire de Fontès*, Montpellier, 1878.

Billange (M.), "La garrigue de Nîmes," *B.S.L.G.*, 1942.

Billaut (M.), Birot (P.), Cavalier (D.) and Pédelaborde (P.), "Problèmes climatiques sur la bordure nord du monde méditerranéen," *Annales de géographie*, 1956.

Biraben (J. N.) and Henry (C.), "La mortalité des jeunes enfants dans les pays méditerranéens," *Population*, 1957.

Birot (P.), *La vie rurale pyrénéenne*, Paris, 1937.

——— and Dresch, *La Méditerranée et le Moyen-Orient*, Paris, 1953.

Blanchard (M.), "Sel et diplomatie," *Annales*, 1960.

Blanchard (R.), "La limite nord de l'olivier dans les Alpes françaises," *La Géographie*, 1910.

———, *Les Alpes occidentales*, Tours, 1938–1956.

Blaquière (H.), "Aspects de l'histoire politique, sociale et économique de Toulouse aux xvie et xviie siècles," *Annales de l'Institut d'études occitanes*, 1960.

Blazin (M.), "Le Minervois et la commune d'Olonzac," *B.S.L.G.*, 1896.

Bloch (C.), "La viticulture languedocienne avant 1789," *B.S.L.G.*, 1896.

Bloch (J.), *Les Tziganes*, Paris, 1953.

Bloch (M.), *Les caractères originaux de l'histoire rurale française*, 2 vols., Paris, 1956 edn.

Bobinska (C.), Madurowicz (H.) and Podraza (A.), "L'économie régionale polonaise au xviiie siècle," *Annales*, 1963.

Bodin (J.), *De la démonomanie des sorciers*, Paris, 1580 and 1587 edns.

Boguet (H.), *Discours des sorciers*, Lyons, 1608.

Bois (D.), *Les plantes alimentaires à travers les âges*, Paris, 1927–1937.

Bois (P.), *Paysans de l'Ouest*, Le Mans, 1960.

Boisguillebert (P. Le Pesant de), *Détail de la France*, 1695.

Boislisle (A. M. de), *Correspondance des contrôleurs généraux des finances avec les Intendants des provinces*, Paris, 1864–1897.

Boisselly (Cl.), *Calcul ou tariffe sur le débordement des monnaies tant d'or que d'argent advenu au pays de Provence, ans 1590–1591–1592–1593*, Aix, 1600.

Boissonnade (P.), "Colbert, son système, et les entreprises industrielles d'État en Languedoc, 1661–1683," *Annales du Midi*, 1902.

———, "Production et commerce des céréales, des vins et eaux-de-vie en Lanquedoc, dans la seconde moitié du xviie siècle," *Annales du Midi*, 1905.

———, "La restauration et le développement de l'industrie en Languedoc au temps de Colbert," *Annales du Midi*, 1906.

———, "L'industrie languedocienne pendant les soixante premières années du xviie siècle," *Annales du Midi*, 1909.

———, *Le socialisme d'État, 1453–1661*, Paris, 1927.

———, "L'essai de restauration des ports en Languedoc an xviie siècle," *Annales du Midi*, 1934.

Bon jardinier (Le), *nouvelle encyclopédie horticole*, Paris, 1947.

Bondois (P.), "La misère sous Louis XIV, la disette de 1662," *R.H.E.S.*, 1924.

Bonnier (G.), *Flore complète illustrée en couleurs de France, Suisse et Belgique*, Neuchâtel, Paris, Brussels, 1911–1934.

Bost (Ch.), *Les prédicants protestants des Cévennes et du Bas-Languedoc*, Paris, 1912.

———, "Les prophètes du Languedoc," *Revue historique*, 136 and 137, 1921.

———, "Les prophètes des Cévennes," *Revue d'histoire et de philosophie religieuse*, 1925.

Bouges (le R. P.), *Histoire ecclésiastique et civile de la ville et diocèse de Carcassonne*, Paris, 1741.

Bourdieu (Cl.), *Sociologie de l'Algérie*, Paris, 1961.

Bousquet (J.), *En Rouergue à travers le temps*, Rodez, 1961.

Bousquet (L.), "Les genres de vie dans le Delta des Bouches-du-Rhône," *B.S.L.G.*, 1922.

Boutelet (B.), "La criminalité dans le baillage de Pont-de-l'Arche," *Annales de Normandie*, 1962.

Boutruche (R.), "La dévastation des campagnes pendant la guerre de Cent ans et la reconstruction agricole de la France," *Publication de la faculté des Lettres de Strasbourg*, 106, 1946.

————, *La crise d'une société; seigneurs et paysans du Bordelais pendant la guerre de Cent ans*, Paris, 1957 edn.

Bozon (P.), "La population de la Cévenne vivaroise," *Revue de géographie alpine*, 1958.

————, *La vie rurale en Vivarais*, Valence, 1961.

Branas (J.), *Éléments de viticulture générale*, Montpellier, 1946.

Braudel (F.), *La Méditerranée et le monde méditerranéen à l'époque de Philippe II*, Paris, 1949.

————, Hémardinquer (J. J.) and Philippe (R.), "Vie matérielle et comportements biologiques," *Annales*, 1961, pp. 545–574.

———— and Romano (R.), *Navires et marchandises à l'entrée du port de Livourne, 1547–1611*, Paris, 1951.

Brémond (Henri), *Histoire littéraire du sentiment religieux en France*, Paris, 1916–1936.

Brun, (A.), *Recherches historiques sur l'introduction du français dans les provinces du Midi*, Paris, 1923.

Brun-Durand (J.), *Dictionnaire biographique de la Drôme*, Grenoble, 1901.

Brutails (J. A.), *Étude sur la condition des populations rurales en Roussillon au Moyen Âge*, Paris, 1891.

Burckhardt (J.), *La civilisation en Italie au temps de la Renaissance*, 2 vols., Paris, 1885.

[Burel], *Mémoires de Jean Burel, bourgeois du Puy*, Le Puy, 1875 edn.

Cabane (M.), "L'olivier dans le Gard," *B.S.L.G.*, 1942.

[Cabrol], "Le livre de notes de Bernard Cabrol, vicaire de Riols à Saint-Pons," edited by J. Sahuc, *Revue d'histoire du diocése de Montpellier*, II, 1910–1911.

Cabrol (E.), *Annales de Villefranche de Rouergue*, Villefranche, 1860.

Calmette (J.) and Vival (P.), *Histoire du Roussillon*, Paris, 1923.

Cambon (P.), *La vente des biens nationaux dans les districts de Béziers et Saint-Pons*, Montpellier, 1951.

The Cambridge Economic History of Europe, Cambridge, 1942–1963.

Camps (G.), "Aux origines de la Berbérie," *Lybica*, 1960.

Camps-Fabrer (Henriette), *L'olivier dans l'Afrique romaine*, Algiers, 1953.

Candolle (A. de), *Origine des plantes cultivées*, Paris, 1883.

Cantaloube (C.), *La Réforme vue d'un village cévenol*, Paris, 1951.

————, "Les origines de la Réforme dans les Cévennes," *Bulletin de la Société de l'histoire du protestantisme français*, 1959.

Cantillon (R.), *Essai sur la nature du commerce en général, Paris*, 1952 edn.

Carles (M.), "Le folklore de Saint-Guilhem-le-Désert," *Folklore*, VI, 1945.

Caron (Cl.), *L'antéchrist démasqué*, Tournon, 1581.

Carpentier (E.), *Orviéto et la peste noire*, Paris, 1962.

———— and Glénisson (J.), "La démographie française au xive siècle," *Annales*, 1962.

Carrière (V.), *Introduction aux études d'histoire ecclésiastique locale*, Paris, 1936.

Cartulaire de l'abbaye de Conques, ed. by G. Desjardins, Paris, 1879.

Cassan (C.), *Les archives municipales d'Aniane*, Montpellier, 1895.

————, *Saint-Guilhem-le-Désert*, Montpellier, 1902.

————, "L'administration communale aux xive et xve siècles dans quelques communautés dépendant de l'abbaye d'Aniane," *Mémoires de la Société d'archéologie de Montpellier*, 1907.

Castellan (G.), "Fourrages et bovins dans l'économie rurale de la Restauration: l'exemple du Rhône," *R.H.E.S.*, 1960.

Caster (G.), *Le commerce du pastel à Toulouse*, Toulouse, 1962.

Castro (J. de), *Géographie de la Faim*, Paris, 1949.

Cavalier (J.), *Mémoires sur la guerre des Cévennes*, Paris, 1918 edn.

Cazalet (H.), *Valleraugue*, Uzès, 1950.

Cazalis de Fondouce (P.), "Faune historique du Bas-Languedoc," *B.S.L.G.*, 1898.

Chabaud (F.), "L'horizon rural à travers les compoix," *Communication au 33e congrès (1959, Bagnols-sur-Cèze) de la Fédération historique du Languedoc-Roussillon.*

Chabrol (J. P.), *Les fous de Dieu*, Paris, 1961.

Chamson (A.), *Le crime des justes*, Paris, 1948 edn.

[Chapelle], *Voyage de Chapelle et Bachaumont*, Paris, 1861 edn.

Charrin (L. de), *Les testaments dans la région de Montpellier*, Montpellier, 1961.

Chaunu (P.), "Sur le front de l'histoire des prix du xvie siècle," *Annales*, 1961.

————, "Au xviie siècle, rythmes et coupures: à propos de la mercuriale de Paris," *Annales*, 1964.

Chaunu (P. and H.), *Séville et l'Atlantique*, Paris, 1955–1957.

Chauvet (M.), "Le folklore languedocien," *Album des vins de France*, 1937.

————, *Occitanie*, Montpellier, 1955.

Chéron (A.) and Sarret (G. de), *Coussergues et les Sarret*, Brussels, 1963.

Chevalier (A.) and Emberger (L.), "Les régions botaniques terrestres," *Encyclopédie française*, V, Paris, 1937.

Chevalier (D.), "Troubles agraires libanais en 1958," *Annales*, 1959.

Chevalier (M.), *La vie humaine dans les Pyrénées ariégeoises*, Paris, 1956.

Chobaut (H.), "Les origines de la sériciculture française," *Mémoires de l'Académie du Vaucluse*, 1940.

Chomel (V.), "La pratique religieuse en Narbonnais (xvᵉ–xviᵉ siècles)," *Bibliothèque École des Chartes*, 1957.

"Chronique inédite de Mauguio," *Mémoires de la Société d'archéologie de Montpellier*, VII, 1881.

"La chronique consulaire de Béziers," *Bulletin de la Société d'archéologie de Béziers*, 3, 1839.

Clamagéran (J.), *Histoire de l'impôt en France*, Paris, 1857–1876.

Claparéde (J.), et al., *Languedoc méditerranéen et Roussillon d'hier et d'aujourd'hui*, Nice, 1947.

Clapham (J.), *A Concise Economic History of Britain*, Cambridge, 1951.

Clark (K.), *L'art du paysage*, Paris, 1961.

Clébert (J. P.), *Les Tziganes*, Paris, 1961.

Clément (P.), *Le Salavès, étude monographique du canton de Sauve (Gard)*, Anduze, 1952.

Cohn (N.), *Les fanatiques de l'Apocalypse* [The Pursuit of the Millenium], Paris, 1962 edn.

Cole (C. W.), *Colbert and a Century of French Mercantilism*, New York, 1939.

Combes (J.), "La constitution de rente à Montpellier au xvᵉ siècle," *Annales de l'Université de Montpellier*, II, 3–4, 1944.

———, "Le port de Sérignan au xivᵉ siècle," *Annales du Midi*, 1950.

———, "Un marchand de Chypre, bourgeois de Montpellier," dans *Études médiévales offertes à A. Fliche*, Montpellier, 1952.

———, "Montpellier et les foires de Pézenas et Montagnac au xivᵉ siècle," *Féd. hist. du Languedoc méditerranéen*, Congrès de Carcassonne, 1952.

———, "Les foires en Languedoc au Moyen Âge," *Annales*, 1958.

Coquelle (P.), "La sédition de Montpellier en 1645," *Annales du Midi*, 1908.

Corvisier (A.), *L'armée française de la fin du xviiᵉ siècle au ministère de Choiseul*, Paris, 1964.

Coste (L.), "Les transformations de Montpellier depuis la fin du xviiᵉ siècle," *B.S.L.G.*, 1891.

Coudy (J.), *Les guerres de religion*, Paris, 1962.

Courtois (C.), *Les Vandales et l'Afrique*, Paris, 1955.

Cousin (V.), *Madame de Longueville pendant la Fronde*, Paris, 1887.

Coutance (A.), *L'olivier*, Paris, 1877.

Craeybeckx (I.), *Un grand commerce d'importation: les vins de France aux anciens Pays-Bas*, Paris, 1958.

Creuzé de Lesser (H.), *Statistique du département de l'Hérault*, Montpellier, 1824.

Dainville (F. de), "Obstacles humains au progrès de l'agriculture montpelliéraine en 1789," *Bulletin de la Société française d'économie rurale*, II, 1950.

————, "L'enquête d'Orry," *Population*, 7, 1952.

————, "La moisson et les travaux de l'aire en Bas-Languedoc," *Arts et traditions populaires*, 1955.

————, "Cartes anciennes du Languedoc," *B.S.L.G.*, 1960.

Dainville (O. de), "Le consistoire de Ganges à la fin du xvie siècle," *Revue d'histoire de l'Église de France*, 18, 1932.

————, "Remarques sur les compoix du Languedoc méditerranéen," *Folklore*, 2, 1939.

Daléchamps (J.), *Histoire générale des plantes*, Lyons, 1615.

Daumas (M.), "Le Lunellois," *B.S.L.G.*, 1952.

Davity (P.), "Languedoc," in *Description des quatre parties du monde*, II, Paris, 1643.

Debien (G.), *En Haut-Poitou: Défricheurs au travail*, Paris, 1952.

Dedieu (J.), *Le rôle politique des protestants français (1685–1715)*, Paris, 1920.

Deffontaines (P.), *Les hommes et leurs travaux dans les pays de la Moyenne Garonne*, Lille, 1932.

Degarne (M.), "La révolte du Rouergue en 1643," xviie *siècle*, 1962.

Degrully (L.), *L'olivier*, Montpellier, Paris, 1906.

Delefortrie (N.) and Morice (J.), *Les revenus départementaux en 1864 et 1954*, Paris, 1959.

Deleuze (S.), *Le climat de Saint-Georges-d'Orques*, Montpellier, 1876.

————, *Saint-Georges-d'Orques*, Montpellier, 1881.

Delisle (L.), *Études sur la condition de la classe agricole en Normandie au Moyen Âge*, Évreux, 1851.

Delumeau (J.), *Vie économique et sociale de Rome au xvie siècle*, Paris, 1959.

————, *L'alun de Rome* (xve–xixe *siècles*), Paris, 1962.

Démians d'Archimbaud (G.), "L'archéologie du village médiéval: exemple anglais et expérience provençale," *Annales*, 1962.

Demougeot (E.), "Le chameau et l'Afrique du Nord romaine," *Annales*, 1960.

Depping (G.), *Correspondance administrative sous le règne de Louis XIV*, Paris, 1850–1855.

Dermigny (L.), *Sète de 1666 à 1880*, Montpellier, 1955.

————, "De Montpellier à La Rochelle: route du commerce, route de la médecine au xviiie siècle," *Annales du Midi*, 1955.

————, "Armement languedocien et trafic du Levant et de Barbarie," *Provence historique*, 1955–1956.

Derrau (M.), "L'intérêt géographique des minutes notariales et des compoix," *Revue de géographie alpine*, 1946.

Des Hours-Farel, "Le Domaine de Méric," *Bulletin de la Société d'agriculture de l'Hérault*, 1865.

Despois (J.), "La culture en terrasses en Afrique du Nord," *Annales*, 1956.

Devereux (G.), "Normal and Abnormal, the Key Problem of Psychiatric Anthropology," in *Some Uses of Anthropology: Theoretical and Applied*, Anthropological Society of Washington, Washington, D.C., 1956.

Devèze (M.), *La vie de la forêt française au* xvie *siècle*, Paris, 1961.

Devic (Cl.) and Vaissette (J.), *Histoire générale de Languedoc*, Toulouse, 1872–1892 edns.

Deyon (P.), "Evolution du régime seigneurial en Picardie," *R.H.M.C.*, 1961.

———, "Variations de la production textile aux xvie et xviiie siècles," *Annales*, 1963.

Dictionnaire des postes de l'Empire, Noyon, 1859.

Dictionnaires topographiques, (the Hérault, the Gard, and the Aude), Paris, 1865, 1868, 1912.

Dictionnaire Vilmorin des plantes potagères, Paris, 1946.

Dintzer (L.), *Nicolas Rémy*, Lyons, 1936.

Dion (R.), *Essai sur la formation du paysage rural français*, Tours, 1934.

———, *Histoire de la vigne et du vin en France*, Paris, 1959.

———, "Tartessos," *Revue historique*, 224, 1960.

Dognon (P.), *Les institutions politiques et administratives du Pays de Languedoc du* xive *siècle aux guerres de religion*, Paris, 1895.

Doucet (R.), "Le grand parti de Lyon au xvie siècle," *Revue historique*, 1933.

———, "Les de Lairan, marchands drapiers à Toulouse," *Annales du Midi*, 1943.

———, "Le commerce et l'industrie de la soie d'après des inventaires lyonnais du xvie siècle," *Mélanges économiques René Gonnard*, Paris, 1946.

Doumenge (F.), "L'habitat en roseau de la côte du Roussillon," *B.S.L.G.*, 1956.

Drouot (H.), *Mayenne et la Bourgogne (1587–1596)*, Paris, 1937.

Dubled (H.), "Mortalités du xive siècle en Alsace," *R.H.E.S.*, 1959.

Dubois (A.), *Les prophètes cévenols*, Strasbourg, 1861.

Duby (G.), *La société aux* xie *et* xiie *siècles dans la région mâconnaise*, Paris, 1953.

———, "Techniques et rendements dans les Alpes du Sud en 1338," *Annales du Midi*, 1958

———, *L'économie rurale et la vie des campagnes dans l'Occident médiéval*, Paris, 1962.

——— and Mandrou (R.), *Histoire de la civilisation française*, 2 vols., Paris, 1958.

Ducasse (A.), *La guerre des Camisards*, Paris, 1962.

Duchaussoy (H.), "Les bans de vendanges de la Région parisienne," *La Météoro-logie*, 1934.

Dugrand (R.), *Villes et campagnes en Bas-Languedoc*, Paris, 1963.

Dulieu (L.), *Essai historique sur l'hôpital Saint-Éloi de Montpellier*, Montpellier, 1953.

Dumas (A.), *La condition des gens mariés dans la famille périgourdine* (xve–xvie *siècles*), Paris, 1908.

Dumont (R.), *Voyages en France d'un agronome*, Paris, 1951.

———, "L'agriculture comparée," in *Larousse agricole*, Paris, 1952.

———, *L'Afrique Noire est mal partie*, Paris, 1962.

Dupont (A.), *Les cités de la Narbònnaise première*, Nîmes, 1942.

———, "La Roque-Aynier," in *Études médiévales offertes à A. Fliche*, Montpellier, 1952.

Dupront (A.), "Problèmes et méthodes d'une histoire de la psychologie collective," *Annales*, 1961.

Durand and Flahault (Ch.), "Les limites de la région méditerranéenne en France," *Bulletin de la Société botanique de France*, 33, 1886.

Durliat (M.), *Histoire du Roussillon*, Paris, 1962.

———, *L'art dans le royaume de Majorque*, Toulouse, 1962.

Duthil (C.), "L'industrie de la soie à Nîmes jusqu'en 1789," *R.H.M.C.*, 10, 1908.

Duthil (L.), *L'état économique du Languedoc (1750–1789)*, Paris, 1911.

Duveau (G.), *La vie ouvrière en France sous le Second Empire*, Paris, 1946.

Éliade (M.), *Le chamanisme*, Paris, 1950.

Engels (F.), *La guerre des paysans en Allemagne*, Paris, 1929.

Enjalbert (H.), "Le commerce de Bordeaux au xviie siècle," *Annales du Midi*, 1950.

———, "Comment naissent les grands crus," *Annales*, 1953.

———, "Économie rurale du Rouergue à la veille de la Révolution," *Annales du Midi*, 1955.

Ernle (Lord), *Histoire rurale de l'Angleterre*, Paris, 1952 edn.

Esmonin (E.), *La taille en Normandie au temps de Colbert*, Paris, 1913.

Estienne (C.) and Liébaut (J.), *L'agriculture et la maison rustique*, Rouen, 1645.

"Évolution de l'élevage ovin," *Chambres d'agriculture*, June 1–15, 1957.

Expilly (Abbé), *Dictionnaire historique, géographique et politique des Gaules et de la France*, Paris, 1762.

Ey (H.), *Études psychiatriques*, Paris, 1948.

———, Bernard (P.) and Brisset (Ch.), *Manuel de psychiatrie*, Paris, 1963.

Faber (J. A.), "Het probleem van de dalende graanaanvoer uit de Oostzeelanden in de tweede helft van de zeventiende eeuw," *A.A.G. Bijdrajen*, 9, 1963.

——— and Baehrel (R.), "Prix nominaux, prix métalliques et formule d'Irving Fischer," *Annales*, 1962.

Fagniez (G.), *L'économie de la France sous Henri IV*, Paris, 1897.

Falgairolles (P.), *Histoire de Vauvert*, Nîmes, 1918.

Faucher (D.), "Campagnes françaises et campagnes méridionales," *Annales du Midi*, 1930, p. 400.

——, *Géographie agraire*, Paris, 1949.

Fucher (O.), *Plaines et bassins du Rhône moyen*, Paris, 1927.

Faure (E.), *La disgrâce de Turgot*, Paris, 1961.

[Faurin], *Journal de Faurin sur les guerres de Castres*, Montpellier, 1878 edn.

Favre (Abbé), *Jean l'an près (1750)*, in *Milhous Moncels*, Nîmes, 1928.

Fay (H. M.), *Lépreux et cagots du Sud-Ouest*, Paris, 1910.

Febvre (L.), *Philippe II et la Franche-Comté*, Paris, 1912.

——, "Patate et pomme de terre," *Annales*, 1940.

——, *Le problème de l'incroyance au xvie siècle*, Paris, 1942.

——, *Au cœur religieux du xvie siècle*, Paris, 1957.

Fel (A.), *Les hautes terres du Massif central*, Paris, 1962.

Feller (F. X. de), *Biographie universelle*, Paris, 1833 edn.

Felloni (G.), "Une monographie d'histoire démographique," *Annales*, 1960.

Féral (P.), *Approches: essais d'histoire économique et sociale de la Gascogne*, Auch, 1957.

Ferres (A.) and Lopez Salinas (A.), "Voyage à Las Hurdes," *Temps modernes*, 1961.

Février (P. A.), "Aspects de la vie agricole en Basse-Provence à la fin du Moyen Âge," *Bulletin philologique et historique, (jusqu'à 1610)*, 1959.

Fleury (M.) and Valmary (P.), "Les progrès de l'instruction élémentaire de Louis XIV à Napoléon III," *Population*, 1957.

Fontenay (M.), "Paysans et marchands ruraux de la vallée de l'Essonne dans la seconde moitié du xviie siècle," *Paris et Ile-de-France*, 1958.

Fort (aîné), *Table de comparaison entre anciens et nouveaux poids et mesures du département de l'Hérault*, Montpellier, *an* XIII.

Foucault (M.), *Histoire de la folie*, Paris, 1961.

Fourquin (G.), *Les campagnes de la Région parisienne à la fin du Moyen Âge*, Paris, 1964.

François Quesnay et la physiocratie, Paris, 1958

Francolini (F.), *Olivicoltura*, Turin, 1923.

Frèche (G.), "Les prix des céréales à Toulouse (1650–1715)," *Recherches d'histoire économique*, directed by G. Besnier, Paris, 1964.

Freud (S.), *Nouvelles conférences sur la psychanalyse*, Paris, 1936.

——, "Deuil et mélancolie," *Revue française de psychanalyse*, 1936.

——, *Études sur l'hystérie*, Paris, 1956 edn. (with Breuer).

——, *Psychologie collective et analyse du Moi*, Paris, 1962 edn.

Furet (F.), "Pour une définition des classes inférieures à l'époque moderne," *Annales*, 1963.

————, Mazauric and Bergeron, "Les sans-culottes et la Révolution française," *Annales*, 1963.

Furon (R.), *Manuel de préhistoire générale*, Paris, 1951.

Gaches, *Mémoires,* ed. by Ch. Pradel, Paris, Albi, 1894.

Gachon (P.), *Les États de Languedoc et l'édit de Béziers*, Paris, 1887.

————, *Histoire du Languedoc*, Paris, 1921.

Gagg (R.), *Kirche im Feuer . . .* , Zurich, 1961.

Galbraith (J.), *L'ère de l'opulence* [The Affluent Society], Paris, 1962 edn.

Gallix (M.), *La vente des Biens nationaux des districts de Montpellier et Lodève*, Montpellier, 1951.

Galtier (G.), "La côte sableuse du Golfe du Lion," *B.S.L.G.*, 1958.

————, *Le vignoble du Languedoc méditerranéen et du Roussillon*, Montpellier, 1960.

[Gamon], *Mémoires d'Achille Gamon*, in *Collection complète des Mémoires relatifs à l'histoire de France*, XXXIV, Paris, 1823.

Ganiage (J.), *Les origines du protectorat français en Tunisie*, Paris, 1959.

Gardette (P.), *Atlas linguistique et ethnographique du Lyonnais*, Lyons, 1950.

Garola (C.), *Les céréales*, Paris, 1914.

Gasparin (Comte de), *Cours d'agriculture*, Paris, 1848.

Gaufridi (J. F. de), *Histoire de Provence*, Aix, 1694.

Gaujal (de), *Études historiques sur le Rouergue*, 1858.

Gaussen (H.), *Géographie des plantes*, Paris, 1933.

Gauthier (E.) and Henry (L.), *La population de Crulai, paroisse normande*, Paris, 1958.

Gaxotte (P.), *La France de Louis XIV*, Paris, 1946.

Geisendorf (P. F.), *Livre des habitants de Genève*, I, Geneva, 1957.

Gentil da Silva (J.), "Villages castillans au xvie siècle," *Annales*, 1963.

George (P.), *La région du Bas-Rhône*, Paris, 1935.

Géraud-Parracha (G.), *Le commerce des vins et des eaux-de-vie en Languedoc sous l'Ancien Régime*, Montpellier, 1957.

Germain (A.), "La Fronde à Montpellier," *Mémoires de l'Académie des Sciences de Montpellier, Section des lettres*, III, 1859–1863, p. 579 ff.

Germain (J.), *Sauve, antique cité*, Montpellier, 1952.

Geslin (H.), *Étude des lois de croissance d'une plante, contribution à l'étude du climat du blé*, Paris, 1944.

————, "L'échaudage physiologique du blé," *Bulletin des engrais*, June, 1955, pp. 12–14.

Gibault (Dr.), *Histoire des légumes*, Paris, 1913.

Gibrat (R.), *Les inégalités économiques*, Paris, 1931.

Gidon (F.), "Un haricot dans la corbeille de noces de Catherine de Médicis?" *Presse médicale*, January 18, 1936.

Gigon (S. C.), *La révolte de la gabelle en Guyenne*, Bordeaux, Paris, 1906.

Gigot (J.), "État des registres d'état civil de la ville de Canet," *Cerca* (Bulletin des archives des Pyrénées-Orientales), 7, spring, 1960.

Giralt Raventos (E.), "En torno al precio del trigo en Barcelona durante el siglo XVI," *Hispania*, 18, 1958.

Girard (A.), "La guerre monétaire," *Annales*, 1940.

Girard (G.), "Peste tellurique et peste de fouissement," *La Presse médicale*, May 30, 1964.

Girard (J.), *L'art de la Provence*, Paris, n.d.

Godard (M.) and Nigond (J.), "Le climat de la vigne dans la région de Montpellier en 1957," *Vigne et vins*, 66, n.d.

Godechot (J.) and Moncassin (S.), "Démographie et subsistances en Languedoc du XVIIIᵉ au début du XIXᵉ siècle," *Bulletin d'histoire économique et sociale de la Révolution française*, 1964.

Godwin (H.), *The History of the British Flora*, Cambridge, 1956.

Gölnitz (A.), *Ulysses belgico-gallicus*, Leyden, 1631 (cf. Malavialle, 1908).

Gorlier (P.), *Le Vigan à travers les âges*, Montpellier, ca. 1950.

Goubert (P.), "Problèmes démographiques en Beauvaisis," *Annales*, 1952.

————, "Une richesse historique: les registres paroissiaux," *Annales*, 1954.

————, *Beauvais et le Beauvaisis au XVIIᵉ siècle*, Paris, 1960.

———— and Denis (M.), *1789: les Français ont la parole*, Paris, 1964.

[Gouberville], *Le Journal du Sire de Gouberville*, ed. by M. de Beaurepaire, Caen, 1892.

Gouhier (P.), "Port-en-Bessin, 1596–1792," *Cahiers des Annales de Normandie*, 1962.

Gouron (A.), *Les métiers en Languedoc au Moyen Âge*, Geneva, 1958.

Gouron (M.), *Les étapes de l'histoire de Nîmes*, Nîmes, 1939.

Gourou (P.), *La terre et l'homme en Extrême-Orient*, Paris, 1940.

Gros (Ch.), "Le plateau du Sommail," *B.S.L.G.*, 1922.

Gros (G.), "La Salvetat," *B.S.L.G.*, 1901.

Guérin (I.), *La vie rurale en Sologne aux XIVᵉ–XVᵉ siècles*, Paris, 1960

Guibal (G.), "Riquet," *Annales du Midi*, 1866.

Guibal-Lanconquié, *Traité du calcul décimal, relativement aux nouveaux poids et mesures*, Béziers, an VII.

Guillemain (B.), *La Cour pontificale d'Avignon (1309–1376)*, Paris, 1962.

Guiraud (L.), *Jacques Cœur*, Montpellier, 1900.

————, *Études sur la Réforme à Montpellier*, 2 vols., *Mémoires de la Société d'archéologie de Montpellier*, VI and VII, 1918–1919.

[Guiscard], *Mémoires du marquis de Guiscard*, Delft, 1705, reedited in *Archives curieuses de l'histoire de France*, XI, by F. Danjou, Paris, 1840.

Gussow (Z.), "Pibloktoq, an Ethno-psychiatric Study," in *The Psychoanalytic Study of Society*, I, New York, 1960.

Guyot (J.), *Viticulture et vinification en France, vignobles de France*, Paris, 1860–1868.

Guyot (L.), *Origine des plantes cultivées*, Paris, 1946.

———— and Gibassier (P.), *Histoire des fleurs*, Paris, 1961.

———— and Guerillot-Vinet (A.), *Les épices*, Paris, 1963.

Hamilton (E. J.), *American Treasure and the Price Revolution in Spain, 1501–1650*, Cambridge, 1936.

Haudricourt (A.) and Jean-Brunhes-Delamare (M.), *L'homme et la charrue à travers les âges*, Paris, 1955.

Hauser (H.), "Étude critique sur la *Rebeine* de Lyon," *Revue historique*, 1896.

————, "La Réforme et les classes populaires en France," *R.H.M.C.*, 1899.

————, *Études sur la Réforme française*, Paris, 1909.

———— and Renaudet (A.), *Les débuts de l'âge moderne*, Paris, 1946.

Hayes (H. K.) and Immer (F. R.), *Methods of Plant Breeding*, New York, 1942.

Hazard (P.), *La crise de la conscience européenne*, Paris, 1935.

Heers (J.), *Gênes au xvᵉ siècle*, Paris, 1961.

Heim (V.), *Handbuch der Gletscherkunde*, Stuttgart, 1885.

Hemardinquer (J. J.), "Essai de carte des graisses de cuisine en France," *Annales*, 1961, p. 747.

Hemingway (E.), *Pour qui sonne le glas* [For Whom the Bell Tolls], Paris, 1949 edn.

Henry (L.), *Anciennes familles genevoises: étude démographique*, Paris, 1956.

Heyd (W.), *Histoire du commerce du Levant au Moyen Âge*, Amsterdam, 1959 edn.

Higounet (C.), "Les bastides du Sud-Ouest," *Information historique*, 2, 1946.

————, "Mouvements de population dans le Midi de la France," *Annales*, 1953.

————, "Une carte agricole de l'Albigeois vers 1260," *Annales du Midi*, 1958.

Hilaire (J.), "Une vente de biens ecclésiastiques au diocèse de Béziers en 1563," *Fédération historique du Languedoc*, Congrès de Carcassonne, 1952.

————, *Le régime des biens entre époux dans la région de Montpellier*, Paris, 1957.

————, "Les aspects communautaires du droit," *Recueil de mémoires et travaux publiés par la Société d'histoire des pays de droit écrit*, IV, 2, 1958–1960.

Histoire du commerce de Marseille, published under the direction of Gaston Rambert, Paris, 1949–1959.

Hobsbawm (E.), "The General Crisis in the 17th Century," *Past and Present*, 1954.

Homo (L.), *Aurélien*, Paris, 1904.

Honoré (C.), "Sécheresses . . . en Basse-Provence," *Var historique et géographique*, 1938.

Hoszowski (S.), "L'Europe centrale devant la Révolution des prix (xvie–xviie siècles)," *Annales*, 1961.

Houssay (F.), "Voyage en Perse," *Revue des Deux Mondes*, January 15, 1887.

Hugues (J. P.), *Histoire de l'Église réformée d'Anduze*, Montpellier, Paris, 1864.

Huizinga (J.), *Le déclin du Moyen Âge* [The Waning of the Middle Ages], Paris, 1932 edn.

Ibn-Al-Awan, *Le livre de l'agriculture*, 3 vols., Paris, 1866 edn.

Imbart de La Tour (P.), *Les origines de la Réforme*, Paris, 1905–1914.

Inventaire sommaire des registres de la Jurade de Bordeaux, Bordeaux, 1895.

Jaberg (K.) and Jud (J.), *Sprach und Sachatlas Italiens*, Zofingen, 1937.

Jacquart (J.), "La Fronde des princes dans la région parisienne et ses conséquences matérielles," *R.H.M.C.*, 1960.

———, "Propriété et exploitation rurale au sud de Paris, au xvie siècle," *B.S.H.M.*, November 6, 1960.

Jannoray (J.), *Ensérune*, Paris, 1955.

Jeannin (P.), *Les marchands au xvie siècle*, Paris, 1957.

———, "Les comptes du Sund comme source pour la construction d'indices généraux de l'activité économique en Europe," *Revue historique*, 1964.

Jeanroy (A.), *Histoire de la poésie occitane*, Toulouse, 1945.

Jones (E.), *Sigmund Freud, Life and Work*, III, London, 1957.

———, *La vie et l'œuvre de Sigmund Freud*, Paris, 1958–1961.

Jordan (J. J. B.), *Histoire de la ville d'Agde*, Montpellier, 1824.

Jourdan (E.), "La côte calcaire du Languedoc entre Nîmes et le Vidourle," *B.S.L.G.*, 1939–1941. Offprint, 1942.

Juillard (E.), *La vie rurale dans la plaine de Basse-Alsace*, Strasbourg, Paris, 1953.

———, Meynier (A.) and Planhol (X. de), *Structures agraires et paysages ruraux*, Nancy, 1957.

Juillard (M.), "La vie populaire à la fin du Moyen Âge en Auvergne (xve siècle)," *Auvergne*, 28, 1951.

Jurieu (P.), *L'accomplissement des prophéties*, Rotterdam, 1686.

———, *Suite de l'accomplissement des prophéties*, Rotterdam, 1687.

———, *Apologie pour l'accomplissement des prophéties*, Rotterdam, 1687.

———, *Lettres pastorales*, Rotterdam, 1688.

———, *The Reflexions of the Reverend and Learned Monsieur Jurieu*, London, 1689.

Kardiner (A.), *The Individual and His Society*, New York, 1939.

Kühnholtz-Lordat (G.), *La terre incendiée*, Nîmes, 1938.

————, "Influence des feux pastoraux dans la région méditerranéenne," *Revue d'agriculture tropicale et de botanique appliquée*, 1956.

Labbé (Ph.), *Sacrosancta consilia*, Paris, 1671–1672.

La Boétie (E. de), *Mémoires*, Paris, 1922 edn.

Laboissière (J. de), *Les commentaires du soldat du Vivarais*, Privas, 1811.

Labrely (R.), "Notice sur la seigneurie de Bourg," *Revue du Vivarais*, 1912.

Labrousse (C. E.), *Esquisse du mouvement des prix et des revenus en France au* xviiie *siècle*, Paris, 1933.

————, *La crise de l'économie française à la fin de l'Ancien Régime et au début de la Révolution*, Paris, 1943.

Laferrière (J.), *Le contrat de Poissy, 1561*, Paris, 1905.

La Gorce (A. de), *Camisards et Dragons du Roi*, Paris, 1964.

[Lalande], *Notes de Michel Lalande, curé de Siran, 1680–1710*, ed. by J. Sahuc, Narbonne, 1898.

Lancre (P. de), *Traité de l'inconstance des mauvais anges*, Paris, 1612.

————, *De l'incrédulité du sortilège*, Paris, 1622.

Landry (A.), "La dépopulation dans l'Antiquité," *Revue historique*, 1936.

Lanternari (V.), *Les mouvements religieux des peuples opprimés*, Paris, 1962.

Lapeyre (H.), *Géographie de l'Espagne morisque*, Paris, 1959.

La Pijardière (M. de), *Les chroniques du Languedoc*, I, Montpellier, 1875.

Lapouge (G. de), "Géographie anthropologique de l'Hérault," *B.S.L.G.*, 1894.

————, "Matériaux pour l'anthropologie de l'Aveyron," *B.S.L.G.*, 1898.

Larenaudie (M. J.), "Les famines en Languedoc aux xive et xve siècles," *Annales du Midi*, 1952.

Latouche (R.), *La vie en Bas-Quercy* (xive–xviiie *siècles*), Toulouse, 1923.

Latreille (A.), Delaruelle (E.) and Palanque (J. R.), *Histoire du catholicisme en France*, Paris, 1957–1962.

Laur (F.), *Le Plateau du Larzac*, Montpellier, 1929.

Laurent (R.), *Les vignerons de la "Côte-d'Or" au* xixe *siècle*, Dijon, 1957–1958.

Lavisse (E.), *Histoire de France*, Paris, 1911.

Le Brun (P.), *Histoire critique des pratiques superstitieuses*, Paris, 1750 edn.

Leclerc (H.), *Les légumes de France*, Paris, 1928.

————, *Les fruits de France*, Paris, 1933.

Leenhardt (A.), *Belles résidences des environs de Montpellier*, Montpellier, 1931 and 1932.

————, *Vieux hôtels montpelliérains*, Bellegarde, 1935.

Lefebvre (G.), *Les paysans du Nord pendant la Révolution française*, Paris, 1924.

Lefebvre (Th.), *Le mode de vie dans les Pyrénées atlantiques orientales*, Paris, 1933.

Legendre (M.), *Las Hurdes*, Bordeaux, 1927.

Le Goff (J.), *La civilisation de l'occident médiéval*, Paris, 1964.

Le Loyer (P.), *Discours des spectres*, Paris, 1608.

Lempereur (L.), *État du diocèse de Rodez en 1771*, Rodez, 1906.

Lenthéric (C.), *Les villes mortes du golfe du Lion*, Paris, 1876.

Léon (P.), paper read to the Première conférence internationale d'histoire économique (Stockholm, 1960), Paris, 1960.

Léonard (E. G.), *Histoire générale du protestantisme*, 3 vols., Paris, 1961–1964.

Leroi-Gourhan (A.), *Évolution et techniques*, vol. II, *Milieu et techniques*, Paris, 1945.

Le Roy Ladurie (E.), "Fluctuations météorologiques et bans de vendanges au xviiie siècle," *Féd. hist. du Languedoc méditerranéen et du Roussillon* (30e et 31e Congrès, Sète, Beaucaire, 1956–1957), Montpellier, n.d., p. 189.

———, "Sur Montpellier et sa campagne aux xvie et xviie siècles," *Annales*, 1957.

———, "Histoire et climat," *Annales*, 1959.

———, "Climat et récoltes aux xviie et xviiie siècles," *Annales*, 1960.

———, "Aspects historiques de la nouvelle climatologie," *Revue historique*, 1961.

———, *Histoire du Languedoc*, Paris, 1962.

———, "La conférence d'Aspen," *Annales*, 1963.

———, "Voies nouvelles pour l'histoire rurale," *Études rurales*, 1964.

———, "Les diagrammes d'Aspen," *Annales*, 1965.

———, "Démographie et funestes secrets: le Languedoc," *Annales d'histoire de la Révolution française*, 1966.

———, "La démographie languedocienne (fin du xviiie, début du xixe siècle)," *Annales d'histoire de la Révolution française*, n.d.

L'Estoile (P. de), *Mémoires*, Paris, 1875 edn.

Lestrade (J.), *Les Huguenots en Comminges*, Paris, 1900.

———, "Les Huguenots dans les paroisses rurales du diocèse de Toulouse," *Revue historique de Toulouse*, 1938.

Levadoux (L.), *La vigne et sa culture,* Paris, 1961.

Levasseur (E.), *La population française*, Paris, 1889–1891.

Leveel (P.), *Histoire de la Touraine*, Paris, 1956.

Lévi-Strauss (C.), *Tristes tropiques*, Paris, 1955 edn.

———, *Anthropologie structurale*, Paris, 1958.

———, "La geste d'Asdiwal," *Les Temps modernes*, March, 1961.

Liger (L.), *La nouvelle Maison rustique*, Paris, 1743 edn.

Linton (R.), *Culture and Mental Disorders*, Springfield, Ill., 1956.

Livet (G.), *L'Intendance d'Alsace sous Louis XIV*, Strasbourg, 1956.

———, *Les guerres de religion*, Paris, 1962.

———, *La guerre de Trente Ans*, Paris, 1963.

Livet (R.), *Habitat rural et structures agraires en Basse-Provence*, Gap, 1962.

[Locke], *Loke's Travels in France, 1675–1679*, ed. by John Lough, Cambridge, 1953.

Loirette (G.), "Catholiques et protestants en Languedoc à la veille des guerres civiles (1560)," *Revue d'histoire de l'Église de France*, 1937.

Lot (F.), "L'état des paroisses et des feux en 1328," *Bibliothèque de l'École des Chartes*, 90, 1929.

Louis (M.), *Préhistoire du Languedoc méditerranéen et du Roussillon*, Paris, 1948.

———— and Taffanel (O. and J.), *Le premier âge du fer languedocien*, Bordighera, 1955–1958.

Loutchitsky (J.), "Assemblée des Réformés de Nîmes, 2 et 3 novembre 1562," *Bulletin de la Société historique du protestantisme français*, 22, 1873.

Louvreleuil (Le P.), *Le fanatisme renouvelé*, Avignon, 1704–1706. Reedition, Avignon, 1868.

————, *Mémoires historiques sur le pays de Gévaudan*, Mende, 1825.

Lubbe (G. de), *Chronique bourdeloise*, Bordeaux, 1619.

Lukacs (G.), *Histoire et conscience de classe*, Paris, 1960 edn.

Lunel (A.), "L'archéologie et les Bohémiens," *L'Arc*, 1959.

Luthard (M.), "Catholiques et protestants à Béziers, 1567–1568," *Revue d'histoire du diocèse de Montpellier*, 3, 1911–1912.

————, "Journal des actes de Jean Plantavit de la Pause, évêque de Lodève, 1626–1630," *Annales du Midi*, 25, 1913.

Magen (A.), "Une émeute à Agen en 1635," *Recueil des travaux de la Société d'agriculture d'Agen*, VII, 1854–1855.

Malavialle (L.), "Une excursion dans la Montagne Noire," *B.S.L.G.*, 1900.

————, "Le Bas-Languedoc en 1626," *B.S.L.G.*, 1908 and 1909.

Malowist (M.), "Le commerce de la Baltique et le problème des luttes sociales en Pologne aux xvᵉ et xviᵉ siècles," in *La Pologne au Xᵉ Congrès international des sciences historiques à Rome*, Warsaw, 1955.

Malthus (T. R.), *Essai sur le principe de population* [Essay on Population], Paris, 1963.

Malzac (L.), *Lasalle, les Lasallois et leurs origines*, Montpellier, 1910.

Mandrou (R.), "Français hors de France aux xviᵉ et xviiᵉ siècles," *Annales*, 1959.

————, *Introduction à la France moderne*, Paris, 1961.

————, Contribution to "Vie matérielle et comportements biologiques," *Annales*, 1961.

Mantran (R.), *Istanbul dans la seconde moitié du* xviiᵉ *siècle*, Paris, 1962.

Marion (E.), *Cri d'alarme*, 1708.

———— and Mazel (A.), "Mémoires inédits," in *Publications of the Huguenot Society of London*, 33, 1931.

Marres (P.), "La production des olives dans l'Hérault," *B.S.L.G.*, 1933.

————, *Les grands Causses*, Tours, 1935.

————, *La vigne et le vin en France*, Paris, 1950.

————, "L'immigration en Bas-Languedoc sous l'Ancien Régime," unedited paper read to the Congrès d'études occitanes de Montpellier, 1962.

Martin (A.), *Notice historique sur Mende*, Marvejols, 1894.

Martin (E.), *Histoire de Lodève*, Montpellier, 1900.

Martino (E. de), *Italie du Sud et magie*, Paris, 1963.

Marty (J.), "Frontignan," *B.S.L.G.*, 1957–1958.

Marx (K.), "Économie politique et philosophie," in *Œuvres philosophiques*, vol. VI, Paris, 1937 edn.

————, *Das Kapital*, Berlin, 1955 edn.

[Mascaro], *Mémoires de Jacme Mascaro*, published in *Bulletin de la Société d'archéologie de Béziers*, I, 1836.

Masson (P.), *Histoire des établissements et du commerce français dans l'Afrique barbaresque (1560–1973)*, Paris, 1903.

————, *Les Bouches-du-Rhône. Encyclopédie départementale*, Paris, 1913–1937 (especially vol. VII, *Agriculture*).

Mathieu (Cl.), *Le commerce des draps et des toiles en Avignon à la fin du* xive *siècle et au* xve *siècle*, Diplome d'études supérieures, unedited, Montpellier, 1960.

Mathiole, *Commentaires sur Dioscoride*, tr. by Desmoulins, Lyons, 1579 edn.

Maurette (F.), *Afrique équatoriale, orientale et australe*, Paris, 1938.

Maurizio (A.), *Histoire de l'alimentation végétale*, Paris, 1932.

Mauro (F.), *Le Portugal et l'Atlantique*, Paris, 1960.

Mazel (A.), *see* Marion (E.).

Mazier, "L'habitat en Costière," *B.S.L.G.*, 1956.

Mazon, *Vivarais et Velay*, Annonay, 1890.

Mazoyer (L.), "Le prophétisme cévenol," *Revue historique*, 197, 1947.

Meiss (M.), *Painting in Florence and Siena after the Black Death*, Princeton, N. J., 1951.

Ménard (L.), *Histoire civile, ecclésiastique et littéraire de la ville de Nismes, avec les preuves*, Paris, 1744–1758.

Merle (L.), *La métairie et l'évolution agraire de la Gâtine poitevine, de la fin du Moyen Âge à la Révolution*, Paris, 1958.

Meuvret (J.), "Les mouvements des prix de 1661 à 1715 et leurs répercussions," *Journal de la société de statistiques de Paris*, 1944.

————, "Les crises de subsistances et la démographie de la France d'Ancien Régime," *Population*, 1946.

————, "Circulation monétaire et utilisation économique de la monnaie dans la France du xvie et due xviie siècle," *Études d'Histoire moderne et contemporaine*, I, 1947.

————, "Agronomie et jardinage au xvie et au xviie siècle," *Mélanges Lucien Febvre*, II, Paris, 1953.

————, "Conjoncture et crise au xviie siècle: l'exemple des prix milanais," *Annales*, 1953.

————, "L'agriculture en Europe aux xviie et xviiie siècles," *Xe Congrès international des sciences historiques, Relazioni*, IV, Rome, 1955.

————, "La conjoncture internationale de 1660 à 1715," *B.S.H.M.*, 1964.

Meynier (A.), *Ségalas, Lévezou châtaigneraie*, Aurillac, 1931.

————, Perpillou (A.), et al., "La carte des communes de France," *Annales*, 1958.

Mezeray (F. de), *Histoire de France depuis Pharamond*, Paris, 1646–1651.

Michel (F.), *Histoire des races maudites de la France et de l'Espagne*, Paris, 1847.

Michelet (J.), *Histoire de France*, Paris, 1893–1898 edn.

Milhau (G.), *Navacelle*, Montpellier, 1955.

Millardet (G.), *Petit atlas linguistique des Landes*, Toulouse, 1910.

Miller (Ph.), *Dictionnaire des jardiniers*, 10 vols., Paris, 1785.

Millerot (T.), *Histoire de la ville de Lunel*, Montpellier, 1882.

Miquel (J.), "Essai sur l'arrondissement de Saint-Pons," *B.S.L.G.*, 1895.

Mireaux (E.), *Une province française au temps du grand Roi: la Brie*, Paris, 1958.

Misson (A.), *Le Théâtre sacré des Cévennes*, Paris, 1847 edn.

Moheau (pseudonym of Montyon), *Recherches et considérations sur la population de la France*, Paris, 1778.

Molitor (U.), "Tractatus utilis de phytonicis mulieribus," in *Mallei Maleficarum*, Lyons, 1669 edn.

Mollat (M.), *Le commerce de la Haute-Normandie au xve siècle et au début du xvie*, Paris, 1950.

Mols (R.), *Introduction à la démographie historique des villes d'Europe* (xive–xviiie siècles), Gembloux, 1954–1956.

Monin (H.), *Essai sur l'histoire administrative du Languedoc pendant l'Intendance de Basville*, Paris, 1884.

————, "La province du Languedoc en 1789," *B.S.L.G.*, 1886.

Montarlot (G.), "Facteurs météorologiques de la végétation de la vigne," offprint of *Annales E.N.A.M.*, 22, 3, p. 236.

————, "Description des sols de l'Hérault," *Annales de l'Institut national de la recherche agronomique*, 1952.

Montaugé (T. de), *L'agriculture et les classes rurales dans le pays toulousain, depuis le milieu du* xviiiᵉ *siècle*, Paris, 1869.

Montchrestien (A. de), *Traité de l'économie politique*, Paris, 1889 edn.

Montel (A.) and Lambert (P.), *Chants populaires du Languedoc*, Paris, 1880.

Montet (P.), *La vie quotidienne en Égypte au temps de Ramsès II*, Paris, 1946.

Moscovici (S.), *Reconversion industrielle et changements sociaux. Un exemple: la chapellerie dans l'Aude*, Paris, 1961.

Mours (S.), *Le Protestantisme en Vivarais et en Velay des origines à nos jours*, Valence, 1949.

――――, *Les églises réformées en France*, Strasbourg, 1958.

――――, *Le protestantisme français*, vol. I, *le* xviᵉ *siècle*, Paris, 1959.

Mousnier (R.), *La vénalité des offices sous Henri IV et Louis XIII*, Rouen, 1945.

――――, "Quelques raisons de la Fronde," *Bulletin de la société d'études du* xviiᵉ *siècle*, 1949, p. 33 ff.

――――, "L'évolution des finances publiques en France et en Angleterre pendant les guerres de la Ligue d'Augsbourg et de la Succession d'Espagne," *Revue historique*, 1951.

――――, "Études sur la population de la France au xviiᵉ siècle," xviiᵉ *siècle*, 1952.

――――, *Les* xviᵉ *et* xviiᵉ *siècles*, Paris, 1954.

――――, "L'âge classique," in *Histoire de France*, published under the direction of M. Reinhard, I, Paris, 1954.

――――, "Recherches sur les soulèvements populaires en France avant la Fronde," *R.H.M.C.*, 1958.

――――, *Paris au* xviiᵉ *siècle*, Paris (C.D.U.), (ca. 1963).

――――, *L'assassinat d'Henri IV*, Paris, 1964.

Musset (R.), *L'élevage du cheval en France*, Paris, 1917.

Nadal (J.) and Giralt-Raventos (E.), *La population catalane de 1353 à 1717*, Paris, 1960.

Nauton (P.), *Atlas linguistique et ethnographique du Massif central*, Paris, 1959.

Nef (J. U.), *The Rise of the British Coal Industry*, 2 vols., London, 1932.

Nelli (R.), *Le Languedoc et le comté de Foix*, Paris, 1958.

Nicod (J.), "L'oléiculture provençale," *Revue de géographie alpine*, 1956, pp. 247–295.

Nicolle (Ch.), *Destin des maladies infectieuses*, Paris, 1939.

Niel (F.), *Montségur*, Paris, 1954.

Niel (P.-G.-J.), *Portraits de personnages français les plus illustres au* xviᵉ *siècle*, Paris, 1848–1856.

Nouaillac (M.), "Henri IV et les Croquants du Limousin," *Bulletin historique et philologique*, 1912.

Le Nouveau de la Quintinye (cf. *Traité des jardins*).

Nynaud (L. de), *De la lycanthropie*, Paris, 1615.

Orange (A.) and Amalbert (M.), *Le mérinos d'Arles*, Antibes, 1924.

Pagézy (J.), *Mémoires sur le port d'Aigues-Mortes*, Paris, 1879–1886.

Palou (J.), *La sorcellerie*, Paris, 1957.

Papon (Abbé), *Histoire générale de Provence*, Paris, 1786.

Pech (F.), *La Bastide-Rouairoux*, Montpellier, 1951.

Pédelaborde (P.), *Le climat du Bassin parisien*, Paris, 1957.

Pégat (F.), "Les consuls de Montpellier, 1640–1657," *Mémoires de l'Académie des sciences de Montpellier, Section des lettres*, V, 1870–1873, p. 569 ff.

Pelc (J.), *Ceny w Gdansku w* XVI *i* XVII *Wieku* [Prices in Gdansk in the 16th and 17th Centuries], Lvov, 1937.

Pelissier (L. G.), "Carpentras au temps de Louis XIV," *Annales du Midi*, 1909.

Pellas (Le Père), *Dictionnaire provençal, avec les termes des arts mécaniques*, Avignon, 1723.

Pépin (I.), "De l'enseignement primaire dans le département de l'Hérault, 1822–1890," *B.S.L.G.*, 1895.

Pepys (S.), *Journal*, Paris, 1948 edn.

Perrot (M.), "Archives policières et militants ouvriers: le Gard," *R.H.E.S.*, 1959.

Perroy (E.), "A l'origine d'une économie contractée: les crises du XIVe siècle," *Annales*, 1949.

———, *Le Moyen Âge*, Paris, 1955.

Pesez (J.) and Le Roy Ladurie (E.), "Les villages disparus en France," *Annales*, 1965 (see *Villages désertés et histoire économique*).

Le Petit Thalamus de Montpellier, Montpellier, 1840 edn.

Peyrat (N.), *Histoire des pasteurs du désert (1685–1789)*, Paris, 1842.

———, *Histoire des Albigeois; les Albigeois et l'Inquisition*, 3 vols., Paris, 1870–1872.

Philippe (R.), "Sur l'histoire de l'alimentation," *Annales*, 1961.

———, "L'étude du ravitaillement de Paris au temps de Lavoisier," *Annales*, 1961.

Picheire (J.), *Histoire d'Agde*, Montpellier, 1960.

[Piemond], *Mémoires d'Eustache Piemond (1572–1608)*, edited by J. Brun-Durand, Valence, 1885.

Piétrement (C. A.), *Les chevaux préhistoriques et historiques*, Paris, 1883.

Pin (M.), *Nicolas Jouany*, Montpellier, 1930.

———, *Jean Cavalier*, Alès, 1936.

Pintard (R.), *Le libertinage érudit*, Paris, 1943.

Plaisse (A.), *La baronnie de Neubourg*, Paris, 1961.

Planhol (X. de), *De la plaine pamphylienne aux lacs pisidiens*, Paris, 1958.

————, "Du Piémont téhéranais à la Caspienne," *B.A.G.F.*, May–June, 1959.

————, "Sur l'agriculture turque," *Revue de géographie de Lyon*, 1960.

Platter (T. and F.), *Zur Sittengeschichte des* xvi *Jahrhunderts*, Leipzig, 1878.

[Platter], *Félix et Thomas Platter à Montpellier, 1552–1559, 1595–1599, notes de voyage de deux deux étudiants bâlois*, Montpellier, 1892.

Poitevin (J.), *Essai sur le climat de Montpellier*, Montpellier, 1803.

Polge (H.), "A propos de la charrue gersoise," *Bulletin de la Société d'archéologie, Gers*, 60, 1959.

Poliakov (Léon), *Histoire de l'antisémitisme*, vol. II, *De Mahomet aux Marranes*, Paris, 1961.

Pollitzer (R.), *La peste*, Organisation mondiale de la santé, Geneva, 1954.

Poncer (M. A.), *Mémoires historiques sur Annonay et le Haut-Vivarais*, Annonay, 1835.

Poncet (J.), "A propos des cultures en terrasses," *Annales*, 1957.

Porchnev (B.), *Les soulèvements populaires en France de 1623 à 1648*, Paris, 1963.

Portal (Ch.), *Documents sur le commerce des draps à Lavaur au* xvi*e siècle*, Albi, 1915.

Porteau (A.) and Vilmorin, *Le bon jardinier*, Almanach, Paris, 1843.

Postan (M.), "The Fifteenth Century," *The Economic History Review*, 1938–1939.

Pouthas (Ch.), *La population française pendant la première moitié du* xix*e siècle*, Paris, 1956.

Prat (G.), "Albi et la peste noire," *Annales du Midi*, 1952.

Prentout (H.), *Les États provinciaux de Normandie*, Caen, 1925.

Puaux (F.), "Le dépeuplement et l'incendie des Hautes-Cévennes," *Bulletin de la Société de l'histoire du protestantisme français*, 63–64, 1914–1915.

————, "Origines, causes et conséquences de la guerre des Camisards," *Revue historique*, 129, 1918.

Puech (A.), *Nîmes à la fin du* xvi*e siècle*, Nîmes, 1884.

————, "Les origines de l'industrie de la soie à Nîmes," *Mémoires de l'Académie du Gard*, 1885.

————, *La léproserie de Nîmes*, Nîmes, 1888.

————, *Livres de raison: les Nîmois au* xvii*e siècle*, Nîmes, 1888.

————, *La Renaissance et la Réforme à Nîmes*, Nîmes, 1893.

Quiqueran de Beaujeu, *La Provence louée*, Lyons, 1614.

Rabelais (F.), *Œuvres complètes*, Paris, (Pléiade edition), 1951.

Racine (J.), *Lettres d'Uzès*, Paris, 1930 edn.

Rascol (P.), *Les paysans de l'Albigeois à la fin de l'Ancien Régime*, Aurillac, 1961.

Ratineau (J.), *Les céréales*, Paris, 1945.

Raveau (P.), *L'agriculture et les classes paysannes dans le Haut-Poitou au* xvie *siécle*, Paris, 1926.

———, *Essai sur la situation économique en Poitou au* xvie *siécle*, Paris, 1931.

Regné (J.), "Gibiers de potence," *Revue du Vivarais*, 1912.

———, "La sorcellerie en Vivarais," *Revue du Vivarais*, 1913.

Reinhard (M. R.) and Armengaud (A.), *Histoire générale de la population mondiale*, Paris, 1961.

Rémi (N.), *Daemonolatriae libri tres*, Lyons, 1595.

Renaud (P.), "Effet des froids du début de l'hiver 1940–1941 sur l'olivier," *Le progrès agricole et viticole*, 14, 1941, p. 235.

———, "L'olivier de confiserie dans l'Hérault," *Annales E.N.A.M.*, 1952.

Renouard (Y.), *Histoire de Florence*, Paris, 1964.

Revoil (J.), "La situation de l'oléiculture en France avant et après le gel de 1956," *Information oléicoles internationales*, October–December, 1958. New series, 4, Madrid.

Reynier (E.), *Histoire de Privas*, Aubenas, 1943.

Ribbe (Ch. de), *La société provençale à la fin du Moyen Âge*, Paris, 1898.

Ribero, paper read to the Congrès d'études occitanes de Montpellier, 1962.

Ricardo (D.), *Principes de l'économie politique* [Principles of Political Economy], in *Œuvres complètes*, Paris, 1847.

Richelet, (P.), *Dictionnaire français contenant les mots et les choses*, Paris, 1680.

[Richeprey], *Journal des voyages en Haute-Guyenne de J. F. H. de Richeprey*, Rodez, 1952 edn.

Richer (P.), *Études cliniques sur la grande hystérie*, Paris, 1885.

Richet (D.), "Le cours officiel des monnaies étrangères circulant en France au xvie siècle," *Revue historique*, 225, 1961.

Rivals (G.), "La Réforme en Bas-Languedoc," *Cahiers d'histoire et d'archéologie*, 13, 1938.

Robert (S.), "Sommières," *B.S.L.G.*, 1956.

Roger-Lureau, *Les doctrines politiques de Jurieu*, Bordeaux, 1904.

Roman (Abbé), *Goudargues, son abbaye, son prieuré*, Nîmes, 1886.

Roman (J.), "La guerre des paysans en Dauphiné," *Bulletin de la Société d'archéologie et de statistique de la Drôme*, 1877.

Romano (R.), "Les prix au Moyen Âge dans le Proche-Orient et l'Occident chrétien," *Annales*, 1963.

———, "Encore la crise de 1619–1622," *Annales*, 1964.

Romier (L.), *Le royaume de Catherine de Médicis*, Paris, 1922.

Rosengarten (Y.), *Le concept sumérien de consommation dans la vie économique et religieuse*, Paris, 1958.

Rostaing (L.), "La navigation du Rhône au xviiie siècle," *Revue du Vivarais*, 1912.

Rostow (W.), paper read to the Première conférence internationale d'histoire économique (Stockholm, 1960), Paris, 1960.

————, *Les étapes de la croissance économique* [The Stages of Economic Growth], Paris, 1962 edn.

Rougerie (J.), *Procès des Communards*, Paris, 1964.

Roupnel (G.), *Histoire de la campagne française*, Paris, 1932.

————, *La ville et la campagne au* xviie *siècle, étude sur les populations du pays dijonnais*, Paris, 1955.

Rouquette (J. B.), *Histoire de Ganges*, Montpellier, 1904.

Rozier (Abbé), *Cours complet d'agriculture*, Paris, 1785. Reedited in 1805 and 1809.

Rudé (G.-E.), "La taxation populaire de mai 1775 (la guerre des farines)," *Annales historiques de la Révolution française*, 1956.

Sahuc (J.), "Solliolis, médecin astrologue à Saint-Pons," *Revue de l'histoire du diocèse de Montpellier*, II, 1910–1911.

Saint-Jacob (P. de), *Les paysans de la Bourgogne du Nord au dernier siècle de l'Ancien Régime*, Paris, 1960.

Santi (L. de) and Vidal (A.), *Deux livres de raison (1517–1560), avec des notes sur les conditions agricoles de l'Albigeois au* xvie *siècle*, Paris, Toulouse, 1896.

Sartre (J. P.), *Critique de la raison dialectique*, Paris, 1960.

Satire Menippée, Paris, 1878 edn.

Saugrain, *Nouveau dénombrement du royaume*, Paris, 1720.

Saumade (G.), *Fabrègues*, Montpellier, 1908.

Saurel (F.), *Antoine Subjet, évêque de Montpellier*, 1898.

Savary des Bruslons (J.), *Dictionnaire universel du commerce*, Copenhagen, 1765.

Sayous (A.) and Combes (J.), "Les commerçants et les capitalistes de Montpellier aux xiiie et xive siècles," *Revue historique*, 1940.

Schnapper (B.), *Les rentes au* xvie *siècle*, Paris, 1958.

Schnerb (R.), *Le* xixe *siècle. L'apogée de l'expansion européenne*, Paris, 1955.

Schram (S.), *Protestantism and Politics in France*, Alençon, 1954.

Sclafert (T.), *Cultures en Haute-Provence*, Paris, 1959.

Scoville (W. C.), *The Persecution of the Huguenots and French Economic Development*, Berkeley, 1960.

Segondy (J.), *Cessenon-sur-Orb*, Montpellier, 1949.

Segui (E.), *Faugères-en-Biterrois*, Nîmes, 1933.

[Séguier], *Diaire ou journal du voyage du chancelier Séguier en Normandie*, Rouen, 1842.

Seguy (J.), *Atlas linguistique et ethnographique de la Gascogne*, Paris, 1956.

Seignolle (Cl.), *Le folklore du Languedoc*, Paris, 1960.

Seriayne, "Statistique du canal du Midi," *B.S.L.G.*, 1878.

Serres (O. de), *Le théâtre d'agriculture et ménage des champs*, Paris, chiefly the edition of 1605.

[Sévigné], *Lettres de Madame de Sévigné*, Paris, 1953 edn.

Seyssel (Cl. de), *Les louanges du roi Louis XII*, Paris, 1508.

Siegfried (A.), "Le groupe protestant cévenol," in *Protestantisme français*, Paris, 1945.

—————, *Géographie électorale de l'Ardèche sous la IIIe République*, Paris, 1949.

Simiand (F.), *Le salaire, l'évolution sociale et la monnaie*, Paris, 1932.

Singer (C.) and Holmyard (E.), *A History of Technology*, Oxford, 1956.

Sion (J.), *Les paysans de la Normandie orientale*, Paris, 1909.

Slicher van Bath (B. H.), *The Agrarian History of Western Europe*, London, 1963.

—————, "Yield Ratios, 1810–1820," *A.A.G. Bijdrajen*, 10, 1963.

Soboul (A.), "La communauté rurale," *Revue de synthèse*, 1957.

—————, *Les sans-culottes parisiens en l'an* II, Paris, 1958.

—————, *Les campagnes montpelliéraines à la fin de l'Ancien Régime: propriétés et cultures d'après les compoix*, Paris, 1958.

Soreau (E.), *L'agriculture du* XVIIᵉ *à la fin du* XVIIIᵉ *siècle*, Paris, 1952.

Sorre (M.), "Répartition de la population en Bas-Languedoc," *B.S.L.G.*, 1906.

—————, "La transhumance dans la région montpelliéraine," *B.S.L.G.*, 1912.

—————, *Étude critique des sources de l'histoire de la viticulture . . . en Bas-Languedoc au* XVIIIᵉ *siècle*, Montpellier, 1913.

Les soupirs de la France esclave qui aspire après la liberté, 1689.

Soutou (A.), "La draille d'Aubrac," *Cahiers ligures*, 1959.

Spont (A.), *Semblançay et la bourgeoisie financière au début du* XVIᵉ *siècle*, Paris, 1895.

Spooner (F.), *Economie mondiale et frappes monétaires en France (1493–1680)*, Paris, 1956.

—————, "Régimes alimentaires d'autrefois," *Annales*, 1961.

Stoianovitch (T.) and Haupt (G.), "Le maïs arrive dans les Balkans," *Annales*, 1962.

"La structure et les rendements du vignoble du Bas-Languedoc," *Études et conjoncture*, 1955.

Taillepied (F.), *Traité de l'apparition des esprits*, Brussels, 1609.

Tapié (V.-L.), *La France de Louis XIII et de Richelieu*, Paris, 1952.

Tarde (J.), *Les chroniques de la ville et du diocèse de Sarlat*, ed. by G. de Gérard, Paris, 1887.

Tawney (R.), *La religion et l'essor du capitalisme* [Religion and the Rise of Capitalism], Paris, 1951.

Teissier (O.), *Archives municipales de Toulon*, Toulon, 1863.

Temple (Sir W.), *Observations upon the United Provinces of the Netherlands*, Cambridge, 1932 edn.

Thiriet (F.), *La Romanie vénitienne au Moyen Age*, Paris, 1959.

Thomas (A.), "Élevage et commerce des porcs au xvᵉ siècle," *Annales du Midi*, 1908.

Thomas (L. J.), "La population du Bas-Languedoc (xiiiᵉ–xivᵉ siècle)," *Annales du Midi*, 1908.

———, "L'émigration temporaire en Bas-Languedoc et Roussillon," *B.S.L.G.*, 1910.

———, "Fortifications de Marsillargues," *Mémoires de la Société d'archéologie de Montpellier*, X, 1932–1934, p. 54.

———, *Montpellier, ville marchande*, Montpellier, 1936.

Tillion (G.), "Dans l'Aurès. Le drame des civilisations archaïques," *Annales*, 1957.

Toujas (R.), "L'apprentissage à Montauban," *Bulletin philologique et historique*, 1955–1956.

———, "Le commerce en 1646, entre Bordeaux et Toulouse," *Annales du Midi*, 1960.

Tournefort (J. Pitton de), *Éléments de botanique*, Paris, 1694.

Toussaert (J.), *Le sentiment religieux en Flandre à la fin du Moyen Âge*, Paris, 1963.

Traité des jardins; ou, le nouveau de La Quintinye, Paris, 1775.

Tregaro (L.), "Les Maures et l'Estérel," *B.S.L.G.*, 1931.

Le Trésor de la cuisine du Bassin méditerranéen, Paris, ca. 1950.

Trocmé and Delafosse. *Le commerce rochelais de la fin du xvᵉ siècle au début du xviiiᵉ siècle*, Paris, 1953.

Tucoo-Chala (P.), *Gaston Phébus et la vicomté de Béarn*, Bordeaux, 1959.

Tudez (M.), *Le développement de la vigne dans la région de Montpellier*, Montpellier, 1934.

Tulippe (O.), *L'habitat rural en Seine-et-Oise*, Liège, 1934.

Utterstrom (G.), "Climatic Fluctuations and Population Problems in Early Modern History," *The Scandinavian Economic History Review*, 1955.

Vallet (R.), "La participation volontaire dans l'hystérie," *L'évolution psychiatrique*, 1963.

Vallois (H. V.), *Anthropologie de la population française*, Toulouse, 1943.

Van der Wee (H.), *The Growth of the Antwerp Market and the European Economy*, The Hague, 1963.

Van Gennep (A.), *Manuel de folklore française*, Paris, 1947.

Varagnac (A.), *L'homme avant l'écriture*, Paris, 1959.

Vauban, *Projet d'une dîme royale*, Paris, 1933 edn.

Vavilov (N. J.), "Sur l'origine de l'agriculture mondiale," *Revue de botanique appliquée et d'agriculture tropicale*, 1932.

Vavilov (N. I.), "The origin, variation, immunity, and breeding of cultivated plants," *Chronica botanica*, 13, 1–6, 1949–1950.

Vénard (M.), *Bourgeois et paysans au* xviiᵉ *siècle*, Paris, 1958.

Vercier (J.), *Culture potagère*, Paris, 1946.

Verlinden (C.), "Mouvement des prix et des salaires en Belgique au xviᵉ siècle," *Annales*, 1955.

Veron de Forbonnais (F.), *Recherches et considérations sur les finances de France*, Basel, 1758.

Vicens Vives (J.), *Manual de historia economica de Espana*, Barcelona, 1959.

———, Regla (J.) and Nadal (J.), "L'Espagne aux xviᵉ et xviiᵉ siècles. L'époque des souverains autrichiens," *Revue historique*, 220, 1958.

Vilar (P.), "Histoire des prix, histoire générale," *Annales*, 1949.

———, "Géographie et histoire statistique, quelques points d'histoire de la viticulture méditerranéenne," in *Éventail de l'histoire vivante*, Paris, 1953.

———, paper read to the Première conférence internationale d'histoire économique (Stockholm, 1960), Paris, 1960.

———, *La Catalogne dans l'Espagne moderne*, Paris, 1962.

Vilback (R. de), *Voyage dans les départements de Languedoc*, Paris, 1825.

Villages désertés et histoire économique, Paris, 1965.

Villars (L. de), *Mémoires*, Paris, 1884–1904 edn.

Villemagne (A.), "Aliénation du temporel du clergé en 1562," *Revue d'histoire du diocèse de Montpellier*, 4 and 5, 1912–1914.

———, *Mélanges historiques*, Montpellier, 1913.

Villeneuve (Comte de), *Statistique des Bouches-du-Rhône*, Marseilles, 1821.

Vincent (Dr.), "La léproserie de Poitiers," *R.H.E.S.*, 1931.

Vissac (R. de), *Antoine du Roure et la révolte de 1670*, Paris, 1895.

Vitalis (A.), "Fleury, les origines, la jeunesse," *Annales du Midi*, 1906.

Voltaire, *Le siècle de Louis XIV*, Paris, 1962 edn.

Vovelle (M.), "Déchristianisation spontanée et déchristianisation provoquée dans le Sud-Est sous la Révolution française," *B.S.H.M.*, 1964.

Wailly (N. de), "Mémoire sur les variations de la livre tournois," *Mémoire de l'Académie des Inscriptions et Belles-Lettres*, 21, part 2, 1857.

Walawender (A.), *Kronika Klesk elementarnych w polsce i w Krajwach Sasiednich w latach, 1450–1586*, Lvov, 1932.

Walter (G.), *Histoire des paysans de France*, Paris, 1963.

Weber (M.), *The Protestant Ethic and the Spirit of Capitalism*, New York, 1951 edn.

———, *Le savant et le politique*, Paris, 1963 edn.

Weill (G.), *Les théories sur le pouvoir royal en France pendant les guerres de religion*, Paris, 1891.

Weulersse (G.), *Le mouvement physiocratique en France*, Paris, 1910.

Weulersse (J.), *Paysans de Syrie et du Proche-Orient*, Paris, 1946.

Wolff (Ph.), *Commerce et marchands de Toulouse*, Paris, 1954.

——, *Les estimes toulousaines aux* xive *et* xve *siècles,* Toulouse, 1956.

——, "Trois études de démographie en France méridionale," in *Studi in onore di Armando Sapori*, Milan, 1957.

——, *Histoire de Toulouse*, Toulouse, 1958.

Young (A.), *Voyages en France*, Paris, 1931 edn.

Zola (É.), *Madeleine Férat*, Paris, 1913 edn.

Zolla (D.), "Les variations du revenu et du prix des terres en France au xviie et au xviiie siècle," *Annales de l'École libre des sciences politiques*, 1893.

Zumthor (P.), *Histoire littéraire de la France médiévale*, Paris, 1954.

Index